Shikwa-e-Hind

Shikwa-e-Hind

THE POLITICAL FUTURE OF INDIAN MUSLIMS

Mujibur Rehman

London · New York · Sydney · Toronto · New Delhi

First published in India by Simon & Schuster India 2024

1 3 5 7 9 10 8 6 4 2

Simon & Schuster India
818, Indraprakash Building,
21, Barakhamba Road,
New Delhi 110001.

www.simonandschuster.co.in

Simon & Schuster: Celebrating 100 Years of Publishing in 2024

Paperback ISBN: 978-81-946464-8-8
eBook ISBN: 978-81-946464-9-5

Typeset in India by SÜRYA, New Delhi
Printed and bound in India by Replika Press Pvt. Ltd.

To

HALIMA, my mother
and
SHAKOOR SAHIB, my most forgiving father

Both warned me very early that the most gorgeous flower of Indian culture, secularism, is in danger, and I must take a firm stand.

CONTENTS

Introduction 1

1. Indian Muslims' Rights to Have Rights and Its Political Context 53
2. The Cultural and Political Lives of South Indian Muslims 96
3. Violence against Muslims and the Idea of 'Banality of Violence' 147
4. Indian Muslim Women: Which Way Now? 199
5. Shaheen Bagh and the Future of India's Citizenship Debate 244
6. The Unending Debate on Muslim Backwardness 279

Conclusion 324

Acknowledgements 358

INTRODUCTION

> 'I do not think simply because a community happens to be a community composed of small numbers it is therefore necessarily a minority for political purposes. A minority which is oppressed or whose rights are denied by the majority, would be a minority that would be fit for consideration for political purposes.'
>
> —Dr BR Ambedkar, *Dr Babasaheb Ambedkar: Writings and Speeches*

India is currently witnessing a massive surge in the popularity of the Hindu Right as a political force. What is at stake, in this scenario, for Indian Muslims?

It is their *political future*.

It is the political future that determines the economic, cultural, and every other aspect of the fate of a community. Those who hold political power, alone hold the key to all forms of decision-making. They determine how the laws of the land are to be framed which in turn affects the economy, the cultural life, and just about everything else in a democratic society. As legendary African American writer, James Baldwin, once described the white domination over American state power as follows, 'They had the judges, the juries, the shotguns, the law—in a word—power. But it was a criminal power, to be feared but not respected—and to be outwitted in any way whatever.' [1]

In the wake of the growing Hindu Right dominance, comparing the situation of Indian Muslims to the African American experience might seem a little far-fetched. Indian Muslims are seen as a community that once ruled India for hundreds of years whereas the

African American community was subjected to slavery for centuries in America. As Cornel West writes in the Preface to his widely read book, *Race Matters*, 'Black people in the United States differ from all other modern people owing to the unprecedented levels of unregulated and unrestrained violence directed at them. No other people have been taught systematically to hate themselves—psychic violence—reinforced by the powers of state and civic coercion—physical violence—for the primary purpose of controlling their minds and exploiting their labour for nearly four hundred years.'[2]

Nonetheless, the forces of supremacist ideology that have been working against these two prominent minorities—Indian Muslims, a religious minority, and African Americans, a racial minority—have a great deal in common in contemporary times. Both communities are confronting challenges in asserting their position for equality and dignity.[3]

In contemporary times, there is a great deal of commonality in their sufferings and struggles. Consider lynchings. African Americans have suffered lynchings for centuries and now Muslims are its prominent victims in India. More and more voices are calling for an economic boycott of Indian Muslims—very recently in Haryana after the Nuh violence.[4] In the past, such boycott calls were made for Muslims in India during the communal violence in the 1980s in Gujarat.[5] And, even before this, several caste panchayats had called for an economic boycott for Muslims during the Hindu-Muslim riot of the late 1920s in Surat and Godhra.[6] Given the toxic environment of anti-Muslim prejudices in the present time, will these boycott calls intensify and lead to segregation in the future? On the question of segregation, it is worth recalling the centuries-old inhumane experiences of Dalits/former untouchables and how the Brahminical caste order denied them basic human dignity. Various forms of practices of untouchability, some may argue, could be viewed as segregation by other means.[7] Indian society is not completely unfamiliar with such extreme practices. This is recognized by Hindu Right leaders as well. In September 2023 at Agrasen Chatravaas, Nagpur, Rashtriya Swayan Sevak Sangh (RSS) chief Mohan Bhagwat said, 'We did not bother when they [Dalits] lived like animals.'[8] In his comparative study of processes of otherisation of Dalits or former untouchables and African Americans, Gyanendra Pandey introduces a concept of prejudices, what he calls 'vernacular prejudices'—'the already known'—which always appears as common sense.[9] And then there is the universal kind. Both forms of prejudices, I suggest, serve as the major source of such extreme practices.

A vigorous debate on how Muslim history is to be interpreted and taught in India, generally discussed as a textbook controversy, has been going on for some years now, prior to 2014 as well. [10] In the US, the subject of Critical Race Theory (CRT) has emerged as a prominent polarizing topic in political discussions.[11] The debate over affirmative action policy is an issue common to both communities too.[12] Thus, there are several issues that seem to be binding the two major minorities, their struggles, and their challenges.

This is why we may very well ask if most of the painful past experiences of violence and degradation of African Americans could become the future experiences of Indian Muslims.

To interrogate the future of Muslims, the comparative insights should not only be drawn from African American experiences. Other cases such as Rohingyas in Burma, Hindus, Sikhs, and Christians or other minorities such as Ahmedias in Pakistan and Bangladesh, Uyghurs in China, and several others could provide valuable insights into the ongoing predicament of Indian Muslims. Quite a few valuable scholarships on this theme are already available. For instance, Aamir R Mufti has sought to compare the Indian Muslim question with the European Jewish question to reflect on the crisis of modern secularism and of postcolonial secularism through the examination of what he calls, 'terrorized and terrifying figures of the minority.'[13] On the other hand, Mahmood Mamdani, articulates the idea of what he calls 'permanent minorities' by reflecting on American natives and their treatment, among others, in a complex process that entails organized violence and systematic exclusion and consequently how the colonial state and nation-state feed and create each other.[14]

On the Limits of the Hindu-Muslim Framework

One crucial caveat in the wider debate and discussion on Hindu majoritarianism is the limitation of the frequently deployed Hindu-Muslim framework in the analysis of Muslim questions in India. This Hindu-Muslim framework conceals more than it reveals. Moreover, it offers some inherent advantages to the Hindu Right. So, we have to ask: Who are the dominant fractions who control and regulate the political, economic, and religious power of the Hindu community? To understand the power dimension of the Hindu community, it is crucial to recognize caste factors—particularly the role of dominant castes. Directly or indirectly, it is the dominant castes that govern this country, even if they are rather small in number or a numerical minority. By all means, they should not be more than 8 to 10 per cent or even much less. India's majoritarian project thus is run by a minority and that is the dominant caste group because they have a decisive say on the Hindu social order. If today the Hindu Right has acquired so much muscle, it is because it enjoys the support of India's dominant caste groups as never before.

Based on fieldwork in states such as Rajasthan, Haryana, Gujarat, and Uttar Pradesh, Amrita Basu suggests that wherever dominant caste groups have supported the Bharatiya Janata Party, violence against Muslims has also risen.[15] Therefore, the caste dimension of the debate, especially the role and contributions of upper castes in legitimizing majoritarianism both domestically and globally through global networks (as part of the global diaspora) deserves special attention. For the Hindu community, it is the caste and caste identity that matters. Ambedkar, in his widely read essay, *Annihilation of Caste*,[16] stresses on this caste aspect of the identity of Hindus as the genuine identity. In contemporary times, Kancha Ilaiah, in his book, *Why I Am Not a Hindu*,[17] presents his resistance to being co-opted by this broad term called the Hindu. The Hindu Right also understands it quite well, but it cleverly wants its broad Hindu identity to consolidate and expand. It has invested decades of mobilization to present the Hindu identity, and create political conditions where it can stitch an electoral majority, which it did in 2014 quite successfully—and it is working amazingly through the politics of aggressive religious polarization in election after election in most cases. This is the reason also why the Hindu Right is so opposed to caste census.[18] Indeed, Gandhi was also opposed to division based on caste.[19] Therefore, the framework needs to be reformulated as a dominant caste-Muslim framework.

So we need to ask the following questions: Why and how did India's dominant castes choose to turn their back on secularism? Were they ever secular? Or was it a reflection of some kind of constraint? Why have they become so anti-Muslim or are they simply indifferent? It is my submission that India enjoyed some variant of secularism until now, because India's upper castes found it reasonable. Now they find Hindutva more reasonable which is the reason for India's turn towards Hindu majoritarianism. Their role in the revival of secular democracy remains vital, and also crucial for the future of Indian Muslims. In other words, all the suggestions about the alliance between Muslims or minorities and Dalits to take on dominant castes have limits and in the long run, might not work.[20]

Indian Muslims: A Religious Minority or Babur's *Santan*?

Two points deserve attention for clarity in any discussion on Indian Muslims and the Hindu Right. Firstly, the Hindu Right does not consider Indian Muslims as a religious minority. In its narrative of a thousand years of slavery, Indian Muslims are seen as part of Islamic colonialism that ran through a large part of medieval India, particularly Mughal rule.[21] While an average Indian drawn mainly from an upper-caste background could become a full citizen having lived and worked for a couple of years in West or North America, Muslims, despite having lived here for centuries, are still considered alien. That Indian Muslims are born in this land and have been living here for ages is not good enough to convince them that Muslims can have equal rights as citizens. Strangely, the upper caste Indians who constitute the global diaspora and have profited out of the modern idea of multiculturalism in Western societies—particularly in America, Britain, Canada, Australia, etc.—have become most passionate supporters of exclusionary Hindu nationalism.[22]

On the other hand, most critics of the Hindu Right, particularly liberal critics, consider Indian Muslims as a religious minority and they deploy the language of minority rights to express their concerns for Indian Muslims. Consider the research of Amar Sohal who examines the lives and works of three iconic Muslim personalities—Abul Kalam Azad, Khan Abdul Gaffar Khan, and Sheikh Abdullah to make a case for Muslim secularity.[23] For the Hindu Right, these iconic figures are simply Babur's *santan*. This distinction in the approach of secularists and the Hindu Right needs to be kept in mind to grasp the nature of ongoing confrontation and exchange, both in the domain of political power and intellectual discourses. What we are witnessing is a lot of cross-talk going on, not a healthy exchange or debate between rival perspectives as there is no meeting point. This is a typical case of ideological warfare, about which I discuss in detail in Chapter 1. Indeed, the Muslim identity issue here could be in some ways compared to what WEB Du Bois described as 'double consciousness'. Du Bois explains in the following words—'this sense of always looking at one's self through the eyes of others, of measuring one's soul by the tape of a world that looks on in amused contempt and pity.'[24]

Secondly, liberal critics carry a general impression that the Hindu Right is against all minorities, religious or otherwise. The Hindu Right (or the Bhartiya Janata Party) is not against all minorities, religious or otherwise, *per se*. The Hindu Right has shown no animosity towards religious minorities such as Jains, Parsis, Buddhists or even Sikhs, etc. Its opposition to the Khalisthan movement should not be viewed as opposition to Sikhism, as the former is a political movement, to which the Hindu Right is as fiercely opposed as it is to Kashmiri separatism. Therefore, the attempt to paint the Hindu Right as anti-minority per se is a misleading formulation. For the Hindu Right, Muslims and Christians are the two prominent religious minorities that are of special concern. And, the reasons for such concerns are also different, which I explain in the following section.

Only Muslims and Christians

Put simply, the core Hindutva ideology believes that India is a Hindu land meant only for Hindu people. Or at best, for people whose religion was born in this land such as Sikhism, Jainism, Buddhism, etc. Following Savarkar's formulations[25], the Hindu Right considers people born to a religion that has its origin outside of India unable to be fully loyal. On top of it, the Hindu Right is deeply suspicious of the long-term goal of people who follow Islam and Christianity. Since both are evangelical religions, the Hindu Right fears that these two communities could transform Hindu India into either a Muslim land or a Christian land in the future. Given that some Muslims have already carved out Pakistan and Bangladesh, and the ongoing secessionist movement in Kashmir, there is empirical evidence to corroborate their fear, which contributes some legitimacy to the propagation of their anti-Muslim, anti-Islam propaganda. This lurking suspicion of Muslim loyalty runs deep and goes beyond the Hindu Right thinking. This is perhaps the reason why no Muslim diplomat has ever been appointed as India's High Commissioner to Pakistan since India's independence.[26] Furthermore, ongoing Christian missionary activities—particularly among Dalits and Adivasis in various parts of India—form the ground of their suspicion. For historical reasons, the Hindu Right is more concerned about Muslims than Christians. In his maiden speech in Parliament, Narendra Modi after the 2014 election alluded to 1000 years of India's slavery, which meant Muslim rule as a foreign rule. And he repeated similar observations in his speech in US Congress on 23 June 2023. He said in the following words, 'We celebrated a remarkable journey of over seventy-five years of freedom, after thousand years of foreign rule in one form or another.'[27] This is how Muslim identity is dragged into India's contentious history in political discussions.

Thus, the ideological project of Hindutva politics seems to be guided by the simple logic: MUSLIMS NO MORE. The multi-pronged attack on everything associated with Muslims—masjid, Waqf land, dargahs, hijab, etc—suggests that the long-term goal is mainly to de-Islamise India. It so happens, most media reports indicate that the only institutions connected with Islam or Muslims like masjids, madrasas, dargahs alone have illegality associated with their land or location. But not with other religions. This singular focus indicates that for the Hindu Right, Islam and Indian Muslims have become lasting trauma. It seems the state is adopting a no-stone-unturned approach to deal with Indian Islam and their institutions. To achieve these goals, the Hindu Right organizations and their regimes seek to consistently delegitimize each and every legitimate need or policy for Muslims as part of 'appeasement politics' or 'vote bank politics.' Neeti Nair, however, responds to this otherwise ludicrous allegation of appeasement as 'Muslim abandonment' politics. It is ludicrous because how could a community supposed to have been pampered for ages by the state and political parties remain the world's most backward religious minority by official reports published again and again? In the words of Neeti Nair, 'The substance of Indian secularism in this founding moment appeared closer to "Muslim abandonment" than to the common right-wing charge of "Muslim appeasement".' [28] In my view, the Hindu Right considers Muslim suffering desirable.

Indian Muslims are often presented in a derogatory way as Babur's *santan* or Aurangzeb's *aulad*. The phrase 'Babur's *santan*' was widely used during the Ayodhya movement in the late 1980s and later. And the phrase 'Aurangzeb ki *aulad*' was used in Maharashtra by its Deputy Chief Minister, Devendra Fadnavis, as recently as in 2023.[29] Both are abusive and derogatory, to say the least. And Indian Muslims have chosen to ignore such abuses. For instance, neither Muslims nor secularists have filed a court case against such abuses as yet even if such accusations have been floating in public for years. Besides above-mentioned types of abuses, there are general prejudices against Muslims that run very deep. And much of the basis of anti-Muslim prejudices are fabricated. Shahid Amin shares interesting insights about various kinds of representations of Muslims by the state and other agencies in an essay titled, *Representing the Musalman: Then and Now, Now and Then,* and seeks to answer the question of what constitutes a Musalman, or more specifically, what he calls 'commonsense about North Indian Musalman.'[30]

For some, the Indian Muslim identity has been problematic because it is a religious identity. That may be true, but it is perceived as a contentious one because it is a historically dense identity. The fact remains that Indian Muslims have always been a numerical minority in the subcontinent, even during the so-called Muslim rule.[31] I describe it as a so-called Muslim rule because there was none. Indeed, the so-called Muslim rule was a rule by a handful of Muslim families/dynasties—often engaged in mutual violence towards each other and their Muslim rivals as well. In Mughal families, there used to be a saying, 'takth ya tabut' (throne or grave).[32] Therefore, the commitment of these Muslim rulers to the Muslim community in general and also to non-Muslim subjects was dictated by considerations of power/throne alone. According to Mohammad Mujeeb, 'The Indian Muslim states were not secular but they were not religious. They were the government of minorities ruling in their interest; apart from the religious affiliation with the masses, they could not even be called communal.'[33] If adherence to religious tradition and law were to be considered, then the Rajput Hindu states were more religious compared to the Muslim states, he further argues.

According to Romila Thapar, the attempt to present the rule by Muslim dynasties as Muslim rule is a misleading claim, which has become the most enduring source of communalism in modern India. Romila Thapar has brought this reasoning to our attention consistently with great clarity in several of her works, the latest being her new title, *Our History, Their History, Whose History?*[34] James Mill wrote the first modern history of India, *The History of British India,* in 1817. According to Thapar, 'Mill maintained that this history was that of two nations, the Hindu and the Muslim, quite distinctly separate and constantly in conflict.'[35] This, according to her, became the source of the two-nation theory and an enduring source of communalism in India.

The manner in which Indian Muslims have been addressed at

different points of time in history—particularly in pre-Muslim rule era—also indicates prejudices people have or had against them for ages. The word 'Muslim' was not used that frequently in Indian languages for many centuries. They were referred to often as Yavanas and Tajiks for the Arabs or those coming from the West.[36] According to Upinder Singh,[37] the earliest reference to the term Musalman seems to be in the 7th-century Buddhist commentary. In Sanskrit *Mahakavyas* and inscriptions, generic terms such as Tajikas, Turushka, Yavana, Parasika, and Mleccha were employed to refer to Muslim rulers and invaders. In the 12th and 13th centuries Sanskrit sources used *hammira* (from the Arabic and Persian Amir) and *surantrana* (from Sultan)—the two terms used for Muslim rulers. It is worth recalling that VD Savarkar composed a poem in 1908 titled, 'Amucha Priyakar Hindustan' (Our Beloved Hindustan) in Marathi and delivered it in London in which he looked at the British and the Muslims as outside colonizers and used the term 'mlecchas' for Muslims in that poem.[38]

On Pasmanda Muslims

In recent times, the phrase Pasmanda Muslims has gained tremendous political currency owing to the rather surprising interest shown by the Bharatiya Janata Party's top leadership. In July 2022, at the national executive meeting of the BJP in Hyderabad, Prime Minister Narendra Modi suggested that the party should have an outreach to Pasmanda Muslims, which is the most backward among the otherwise backward Muslims. This Pasmanda debate refers to the presence of castes among Muslims, though Islam does not recognize caste given its egalitarian philosophy. However, in India, caste among Muslims is a reality just as it is among other non-Hindu religions such as Christianity or Sikhism. Thus, caste is a unique gift to Indian Islam. Officially, it was recognized in the Sachar Report published in 2006. The Hindu Right dismissed the Sachar report as part of vote bank politics at the time of its publication and even some of the BJP leaders criticized the document as intended to plant more seeds of partition in India (for more details on this, see Ch. 6 in this book).

The term Pasmanda is a combination of two Persian words: *Pas* meaning left and *Manda* meaning behind. In other words, it means, *Left Behind*—left behind compared to other castes such as Shaikhs, Sayyids, and Pathans among Muslims. Ali Anwar, a journalist turned politician, is known to have used the term for the first time in the late 1990s. He started an organization called Pasmanda Muslim Mahaz (PMM) which was renamed as All India Pasmanda Muslim Mahaz (AIPMM).[39]

Who are Pasmanda Muslims?

This remains a debatable point from many perspectives. It is generally assumed that Pasmandas are Muslims of Hindu heritage including people of lower-caste origin. How many? Again, some suggest it is around 80 per cent or even more. Without a doubt, a vast number of Indian Muslims are of Hindu heritage but there is little scientific research to suggest who is converted from which specific caste etc. Imtiaz Ahmad has an interesting take on castes among Muslims in India. Ahmad writes, 'It would be futile to argue that this can be solely explained in terms of Hindu influence or Islam's contact with other cultures in the course of its journey into India. It would appear that the caste phenomenon among Muslims must be explained both in terms of external as well as indigenous influences.'[40] Imtiaz Ahmad's formulation makes sense but given that caste and occupations are historically tied according to Hindu tradition, it is plausible when people of Hindu heritage embraced Islam, they retained their occupations because the new faith did not alter the political economy in which these new converts lived. For instance, there are Hindu Patels and Muslim Patels like the late Ahmed Patel, the trusted aide of Sonia Gandhi, or Munaf Patel, an Indian fast bowler in cricket. Since the caste system is not so rigid among Muslims, it is not that hard for a Shaikh to become a Saiyid or a Pathan completely owing to a change of mind. As Richard Eaton writes, 'A famous proverb, known throughout Bengal and northern India and uttered usually with a smile, implicitly links social status with Islamically legitimated titles:

The first year I was a Shaikh, the second year a Khan.
This year if the price of grain is low, I'll become a Saiyid.'[41]

Research suggests that there was always what Raiffudin Ahmed describes as 'brisk upward mobility of the lower orders—their effort to gain entry into one of the four respectable social groups—Sayed, Shaikh, Mughal and Pathan.'[42] This is quite apparent from census reports. Ahmed writes:

> The number of Shaikhs and three other categories increased phenomenally, while the occupational caste groups registered a sharp decline. In 1872, the number of claimants to these 'Muslim ranks' for the whole of Bengal, including Sylhet and Cachar, was shown as 2,66,378 (of this, 2,32,189 were returned as Shaikhs, 9,858 as Syeds, and 2,205 as Mughuls) out of a total population of 17,609,135. By 1901, these numbers increased so dramatically that those claiming to be Shaikhs alone were 19,527,221 in a total Muslim population of slightly over twenty-one and half a million in the four divisions of Bengal Proper, excluding Sylhet and Chachar.[43]

The moot point is that caste among Muslims is not a replication of caste among Hindus. The most persuasive distinction between castes among Muslims and castes among Hindus was made by BR Ambedkar in his famous undelivered speech, *Annihilation of Caste* (1936). He emphatically clarifies the difference between caste among Hindus and non-Hindus such as Mohammedans (Muslims) as: 'Caste among the non-Hindus has no religious consecration, but among the Hindus most decidedly it has. Among the non-Hindus caste is only a practice, not a sacred institution. They did not originate it. With them, it is only a survival mechanism.'[44] He further emphasizes that a breach of caste among Hindus always has consequences, which is not the case with Mohammedans (Muslims). However, this does not mean that there are no socio-economic differences around caste lines among Muslims. But this is not exactly the way the Hindu Right paints it. Whatever discrimination exists, it is owing to a lack of proper Islamization among Indian Muslims as a result of which they fail to recognize the egalitarian philosophy of Islam.

Muslim Sects: Sunnis, Shias, etc.

Islam is a centuries-old Abrahamic religion like Christianity or Judaism. Over the years, based on varied interpretations, several sects have emerged. While claiming to be Muslims, people of various sects are also competing with each other for a place to claim that they represent a true version of Islam. In India, Sunni Muslims are a preponderant majority, and there are Shias with some reasonable numbers.

The Indian subcontinent is home to the second largest Shiite population after Iran. Bengal, Awadh, and Hyderabad were Shia centers of Muslim power that emerged after the Mughal era. Figure 1.1 below based on the 1921 census gives some indication of Shia population compared to Sunni. No doubt, there must have been some change, but that change does not challenge the claim that India's Muslim population is preponderantly Sunni. According to Justin Jones, 'Of earlier influence and importance were the Shi'a informed dynasties in the Deccani south, such as Sultanates of Bijapur (c.1489-1686), Golconda (1518-1617) and Ahmadnagar (1496-1636); indeed, it was here, rather than in North India that many established Shi'a cultural forms, such as majlis sermon, and marsiya poetry, first developed.'[45] Over time, it was associated with landed elites of Sindh, Punjab, Bengal, Bombay, and also with urban Muslims. Ahmedias are very small in number but they face tremendous hostility, particularly from some Sunni clergy, but the Indian situation is not as bad as in Pakistan where Ahmedias face severe persecution. In short, the Muslim politics of India is mainly Sunni Muslim politics.

While there is some history of conflict between the two sects, its legacy continues to shape the present generation of leadership and its people to some measure. Overall, the relationship between the two sects is reasonably normal. According to Jamal Mallick, 'Ulema of both sects dwelt openly on the superiority of their faith. Sunni revivalism was directed against non-Muslims and the Shia ruling class. Thus the beginning of the twentieth century saw frequent Sunni-Shia clashes—especially in the United Provinces.'[46] But the conflict between the two sects predates the 20th century. This conflict between Shia and Sunni was witnessed in the 1880s, 1890s, and in 1897-1988.[47] In 1938-39, Lucknow was a site of a violent clash between two sects. In the South, according to Fakhri, there is no such conflict between Shias and Sunnis, and that is how Islam in the South is distinctly different from the North.[48]

The response to the Pakistan movement by Shias is quite interesting. Some of the prominent Shia religious and political figures were fiercely opposed to the Pakistan movement. Hosseinbhoy Lalji, who served as the President of the Shia political conference, an organization with massive support from the Shia population, vehemently argued that Pakistan was going to be a Sunnistan, and thus the religious rights of Shias were going to be in danger. Justin Jones thus has concluded that the Pakistan movement 'was largely unsuccessful in crafting an ecumenical *qaumiyyat* that could transcend Shia-Sunni categories'[49] and their reaction was 'marked by, at best, a degree of ambivalence.'[50]

FIGURE 1.1

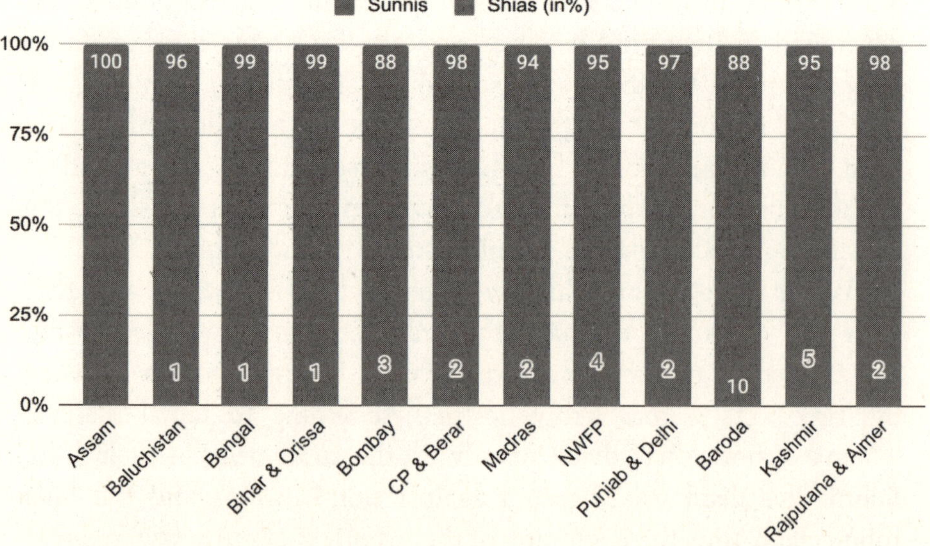

(Source: Census Report, 1921. The lower percentages are indicative of Shias.)

Some of the prominent Muslim faces from the Hindu Right, say the BJP, are of Shia heritage. For instance, Mukhtar Abbas Naqvi, a member of the Modi cabinet, is a person of Shia heritage. Owing to the friction between the two sects, some are of the view that many early enthusiastic supporters of the Hindu Right were Shias. According to Patrick Eisenlohr, a scholar who researches on Shia Muslims, 'My interlocutors described their main "others" to be Sunnis with anti-Shia tendencies, who would be labeled "Wahhabi", regardless of whether they are Wahhabi or not. Surprisingly, one was not too concerned about Hindus. The recent expansion of digital mediascapes has only reinforced this trend, I think.'[51] He further explains, 'However, in my view, whether this undeniable sectarian cleavage translates into support for the BJP is another question altogether. It is, or at least during my research, that was not the case in Mumbai (also in relation to the Shiv Sena). In UP, however, there are long standing links between Shia ulema and the BJP that long predate the Modi government, so this association between some Shia and the BJP is there in the north. But it cannot be generalized across India. It is correct, in my view, that the sectarian difference also motivates alignment with different political forces, but it does not necessarily mean support for the BJP, the fact that this seems to be the case in Lucknow does not mean it happens in Mumbai or Hyderabad or Kolkata, too.'[52]

To take the analysis further, there are also critics of the BJP who are of Shia heritage. For instance, Mushirul Hasan, a noted historian and a Left-liberal intellectual, is of Shia heritage and was a consistent critic of the Hindu Right or the BJP. Indeed, even before the arrival of the Modi government in 2014, Mushirul Hasan expressed deep concern about the future of Muslims in India. He said, 'Being a Muslim in India will become more difficult after 16 May, the day the Lok Sabha election results will be declared.'[53] The context for the remark is the opinion polls that had shown Narendra Modi as the front-runner in the elections in 2014. 'Produce 500 books of this kind but I assure you it's not going to be accepted. Muslims have been seen in a certain way,' Hasan said.[54] 'The mindset is such that such a book is not going to interest people because Islam is what Islam is, Muslims are what Muslims are and they can never be seen as active participants in the local culture. They can never be seen as different from the larger pan-Islamic community.'[55] Mr Hasan asserted that the politics of religious polarization and stereotypes would make any serious intellectual discourse on Islam, Muslims, secularism, minority rights, etc. redundant.

I would agree with Patrick Eisenlohr here. There may be circumstantial evidence pertaining to Shia support for the BJP in some locations, but to generalize it will be to take the issue a bit far. Interestingly, there are also Sunni Muslims who have been supportive of the BJP or Modi regime. For instance, the present Governor of Kerala, Arif Mohammad Khan, or MJ Akbar—both were darlings of India's liberals in the 1980s. My conclusion is that even if there are sectarian divisions and some animosity or mistrust, there is a growing realization that the Hindu Right has a hostile ideological project towards Muslims in general and they need to develop a critique against it.

But, if the Hindu Right is so much opposed to Muslims, why is it that some Muslims, whether Sunnis or Shias, support the Hindu Right, or join the BJP, say like Tariq Mansoor,[56] former Vice Chancellor of Aligarh Muslim University (AMU)? In the past, there were Muslim leaders such as Sikander Bakht who worked closely with Atal Bihari Vajpayee and was a prominent Muslim face for years since the founding of the BJP. As the BJP expands its hold on power and establishes monopoly, there are Muslim personalities who are willing to compromise on the BJP's terms. Life as a dissenter is not easy. But there is also another problem with Muslims in India and their relationship with political parties. No political party wants Muslims to be Muslims. Each one wants them to be a Muslim of their kind. So, a poor Muslim is left with little choice but to negotiate a compromise that he or she considers best. For instance, in the Congress party, a Muslim has to be a loyal member of the Gandhi dynasty or in a communist party, a Muslim has to be a nominal Muslim who would officially proclaim not to have anything to do with Islam or its practices or rituals. Therefore, each political party presents a challenge to Muslims and the choice for a Muslim is not absolute, it is relative. In other words, in free India, Muslim identity was never free and its acceptance in the political domain has been dictated by narrow political considerations. To answer our specific question—why has the BJP embraced a few Muslims—one reason could be that the party is looking for Muslims of its kind or Hindutvawadi Muslims. If Muslims fulfill this requirement, there is some space for them.

On the Veil Question

The issue of the veil or hijab seems to have excited the Hindu Right and there were considerable political and judicial activities in this regard in Karnataka. I discuss this in detail in Chapter 2 which deals with the Muslims in South India. Some observations are in order at this stage. While the veil or hijab issue has been a subject of global debate, in India there is enough empirical evidence to suggest that all Muslim women do not wear a veil or hijab. Some of this could be seen as a class issue as well. This is also the case with the evolution of global Islam. Arab traveller Ibn Battuta (d.1377) was surprised to see unveiled women in southern Anatolia, Central Asia, the Maldives, and western Sudan. The free movement of Turkish women in Central Asia startled him as well.

Writing on Bengal and its Islamization process, Richard Eaton[57] arrives at the conclusion that the purdah system gradually evolved and became part of Muslim lives. And yet there have been considerable variations. Around 1595, referring to Bengal, Abul Fazl wrote 'men and women, for the most part, go naked wearing a cloth (lungi) about the loins.' Eaton argues that this suggests that 'neither the veiling nor the seclusion of women had yet taken hold.'[58]

The most fascinating evidence that Richard Eaton presents is a quote from a Ballad called *Dewana Madina,* composed by Mansur Baiyeoti sometime around 1700. The lament of a Muslim peasant woman for her husband presents very interesting insights into the close bonding and relationships between male and female members working together and no evidence of veil present in it. 'Oh Allah,' the peasant woman sobbed, 'in December, the biting cold made us tremble in our limbs; my husband used to rise early at cock-crow and water the fields of shali crops. I carried fire to the fields and when the cold became unbearable we both sat near the fire and warmed ourselves. We reaped the shali crops together in great haste and with great care. How happy we were when after the day's work we retired to rest in our home.'[59]

Muslims and their Political Moments

This new era of Hindu Right domination presents high risks for the political future of Indian Muslims. I describe it as the inauguration of the *third political moment for Indian Muslims* in the wider context of their historical relationships with Indian society and people of other faiths, particularly the Hindu majority.[60] During this period, the supposed relationship of equality between Hindus and Muslims as scripted in the constitution is increasingly replaced by the domineering tendencies of a Hindu majority—and the promised fraternity between these two communities is coloured by hostility and violence, giving it a systemic form under a majoritarian state. The first political moment occurred in 1857, and the second one was witnessed in 1947.

In 1857, with a British victory and complete suppression of the Sepoy Mutiny, a realization dawned among the Muslim community leaders that the Mughal rule was over forever. Therefore, Muslims needed to explore new methods of negotiation under British colonial rule. Roughly a little more than three decades after the catastrophic end of the Sepoy Mutiny, two broad responses were formulated by Muslim leaders. The first one was by Sir Sayyid Ahmad Khan, who led the Aligarh movement, and the second one was what is known as the Deoband movement. Sir Sayyid argued that Muslims must engage in modern Western education, and helped establish Aligarh Muslim

University (AMU) to advance this process.[61] The second response pertained to the preservation of the Islamic way of life, various forms of religious traditions and rituals, leading to the establishment of the Deoband seminary. The official policy by the Deoband administration not to accept support from the colonial state was dictated by the reason that it could implement its vision without colonial interference which state patronage might result in.[62]

The second political moment was in 1947. During this political moment, the Indian National Congress (INC) and its secular political allies were able to convince an overwhelming number of Muslims to retain India as their homeland and reject Pakistan. For Indian Muslims, this moment was defined by the promise that they would enjoy all the benefits: political, economic, cultural, and social in their fullest sense like Hindus in secular India, or even more than what the Muslim League could promise in Pakistan. The consistent appeal by Congress and other secular parties encouraged an overwhelming number of Indian Muslims to choose to stay back in secular India. The secular parties led by the Congress party did its best to fulfill this promise theoretically by recognizing and providing these rights in the Indian Constitution that came into existence on 26 January 1950. Political developments since the days of the Ayodhya movement, particularly since the mid-1980s, have sought to undermine some of these Constitutional promises.[63] Since 2014, this has taken deeper roots and is increasingly taking on an institutionalized form. The passage of the CAA in November 2019 is one of the prominent instances.

Muslim Conditions Prior to Hindu Right's Domination

The political circumstances for Indian Muslims, it needs to be underscored, were not completely ideal or full of democratic energy before the rise of the Hindu Right since the late 1980s. Signs of deep-seated mistrust for Indian Muslims by the Indian state were witnessed from the early days of the Republic. Immediately prior to the Partition's horrific large-scale violence, Sardar Vallabhhai Patel ordered the removal of Muslims from Delhi police in his official capacity in the 1946 interim Government. After Partition violence erupted, Muslim police were stripped of their weapons under the accusation of being communal in parts of Uttar Pradesh and Punjab. This was not a one-time affair either. According to Paul Brass, the government of Pandit Govind Ballav Pant after independence took drastic measures to reduce the number of Muslims in the police forces and in most other government departments where they were over-represented in relation to their percentage of the population. This led to the considerable under-representation of Muslims in all branches of government in Uttar Pradesh for the next half century and continues.[64] This, according to Brass, is also the reason why a disproportionate number of Muslims variably lost lives and property in riots in post-independent Uttar Pradesh. The Provincial Armed Constabulary (PAC) is often accused of playing a partisan role during Hindu-Muslim riots in Uttar Pradesh. Only during the time of VP Singh as the chief minister of Uttar Pradesh, were there some efforts to hire Muslims in PAC.[65]

In Hyderabad, after the Police Action of 1948, there was a severe reduction of Muslim employees in state services from 85% to 50% in a period of six months only. According to Taylor Sherman, 'As a whole, the reorganization of civil services brought about in Indian bureaucracy that seem to be underwritten by doubts whether Muslims could loyally serve India.'[66] No doubt Muslims did face discrimination and violence in the era prior to the electoral dominance of the BJP or the Hindu Right, which are documented in various scientific academic publications, including in various reports such as Gopal Singh Panel Report (1983) and Sachar Report (2006). (Please see a detailed discussion on Muslim Backwardness in Chapter 6 of this book). But the scale, intensity, and nature of discrimination and violation have exponentially risen in so many dimensions that the present era looks more like a *State against Indian Muslims* situation.

On the Politics of Minoritization of Indian Muslims

While Muslims have been a demographic minority in India, their political positioning in post-1947 India has been particularly unique and vulnerable. The minoritization of Indian Muslims in a political sense began with the end of the Great Rebellion of 1857. According to Ilyse R Morgenstein Fuest, 'The simplification of vastly diverse Muslim communities into a singular entity is the process of minoritization, the process by which the ruling elite came to perceive Muslims of various and differing religious practices, classes, castes, as a unified collective and as a distinctive problem.'[67] Minoritization, she further explains, refers not to a demographic reality, but rather to the systematic process by which a ruling elite denies one group access to power through local, national, or, as in this case, imperial politics. She further elaborates that this whole process of minoritization of Muslims was an imperial project which first found justification in Sir WW Hunter's work, *Indian Musalmans: Are They Bound in Conscience to Rebel Against the Queen.*[68] In this text, Hunter often described Muslims as agitators, rebels, and traitors. The crucial result of this intellectual effort has been to make Muslims a minority—outsiders, disempowered, both unique and problematic.[69] But this has consequences. According to Ayesha Jalal, 'But the depiction of Muslims as the instigators of the rebellion and the selective action against those living in Delhi created a powerful impression of the uneasy coexistence of Indian Islam with British colonialism.'[70] I would improvise Ayesha Jalal's argument and suggest that the Hindu Right also found the co-existence deeply uneasy and traumatic despite enormous contributions Indian Muslims have made as artists, writers, political leaders, sportspeople, and in various walks of life. They have not only excelled but have set a very high standard.

In all societies, democratic or otherwise, the governing elites are invariably a numerical minority. What helps ruling elites protect their interests is their ability or skill to hold on to political/state power. The problem arises when a community that is numerically a minority fails to negotiate with power to protect its interests and consequently finds itself disempowered. The problem aggravates when the community is not just a minority, but a significant minority, and becomes a front for the rights of other minorities, which is a unique situation in which Indian Muslims are placed in modern India. Arjun Appadurai presents crucial insights into this conundrum in his book, *Fear of Small Numbers*.[71] In the case of Indian Muslims, the reason for the mistrust that advocates of Hindu Rashtra have actually several reasons including Muslim history,[72] cultural habits (such as beef eating),[73] and family size[74] because there is a campaign which claims that Muslims have large families because they intend to over-populate and convert India into a Muslim land. Therefore, what plays a greater role is not just fear, as Appadurai claims, but hatred and anger for Muslims and their role in Indian history.

Since 9/11, there has been a massive surge of Islamophobia all over the world, particularly in the West. According to political theorist, Anne Norton, 'In our time, the figure of Muslim has become the axis where questions of political philosophy and political theology, politics and ethics meet. Islam is marked as the pre-eminent danger to the politics of Christians, Jews and secular humanists, to women, sex, and sexuality; to the values and institutions of the Enlightenment.'[75] With regard to Muslims in India, the concerns are not simply owing to the Islamophobia that has swept the West and the rest of the world. Some similarities with such concerns between India and the West exist but the Islamophobia that arises from Hindutva is unique, more pernicious and has deeper roots in South Asian history, which is why the consequent suffering and political implications are also grave.[76] The Muslim identity has been not just a densely historical identity, it is also a *historically dense identity*.

With numerous layers defined by language, ethnicity, region etc, Muslims have the most heterogeneous identity, representing India's quintessential diversity. And yet, Muslims are perceived as the most enduring well-grounded threat to the majoritarian project of Hindu Rashtra, articulated most persuasively in the writings of VD Savarkar.[77] Historian Shruti Kapila presents her analysis of Savarkar's ideas of Hindutva as follows, 'Hindutva's idea of territoriality was informed by the perception that India represented discrete forms of privation for Muslims and for Hindus respectively: a loss of sacrality for the former, and the loss of "centre of gravity" for the latter.'[78]

As a religious minority, the community has several limitations, but it has also had political power that no other religious minority in India ever had. For instance, Indian Muslims are the only religious minority in the continent that was able to carve out two independent sovereign nations: Pakistan (1947)[79] and Bangladesh (1971).[80] This shows the Muslim community's exceptional political prowess compared to others such as Sikhs or Kashmiri Muslims or various groups in the Northeast who have nurtured similar ambitions for years. The Indian state, which is over-developed in matters of security, was able to crush the Sikh-led Khalistan movement,[81] and has contained Kashmiri separatism[82] and other similar movements in Northeast India.[83] We may very well ask why a community that could carve out two countries fails to even organize a worthwhile political protest when its innocent members are lynched.

The lynching of Muslims that began with Mohammad Akhlaq in 2015 reveals that the so-called cow-vigilante groups are indeed Muslim vigilante groups.[84] Two major state governments, Devendra Fadnavis-led BJP government (2014-2019) in Maharashtra and Yogi Adityanath-led BJP government (2017—) in Uttar Pradesh, decided to ban cow slaughter rather swiftly without offering any alternative livelihood to thousands of Muslims engaged in the profession. They were pushed to the abyss of destitution overnight. Sadly, the Muslim community made no effort to register a protest when this happened and the passivity among a preponderant majority of Muslims on this issue reflects their lack of awareness of their political rights.

The anti-CAA protests, particularly the Shaheen Bagh movement, were an impressive burst of Muslim anger, but it didn't amount to much. This Muslim women-led movement, some argue, has challenged stereotypes regarding Muslim women, and their traditional submissive image. However, the protest didn't look like a protest by a community of 200 million strong in number, a population greater than the population of Germany and Great Britain put together. Anyone who has followed the farmer's movement and seen the resources and infrastructure of the movement or its main site can easily decipher the massive difference in the organizational resources of both movements. It is not my objective to trivialize the Shaheen Bagh movement or the role of women or the fresh democratic spirit it brought into India's politics of resistance as an inherent part of Indian democracy. However, it could have been on a far greater scale given the sheer numbers of the community. It only reflects the poor political organization and awareness of the Indian Muslim community today.

A large number of victims of lynching are Muslims and yet the protests against lynching are mainly led by artists, intellectuals, and activists—thus, a secular protest. The same could be said about the anti-CAA protests all over India, which also received some support from political parties. The community has little sense of its political power today, let alone know how to make use of it as a political weapon in a competitive electoral democracy. The community's lack of self-awareness regarding its political strength is another major cause for its contemporary predicament.

Political Space in the Age of the Hindu Right

As I hinted, my focus has been on the political future in the wake of the rise of the Hindu Right, particularly, the BJP. The Hindu Right, it is now apparent, has become a hegemonic force, and is likely to remain a dominant political force for years to come regardless of the electoral results of the 2024 parliamentary elections or any election afterwards. Scholars such as Katharine Adeny[85] and Christophe Jaffrelot[86] have demonstrated with great clarity that India is increasingly becoming what they call an 'ethnic democracy.'

Currently, roughly more than 200 million Muslims live in India, which is more than the population of France and Great Britain together and also, more than half of the American population.

Figure 1.2 based on the census of 2011 shows the state wise distributions of Muslim population. Unfortunately, the census of 2021 is yet to be out, which is why we have to extrapolate to figure out what could be the tentative Muslim population at present.

FIGURE 1.2

Muslims Population as per Census 2011 (In %) and Share in Total Muslims in India (%)

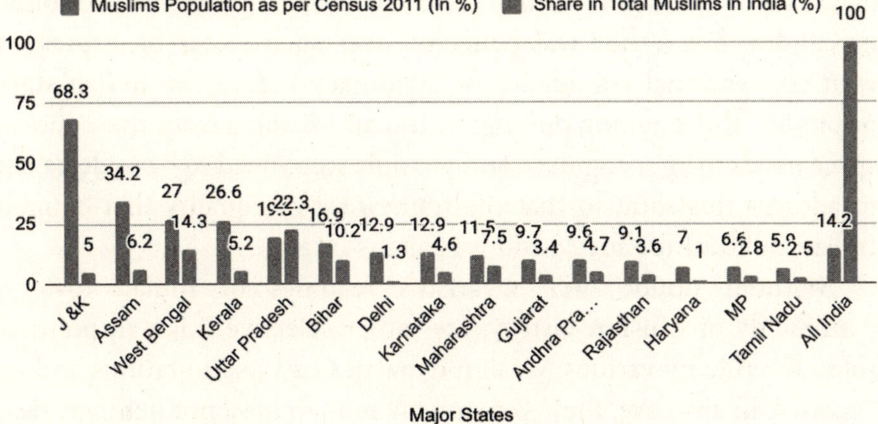

(Source: Census Report, 2011, Government of India, New Delhi)

Prior to the advent of Prime Minister Narendra Modi led BJP in 2014, the United Progressive Alliance (UPA) government led by Dr Manmohan Singh published a report widely known as Sachar Report in 2006. For the first time, any Indian government since independence published a report exclusively on the socio-economic conditions of Indian Muslims. [87] On this Javed Alam wrote, 'Many of us who have been using the survey data of the Centre for the Study of Developing Societies (CSDS) on class formation within the different communities have written on lines quite similar to what the Sachar Committee has done now. What puts its findings on an altogether different plane is not just its thoroughness but also the official stamp it carries.'[88] There are other issues dealing with the cultural aspect of Muslim identity such as hijab, triple talaq, or Urdu language, which have been a part of India's national debate.[89] On such issues, an impressive array of scholarships is also available.

In this age of the Hindu Right, there are visible signs of the political future getting undermined systematically so that Indian Muslims are no longer seen to be politically equal. And their political voice is shrinking. The major reason for it is their fast decline of representation in major policy-making bodies such as the Parliament or the Assembly. If the Muslim community is not seen as politically equal, then the modern Indian state will neither address its economic or cultural future nor will concerns over such issues be expressed with conventional confidence or legitimacy before the Indian state or public. This ongoing purging of Indian Muslims from the political space needs to be recognized and possible steps need to be undertaken to address this slide so that the framework of equality that defined Indian political life for Muslims remains intact.

Without doubt, VD Savarkar's readings of Indian history, particularly of Muslim history, are rather selective. Like all political rules, the rule by various Muslim dynasties had its limitations and its excesses. In any case, they were mostly monarchies, not democracies; not based on the idea of citizens or their rights at all. This is not just true about Muslims but also about non-Muslim rules. For instance, Odisha was once ruled by Marathas for many decades, and they committed unspeakable atrocities against native Oriyas who were their subjects. According to legendary Oriya writer, Fakir Mohan Senapati, comparatively speaking, the excesses committed by colonial British rulers would pale before what the Marathas did to their Oriya subjects.[90]

According to historian Jadunath Sarkar,[91] there were ten specific gifts of the Muslim age to India:

1. Restoration of touch with the outer world, which included the revival of the Indian navy and sea trade, both of which had been lost since the decline of the Cholas.
2. Internal peace over a large part of India, especially north of the Vindhyas.

3. Uniformity secured by the imposition of the same type of administration.
4. Uniformity of social manners and dress among the upper classes irrespective of creed.
5. Indo-Saracen art, in which medieval Hindu and Chinese schools were blended. Also, a new style of architecture, and promotion of industries of a refined kind (shawls, inlaying work, kinkhab, muslin, carpets, etc.).
6. A common lingua franca, called Hindustani or Rekhta, and an official prose style (mostly the creation of Hindu Munshis writing Persian, and even borrowed by Maratha chitnises for their own vernacular).
7. Rise of our vernacular literature, as the fruits of peace and economic prosperity, under the empire of Delhi.
8. Monotheistic religious revival and Sufism.
9. Historical literature.
10. Improvements in the art of war and civilization in general.

Ever since the BJP's rise in Indian electoral politics in the late 1980s, an attempt was made to compare the Hindu Right and its politics with European fascism with an objective to scare Indian voters away from the BJP or the Hindu Right in general. Instead of seeing the voters moving away from the BJP, we have witnessed a consistent rise in its support base and the Party today remains the most dominant party in India. No doubt, some valuable insights could be drawn from such comparisons, but it has not worked electorally. In any case, a vast bulk of India's uneducated voters may not know about Nazi Germany and such criticisms no matter how important perhaps remain elitist.[92] There might be intellectual merit in the comparison between fascism and the European politics of the 1930s and India's Hindu majoritarian ideology, but its electoral appeal is of little consequence. The Italian scholar, Marzia Casolari, in *In the Shade of the Swastika: The Ambiguous Relationship of Indian Nationalism and Nazi- fascism,* observes, 'Hindu organizations adopted two main political lines in the period between 1920 and 1940. On the one hand, the "race" issue was maximized, finding its fullest expression in the Hindutva discourse, which had much in common with widespread racial ideas in Europe, at the time. On the other hand, Hindu organizations made remarkable efforts to convince public opinion that the Hindu population lacked a sense of militancy. According to them, Hindu society should be militarized with an anti-Muslim scope. From the 1920s onwards, Muslims became the main target of Hindu policy and Muslims started to be perceived and described as more threatening than the British rulers.'[93]

On the Idea of Political Future

I want to focus on the political future specifically, not just the general future of Indian Muslims that has been vigorously debated and written about, both prior to and post 1947.[94] In the post-1947 period, some notable scholarship available on this question are regarding the general future of Indian Muslims, including works by scholars such as Mohammad Mujeeb, S Abid Hussain, Mushirul Hasan, Asghar Ali Engineer, Moin Sakir, AG Noorani, and many others, including publications by intellectual politicians such as Rafiq Zakaria and Salman Khurshid. Furthermore, some scholars have worked on particular dimensions of Indian Muslim issues, say, on partition, and related issues of South Asian Muslim history by Ayesha Jalal, Muslims in cities and on discrimination by Christopher Jaffrelot, on institutions such as Deoband by Barbara Metcalf, on the history of Indian Islam or political Islam, by Francis Robinson, Faisal Devji, Mohammad Ayoob and others, or Muslims in specific cities like Hyderabad by Taylor Sherman, or secularism by Romila Thapar, Akeel Bilgrami, Rajeev Bhargava, on Communalism or ethnic violence by Paul Brass, Gyanendra Pandey, Steven Wilkinson, Sudhir Kakar, Ashutosh Varshney, on women by Slyvia Vatuk, Zoya Hasan, or Women Madrasa by Usha Sanyal, or Muslim sects by Justine Jones, on constitution or citizenship question by Upendra Baxi, Nirja Jayal Gopal etc.[95] It is not possible to mention such a rich list of scholars writing on multiple dimensions of Muslim lives but their seminal works have profoundly shaped the scholarship on Muslim conditions and in that particular sense general future of Indian Muslims.

The basic distinction I wish to draw here between the political future and the general future of Indian Muslims is defined by their place in the Indian polity that assigns and protects the rights and privileges of Muslim citizens. What drives the narrative is, primarily, the question of whether Indian Muslims should be treated as an equal stakeholder or not in Indian polity. The question of economic or cultural future becomes redundant or obsolete unless there is a robust political future. More specifically, it implies that Indian Muslims need to be treated as political equals, laying down a framework in which the modern Indian state considers its obligation to address a variety of futures. Without political equality, such concerns might be treated with general empathy or even be ignored completely. According to the Indian Constitution,[96] Indian Muslims are treated as political equals, which is what India's secular polity promised after India's independence, encouraging more than 35 million Indian Muslims at the time of Partition to choose India as their motherland over Pakistan. That political and constitutional arrangement is now under sustained threat with the Hindu Right's growing electoral and political dominance.

By political future, it is implied that the future is reflected in multi-layered relationships that Indian Muslims have forged with the Indian state through various institutions—from the parliament to the panchayat. These relationships, in turn, shape their engagements with Indian society: their place in political processes, their legal and political entitlements to various forms of rights as equal citizens, say, for instance, the right to life, equal opportunity, or to practice their faith without any fear, right for a dignified life or to have access to due process of law, etc. In a nutshell, this implies the notion of citizenship in its political avatar as the bundle of rights—not just inscribed in the wonderful words of the Indian Constitution, but as practised in the day-to-day lives of Indian Muslims. Though these rights are promised in the Indian Constitution endorsed on 26 January 1950, their benefits have been denied over the years in some form or other,[97] and increasingly so after 2014, to Indian Muslims and many other marginalized groups. Owing to this reason, scholars such as Christophe Jaffrelot and others have argued in recent years that India has embarked on an unrestrained march to become a majoritarian state.[98]

Only when the political future is ensured, will Indian Muslims be empowered to bargain and negotiate their economic or cultural future. The systematic weakening of the political future would cause Indian Muslims to gravitate towards destitution, a permanent state of misery, a life of no rights, and endless persecution. An attempt is being made to make Muslims and secular citizens aware that politics matter because political power matters. In the end, citizens live under the shadow of political power or state power, whose arms are long. Therefore, Muslims and all citizens really should be aware of who are the governing elites of the society, their intentions, their commitment to the rights of citizens of various backgrounds, and their long-term objectives. To paraphrase Michel Foucault, they should have 'knowledge of power and power of the knowledge.'[99] Power is a very dynamic phenomenon both as a structure and as a process. It is constantly shaped by multiple forces whose understanding and appreciation are vital for all citizens, in this particular context, Indian Muslims.

Part of the reason why Indian Muslims today have found themselves cornered and stand with their backs to the wall, is because of their lack of awareness of these changing dynamics of political power/state power. To put it bluntly, the average Muslim in India today is confused, lives under unprecedented fear, and has no comprehensive knowledge of what is unfolding in his/her nation or democracy—and what it means for his or her life or future generations. Lost completely in the maze of outdated rhetoric of failed or increasingly irrelevant secular political elites, and their promise of an elusive safe future in the face of a wide variety of random or organized violence, Indian Muslims remain bewildered in their homeland, often consoling themselves privately that these political developments are reflective of short-term political turmoil and a return to the old days in a few years might happen! The truth is a tectonic shift that has caused India's ideological shift towards the Hindu Right for the long haul, and those old days of the so-called secular India are decisively things of the past now!

Indian Muslims: Which Way Now?

For politically aware South Asian Muslims—particularly from India, Pakistan, Bangladesh, and their Muslim diasporas in various regions of the world—Sir Sayyid Ahmad Khan (1817-1898) remains an iconic figure, a revered social reformer, and a source of inspiration.[100] In the words of Ayesha Jalal, 'Sir Sayyid Ahmad Khan took it upon himself to shepherd a straying flock of co-religionists into greener pastures within the colonial system.'[101] Another Sir Sayyid is the need of the hour is how scholars, Muslim public figures, and Muslims generally, often exhort while reflecting on the current predicament of Indian Muslims, almost like the ultimate prayer. During the post-mutiny period, Sir Sayyid made cogent arguments about Muslims needing to come to terms with modernity, reconcile with Western education, and prepare for unprecedented reform in the colonial era. He urged for a paradigmatic shift in Muslim thinking and their approach to life in the changed context. According to KA Nizami, Sir Sayyid found a panacea in education for all types of social, political, and economic ills inflicting Indian Muslims. Addressing a meeting in Amritsar on 29 January 1884, Sir Sayyid said, 'If the Government has not given some of our rights to us as yet for which we may have a grudge, higher education is a thing, which, willy-nilly would oblige them to give (those rights) to us.'[102]

As an institution builder, Sir Sayyid led the Aligarh movement,[103] established Aligarh Muslim University (AMU), and suggested ways to grapple with the unprecedented challenges that Muslims living under British India during the post-Mutiny period confronted. While appearing before the Education Commission, when he was asked if religious prejudices alone had kept the Muslims from English education, Sir Sayyid highlighted political traditions, social customs, religious beliefs, and poverty as the main causes.[104] In setting up MAO College, which eventually became Aligarh Muslim University (AMU), his ideal was an institution modeled on Oxford and Cambridge. While the institution was mainly intended to cater to the needs of Muslims, it was open to all Indians. Sir Sayyid never wanted AMU to be a communal institution but hoped it would be a community institution. A large number of his Hindu friends contributed to the college fund. The Rajas of Benaras, Vizyanagram, and Patiala made generous contributions. Out of the 50 rooms built, at least nine were built by Hindu donors like Chaudhury Shir Singh, Raja Dev Narain Singh, and Lala Phul Chand. On the slabs of the Strachey Hall, there appeared ten names of Hindu donors. In 1898 when Sayyid passed away, there were 285 students out of which 64 were Hindus.[105]

In the context of Hindutva politics, first of all, we need to reflect on the historical imaginations of these two prominent political categories and their political trajectories: Indian Muslims of Sir Sayyid's times and the ones of contemporary India. In part, a look at the various interconnected factors that created multiple Muslim identities out of Sir Sayyid's Muslim political category might shed light on the present-day political future of Indian Muslims. At this juncture, it appears that the political future of Indian Muslims is gloomy, marked by the dilution of rights, growing persecution, and target of sustained violence by both state and non-state actors who consider themselves torchbearers of majoritarian ideology.

The Indian Muslims of British India for whom Sir Sayyid showed concern during the post-Mutiny era and the present-day Indian Muslims are distinct political categories. The present-day Muslims residing in India are roughly 200 million (14.2 per cent according to the 2011 census)—a fraction of the vast population of a political community that Sir Sayyid worked for in the latter part of the 19th century. The Muslims of Sir Sayyid's period resided in an extended geographical region that covered the boundaries of present-day India, Pakistan, Bangladesh, and beyond and now are identified more loosely as South Asian Muslims. They also have state-specific names such as Mohajirs in Pakistan, Bangladeshi refugees in India, etc. Sir Sayyid could not have envisaged that the Muslim identity of his time could implode into such varied forms—and even be antagonistic to each other. Likewise, Mohammad Ali Jinnah, who tirelessly fought for a Muslim homeland during the 20th century also did not foresee, for instance, that Muslim identities could take the shape of identities such as Bangladeshi or Bangladeshi refugees. The two-nation theory that Jinnah championed in his Presidential address to the Muslim League in 1940 has become three nations in the same continent.

- How have these political reconfigurations that led to new identities impacted the fate of Indian Muslim identity today?
- What are the possibilities available to Indian Muslims now to negotiate their constitutional rights in the context of Hindu majoritarianism?

Since the Sepoy Mutiny of 1857[106] to the present day—roughly 170 years—numerous factors such as the politics of colonialism and Muslim nationalism/separatism, migration, politics of secularism, and majoritarianism,[107] have led to various political formations.[108] Consequently, these factors have created multiple political identities for Muslims that are often in conflict with each other. This implosion of Indian Muslim identities has been an enduring source of overt and not-so-overt Muslim consciousnesses. These fragmentations have caused further strains within non-Muslim identities—particularly with Hindu identities in the region, with terrible political consequences.

On paper, Muslims are citizens, but their rights, entitlements, and legitimate claims are fast eroding in the political space. Secular political parties see them as electoral liabilities. The less they talk about Muslims or their issues, the better their prospect of being appreciated by the majority. And the propaganda machine of communal parties presents them as pampered beneficiaries of vote bank politics. And so-called secular leaders often justify their silence on legitimate Muslim citizens' causes as a strategy to take on the Hindu Right's aggressive assault on Muslims. Take, for example, the Aam Admi Party (AAP) and its position on the Delhi riots or the Shaheen Bagh movement. Neither Arvind Kejriwal nor his colleagues such as Manish Sisodia or Sanjay Singh or Aatishi Marlena are bigoted politicians but they are not vocal in their stand on the Muslims of Delhi. It became apparent during the Delhi riot and anti-CAA movement. There are plenty of similar examples in various other so-called secular parties. With their silence, they are weakening the political voice for Muslims and also India's secular fabric. For instance, it is impossible to find a forthright leader like Nehru to stand for Muslim safety. In his book, *India Wins Freedom,* Maulana Abul Kalam Azad recalls a fascinating episode in which Nehru stresses on Muslim security during an episode of violence in Delhi even though Sardar Patel was hesitant to acknowledge the biases of Hindu officials or their complicity in targeting innocent Muslims.

Maulana Azad writes, 'I remember distinctly on one occasion when the three of us were sitting with Gandhiji. Jawaharlal said with deep sorrow that he could not tolerate the situation in Delhi where Muslim citizens were killed like cats and dogs. He felt humiliated that he was helpless and could not save them. His conscience would not let him rest, for what answer could he give when people complained about these terrible happenings? Jawaharlal repeated several times that he found the situation intolerable and his conscience would not let him rest. We were completely taken aback by Sardar Patel's reaction. At a time when Muslims were being murdered in Delhi in open daylight, he calmly told Gandhiji that Jawaharlal's complaints were completely incomprehensible.'[109]

In today's India, there is no secular leader who could be assertive or candid regarding Muslim security. It is no surprise that major so-called secular political parties barely organized protests on bulldozer justice etc., or raised voices for the Gurgaon namaz controversy in a country where Muslims have been allowed to offer prayer peacefully for ages as signs of cultural accommodation. They all seem to be non-issues for secular parties.

There are enough anecdotal accounts and research to suggest a majority of Muslims, of all classes, are hesitant to participate in politics—especially, electoral politics. A vast bulk of them seem to be interested in *deen* (life after death), not *duniya* (worldly life)—and there are regular mobilizations about this approach by Maulanas and various Jammats or organizations who are happy to leave the matter to the *uparwala,* meaning Allah or God. Put crudely, they just do not want to be political activists or people who have a say in political power, its content or direction, which could be possible only by direct engagement in politics as a vocation. To hold politics with contempt, and indifference, or view it as a demeaning act would only make Muslims further irrelevant in decision-making processes and deny them the fruits of state power. They would run the risk of being ignored and eventually destroyed. Life for the Muslim community at the margins of the state is plausible, but it would be a life of extreme marginality: brutish, violent, and short. It would be the life of a condemned lot, in a state of powerlessness, an easy target of violence, prejudices and discrimination, and without any weapon to fight these dark forces. Often, they may face surveillance, detention, and unlawful searches by the state or even non-state actors. In society, they may face boycotts, segregation, random violence and lynchings. According to media reports, Muslims in much of India are facing these unfortunate experiences almost on a day-to-day basis—far more frequently these days than in the past. They are perceived or presented as perpetrators of violence and violators of law, even if they are at the receiving end. Almost a new pattern, it seems, has emerged as a new normal in Indian politics. Indian Muslims are seen as a problem, a threat, or even an internal enemy, who need to be dealt with for political, social, historical, and ideological reasons.

The most important privilege as a citizen in a democratic society, and we are talking especially of Muslims in this scenario, is to enjoy the bundle of rights that empower them to lead a dignified life—not just to have them in rule books (say, in the Indian Constitution) but to have the political ability to make use of them when necessary or demand them when these rights are violated or diluted. This is possible only when they have the ability to negotiate creatively with political power so that those who are hostile to Muslim identity (for whatever reasons) feel the moral obligation to respect their rights and let them lead a dignified life. Indian Muslims are fast emerging as the new untouchables of Indian politics. For Indian Muslims, it is time to take a deep breath, recognize the new political reality, and figure out how they can assert their legitimate place in the Indian democracy to ensure their future as equals with other citizens, and their dignity is protected. A Muslim child should have the freedom to dream of becoming India's Prime Minister if he or she is competent, and religion should not come in its way from denying him or her. Such a political possibility could be explored only if India could be able to revive its secular polity, which was a constitutional dream that is now incurably wounded. And Indians are appreciated for their ability and not targeted for their identities.

Literature Survey

An impressive body of scholarship on various dimensions of identity issues of Indian Muslims and their challenges have emerged from scholars, public figures, journalists, activists, and others since India's independence. And, indeed, prior to 1947 as well. The writings, speeches, and political activities of prominent Muslim figures such as Maulana Abul Kalam Azad, Mohammad Iqbal, Mohammad Ali Jinnah, Khan Abdul Gaffar Khan, Shaikh Mujibur Rehman, Zakir Hussain, together with the writings and political interventions of Mahatma Gandhi, Jawaharlal Nehru, BR Ambedkar, Sardar Patel, VD Savarkar, and many others continue to shape the analysis of Muslim politics. Given that the Muslim identity is such a historically dense and multi-layered identity, contemporary concerns are often analyzed by digging into history. Ironically, the Hindu Right takes a rather deep interest in Indian history, but as Romila Thapar explains, 'Contributions to the past came from varying sources. But for Hindutva, the past of only Hindu communities is of any real consequence. For Hindutva current politics has to be conducive to bring about the Hindu Rashtra.'[110]

I begin my analysis with critical reflections on the scholarship before 1947 to lay out the historical context. WW Hunter's *Indian Musalmans* was written mainly to explain Muslim rebelliousness. It was a major concern for the colonial state owing to the role that Muslims played in the Sepoy Mutiny of 1857. Based on fieldwork in Bengal, Mr Hunter, a colonial civil servant, argued that Muslims had not profited from the British efforts to spread modern education in India, which Hunter argued was owing to their rebelliousness and backwardness. Sir Sayyid Ahmad Khan was deeply concerned about how Indian Muslims should recalibrate their approach to grapple with the post-Mutiny period. Sir Sayyid emphasized mainly on modern education, and actively discouraged Muslims from joining politics and was particularly opposed to the politics of the Congress.

Philosopher Mohammed Iqbal's (1877-1938) writings expressed deep concern about Muslims' future too. Three significant poems from this period, 'Shikwah' (The Complaint), 'Jawāb-e-shikwah' (The Answer to the Complaint), and 'Khizr-e rāh' (Khizr, the Guide), were published later in 1924 in the Urdu collection *Bāng-e darā* (The Call of the Bell). Iqbal presented the anguish of Muslim powerlessness in these works.[111] His philosophical arguments found expression in *The Reconstruction of Religious Thought in Islam* (1934), a volume based on six lectures delivered in 1928-29 in Madras, Hyderabad, and Aligarh. The Muslim community according to Iqbal, through the exercise of *ijtihad*—the principle of legal advancement—needed to devise new social and political institutions. Additionally, he also talked about a theory of *ijmā* (consensus).

In the post-1947 period, a diverse range of scholarship on the subject of Muslim conditions and their future emerged. Some events such as the Ayodhya movement, the demolition of Babri Masjid on 6 December 1992, the Gujarat riots of 2002, the Sachar Report of 2006, and the rise of Modi, particularly his massive victory in 2014 and 2019, have presented crucial contexts for burgeoning scholarship in multiple languages on this theme.

S Abid Hussain's *The Destiny of Indian Muslims,*[112] Mohammed Mujeeb's *Indian Muslims,* and Mushirul Hasan's *Legacy of a Divided Nation,*[113] among others, deserve special attention. Written in the post-Babri Masjid era,[114] a turning point in India's secular life, Mushirul Hasan's book has addressed issues in the context of the rise of Hindutva. Written in the 1990s, Hindutva was still in its early phases and there was hope for a secular fightback, which no longer seems to be the case in India. My book covers a longer period, at a time when Hindutva politics has now flowered and matured, and secular fightback appears rather feeble or some would say almost non-existence. The unraveling of the INDIA alliance prior to the 2024 election is a good example of the commitment to fight for secular India that was so dear to India's founding fathers.

The works of two scholar-politicians, Rafiq Zakaria and Salman Khurshid, are also worth commenting on. Rafiq Zakaria's *Indian Muslims: Where Have They Gone Wrong?*[115] addresses a wide variety of issues central to Indian Muslim lives. The book addresses the legacies of Pakistan—and further argues that its creation has aggravated the problems of the Muslim community. It further recognizes that there are issues of backwardness, particularly in restricting women from becoming independent. Since the book was published after the 2002 Gujarat violence, deep concerns about growing Hindu fundamentalism remain part of the narrative. Salman Khurshid's book, *Visible Muslim, Invisible Citizens,*[116] covers a wide range of themes such as the Babri Masjid dispute, Aligarh Muslim University, riots, Pakistan, the Rajinder Sachar Commission report, and so on. In a chapter titled 'The Shrinking Space', the author has extensively commented on the debate triggered by opinion pieces written by Harsh Mander and Ramachandra Guha.[117] This discussion not only reflects how secularism and Muslim issues are debated, it also exposes the limits of liberal articulation of these issues. It argues how full citizenship and the rights accompanied by it continue to elude Muslims in India.

Asghar Ali Engineer is no doubt the most prominent Muslim scholar-activist in modern India, whose seminal contributions to Muslim issues and their challenges are available in a vast number of scholarly publications. The fact that he was assaulted six times indicates not only how committed he was, but also how his interventions provoked his critics, particularly Bohra fundamentalists. His autobiography, *A Living Faith,*[118] sheds crucial insights into his understanding of Muslim issues, secularism, religious fundamentalism among Hindus and Muslims, etc. Another scholar worth mentioning is Imtiaz Ahmad,[119] who pioneered the works on Indian Muslims and their social stratification. His major contribution includes four edited volumes titled *Caste and Social Stratification among Muslims in India.*[120]

Two other works crucial to pay attention to are Christophe Jaffrelot and Laurent Gayer's *Muslims in Indian Cities: Trajectories of Marginalization,*[121] and Roger Jaffrey and Ronojoy Sen's *Being Muslim in South Asia: Diversity and daily life.*[122] Both volumes have shown how Muslims, like any other community, often negotiate their lives depending on the local contexts, but are driven by the larger cause of Islam, etc. Some works deal more directly with how state policies have impacted the lives of Muslims. Zoya Hasan's book, *Politics of Inclusion: Caste, Communities, and Affirmative Action,*[123] is one such significant intervention.

The work of historian Raziuddin Aquil, *The Muslim Question,*[124] presents fascinating perspectives into Indian Muslim lives and their challenges. While seeking to explain Islam, its history and its current predicament, the author reminds us that the violent political and Islamist groups have a history of their own and are not a typically modern problem. What I find particularly interesting is his suggestion to read ancient Islamic thought and understand the revival of the philosophy of Ibns Rushds to address present and future problems.

The publication of the Sachar Committee Report in 2006 and the debate that ensued has also led to the publication titled *Institutionalising Constitutional Rights: Post-Sachar Committee Report* by Abu Saleh Shariff. The author attempts a critical assessment of the impact of 'post-Sachar' policies, and seeks to bridge the gaps in empirical measurements. The book recommends policies and institutions required to ensure the constitutional right to equal opportunity for all Indian citizens, especially minorities, such as setting up an Equal Opportunity Commission(EOC). It further asks for systematically computing a diversity index to improve the process of assimilation of the deprived groups, including the minorities, into the national mainstream.

Gujarat riots in 2002 also became a major reference point in some of the scholarship on Indian Muslims. Sanjeevini Badigar Lokhande's *Communal Violence, Forced Migration, and the State Gujarat Since 2002*[125] is one such volume. Raheel Dhatiwala's *Keeping the Peace: Spatial Difference In the Hindu-Muslim Violence in Gujarat in 2002*[126] is another crucial scientific narrative on the subject. Two important works that examine Muslim lives in India in the context of liberalization and globalization are Maidul Islam's *Indian Muslim(s) After Liberalization,*[127] and Tabassum Ruhi Khan's *Beyond Hybridity and Fundamentalism.*[128] Maidul Islam argues that the 'Muslim question' in India is not articulated in terms of demands for equity. The book tries to explore connections between multiple forms of Muslim marginalization, the socio-economic realities facing the community, and the formation of modern Muslim identity in the country. While post-liberalization economic policies have created economic inequality and joblessness for a significant population including Muslims, the political leadership camouflages real issues of backwardness, prejudice, and social exclusion, with the rhetoric of identity and security.

Hilal Ahmed's *Siyasi Muslims: A Story of Political Islam in India*[129] raises the following question: How do we make sense of the Muslims of India? The book seeks to analyze the imagined conflict between Islam and modernity affecting the Muslims' political behaviour in India. The author also examines how Muslim religious institutions, such as mosques and madrasas, are involved in politics and whether

Muslim political behaviour is shaped by the intervention of these institutions.

Two other books are of relevance: Saeed Naqvi's *Being the Other: The Muslim in India*[130] and Rakhshanda Jalil's *But You Don't Look Like a Muslim.*[131] Saeed Naqvi is a senior journalist who has reported and commented on many crucial moments of modern Indian politics. Rakhshanda Jalil has raised many pertinent questions on what it means to be a Muslim in India and what are the challenges in leading a life with a secular idea. Among other new works, Ghazala Wahab's *Born A Muslim: Some Truths about Islam in India*[132] is a combination of a personal memoir and her analysis of the history of politics of Islam and Muslims in India.

While my volume draws insights from some of the works discussed here, this book raises some fundamental questions, about why and how Indian Muslims have been edged out of India's power structure, the ideological reasons behind it, and why and how Hindu majoritarianism is going to reconfigure Indian Muslims' relationships with the state as well as society. And how they need to face this challenge in the new period which I describe as the *third political moment.*

The volume has six chapters in addition to the *Introduction* and *Conclusion*. The first chapter, 'Majoritarian *Zulm* (Tyranny) and Muslim's Right to Have Rights', examines the challenges in the evolving majoritarian polity regarding the state and fate of the rights of Indian Muslims as citizens. It reflects on the overall trend of Indian polity and how the ideological warfare is unfolding and also has given the Hindu Right an upper hand. It situates the Muslim question in that wider context. The second chapter titled 'The Cultural and Political Lives of South Indian Muslims' discusses Muslims in India's South, which is generally a neglected or often excluded theme in the writings of Indian Muslims. It is widely recognized that the Muslim puzzle is often generalized through the lens of Muslims in North India alone. In that sense, this is a significant departure in the analysis of Indian Muslims. The third chapter titled, 'Violence against Muslims and the Idea of "Banality of Violence"' discusses various forms of violence that are unleashed on Indian Muslims—and how a new environment of violence is presently created with the unprecedented rise of the Hindu Right. It makes many Muslims in India feel as if the state is against them. Ever since the passage of the Triple Talaq Bill (TTB), there has been a massive interest to find out why the Hindu Right, which is generally seen as anti-Muslim has been too eager to support pro-Muslim women's measures. In a chapter titled, 'Muslim Women: Which Way Now?' I explore various aspects of this debate. The chapter titled 'Shaheen Bagh and the Future of the Citizenship Debate' is on the citizenship question and how the legacy of Shaheen Bagh is going to shape it. Finally, the never-ending debate on Muslim backwardness is closely examined in a chapter titled 'The Unending Debate on Muslim Backwardness' in the context of the rise of Hindu majoritarianism.

Notes

1 Baldwin, James. 2021. 'Letter From A Region In My Mind' in *The Matter of Black Lives.* Edited by Jelani Cobb and Devid Remnick. 3-59. London: Willian Collins (an imprint of Harper Collins). P. 8.

2 West, Cornel. 1994. *Race Matters.* New York: Vintage. Pp. VII.

3 For a comprehensive understanding of the challenges that African Americans are seeking to deal with, see, Shelby, Tommy and Terry, Brandon. M. 2018. *To Shape A New World: Essays on the Political Philosophy of Martin Luther King, Jr.* Cambridge: Harvard University Press.

4 Ojha, Arvind. 2020. '14 Haryana Panchayats decide to "boycott Muslims" after clashes, inform police'. Available at: http://www.indiatoday.in. (accessed on 13 November 2023).

5 See Sud, Nikita. 2008. 'Secularism and the Gujarat State:1960-2005' *Modern Asian Studies.* 42, 6: 1251-1281.

6 Yagnik, Achyut and Sheth, Suchitra. 2005. *The Shaping of Modern Gujarat.* New Delhi: Penguin. P. 212.

7 On the relationship between caste and race, see, Wilkerson, Isabel. 2020. *Caste: The Lies That Divide Us.* New York: Allen Lane, (an imprint of Penguin Books). For a critical understanding of what caste is and its implications, see Ambedkar, BR (first published in 1936). *Annihilation*

of Caste. New Delhi: Navayana. Also for a comprehensive understanding of Ambedkar's contribution to justice, see. Baxi, Upendra. 1992. 'Emancipation As Justice: Babsaheb Ambedkar's legacy And Vision.' In *Ambedkar and Social Justice.* Vol 1. New Delhi: Director of Publications Division, MINISTRY OF INFORMATION AND BROADCASTING, GOVERNMENT OF INDIA. Pp. 13-41.

8 Prabal, AJ. 2023. 'Suffer for 200 years and be ready to atone for 2000 years of caste discrimination'. Available at: http://www.nationalheraldindia.com (acccessed on 13 November 2023). It is reported that Mr Bhagwat said that reservations mandated by the Constitution should continue, it was more a question of dignity and respect rather than political and economic parity. *Samman, Samvedna, Samvad* (respect, empathy, and dialogue) were what was needed.

9 See, Pandey, Gyanendra. 2013. *A History of Prejudice: Race, Caste, and Difference in India and the United States.* Cambridge: Cambridge University Press. P. 2. Pandey basically suggests two types of prejudices: vernacular and universal. The vernacular is reflected in calculated behaviour—racism, casteism, patriarchy so on and so forth which state could measure and contain. The universal type is invisible but is everywhere and nowhere.

10 Considerable debate over this topic has taken place since 1990s. Some valuable works on this: Mukherjee, Aditya. 2008. *RSS, School Texts and the Murder of Mahatma Gandhi: The Hindu Communal Project.* New Delhi: Sage Publications; also the chapter on this by Nussbaum, Martha. 2008. *The Clash Within: Democracy, Religious Violence and India's Future.* Cambridge: Harvard University Press. Lal, Vinay. 2003. *The History of History: Politics and Scholarships in Modern India.* New Delhi: Oxford University Press.

11 For recent debate on this see, Ray, Victor. 2022. *On Critical Race Theory: Why It Matters and Why You Should Care.* New York: Random House. Schuessler, Jeniffer. 2021. 'Bans on Critical Race Theory Threatens Free Speech, Advocacy Group Says.' Available at: http://www.nytimes.com (accessed on 10 February 2024). Also, Robb, Peter.1995. (ed.) *The Concept of Race in South Asia.* New Delhi: Oxford University Press.

12 For a succinct view on Muslim reservation question, see Hasan, Zoya. 2005. 'Reservations for Muslims.' Available at: http://www.india-seminar.com (accessed on 10 February 2024). See the essays by Sukhdeo Thorat, Christopher Jaffrelot and Gurpreet Mahajan, in this special issue of Seminar magazine that focusses on reservation and private sector. For a more detailed analysis on various dimensions of affirmative action policy

and Indian Muslims, see Hasan, Zoya. 2011. *Politics of inclusion: caste, minorities and affirmative action.* New Delhi: Oxford University Press.

13 See, Mufti, Aamir. R. 2007. *Enlightenment in the Colony: The Jewish Question and the Crisis of postcolonial culture.* Princeton: Princeton University Press.

14 Mamdani, Mahmood. 2013. *Neither Settler Nor Native: The Making and Unmaking of Permanent Minorities.* Cambridge: Harvard University Press. His analysis of how genocide and internment was deployed by the White American state to create a permanent native underclass.

15 See, Basu, Amrita. 2015. *Violent Conjectures of Democratic India.* Cambridge: Cambridge University Press.

16 Ambedkar, BR. 2015. (First published in 1936). *Annihilation of Caste.* New Delhi: Navayana.

17 Shepherd, Kancha Ilaiah. 2018. *Why I am Not a Hindu: A Sudra Critique of Hindutva Philosophy, Culture, and Political Economy.* New Delhi: Sage Publications.

18 Rehman, Mujibur. 2023. 'The Politics of Caste Census, Its impact on secularism.' Available at: http://www.thehindu.com (accessed on 10 February 2024).

19 For a detailed discussion on this see, Zelliot, Eleanor. 1992. *From Untouchable to Dalit: Essays on Ambedkar Movement.* New Delhi: Manohar Publications. Especially the section dealing with Round Table conference.

20 I have shared my insights into why Muslim-Dalit alliance is a counterweight to Hindu majoritarianism in the Conclusion of this volume.

21 For understanding various dimensions of mughal rule, see, Dalrymple, William. 2007. *The Last Mughal: The fall of a dynasty: Delhi, 1857* New Delhi: Penguin; Also, Athar, Ali. 2023. *Army Organization, Military Technology, and Warfare During the Delhi Sultanate.* New Delhi: Manohar; Gandhi, Supriya. 2020. *The Emperor Who Never Was: Dara Shukoh In Mughal India.* Cambridge: Harvard University Press.

22 Chakravorty, Sanjoy, Kapur, Devesh and Nirvikar Singh. 2017. *The Other One Perent: Indians in America.* New Delhi: Oxford University Press.

23 Sohal, Amar. 2024. *The Muslim Secular: Party and Politics of India's Partition.* New Delhi: Oxford University Press. This is a very important work not just to demolish the argument that Muslim leaders were separatists, but some of them fiercely worked for a secular India.

24 Dubois, WEB. 2018. *The Souls of Black Folk.* New Delhi: Gyan Publishing House. P. 4.

25 See, Savarkar, VD. 2023. *Essentials of Hindutva.* New Delhi: Abhisek

Publications. For a closer examination of what Hindutva means, see, Sharma, Jyotirmaya. 2023. *Hindutva: Exploring the Idea of Hindu Nationalism.* New Delhi: Context (a division of Westland Books). Also see the chapter on Savarkar by Kapila, Shruti. 2021. *Violent Fraternity: Indian Political Thought in Global Age.* Princeton: Princeton Univeristy Press. Also see, Chaturvedi, Vinayak. 2023. *Hindutva and Violence: VD Savarkar and Politics of History.* New Delhi: Permanent Black.

26 Hamid Ansari was considered for High Commissionership for Pakistan according to rumours in power corridors during the Prime Ministership of Rajiv Gandhi, and it stayed as rumours. Mr Ansari served as India's Vice President for two terms under the UPA government.

27 See, 'Address by Prime Minister, Sri Narendra Modi to the Joint Session of the US Congress.' 23 June, 2023. Available at: http://www.mea.gov.in (accessed on 10 January 2024).

28 Nair, Neeti. 2023. *Hurt Sentiments: Secularism and Belonging in South Asia.* Cambridge: Harvard University Press. P. 75.

29 Sahu, SN. 2023. 'Fadnavis's 'Aurangzeb Ki Aulad' utterance yet another attempt to promote majoritarianism.' Available at: http://www.thewire.in (accessed on 24 January 2024).

30 Amin, Shahid. 2005. 'Representing the Musalman: Then and Now, Now and Then' in Mayaram, Shail, Pandian, S.S., Skaria, Ajay. (Ed). *Muslims, Dalits and the Fabrications of History.* New Delhi: Permanent Black and Ravi Dayal Publishers. P. 3.

31 Eaton, Richard. 2019. *India in the Persianate Age: 1000-1765.* London: Allen Lane.

32 Nizami, KA. 1966. *Sayyid Ahmed Khan.* New Delhi: Publications Division. Ministry of Information and Broadcasting. Government of India.

33 Mujeeb, Mohammad. 2017 (first published 1967). *Indian Muslims.* New Delhi: Munshilal Manoharlal Publishers. P. 557.

34 Thapar, Romila. 2023. *Our History, Their History, Whose History.* London: Seagull Books.

35 Ibid. P. 44.

36 Ibid. P. 53.

37 Singh, Upinder. 2024. *A History of Ancient And Early Medieval India: From the Stone Age to the 12th Century.* New Delhi: Pearson. P. 748.

38 Asif, Manan Ahmed. 2020. *The Loss of HINDUSTAN: the Invention of India.* Cambridge: Harvard University Press. P. 9.

39 Deshpande, Prashant Prabhakar. 2023. 'PM Modi's outreach to the wider Muslim society- an honest effort to bring Muslim society into the

national mainstream.' Available at: http://www.timesofindia.indiatimes.com (accessed on 24 January 2024).

40 Ahmad, Imtiaz. 2018 (first published in 1973). *Caste and Social Stratification Among Muslims in India.* New Delhi: Aakar Books. P. XXIX.

41 See, Eaton, Richard. 1993. *The Rise of Islam and the Bengal Frontier 1204-1760.* New Delhi: Oxford University Press. P. 315.

42 For a detailed discussion on this see, Ahmed, Rafiuddin. 1982. *Bengal Muslims, 1871-1906: A Quest for Identity.* New Delhi: Oxford University Press.

43 Ibid.

44 See, Ambedkar, BR. 2015. *Annihilation of Caste: Annotated Critical Edition.* New Delhi: Navayana. P. 281.

45 See, Jones, Justin. 2012. *Shi'a Islam in Colonial India: Religion, Community and Sectarianism.* New Delhi: Cambridge University Press, p. 5.

46 Ibid. p. 110.

47 Hasan, Mushirul. 1997. 'Traditional Rites and Contested Meanings.' In Graff, Violette. 1997. *Lucknow: Memories of a City.* P. 122.

48 Fakhri, SM Abdul Khader. 2008. *Dravidian Sahibs and Brahmin Maulanas: The Politics of the Muslims of Tamil Nadu, 1930-1967.* New Delhi: Manohar.

49 See, Jones, Justin. 2017. 'The Pakistan That is Going to be Sunnistan': Indian Shi'a Responses to the Pakistan Movement' in Qasmi, Ali Usman and Robb, Megan Eaton. (Ed.) *Muslims Against the Muslim League: Critiques of the Idea of Pakistan.* Cambridge: Cambridge University Press. P. 375.

50 Ibid. P. 375.

51 Email communication with the author on 18 February, 2024.

52 Ibid.

53 See the report, Masoodi, Ashwaq. 2014. 'Being Muslim will be tougher after 16 May: Historian Mushirul Hasan.' Available at: http://www.livemint.com (accessed on 10 June 2020).

54 Ibid.

55 Ibid.

56 See, Yadav, J.P. 2023. 'BJP appoints former AMU Vice Chancellor Tariq Mansoor as party vice president'. Available at: http://www.telegraphindia.com (accessed on 10 January 2024).

57 Eaton, Richard. 1994. *The Rise of Islam and the Bengal Frontier, 1204-1760.* New Delhi: Oxford University Press. Especially see the chapter, 'The Rooting of Islam in Bengal.' Pp. 297-301.

58 Ibid. p. 299.

59 Dinesh Chandra Sen, Trans and Ed. *Eastern Bengal Ballads,* 1. pt. 1: 3 (originally quoted in Eaton).

60 I first discussed this idea of the political moment in an essay titled, 'Muslim Political Behavior' published in Rehman, Mujibur. (Ed.). 2018. *Rise of Saffron Power: Reflections on Indian Politics.* New Delhi: Routledge. The paper was presented at the Annual Meeting of the European South Asian Association (EASAS) at Zurich, Switzerland held in July 2014. Among others, comments on the paper shared by several scholars were helpful which includes: Dietmar Rothermund, Ted Wright, Katharine Adeny, Yunus Samad and Gur Harpal Singh.

61 On Aligarh movement and its afterlife, see the following amongst others, Lelyveld, David. 2003. *Aligarh's First Generation: Muslim Solidarity in British India.* New Delhi: Oxford University Press. Also, a recent book by Wajihuddin, Mohammad. 2021. *Aligarh Muslim University: The Making of a Modern Indian Muslim.* New Delhi: Harper Collins. Also, see, Hussain, Khuram. 2019. *Islam as Critique: Sayyid Ahmad Khan and the Challenge of Modernity.* New York: Bloombsbury Academic.

62 The most important work on the Deoband movement is by Metcalf, Barbara. 2002. *Islamic Revival in British India: Deoband: 1860-1900.* New Delhi: Oxford University Press.

63 For a rich discussion, see Gopal, Sarvapalli. (Ed.). 1992. *The Anatomy of a Confrontation: Ayodhya and Rise of Communal Politics in India.* London: Zed Books.

64 Brass, Paul 2011. *An Indian Political Life: Charan Singh and the Congress Politics. 1937-1961.* Sage Publications. P. 52.

65 See, Rai, Vibhuti Narain. 2016. *Hashimpura 22 May.* New Delhi: Penguin.

66 Sherman, Taylor. 2022. *Nehru's India: A History in Seven Myths.* Princeton: Princeton University Press. P. 64.

67 Fuerst, Illyse R Morgenstein. 2021. *Indian Muslim Minorities and the 1857 Rebellion: Religion, Rebels, and Jihad.* London: Bloomsbury.

68 Sir WW Hunter's work, *Indian Musalmans: Are They Bound in Conscience to Rebel Against the Queen.*

69 Fuerest, Illyse R Morgenstein. 2021. *Indian Muslim Minorities and the 1857 Rebellion: Religion, Rebels, and Jihad.* London: Bloomsbury. Pp. 49-52.

70 Jalal, Ayesha. 2000. *Self and Sovereignty: Individual and community in South Asian Islam since 1850.* London: Routledge. P. 58.

71 Appadurai, Arjun. 2006. *Fear of Small Numbers.* Duke: Duke University Press.

72 Hindu Right views Muslim history in particularly adversarial ways.

73 Muslims eat beef whereas Hindus worship cows. This has been a matter of mistrust between the two communities and there have been organized anti-cow slaughter movements in various parts of India for many years. This has also been the reason for ethnic violence.

74 It is generally argued by the Hindu Right that Muslims deliberately opt for large families so that they can overtake the Hindu population. A very useful empirical analysis that debunks this myth is by Qureshi, SY. 2021. *Population Myth: Islam, Family Planning and Politics in India.* New Delhi: Harper Collins.

75 Norton, Anne. 2013. *On the Muslim Question.* Princeton: Princeton University Press. P. 9.

76 Shaikh Mujibur Rehman. 'The Many Faces of Islamophobia.' *The Hindu.* 2 September 2023.

77 Also, see some of the recent works on Savarkar, his ideas and life. See, Vikram Sampath. 2019. *Savarkar: Echoes of a forgotten past.* New Delhi. Penguin Viking.

78 Kapila, Shruti. 2021. *Violent Fraternity: Indian Political Thought in Global Age.* Princeton: Princeton University Press. P. 115.

79 For a useful scholarly account on Pakistan see, Shaikh, Farzana. 2009. *Making sense of Pakistan.* London: Hurst and Co.

80 Some of the important works on Bangladesh liberation include Raghavan, Srinath. 2015. *1971: A Global History of the Creation of Bangladesh.* New Delhi: Orient Blackswan; Bass, Gary J. 2014. *The Blood Telegram: India's Secret War in Bangladesh.* London: Random House; Zakaria, Anam. *1971: A People's History from Bangladesh, Pakistan, and India.* London: Vintage.

81 Singh, Gur Harpal. 2000. *Ethnic Conflict in India: A Case Study of Punjab.* London: Palgrave Macmillan. Also, see Singh, Gur Harpal. 1996. *Punjabi Identity: Continuity and Change.* New Delhi: Manohar.

82 Recent intervention by the Indian state to take over Kashmir by removing article 370 and converting it to a union territory.

83 See, Hazarika, Sanjoy. 2018. *Strangers No More.* New Delhi: Aleph; also, Baruah, Sanib. 2001. *India Against Itself: Assam and Politics of Nationality.* New Delhi: Oxford University Press.

84 Rehman, Shaikh Mujibur. 2018. 'A new vulnerability.' http://www.thehindu.com (accessed on 10 February 2024).

85 See, Adeny, Katharine. 2021. 'How Can We Model Ethnic Democracy? An application to contemporary India.' *Nations and Nationalism.* Vol 27. Issue. 2. Pp. 393-411.

86 Jaffrelot, Christophe. 2019. *Modi's India: Hindu Nationalism and The Rise of Ethnic Democracy.* Princeton: Princeton University Press. See particularly Part II of the volume titled, *'The World's Largest De Facto Ethnic Democracy.'* Pp. 155-248.
87 The Report was commissioned in 2005 and was submitted in 2006. Since Justice Rajinder Sachar was the chairperson of the Report, it is widely referred to as the Sachar Report. Other members of the Committee include Dr Abu Shaleh Shariff (Member-Secretary), TK Ommen, Rakesh Basant and a few others.
88 Alam, Javed. 2005. 'A Turning Point in History.' Available at: http://www.frontline.thehindu.com (accessed on 15 September 2023).
89 These issues are also discussed in detail in some of the chapters here.
90 In his autobiography Fakir Mohan Senapati recounts this story.
91 See, Sarkar, Sir Jadunath. 2023. (first published 1960.) *India: Through the Ages: A Survey of the Growth of Indian Life and Thought.* New Delhi: Manohar Publications. Pp. 42-43.
92 See, Chandra, Abhimanyu. 2020. 'Modi is a bigger cult figure than Savarkar or Vajpayee: Jamia professor Mujibur Rehman.' Available at: http://www.caravanmagazine.in (accessed on 10 November 2023).
93 Casolari, Marzia. 2020. *In the Shadow of the Swastika: The Relationships betweenIndian Radical Nationalism, Italian Fascism and Nazism.* New Delhi: Routledge.
94 It could be argued that the main factor that motivated the separate homeland debate was the deep concern for the political future of Indian Muslims in post British free India. Since free India was going to be a democracy led by a majority rule, it was feared the Hindu majority would have a natural advantage in the governing of India.
95 There is also vast number of young scholars at the doctoral and post-doctoral level working on various dimensions of Muslim question. I have engaged with their research in building up my narrative.
96 On various dimensions of the Indian Constitution and how it has fared, see, Austin Guneville. 1999. *Working in a Democratic Constitution: A History of Indian Experience.* New Delhi: Oxford University Press.
97 Not just Indian Muslims, there are others such as Dalits, and tribals who have also experienced such widespread violations of their rights. Clearly, the Indian state has shown class bias. The case of Indian Muslims could be unique owing to the fact it is a major religious minority with a distinct history, which is the reason for it being a political target by the Hindu Right.

98 See, Rehman, Shaikh Mujibur. 2019. 'Rule of the Majority'. Available at: http://www.frontline.thehindu.com (accessed on 10 February 2024). Also, Chatterji. A.P., and others. (Ed.). *The Majoritarian State: How Hindu Nationalism is Changing India.* New Delhi: Harper Collins.

99 Foucault, Michel. 2002. *Power: Essential Works 1954-84.* London: Penguin Random House.

100 For an incisive analysis on Sir Sayyid, see Yasmeen Saikia and M Raisur Rahman. (Ed.). 2019. *The Cambridge Companion to Sayyid Ahmad Khan.* Cambridge: Cambridge University Press.

101 Jalal, Ayesha. 2000. *Self and Sovereignty: Individual and Community in South Asian Islam since 1850.* New York: Routledge. P.61.

102 Lectures. (cited in KA Nizami. 1966. New Delhi: Publications Division. Ministry of Information and Broadcasting. Government of India. P. 189).

103 For understanding the legacy of this movement, see the chapter, 'Defining Boundaries: Modernist interpretations and the new intellectual structures' in Hasan, Mushirul. 1997. *Legacy of a Divided Nation: Indian Muslims Since Independence.* New Delhi: Oxford University Press. Pp. 223- 252. Also see David, Lelyveld. 2003. *Aligarh's First Generation: Muslim Solidarity in British India.* New Delhi: Oxford University Press.

104 Nizami, KA. 1966. *Sayyid Ahmad Khan.* New Delhi: Publications Division. Ministry of Information and Broadcasting. Government of India P. 72.

105 Ibid. P. 70.

106 There are multiple interpretations of this momentous event of Indian history. Veer Savarkar. 2019. *India's first war of independence.* New Delhi: Abhisekh. This presents Hindu Right perspectives. Also see Bipan Chandra and others. (Ed.). 2016. *India's Struggle for Independence.* New Delhi: Penguin.

107 On the issue of majoritarianism see, Appadurai, Arjun. 2006. *Fear of Small Numbers.* London: Seagull. Also see, Robinson, Francis. 2007. *Separatism Among Indian Muslims: The Politics of the United Provinces Muslims, 1860-1923.* Cambridge: Cambridge University Press.

108 Some of the important works are: Bose, Sugato and Jalal, Ayesha. 2017. *Modern South Asia.* New Delhi: Taylor and Francis. Also, Sugato Bose and Ayesha Jalal. 1997. *Nationalism Democracy and Development: State and Politics in India.* New Delhi: Oxford University Press.

109 Azad, Mualana Abul Kalam. 2022. (first published in 1959). 'India Wins Freedom: The Complete Version.' New Delhi: Orient Blackswan. Complete version first published in 1988. P. 232. See the chapter 'Divided India' in this volume for a detailed discussion. Pp. 224-242.

110 Salam, Ziya Us. 2023. 'For Hindutva, Only the Hindu Past is Relevant, says Romila Thapar, author of The Future in the Past: Essays & Reflections.' Available at: http://www.thehindu.com (accessed on 10 February 2024).

111 See Mcdonough, Sheila D. 2024. 'Mohammad Iqbal: Poet, Philosopher'. Available at: http:// www.britannica.com. (accessed on 22 February 2024).

112 Hussain, S Abid. 1965. *The Destiny of Indian Muslims.* New Delhi: Asia Publishing House.

113 Mushirul Hasan has another edited volume titled, *Living With Secularism: Destiny of Indian Muslims* (Manohar 2017). For his main ideas of Indian Muslims, see, Hasan, Mushirul. 1997. *Legacy of a Divided Nation.* New Delhi: Oxford University Press.

114 Babri Masjid demolition on 6 December 1992, is the major turning point in Indian Muslims' lives, and continues to shape the politics that directly impact their future.

115 Zakaria, Rafiq. 2004. *Indian Muslims: Where Have they Gone Wrong?* Mumbai: Popular Prakashan.

116 Khurshid, Salman. 2019. *Visible Muslim, Invisible Citizens.* New Delhi: Rupa Publications.

117 See, Palshikar, Suhas. 2018. 'Citizenship Rights, Not burka: Why the Harsh Mander- Ramachandra Guha debate must continue—and expand.'. Available at: http://www.indianexpress.com (accessed on 10 February 2024).

118 Engineer, Asghar Ali. 2012. *A Living Faith.* New Delhi: Orient Blackswan.

119 See my obituary, Rehman, Mujibur. 2024. The Social Scientist.

120 Imtiaz, Ahmed. 1978. *Caste and Social Stratification among Muslims in India.* New Delhi: Manohar.

121 Jaffrelot, Christophe and Laurent Gayer. (Ed.). 2012. *Muslims in Indian Cities: Trajectories of Marginalization.* New Delhi: Manohar.

122 Jaffrey, Roger and Ronojoy Sen. (Ed.). 2014. *Being Muslim in South Asia: Diversity and daily life.* New Delhi: Oxford University Press.

123 Hasan, Zoya. 2011. *Politics of Inclusion: Caste, Communities, and Affirmative Action.* New Delhi: Oxford University Press.

124 Aquil, Raziuddin. 2017. *The Muslim Question: Understanding Islam and Indian History.* New Delhi: Penguin Random House.

125 Badigar Lokhande, Sanjeev. 2016. *Communal Violence, Forced Migration, and the State Gujarat Since 2002.* Cambridge: Cambridge University Press.

126 Dhattiwala, Raheel. 2020. *Keeping the Peace: Spatial Difference In the*

Hindu-Muslim Violence in Gujarat in 2002. Cambridge: Cambridge University Press.

127 Islam, Maidul. 2018. *Indian Muslim(s) After Liberalization*. New Delhi: Oxford University Press.

128 Khan, Tabassum Ruhi. 2015. *Beyond Hybridity and Fundamentalism: Emerging Muslim identity in Globalized India*. New Delhi: Oxford University Press.

129 Ahmad, Hilal. 2019. *Siyasi Muslims: A Story of Political Islam in India*. New Delhi: Penguin.

130 Naqvi, Saeed. 2016. *Being the Other: The Muslim in India*. New Delhi: Aleph.

131 Jalil, Rakhshanda. 2019. *But You Don't Look Like a Muslim*. New Delhi: Harper Collins.

132 Wahab, Ghazala. 2021. *Born A Muslim: Some truths about Islam in India*. New Delhi: Aleph.

1

INDIAN MUSLIMS' RIGHTS TO HAVE RIGHTS AND ITS POLITICAL CONTEXT

> 'The calamity of the rightless is not that they are deprived of life, liberty and the pursuit of happiness, or of equality before the law and freedom of opinion—formulas which were designed to solve problems within given communities—but they no longer belong to any community whatsoever.'
>
> —Hanna Arendt, *The Origins of Totalitarianism*

Indian Muslims are currently living under pervasive fear in an India that is increasingly embracing Hindu majoritarian politics. Finding themselves as targets of lynching, bulldozer justice, frequent riots for trivial or often for no reason, and subject to random violence in this new majoritarian state, they have started asking if they have any rights at all as citizens in India.

The Indian state's decision to approve the pardon of 11 perpetrators against gang rape victim Bilkis Bano during the 2002 Gujarat riots on 15 August 2022 and facilitate their release is one of the prominent examples that shows that the arc of justice has stopped bending towards fairness for Indian Muslims. India's Supreme Court overturned this decision of the government on 8 January 2024, but the intent of the government is what is central to our analysis. Despite public outcry, that the Indian state remained firm on its decision for close to a year and a half speaks volumes of its intent. In this broad scenario, Muslim citizens are experiencing substantial erosion of rights and their 'Right to Have Rights' is constantly challenged.

The phrase 'Right to Have Rights' was formulated by German philosopher Hanna Arendt—a phrase of tremendous theoretical and intellectual potential—which needs to be unpacked in order to make sense of what is unfolding in India today. In *Origins of Totalitarianism,*[1] Arendt wrote, 'We become aware of the existence of a right to have rights (and that means to live in a framework where one is judged by one's actions and opinions) and a right to belong to some kind of organized community, only when millions of people emerge who had lost and could not regain these rights because of the new global situation.'[2]

Syela Benhabib analyzes further the phrase, *Right to have Rights.* It is apparent that the word 'right' is deployed twice in this phrase. So, Benhabib asks, 'Is the concept of "right" being used equivalently in two halves of the phrase?' The first use, she says, 'is addressed to humanity as such and enjoins us to recognize membership in some human group.'[3] She further explains that what is involved here 'is a moral claim to a membership and certain form of treatment compatible with the claim of membership.'[4] The second use of 'right' is in its juridico-civil usage and could be described as 'civil and political' rights or as citizens' rights. In this particular usage, according to Benhabib, there is a 'triangular relationship between the person who is entitled to rights, others upon whom this obligation creates a duty, and the protection of this rights claim and through its enforcement through some established legal organ, most commonly the state and its apparatus.'[5] This second use of 'right' is pursued on the prior claim of membership. Therefore, she explains, 'To have a right, when one is already a member of an organized political and legal community, means that I have a claim to do or not to do A, and you have no obligation not to hinder me from doing or not doing A.' This second category of rights, according to her, 'entitles persons to engage or not in a course of action, and such entitlements create reciprocal obligations. Rights and obligations are corresponded: rights discourse takes place among the consociates of a community.'[6]

Since Indian Muslims are seen as a religious minority, they enjoy minority rights, which is how a whole set of rights were created and embraced in the Indian Constitution based on debates in the Constituent Assembly.[7] Given that majoritarian Hindutva polity does not recognize minority rights, it has systematically attacked the rights of Indian Muslims as part of vote bank politics for decades. What is crucial to note is that there is no place for minority rights as such in the overall discourse of rights by Hindutva polity, which deems minority rights as divisive and thus antithetical to majoritarian polity. Additionally, Hindutva polity views Indian Muslims as a historical entity with an established record of oppression against Hindu society. That is why it is necessary to understand the complex relationship between Indian Muslims and Hindutva polity or Hindu majoritarianism. And how its growth has contributed to the changing fortunes of Indian Muslims and is redefining the basic character of Indian democracy.

Separation of Powers: Not Working

In India's liberal democracy, the conventional logic that the separation of powers between executive, legislature, and judiciary would protect the rights of average citizens (in this case Indian Muslims) is becoming increasingly non-functional. This is what is giving Indian democracy a body blow, not just to minority rights or the Muslim future. Even distinguished members of the Indian judiciary have started throwing up their arms about the efficacy of India's liberal polity—especially its ability to deliver justice. This non-functionality of separation of powers is the most crucial reason why Hindu majoritarianism has become the only game in town. Often recognized in the form of decay of institutions, it has deeper roots and predates the arrival of the BJP in national politics. In a rather benign way, Atul Kohli presented empirical evidence for what he described as a 'growing crisis of governability' in the late 1980s.[8] We need to take a pause before we put all the blame on the Hindu Right political forces to make sense of how and what led to such a dangerous turn. If you look at the emergency of 1975-1977 as an aberration and turn a blind eye to the phenomena of the 'decay' of institutions prior to and after the emergency—we may not go very far in making sense of why Indian voters continue to support Hindu majoritarianism.

Indian Case: Not Part of Global Pattern

Crisis in liberal democracy, some argue, is part of a global pattern. Put simply, Hindu majoritarianism is expanding because identical forces are also gaining ground elsewhere in Europe, Latin America, and North America. However, I'd disagree with the argument that the roots of Hindu majoritarianism lie in global factors. The global tendencies may be a small part of the story, but the Indian case is unique and indigenous. The Hindu Right would have risen and expanded in any case given its commitment and elaborate and systematic organizational activities in multiple spheres for decades. It did receive some support from global developments. For instance, Islamophobia owing to 9/11 helped the Hindu Right to legitimize its version of anti-Islamism. Or the global story of Islamic terrorism created a favourable climate to justify its measures against Kashmir. Some circumstantial factors might have helped expedite the rise of Hindu majoritarianism but the Hindu Right movement of India is primarily an indigenous ideological movement. According to the proponents of Hindutva politics, they are not undermining institutions, instead they are rescuing institutions from Western influence and corrupt secularists who have disregarded Hindu culture since India's independence. Votaries of Hindutva politics would further argue to address the concerns of religious minorities such as Muslims or Christians that they are indeed creating a new version of cultural accommodation in India by encouraging minorities to respect Indian culture. What was presented to the world as minority rights, according to Hindutva votaries, is indeed reckless pampering of Muslims and Christians.

Ever since the rise of Donald Trump and other populist leaders in the West and elsewhere, a great deal of scholarly writings on the of crisis of liberalism has emerged. Jan-Werner Mueller explained it beautifully in a column titled *Liberalism's Forever Crisis.*[9] Ever since British voters voted to pull out from the European Union and American voters' decided to vote for Mr Trump in 2016, liberalism is seen in crisis, wrote Mueller. But, 'Which liberalism? Are we talking about the set of ideals or institutions such as the much criticized "liberal global order," or only about recent policies pursued in several Western countries, which may or may not have anything to do with a political philosophy plausibly labelled liberalism?' asks Mueller.[10]

To understand various strands of liberalism and challenges that liberal democracy are facing, the writings of two scholars, AC Grayling and Pierre Rosanvallon, could be immensely useful. Both focus their analysis mainly on Western democracies. Rosanvallon offers a fascinating narrative about democracy beyond elections. The puzzle he seeks to address is captured in the opening sentence itself, which is, 'Our regimes are democratic but we are not governed democratically.'[11] AC Grayling, however, addresses more directly the challenges arising from the British voters' decision to withdraw from European voters and election of Donald Trump in America. In a chapter titled, 'Why It Has Gone Wrong,'[12] Graying cites three reasons why the representative government in liberal democracy has failed to live up to expectations. The first relates to the functioning of institutions, and the second is about 'those in whose hands lies the ultimate source of legitimation of the democratic order—the electorate.'[13] And finally, the third factor is the agencies with partisan interests who do not want open competition with competent rivals and therefore manipulate both the institutions and the electorate. In the Conclusion, Grayling offers a set of solutions to fix the problems associated with the system of representative government. While the works of both of these scholars are of tremendous value in making sense of Western scholarship, their concerns may not address the challenge that Indian democracy faces—the reason: the Indian case is a reflection of a deeply ideological movement, which has its own version of governance, and the Hindu Right celebrates it as a unique version of democracy.

When Narendra Modi became India's Prime Minister, some compared him with Donald Trump. Martha C Nussbaum and Zoya Hasan wrote a column in a major Indian daily, *The Indian Express*, on 24 July 2017 titled, 'India and the US, Spot the Difference'. But the comparison between the two cannot be stretched beyond a point. Even they recognized in the same column, 'Modi is disciplined and works to a plan. He has patience and a long attention span. He does appear to enjoy the adulation, but not in the manner of the narcissist: he does not let him turn away from his ideological programme.'[14]

Ideological Warfare

Some scholars who study Hindutva politics or majoritarian politics assume that the BJP is like any other party, and is expected to follow the Constitution. And its policy interventions are meant only for the pursuit of political power. This is the reason why they often accuse the Hindu Right regimes and their organizations of violating the Indian Constitution. But the truth is that the BJP is distinctly an ideological party. And the BJP's ambitions are not limited to just grabbing state power, but to bringing about the cultural and political transformation of society. Without a doubt, India is in the midst of an ideological warfare, and the Hindu Right at present enjoys a comparative advantage, with its organizational strength, resources and effective strategies. Therefore, the best way to understand Muslim issues is to view it from the vantage point of ideological struggle, and how the Hindu Right has formulated strategies to convert Muslims from *citizens* to *subjects*.

Historically speaking, the Hindu Right's goal to establish a majoritarian state could be traced to the politics of early 20th century of British India. During the 1920s three dominant ideological forces found their feet in the political landscape of British India. They worked in tandem with each other in their shared objective to free

India from the yoke of British rule. At the same time, each of them sought to deploy a distinct ideological brush to paint a new India once the British departed: the Congress for a secular India, for people of all faiths; the Muslim League for an Islamic Pakistan, a Muslim homeland; and the Hindu Right for a Hindu Rashtra, a homeland only for Hindus.

The Indian National Congress (INC) party with an extensive mass base, together with other secular parties was working for a secular India. Their singular goal was to create a nation in which people of all religions could live harmoniously with equal rights. Then, there was the Muslim League led by Mohammed Ali Jinnah (1876-1948) which fought for a separate homeland for Muslims called Pakistan. Jinnah made a case for it in the League's 1940 Lahore resolution and argued that Muslims are a separate nation by themselves, not to be seen as a religious minority.[15] The Hindu Right was the third political force, which considered India mainly a Hindu land and viewed Muslims and Christians as outsiders. It advocated for a Hindu Rashtra, an idea articulated in the writings of VD Savarkar.[16] This third force operated through various organizations and individuals to advance its ideological goal, and its most prominent political platform in the past few decades has been the BJP, set up in 1980.[17]

Among all the organizations that have remained active partners in the promotion of the Hindu Right's ideological goal, Rastriya Swayan Sevak Sangh (RSS), set up in 1925 has been the most prominent one.[18] Though RSS remains officially a cultural organization, the BJP's website recognizes it as its mentor.[19] Two of the RSS's former members have become India's Prime Ministers, Atal Bihari Vajpayee[20] (1998-2004), and Narendra Modi[21] (2014-present), indicating RSS's growing clout in the Indian polity. Given the growing electoral strength, many more future Prime Ministers of India are likely to come from the RSS background. Several RSS members serve as Chief Ministers, members of the Indian Cabinet, governors, and many other key positions of the political power structure that control the breath of Indian democracy. By all accounts, the political trends signifying the electoral and political domination of the Hindu Right seem irreversible.

On 15 August 1947, India was partitioned on religious lines. With this, the first two ideological forces found considerable success with the creation of secular India—at least in its Constitution, and Pakistan, a Muslim homeland. The third ideological force, the Hindu Right remained a marginal force. Mahatma Gandhi's assassination on 30 January 1948, which led to the ban of the RSS pushed it further into the margins.[22] Congress and other secular parties, for instance, Janata Party (1975-1977) and the National Front (1989-1991), largely governed India till the late 1980s and around the same time, the BJP emerged as a major political formation.

Till the mid-1990s, the Hindu Right was not seen as a threat to Indian nationhood by the supposedly secular political forces, who had no issues in aligning with the BJP and its predecessor, Bharatiya Jana Sangh (BJS). Such electoral alliances took place in the 1977 parliamentary elections and again in 1989 parliamentary elections presuming that the Hindu Right could be contained. In 1996, the BJP met with organized resistance when Vajpayee failed to cobble together a government despite being the single largest party and his government had to collapse in 13 days. Until then, the secular parties and various regimes they formed at all levels were convinced that owing to its exclusionary agenda, the BJP could not emerge as a dominant force in India, let alone win parliamentary elections or form a government on its own. What gave confidence to secular political parties and secular scholars to subscribe to such a view is the firm belief that India is a diverse country and that diversity has built-in resistance against such an exclusionary agenda. The results of the 2014 parliamentary election that elected Prime Minister Modi exploded that myth and his return in the 2019 parliamentary election and the high prospect of return in the 2024 parliamentary election signifies an unprecedented voter realignment in favor of the Hindu Right.[23]

Among the factors that led to the BJP's rise is the lack of

competition in the available non-Congress political space in the Indian electoral landscape. It happened because the non-Congress parties failed to emerge as an enduring opposition coalition. For instance, the secular parties of the non-Congress coalition who managed to pull up a historic win in the 1977 election under the leadership of Jai Prakash Narayan and formed the Janata Party government (1977-1980) imploded leading to the return of Indira Gandhi in 1980. A similar experiment, mainly led by a Congress rebel, VP Singh, in 1989 collapsed owing to ideological contradictions with the BJP, a coalition partner. Equally frustrating was the repetition that was witnessed during the 1996-1998 coalition experiment by non-Congress, non-BJP forces, which saw two short-term Prime Ministers, Deve Gowda[24] and IK Gujral.[25] This series of failures by the non-Congress governments destroyed the credibility of the non-Congress, non-BJP opposition alliance in the eyes of voters, thus killing the prospect of any potential third force outside the Congress and the BJP fold. The last time some serious conversation took place around the third force was before the 2009 election. The absence of a serious contender for a third force created a clear opportunity for the BJP to profit out of anti-Congressism, which has become an ideology in itself in Indian politics prominently since 1977. No one should assume that Indian voters were desperate to embrace Hindutva. They were never for Hindutva—not in the past and not even now. The latter is evident by the fact that whenever a serious contender emerges in state elections, the BJP has failed to win. For instance, Delhi 2020, West Bengal 2021, or Karnataka 2023. There are enough surveys to suggest people often vote for the BJP as they do not have a reasonable alternative against the Congress. The failure of a non-Congress secular opposition to emerge as a lasting coalition is a big factor in the BJP's rise, and this is not adequately acknowledged in the political analysis of the failure of India's secular project.

Since the mid-1990s, after the failure of the United Front government (1996-1998), India moved towards bipolar polity in which two coalition formations—National Democratic Alliance

(NDA) and United Progressive Alliance (UPA)—remained major rivals for national power. A perception was built that India was destined for coalition politics for a long time, but the emergence of Narendra Modi changed that scenario forever.[26] Along with this change, dramatic transformations in the fortunes of Indian Muslims have happened.

The Hindu Right forces, it is apparent, have operated within the rules set up by the secular political forces, employing various methods of trial and error, but never losing sight of its ultimate goal: the Hindu Rashtra/the Hindu state. They worked at multiple levels of formal and informal politics and have decisively outsmarted their secular challengers in most regions of India. Presently, the Hindu Right is securely poised at a knocking distance from accomplishing its ultimate goal of making India officially a Hindu Rashtra. Formulated mainly in the line of VD Savarkar's idea of Hindutva, the political strategies have evolved over the years, as a response to changing realities of Indian politics. This extraordinary political accomplishment by the Hindu Right has raised new threats for Indian Muslims, the alleged outsiders, risking their political future as never before.

From the 1980s to Today—The Position of Indian Muslims

Since the late 1980s, the steep growth of Hindu majoritarianism and the concomitant rise of the BJP has reconfigured Indian Muslims' relationship with the state as well as society.[27] Established in 1980,[28] the BJP fought its first parliamentary election in 1980 and won only two seats in 1984. Two of its stalwarts, Atal Bihari Vajpayee, who became India's Prime Minister (1998-2004), and LK Advani, who led the Rath Yatra which transformed the BJP into a party of mass base, both lost in the 1984 election.

The two BJP candidates who won were Chandupatla Janga Reddy from the Hanamkonda parliamentary constituency of Andhra Pradesh and AK Patil from the Mehsana constituency of Gujarat.

TABLE 1.1

Results of 2 Seats on Which BJP Won in 1984

State: Andhra Pradesh

Constituency: Hanamkonda

S. No.	Candidate	Party	Result	Votes	Vote Share %
1.	Chandupatla Janga Reddy	BJP	Won	263762	52.40
2.	P.V. Narasimha Rao	INC	Loss	209564	41.63

State: Gujarat

Constituency: Mehsana

S. No.	Candidate	Party	Result	Votes	Vote Share%
1.	A.K. Patel	BJP	Won	287555	52.86
2.	Rayanka Sagarbhai Kalyanbhai	INC	Loss	243659	44.79

But the 1984 election was an unusual one. Fought immediately after Indira Gandhi's brutal assassination, it was also called Shok Sabha,[29] not the Lok Sabha election. The Congress party won 404 seats with a vote share of 49.10 per cent, the highest any party had both before 1984 and after in modern India.

The sympathy wave for Indira Gandhi ran so deep during the 1984 parliamentary election that former West Bengal Chief Minister, Jyoti Basu, famously remarked that the dead Indira Gandhi seemed more powerful than the one who was alive. Had the BJP entered the election fray under normal circumstances, the party might have won more than two seats and even a greater vote share. With only two seats the party was seen as an insignificant force, but its vote share was 7.74 per cent. This vote share is greater than the vote share of the two communist parties in 2004 (7.07% [CPI(M)=5.66% and CPI=1.41%]) but their combined strength of seats in Parliament was: CPI (10 seats) and CPI(I) (43 seats) = total 53 seats. Though perceived as an insignificant political force, the BJP indeed had a decent foundational social base, though widely dispersed, to build on, which is what it did with great sophistication and commitment in subsequent years.

Between 1984, when they held only two seats, and 2014, when they gained 272 seats in the Indian Parliament, the BJP's political rise is unrivalled in India's modern political history. Among the many factors that contributed to its spectacular rise, the prominent seems to be the party's position concerning Muslims or Muslim issues. Among the strategies the party employed, the politics of religious polarization remains at the epicentre, which electorally helped the party and continues to do so. A report appeared in 2014 in *The Economic Times* titled 'BJP Gains in Polls after every riot, says Yale study'[30] that cited a research article published by a group of young political scientists from Yale University. Political polarization, according to research published under the title: 'Do Parties Matter for Ethnic Violence? Evidence from India' co-authored by Gareth Nellis, Michael Weaver, and Steven Rosenweig,[31] shows how riots help the BJP electorally. This is not to suggest that the politics of religious polarization revolving around Muslims has the capacity to help the BJP win the election. On several occasions, this strategy has backfired in a big way, particularly in state elections. For instance, in Karnataka Assembly Elections in 2023, Himachal Pradesh Assembly Elections in 2023, Bengal Assembly Elections 2021, Delhi Assembly Elections 2020, and many others. In all these instances, the BJP deployed the high-pitch strategy of politics of polarization but it didn't work. Given that it is part of its ideological campaign, despite electoral setbacks, it remains an integral part of the electoral arsenal. Consequently, we hear Amit Shah, India's Home Minister say, 'Reservations for Muslims is against the Constitution.'[32] But discrimination or violence against Muslims is against the Constitution as well, which no one hears from the Hindu Right or its political leadership.

In the words of Mohan Bhagwat, 'You see, the Hindu society has been at war for 1000 years. This fight has been going on against foreign aggressions, foreign influences, and foreign conspiracies. Sangh has offered its support to this cause, and so have others. Many have spoken about it. It is because of all these that the Hindu society has awakened. It is but natural for those at war to be aggressive.'[33] This should give some sense of why the Hindu-Muslim relations have gone into this conflict-ridden phase.

Table 1.5 contains the data showing the BJP's rise to political power until the last 2019 parliamentary elections. In this election, the party won the highest number of seats in its history, giving the party a great majority on its own to govern and set its agenda. On the rise of the Hindu Right, Akeel Bilgrami writes, 'But the roots of Hindutva nationalism were laid in the late 1970s and 1980s and from these, one can demonstrate determinable causal pathways and narratives to the phenomenon we have been landed within contemporary India.'[34] While this is a valuable perspective, the problem with this analysis is: How is it that the 'roots' of the Hindu right could grow during this period but not the roots of secular politics?

In my view, broadly, three turning points could be identified in the BJP's evolution from a marginal force to becoming the single largest party in modern India—and each has to do with its position on Muslim or Muslim-related issues.[35]

The first was the 1989 election. Fought at the height of the Ayodhya movement in which the BJP, particularly LK Advani,[36] chose to offer the movement the required leadership, and the party reaped enormous electoral benefits. The BJP made a significant jump from 2 to 85 seats in Parliament. Its vote share also moved from 7.74 per cent to 11.6 per cent.

The second turning point was in 1996. Having emerged as the single largest party with a vote share of 20.29 per cent, the party unsuccessfully tried to form a government under Atal Bihari Vajpayee. A moderate leader like Vajpayee failed to cobble together the first-ever BJP government in 1996, which lasted only 13 days. The BJP's national isolation was owing to its position on three controversial issues: 1) the removal of Article 370 from Kashmir; 2) the setting up of Ram Mandir in Ayodhya; and 3) the Uniform Civil Code (UCC). Owing to its hardline position on these issues, the party realized it was isolated, and decided to opt for a strategic retreat, which helped it to emerge as a group leader of the non-Congress coalition group called National Democratic Alliance (NDA) as India entered coalition politics. As things stand now, out of these three issues, two of them have been realized. Article 370 has been removed[37] and the Ram Temple has been inaugurated on 22 January 2024 based on an unprecedented judgement given by India's honourable Supreme Court.[38] The effort to implement the third is on and this is apparent in the way the BJP leadership is raising the issue in various state elections. The UCC was a major agenda for the BJP in the state election campaign of Himachal Pradesh[39] and Karnataka[40] and leaders in other BJP-ruled states have been raising the UCC issue. Uttarakhand has passed its version of the Uniform Civil Code.[41]

But during the mid-1990s, the short-term compromise helped the BJP to run the country from 1998 to 2004 with its coalition partners,[42] most of them secular parties such as Mamata Banerjee-led TMC; Farooq Abdullah-led National Conference (NC), and Nitish Kumar-led Janata Dal (U). These parties increasingly got acclimatized to the BJP's ideological politics, which weakened their credibility to make a case against Hindutva and the BJP. Nitish Kumar's JD(U) is now part of the NDA alliance and very much an integral part of the Hindu Right political alliance.

The 2014 election constituted the third turning point,[43] when the charismatic Narendra Modi created a broad social base that voted the party into power. The Hindutva agenda, however, remained intact, and in the background—but surfaced once the party was in power and became apparent after its resounding victory in 2019. Ramachandra Guha makes an apt observation in a column titled, 'Three Traits of Modi that has cost India dearly' in 2020. He explains why India's reasonably decent people have been backing Modi despite many challenges.

> Tragically, these well-meaning Indians were mistaken in giving Narendra Modi the benefit of the doubt. The third reason that Modi has been such a disappointment as Prime Minister is that

> he remains a sectarian Sanghi at heart. In his public statements, he has been careful not to appear outrightly communal—though even here he can slip, as in his notorious remark that he could identify those protesting against the Citizenship Amendment Act by the clothes they wore. [44]

During the Modi-led BJP reign since 2014, India's major religious minorities—particularly Muslims and Christians—have met with violence, hostility, and discrimination as never before. Muslims have been singled out more prominently compared to Christians. They are targets of lynching and are alleged to be part of various other projects such as love jihad, land jihad, religious conversion cases, etc. The anti-Muslim violence has increased since 2014 compared to what it was under Atal Bihari Vajpayee.[45] Owing to this difference, Vajpayee is often described as far more accommodating—even as secular by his opponents. On the day Vajpayee died, *The Hindu* described him as a secular leader. Several of Vajpayee's contemporaries, however, were deeply suspicious of the BJP's Hindu majoritarianism ideology and its Hindu Rashtra project, which is why Atal Bihari Vajpayee was fiercely opposed when he attempted to muster support from parties and leaders to form a coalition government in 1996. Vajpayee had often fought big political battles shoulder to shoulder with several stalwarts[46] of non-Congress parties, for instance, during the anti-Emergency movement in 1977, and later in 1989 to defeat the Rajiv Gandhi government.

The high tide of constant demonization of Indian Muslims has grown stronger because the Indian state has either remained indifferent or complicit in this campaign against Muslims. This was not only unleashed by the Hindu Right organizations, their cadres, and other like-minded organizations but by a powerful section of the Indian media. While hearing a series of cases of inaction by the state on hate speeches against Muslims and Christians, a bench of Supreme Court Justices, Justice KM Joseph and BV Nagarathna said, 'This is a complete menace and nothing short of it... We should all be careful about the seriousness of hate speech. We should not end up creating a Frankenstein's monster that will gobble (us) up.'[47]

Lynching is one of the worst forms of violence Indian Muslims are facing regularly. Senior journalist, Zia Us Salam's *Lynch Files: The Forgotten Saga of Victims of Hate Crime* documents the gory details of these inhuman crimes.[48] In July 2018, India's Supreme Court (a three-judge bench led by Justice Deepak Mishra and also comprising Justices AM Khanwilkar and DY Chandrachud[49]) asked the Modi government to come out with a separate law on lynching, which should instill a sense of fear in the perpetrators.[50] The Modi government has remained indifferent to this suggestion of India's highest court for more than four years, but has shown great alacrity to take measures to build Ram Mandir at the disputed site in Ayodhya revealing the Indian state's growing indifference towards Muslim lives and dignity. The judgment for Ayodhya was given on 9 November 2019, which was more than a year later, and the Modi government acted with tremendous commitment for obvious political reasons.[51] And the Ayodhya temple is now built and stands in glory. In December 2023, the government, in its attempt to decolonize the law, made some effort to make laws against lynching. Leave aside the Hindu Right or the BJP, the secular parties largely remained indifferent and barely made any noise on this Court judgement. They seemed obsessed with Adani's issue instead as if the other top corporate entities were paragons of virtues.

The nature and intensity of various Muslim demonizing campaigns vary from state to state and region to region. It is reported that there are different kinds of Hindutva laboratories, each with their distinct attributes and often identified as the Yogi Model, Gujarat model, Karnataka model, etc. A disturbing national pattern has been established and appears irreversible. The potential of the Hindu majoritarian forces to undermine the political future of Indian Muslims even as a non-state power raises greater concern.

Given the centrality of the state's role in a democratic society, it is impossible to foresee a society without a state. According to Harold Laski, 'Without the state, there will be anarchy.'[52] Even within the state, a set of anarchic conditions always exists. For instance, a majoritarian state could create conditions of anarchy for the religious minorities it seeks to target. An increasingly majoritarian Indian state has different narratives for different minorities depending on its perception of a particular minority, which it might seek to accommodate if perceived as non-threatening. Hence, Jains and Buddhists fall in the category of accommodation whereas Muslims and Christians fall under the category of exclusion.

The key point of my argument is: Indian Muslims would be able to safeguard their other interests, such as economic or cultural or of any other kind, only by becoming part of the political power structure. It means Muslims' presence in powerful decision-making bodies such as Parliament, Assembly, City Councils, Panchayat Raj, etc., in addition to bureaucracy—from national to local. But the Hindu Right has deliberately made an effort to push Muslims away from the political power structure. It has taken measures that have substantially reduced their numbers in bodies such as the Parliament or Assembly and weakened their political voice. This is apparent in the deliberate denial of Muslims from fielding them as candidates in various elections from Parliament to Assembly or any other elections in various states by the BJP. It has resulted in a massive decline of Muslim representatives in Parliaments and Assemblies (see Figure 1.2). The majoritarian agenda is to create a Muslim community without its own leadership, its political class, and thus no voice of its own.

Since the Gujarat violence in 2002, Narendra Modi has been questioned over the Muslim exclusion issue. In the *India Today Conclave* in 2008, Mr Modi was challenged by Congress leader Digvijay Singh, and Farooq Abdullah was also present on the panel.[53] According to Prime Minister Modi, his decision not to field Muslim candidates was not dictated by any communal consideration but such decisions were made purely by winnability criteria. But the notion of winnability is a subjective one. To give one example from innumerable existing ones, Mr Arun Jaitley was considered a candidate who could win which is why he was fielded in Amritsar in the 2014 parliamentary election, former finance minister of Prime Minister Narendra Modi, and yet he lost. Likewise, in elections under Modi, there are many ministers who on their own might not be able to win a seat owing to a lack of a mass base. No doubt, the real intent was to deny Muslims the opportunity to compete for a place in India's political power structure, a significant move for their disenfranchisement.

The fact remains that the BJP did not field a single Muslim candidate in Gujarat Assembly elections in 2002, 2007, 2012, and 2022. As a result, with no Muslim MLAs from the BJP, cabinet after cabinet in Gujarat had no Muslims in its ranks. This is the circle of exclusion from the power structure. The story was the same in the Assembly elections of Karnataka in 2018 and 2023 for the BJP and Uttar Pradesh in 2014 and 2017.

FIGURE 1.2

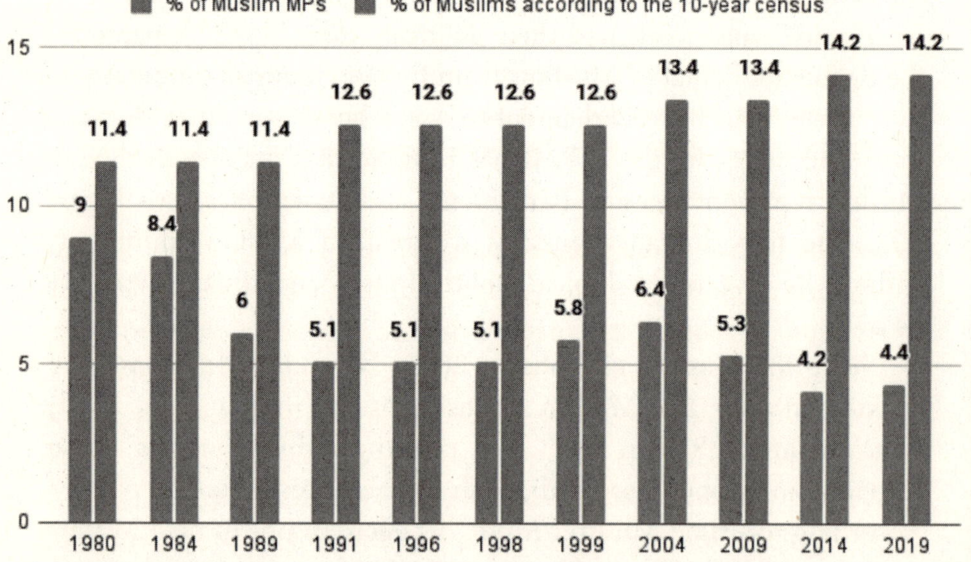

(Source: Election Commission Website. Government of India, New Delhi)

A dramatic decline of Muslim representation in political institutions like Parliament became stark in the 2014 parliamentary elections and was repeated in 2019. In 2014, no Muslim was elected from Uttar

Pradesh because the BJP did not field a single Muslim in the state where it won 71 seats, and again in 2019, the BJP fielded no Muslim in Uttar Pradesh, but 6 Muslim MPs were elected from Uttar Pradesh, 3 each from Bahujan Samaj Party (BSP) and Samajwadi Party (SP).[54] On the other hand, the Congress had fielded six Muslim candidates in Uttar Pradesh, and all lost. Other Muslim MPs came from states such as Jammu and Kashmir, Punjab, Kerala, Maharashtra, Telangana, and the Union Territory of Lakshadweep.[55] Not offering tickets to Muslims to run for office is part of the deliberate electoral strategy of the BJP. According to Christophe Jaffrelot[56]:

> The BJP's decision not to field any Muslim candidates aims to liberate the party entirely from the "Muslim vote" that it accuses other parties of wooing for electoral gain at the expense of the Hindu majority. The low representation of Muslims also stems from other parties, who are reluctant to field Muslim candidates in constituencies other than those with a high concentration of Muslim voters. This tactic was especially clear in the Congress' case, which the BJP accused of cultivating a Muslim vote bank by showing concern for their social and economic condition—a false concern if one goes by the impoverishment of Muslims in the UPA regime.

When the BJP, as India's largest party, adopts a policy of not fielding Muslims as an electoral strategy, it is plausible other parties would begin to emulate it, resulting in a massive decline of Muslim representatives from political institutions such as Parliament, Assembly, etc. Consequently, the Muslim political class would progressively shrink making the community lose its independent political voice, which is the end game that the Hindu Right is working towards. Such a scenario of weakened political voice would help a majoritarian polity to force a minority community to live under its terms.

FIGURE 1.3

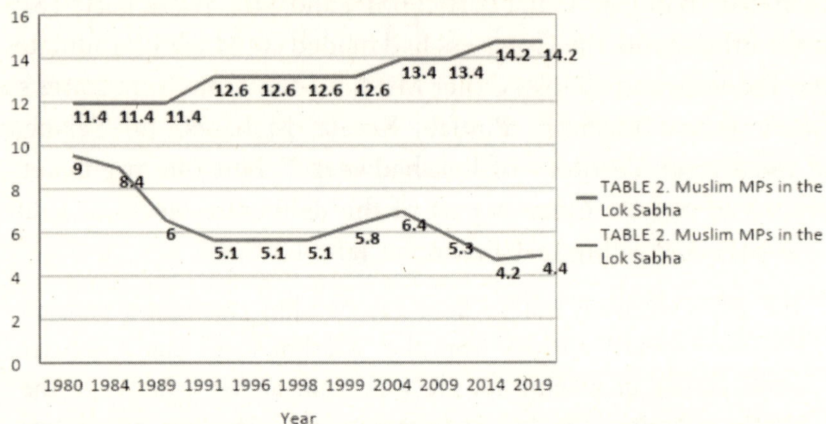

(Source: Election Commission Website, Government of India, New Delhi).

That such exclusionary strategies could be devised by champions of Hindu majoritarianism was foreseen by leaders of India's minority communities during the Partition debate. They demanded communal electorates and reservations of seats like those of Scheduled Castes (SCs) and Scheduled Tribes (STs). Sardar Vallabhbhai Patel (1875-1950), as the Chairman of the advisory committee on minorities in the Constituent Assembly, took steps to abolish communal quotas in legislatures and communal electorates. According to Rajmohan Gandhi, author of *Patel: A Life,*[57] this was because representatives of minority communities supported the idea (as it was widely perceived at the time) that it was the communal electorate system that sowed the seeds for Partition.

It is crucial to recall here that Sardar Patel was fiercely opposed to the idea of reserved seats for minorities, a practice that could have prevented the present scenario of the under-representation of Muslims in India's representative institutions such as Parliament or Assembly. Patel argued that a minority community, if it speaks in one voice, might be able to achieve its demands, but it would lose the goodwill of the majority. All major minorities—Muslims, Christians, Sikhs, Parsis, Anglo-Indians—were persuaded by Patel to forfeit the demand for reservation of seats. The advisory committee moved a resolution on 11 May 1949, that there would be no reservations except for SCs and STs, but there was no consensus. It was put to vote and a resolution was passed with 58 votes in favour and three against. Interestingly, Patel even won over Begum Aizaz Rasul of Uttar Pradesh, a former Muslim League member, and Maulana Azad took time but finally agreed.

What is striking to take note of in this deliberation is that different minority communities had different reasons for accepting Patel's proposal during the debate. For instance, Christians were promised that they would be given the freedom to propagate messages of Jesus or Christianity. During this debate, Patel said, 'I want the consent of all minorities to change the course of history... Whatever may be the credit for having won a Muslim homeland, please do not forget what the poor Muslims have suffered. I respectfully appeal to the believers of the two-nation theory to go and enjoy the fruits of their freedom and leave us in peace.'[58] In this new age of cow vigilantism, Ghar Wapsi, love jihad, it is worth asking: Where is Sardar Patel's promised peace?

Over the years, Muslims have remained underrepresented. This has been the worst-kept secret of Indian democracy that predates the advent of the BJP as a political party. According to Nirja Jayal, some studies argue that 'it is the Congress that must take the blame for the under-representation of Muslims.'[59] In the first five Lok Sabha elections (1952-1971), the Congress nominations for Muslims remained between 4.29 per cent and 5.74 per cent. In these elections, Muslim candidates belonging to the Congress managed to win even in constituencies where the Muslim population was only 3 per cent and 18 per cent (Ansari, 2003: 134). In the post-emergency election in 1977, for the first time Congress represented 7.52 per cent of Muslim candidates. However, Muslim votes went against Muslim candidates even if they were Congress nominees. The subsequent two elections held in 1980 and 1984 saw a massive pro-Congress wave and the number of Muslims elected reached the highest number. Since 1989, a decline of Muslim representation has been seen in subsequent elections say in 1991, 1996, and 1998. In 1996, the election that was held after the demolition of Babri Masjid, the Congress lost Muslim support, from 38 per cent in 1991 to 34 per cent in 1996.

In the parliamentary election in 1998 and 1999, Muslim support for the Congress party was 43 per cent and 50 per cent respectively, which is a significant rise from the past elections, particularly from 1996. This could be because the anger of Muslim voters against the complicity of the Congress party after the demolition of Babri Masjid had receded. On the question of the special relationship of Muslim voters with the Congress party, Nirja Jayal argues, 'While it may have held true till Nehru's time, it is of doubtful validity from the early 1960s onwards.'[60]

In institutions such as the Parliament, Assembly, Judiciary, Police, or any other, Indian Muslims have remained underrepresented and yet they were not anxious about this underrepresentation because they believed that since they were promised equal rights in the Constitution, their future was secure with some ups and downs during their political journey in Indian democracy. That faith in the Indian Constitution's potential to grant them dignified lives has proved to be naïve, misleading, and even delusional. In an incisive review of Madhav Khosla's *India's Founding Moment: The Constitution of a Most Surprising Democracy*,[61] Shruti Kapila has argued that the Indian Constitution has failed its minorities.[62]

Indeed, some scholars have raised concerns over the secular aspects of the Indian Constitution. According to James Chiriankadat, 'An irony of independent India's birth as a secular state was that the midwife—the Constituent Assembly—represented the outcome of communal politics that dominated the last years of British India.'[63] The Assembly, he further argues, did not represent a microcosm of Indian society. It was over-represented by the upper castes, especially among members from western India and the Hindi-speaking north.

Brahmins, who formed about five per cent of the population, accounted for around a quarter. Only 15 women ever sat in the Assembly whereas only one in six Indians was literate. An analysis of the membership of the Provincial Parliament reveals that 68 per cent of the members were graduates (13 per cent have received their degrees from abroad) with a further 18 per cent having attended college or high school. Table 1.4 contains the details in terms of caste and community composition of the Assembly.

TABLE 1.4

Members Serving in the Constituent Assembly :(1946-1949)
(by Caste and Religion)

Caste or Religion	*No of Members*	*Percent of Total*
Hindu (Non-Brahmin)	122	30
Hindu (Brahmin)	95	23.3
Hindu (Caste unknown)	53	13
Hindu (Nepali Gorkha)	2	0.5
Scheduled Caste	33	8.1
Sikh	14	3.4
Jain	4	1
Bhahmo Samaj	3	0.7
Tribal	5	1.2
Muslim	45	11.2
Christian	12	2.9
Christian (Anglo Indian)	4	1
Zorashtrian (Parsi)	6	1.5
Unidentified	9	2.2
Total	**407**	**100**

Note: This includes all those who served in the Assembly (it had 307 members in 1949)
(*Source:* Reproduced from the essay by Chiriankadat, James. 2000. 'Creating a Secular State in a Religious Country: The Debate in Indian Constituent Assembly.' Commonwealth and Comparative Politics.38(2))

From its side, the Hindu Right has explained its views on Muslims. Often, there were statements from leaders of various Hindu Right organizations such as the BJP and RSS, asserting that they do not intend to annihilate the community. RSS chief Mohan Bhagwat's statement is perhaps the most articulate one on the issue of the place of Muslims in Hindutva politics. In September 2018, Mr Bhagwat made an explicit statement on the place of Muslims in Hindutva ideology on the second day of a three-day RSS lecture series in New Delhi[64] which was arranged as a response to Rahul Gandhi's comparison of RSS with ISIS at his lecture at the International Institute of Strategic Studies (IISS), London, few weeks before and Mr Bhagwat clarified, 'Hindu Rashtra does not mean that it has no place for Muslims. The day it is said Muslims are unwanted here, the concept of Hindutva will cease to exist.'[65] What remained clouded in this rather explicit observation is:

What is the precise place of Muslims?

Will they remain equal?

Or will they become another category of Dalits?

Dalits have also been part of Hindu society for centuries—but their place remains at the distant bottom, in the far corner of a village, and their lives are controlled by various traditions and customs that the Brahminical order dictates. And that life is nothing less than slavery!

What Does It Mean for Muslims?

The rise of Hindu majoritarianism and its backlash might force Indian Muslims to survive in diminished numbers, with socio-economic conditions far worse than what has already hit them. Some minorities elsewhere in the world have faced similar threats in the past and others are still confronting them.

But a majoritarian state can make Muslim suffering legitimate because discrimination and violence carry official sanction as has been the case with Burma or Pakistan, but not with a constitutional state. Indeed, Indian Muslims or Christians have recorded suffering from riots or discrimination under a secular state in the past seventy years implying how even a secular state cannot fulfil all the promises it makes to a religious minority. A key question could be: If there is suffering and violence under any circumstance, then what is so unique about a majoritarian state? The fact is: in the case of democratic states, suffering is largely owing to enforcement-related issues; whereas in the case of a majoritarian state, it is directly owing to official policy.

The most crucial lesson that emerges from Indian Muslim experiences is that a religious minority can suffer despite constitutional protections. Despite the suffering, Indian Muslims have had the confidence that they have all the rights that the Indian state's founding fathers who drafted the Constitution ensured as a core set of rights, such as minority rights and human rights. Under the majoritarian state, no such confidence exists. Sabyasachi Bhattacharya in his Presidential address to the Indian History Congress at Malda, in 2016, highlighted this argument in his attempt to explain why the word secular was missing from the Indian Constitution that was adopted in 1950. In case of violations, these could be addressed and corrected by institutions such as the media and judiciary, who could work as a custodian in situations of state failure. However, that trust in the role of custodians is increasingly shattered among Muslims as well as among progressive-minded secular citizens.

In the wake of a Hindu Right ideological movement, those enshrined rights could be set aside or minorities could be victimized, and their political voice could be silenced, as evident in a series of cases following the anti-CAA protests in 2019 and afterwards. Therefore, what matters is not what the Constitution promises, but who controls the state or state power. A party with a majoritarian ideology could manipulate state behaviour in such a fashion that the minority rights enshrined in the Constitution could become inconsequential eventually. The political elites could remain completely insensitive to how history could look at them or even how the world looks at them. Amartya Sen reminded us about such developments in a column as follows[66]:

> No government lasts forever, even though the ruling groups might have the illusion that they would. The terrible departures

> from acceptable norms that the government may be able to push through right now may not be viewed in quite the same way in the future. Faiz Ahmed Faiz's famous poem "Hum Dekhenge", written in protest against President Zia ul Haq's rule pointed to a time in the future when today's deeds would be judged differently. Zia was all-powerful then, but how is he viewed today? And how are the politically invincible authoritarian rulers of Latin America of the past typically seen today? Are powerful rulers in India thoroughly indifferent to judgments that history will make?

In other words, the character of the state might be of a particular kind in its official version but its behavioural response could just be the opposite. In an important essay, Thomas Blom Hansen draws attention to how during Modi's regime a majoritarian ideology was pursued with the help of laws that were supposedly framed under secular regimes.[67] Consider the most controversial—the Citizenship Amendment Act (CAA). It is built on laws that were once passed by the UPA regime which was not an ideal secular regime but not a majoritarian regime either. Often, even the most empowering document like the Indian Constitution appears inconsequential in shaping state conduct, as has been apparent in recent interventions in Kashmir or enactment of laws such as the CAA. Those who run the state can be creative by tinkering with old laws, manipulating institutions such as the judiciary or media, and creating a consensus about their ideological goal. In practical terms, the nature of the state is eventually reflected according to the nature of the people who run it, particularly their political masters, who enjoy the upper hand and could dictate terms for the bureaucracy, and in turn, for the state.

TABLE 1.5

Vote Shares and Seats: Congress and BJP (1952-2019)

S. No.	Year of Election	Total Seats	INC		BJS/BJP	
			Seats	% of Vote	Seats	% of Vote
1	1952	489	364	45.0	3	3.1
2	1957	494	371	47.8	4	5.9
3	1962	494	361	44.7	14	6.4
4	1967	520	283	40.8	35	9.4
5	1971	518	352	43.7	22	7.4
6	1977	542	154	34.5	-	-
7	1980	542	353	42.7	-	-
8	1984	542	415	48.1	2	7.4
9	1989	543	197	39.5	86	11.5
10.	1991	543	232	36.5	120	20.1
11	1996	543	140	28.8	162	20.3
12	1998	543	141	25.8	182	25.6
13	1999	543	111	28.3	182	23.8
14	2004	543	145	26.69	138	22.16
15	2009	543	206	28.55	116	18.80
16	2014	543	44	19.52	282	31.34
17	2019	543	52	19.7	303	37.76

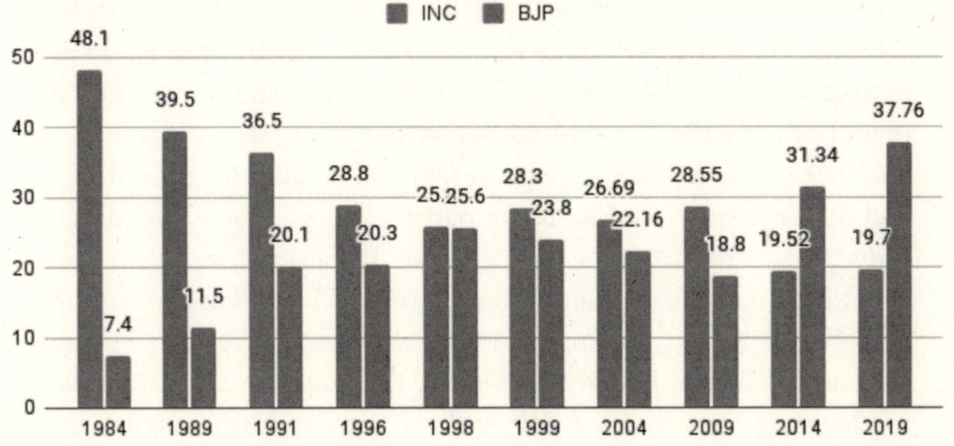

The political future of Indian Muslims is strongly tied to the future of the Hindu Right inversely. Stronger is the political force of the Hindu Right, and gloomier is the future of Indian Muslims. We need to make some sense of various political scenarios of the Hindu Right at this stage just to arrive at the possible political outcome. Compared to its recent history, particularly since the late 1980s, the Hindu Right was under constraint during the coalition era. Since 2014 that era of coalition has ended, and more importantly, the rival coalition for secular politics led by the Congress party has disintegrated. Besides the Congress party itself, from which many of its old and new leaders have moved out to other parties such as the Trinamool Congress (TMC) or National Congress Party (NCP), some of the regional parties have also gone through an internal split, like the NCP.

Another good example is the way several constituents of the anti-BJP coalition, India Alliance, have moved away—including the JD(U) of Nitish Kumar (joining the BJP)—with which it was planning to fight the parliamentary election. Comparing the voting pattern of the BJP and the Congress(I) leaders of the two coalitions—it is apparent that it is unlikely the Congress will be able to gather even one-third of the parliamentary seats that the BJP is winning on its own. It also implies there is no substantial revival of the Congress party in the near future. Consider this: the vote share of the Congress party in 2019 was 19.7, greater than the BJP's vote share in 2009 which was 18.8. And now the BJP's vote share is 37. 76, which is almost double its vote share in 2009 (see Table 1.5). This is evidence of a significant revival of the party. Can the Congress party add, say 10 per cent, to its 2019 parliamentary election vote share in 2024? I have doubts, and this is despite the Yatras the party is doing, which according to the report, is receiving a good response. It does not mean the party won't have more seats than what it has today. It is plausible the party may have a win in this or that state, which we have seen in states such as Telangana, Himachal Pradesh, Karnataka, etc. But, its ability to challenge the Modi-led BJP at the Centre is very limited, which has enormous implications for Muslim politics and Indian Muslims. Clearly, the hegemony of the BJP is likely to be the most dominant trend, which further indicates the flowering of Hindutva polity that will be accompanied by violence and atrocities of the kind that we have witnessed in Nuh in Haryana[68] or Haldwani in Uttarakhand.[69] To understand the BJP's or the Hindu Right's expansion with further clarity, the politics of two states, Gujarat and Uttar Pradesh, is key.

Politics of the Two States of Uttar Pradesh and Gujarat

From the point of view of how the destiny of Indian Muslims moved from the hands of a secular state to a majoritarian state we need to understand the master strategy that the Hindu Right deployed in mobilising the masses in two Indian states for years: Uttar Pradesh and Gujarat. In terms of socio-cultural conditions and political economy, there are strong similarities as well as sharp differences between these two states. These states have provided the anchor—first laying down the foundation—and subsequently, playing a large role in the expansion of Hindu majoritarianism. In the process they have created new models to deal with Muslims: Gujarat model and Yogi model, respectively. What is important to underline is that there would not have been a Yogi model had there been no Gujarat model!

In scholarly analysis, the role of the Ayodhya movement and the polarization it caused is well acknowledged. While both the states have a long history of Hindu-Muslim violence, Uttar Pradesh was the hotbed of communal politics and had witnessed the devastating impact of the Partition of India. Gujarat, the birthplace of Mahatma Gandhi, did not face much impact of Partition. The Hindu Right was able to gradually convert this relatively peaceful state from the point of view of Hindu-Muslim relations into a Hindutva laboratory.[70] On the other hand, Uttar Pradesh witnessed a sharp rise in the electoral base of the BJP in the late 1980s owing to the Ayodhya movement and later faced stiff challenges with the emergence of caste-based parties: Bahujan Samaj Party (BSP) and Samajwadi Party (SP). The alliance between the two caste-based parties raised hopes among secularists for a potent weapon to fight Hindu majoritarianism. It appeared to have some impact for a few years, but eventually, in 2014, the Hindu Right was able to consolidate and expand its social base transcending the caste divisions. In achieving this goal, Narendra Modi and his campaign driven by the Gujarat model played a vital role.

There was almost a similar threat from caste polarization that appeared in Gujarat with the Congress party's KHAM strategy,[71] but the Hindu Right was able to transcend it more conveniently as no such caste-based parties of the Uttar Pradesh type sprung up in Gujarat. LK Advani's Rath Yatra from Somnath to Ayodhya in 1990 and then the Babri Masjid demolition on 6 December 1992 created a new wave of religious polarization in Gujarat. In post-independent India the major turning point in Hindu-Muslim relations in Gujarat came with the 1969 riots. Between 1960 and 1995, the state largely had unstable governments. The only Congress chief minister who completed full term was Madhav Singh Solanki, and on four occasions the state was under President's rule. (Yagnik and Seth, 2005).

The RSS opened its branches in Gujarat in 1944, but it was in the 1960s that the impact of the Hindu Right organizations began to be felt in Gujarat's society. The Reddy Commission that investigated the 1969 riots first took note of it in its report. The 1974 Navanirman student movement presented the Jana Sangh an opportunity to mobilize people and then the party joined Jayaprakash Narayan's anti-emergency movement. In the 1975 elections, the Jana Sangh was able to win 18 of the 40 seats it fought. According to Achyut Yagnik and Suchitra Seth, 'More than the seats, for the first time since independence, Jana Sangh won wide-ranging acceptance and credibility from the middle-class upper castes because of its alliance with Congress(O) and Jayaprakash Narayan.'[72]

What also played a role is a series of Yatras that was undertaken by various Hindu Right organizations in Gujarat. Vishwa Hindu Parishad (VHP) started in 1983 and launched the Gangajal Yatra or Ektamata Yatra from Ganga Sagar in West Bengal to Somnath in Gujarat and also from Haridwar to the foothills of the Himalayas to Rameswaram in Tamil Nadu. In 1987, there was the Ram-Janaki Dharma Yatra which took place throughout Gujarat. This triggered Hindu-Muslim riots in several places such as Sabarkantha and Kheda districts. During this Yatra, for the first time, tribals attacked Muslims in places like Vipur town. This was followed by Ramshila Pujan by the VHP in 1989, which had a tremendous impact on Gujarati society. This Yatra also led to Hindu-Muslim riots in which 180 towns and villages were affected. Then in 1990, there was Ram Jyoti and Vijaya Dashami Yatra. Then there was LK Advani's Somnath to Ayodhya Yatra in 1990 again, which had an impact beyond Gujarat and has played a vital role in transforming India into a majoritarian state. After Advani's arrest, there was a bandh call by the BJP and VHP. It was followed by large-scale riots and 220 people were killed. By this time, religious polarization between Muslims, Hindus, and tribals was complete. It is in this background that the 2002 Gujarat riot and religious polarization that ensued needs to be viewed.

In 1995, the BJP was able to form the first government of its own. By then, what Ward Berenschot calls 'riot network' was well established and began flourishing. According to Berenschot, 'Riot networks are not just institutional riot systems, they are versatile patronage networks: the linkage between the actors who organize and instigate riots are a product of difficulties that citizens face when dealing with state institutions.'[73] What happened in 2002, particularly the silence of the Gujarati society broadly and its decision to return Narendra Modi and the BJP back to power in the Assembly election, needs to be seen against this background.[74]

While the Hindu Right contributed to anti-Muslim prejudices and politics of polarization created hostile conditions for Muslims, Narendra Modi maintained a special friendship with Bohra community, also from Muslim heritage. A group of Bohras are often seen in most of the public gatherings he addressed abroad. In a book titled *No Birds Passage* (2023), Michael O Sullivan presents a fascinating account of Gujarati Muslim communities, particularly Bohras, Khojas, and Memons. Though they constitute less than one per cent of South

Asia's Muslim population, they control a disproportionately large chunk of Muslim-owned firms, which he calls Muslim capitalism.[75]

Uttar Pradesh, however, has a longer history of the politics of religious polarization across Hindu-Muslim lines, particularly owing to the Pakistan movement and also Partition. It also has celebrated what is generally known as Ganga-Jamuna tehzeeb. According to Zoya Hasan, 'Uttar Pradesh, the heart of India has been the nerve centre of Indian politics since the late nineteenth century. Banaras, Allahabad, and Aligarh, along with other towns, were at the forefront of anti-colonial struggles in the last three decades of British rule. Several of the most illustrious leaders of the Congress were drawn from the province. Similarly, the demand for a separate homeland was made by UP Muslims who are at the centre of the separatist movement.'[76] After independence, the state was governed by the Congress party but is now under the BJP rule since 2017 continuously under Yogi Adityanath. With the rise of issues like lynching, a ban on cow slaughter, frequent small-scale riots, madrasa surveys, there has been growing irreparable strain in Hindu-Muslim relations both at the level of society and state.

Among the numerous factors that contributed to the BJP's expansion and consolidation is also the manner in which the party has been able to bring Dalits into its fold and has created voter alignment with the Dalits. There has been a concerted campaign to disrupt the composite living culture between Muslims and Dalits and othering of Muslims, according to Sudha Pai and Sajjan Kumar.[77] Pasis, Musahars, and Nishads were persuaded by the stories of *Ramayana*. These initiatives have borne fruit over the years and are reflected in the election results. In the 2014 parliamentary elections there was a substantial shift of Dalit and backward caste votes which was repeated in the 2017 Assembly elections and later in the 2019 parliamentary elections. In 2014, the party received 18 per cent of Jatav votes and 45 per cent of small Dalit group votes, and in 2017, it received 7 per cent of Jatav votes and 37 per cent of votes from smaller Dalit groups, and in 2019 Parliamentary elections, the party received 17 per cent Jatav votes and 48 per cent of votes from smaller Dalit groups, which helped the party to receive close to 50 per cent of votes, though the number of seats declined to 62 seats compared to 71 in 2014 parliamentary election, in which not a single Muslim MP was elected to Lok Sabha from Uttar Pradesh since India's independence.[78] It needs to be mentioned here that close to 68 per cent of Jatavs voted for the BSP in 2014 and there was a decline of 16 per cent of Jatav votes in 2019 for the BSP. It is also important to underline here that Dalit mobilization by the BJP is different from the way BSP has undertaken the task. According to Badri Narayan, 'While the BJP is reshaping these in terms of the Dalit contribution to the Hindu past, history and Hindu struggle against the Muslims, the BSP is using these as a proof of the better governance of Dalits, their contribution in the nation making process and, most importantly, to retail the memory of exclusion, oppression, and deprivation.'[79]

The first major significant churning among Muslim voters took place in Uttar Pradesh during the anti-Emergency movement in the 1970s, and it is argued by many scholars it was the Muslim voters who played a critical role in the defeat of Indira Gandhi in 1977. But the politics of soft Hindutva that the Rajiv Gandhi government played on the Babri Masjid issue, alienated many Muslim voters in subsequent years. And, the Muslim voters mainly were divided between the Samajwadi Party (SP) and the Bahujan Samaj Party (BSP). Occasionally, there are new Muslim parties like the Peace Party. This party also tried their fortune but not very successfully. The failure to send a single Muslim MP to Parliament in 2014 has created new anxieties among politically aware Muslim voters.[80] Some of the Muslim political formations such as AIMIM and AIUML have joined the fray to seek some support for their parties. They were rejected in 2017 and also in 2019 when most voters voted for candidates that could defeat the BJP. In 2024, it will be seen if the Pasmanda agenda of the BJP succeeds in giving a new spin to Muslim voters in Uttar Pradesh or not.

In the foregoing analysis, it is apparent that India's dream to establish a secular state was systematically challenged by the Hindu Right by deploying varied strategies in different regions of India. What was tried out in Uttar Pradesh was significantly different from what was employed in Gujarat. Likewise, the challenges it posed for Muslims in Uttar Pradesh have also been different from what Muslims experienced in Gujarat. The fact is, without the making of the legend called Narendra Modi in Gujarat, the revival of Hindu majoritarianism in Uttar Pradesh might not have happened. In a way, the Gujarat model revived Uttar Pradesh's declining fortune as apparent in the consistent decline of vote share in various Assembly and Parliamentary elections in Uttar Pradesh. In the 1998 parliamentary elections, the vote share was more than 36 per cent, which was reduced to 17.5 per cent in the 2009 Parliamentary election. Likewise, the BJP's vote share was 33.3 per cent in 1993 and that was reduced to 15 per cent in the 2012 Assembly election. By choosing to run from the Varanasi constituency in 2014, Narendra Modi was able to create a new context for the UP voters to consider his version of Hindu majoritarianism. A significant jump took place in the 2014 election to 42.63 per cent from little more than 17 per cent in 2009 and in 2019 it was close to 50 per cent. The rise in vote share of the BJP in Assembly elections in 2022 is 41.29 per cent, which was only 15 per cent in 2012.

Retrospectively speaking, the chances of containing Narendra Modi were there during the UPA government from 2004 to 2014. The Gujarat Assembly elections in 2002, 2007, and 2012 were not fought by the Congress party with the commitment to defeat Mr Modi during the period, instead he was given a walkover. Secular parties like the Congress was barely able to put up a campaign against the BJP. Gujarat is the base of many prominent corporates so it also opened the opportunity for Narendra Modi to build a special rapport with India's big capital which played a role in funding the elections. So, there was an opportunity to restrain the Hindu Right but they are now lost opportunities. Such a trend emerged because the UPA was not part of the ideological struggle. It only offered lip service to

FIGURE 1.6

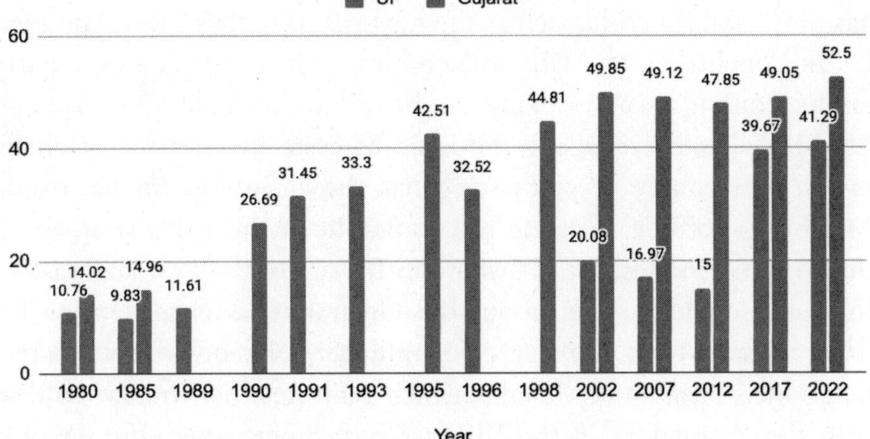

FIGURE 1.7

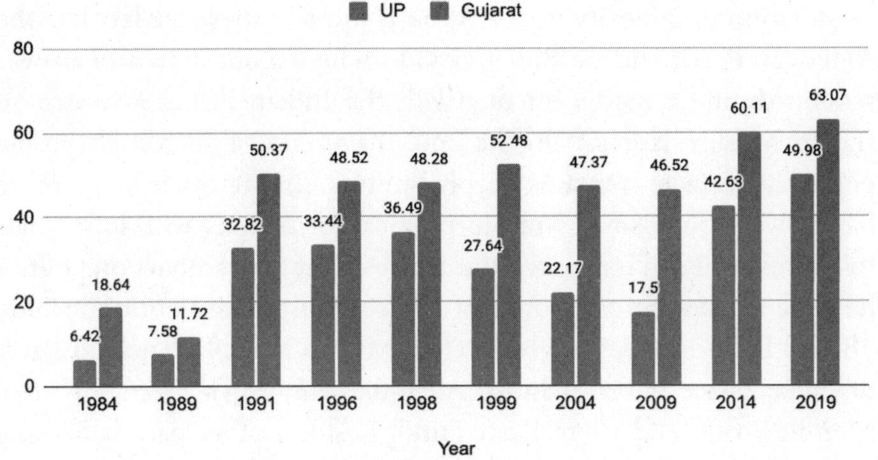

secularism. It is apparent by the fact that the most prominent threat to the UPA was Jagan Reddy, who eventually became the Chief Minister of Andhra Pradesh on his own, not Narendra Modi, who has now established himself as the nemesis of India's secular politics.

In conclusion, the BJP will continue to be a hegemonic party in the coming years, looking at the trends in Table 2.5. Though Mr Modi has been raising the issue of caste in Islam occasionally in the past couple of years—and has shown interest in Pasmanda Muslims—nothing concrete has come out as the BJP's strategy on this in Uttar Pradesh or elsewhere in India. On the Pasmanda issue, the same could be said about the Gujarat experience. During his days as three-term Gujarat chief minister, Narendra Modi barely mentioned Pasmanda Muslims which indicates this strategy to deal with the Pasmandas in the BJP is a rather new one. One possible reason could be owing to the pressure coming from global human rights groups and also a few Western governments. Given India's strategic importance in the wake of rising China, aggressive Russia and broken Pakistan (or to use Nawaz Sharif's description, *zakhmi* Pakistan), Western governments cannot afford to confront India with its violation of minority rights. At best, some of these leaders like the American President Joe Biden, could arrange a question and answer session during a media briefing with the Indian Prime Minister on Indian Muslim issues.[81] In the end, the utility of such high profile political spectacles remains deeply limited. On the other hand, there have always been small Muslim political formations with lofty goals to address Muslim issues in Uttar Pradesh but their impact on politics has been insignificant. Some of these political formations include The All India Muslim Majlis, Ittehad Millat Council, Pancham Party of India, Peace Party of India, All India Minorities Front, Bhartiya Momin Front, and Islam Party Hind. Besides, other parties like the Indian Union of Muslim League (IUML) and AIMIM have taken part in UP elections hoping to expand their national footprint. These parties have not received any support from Muslim voters in Uttar Pradesh since 1947. Muslim voters have mainly supported non-BJP secular parties. For instance, AIMIM fought two Assembly elections in 2017 and again in 2022, and it did not receive any support. According to some analysis, AIMIM did divide votes that helped the BJP in some constituencies in the 2022 Uttar Pradesh elections.

TABLE 1.8

AIMIM in Uttar Pradesh Assembly Elections

Election Year	*Total Seats*	*Candidates fielded*	*Won*	*Forfeited deposit*	*Vote Share (%)*
2017	403	38	0	37	0.24
2022	403	95	0	95	0.49

From Table 1.8, it can be safely argued that Muslims are not looking for a Muslim party to deal with their issues even in present-day India. While this presents robust evidence of Indian Muslims' secular voting behaviour, the Hindu Right remains deeply sceptical about Muslim loyalty. In a nutshell, Gujarat and Uttar Pradesh would continue to be role models for other states in matters of dealing with Muslims, which the Hindu Right would celebrate as the end of appeasement politics while Muslims will look at them as majoritarian *zulm* (tyranny). These two states will remain two key pillars in the Hindu majoritarian project, though other states such as Assam or Uttarkhand might add distinct trajectories to the unfolding versions of Hindu majoritarianism.

Notes

1 Arendt, Hannah. 1994. *The Origins of Totalitarianism*. London: Penguin Random House. The book was originally published as *the Burden of Our Time* in Britain in 1951.

2 Originally quoted in Benhabib, Syela. 2004. *The Rights of Others: Aliens, Residents, Citizens*. Cambridge: Cambridge University Press. P. 50. For detailed discussion see Chapter 2 titled, '"The right to have rights': Hanna Arendt on the contradictions of the nation-state.' Pp. 49-70.

3 Ibid. P. 56.

4 Ibid. P. 56.

5 Ibid. 57.
6 Ibid. 57.
7 Bajpai, Rochana. 2016. *Debating Difference: Group Rights and Liberal Democracy in India.* New Delhi: Oxford University Press.
8 See Kohli, Atul. 1991. *Democracy and Discontent: India's Growing Crisis of Governability.* Cambridge: Cambridge University Press.
9 See Mueller, Jan-Werner. 2024. 'Liberalism's forever Crisis.' Available at: http://www.project-syndicate.org.(accessed on 10 February 2024).
10 Ibid.
11 Rosanvallon, Pierre. 2018. *Good Government: Democracy Beyond Elections.* Cambridge: Harvard University Press. P. 1.
12 Grayling, AC. 2018. *Democracy and Its Crisis.* London: One World.
13 Ibid. P.131.
14 Hasan, Zoya and Nussbaum, Martha C. 2017. 'India and the US, Spot the Difference.' Available at: http://www.indianexpress.com (accessed on 10 February 2024).
15 See an insightful discussion on this in Chapter 3 in *Making a Separate Nation.* Mushirul Hasan. 1997. New Delhi: Oxford University Press. Pp. 53-99.
16 Veer Savarkar's books include *Six Glorious Epochs of Indian History* (Abhishek 2019); *India's War of Independence 1857* (Abhishek 2019); also, see Sampath, Vikram. 2019. *Savarkar: Echoes of Forgotten Past, 1883-1924.* New Delhi: Penguin; see Sharma, Jyotirmaya. 2019. *Hindutva: Exploring the Idea of Hindu Nationalism.* New Delhi: Context.
17 Among the major works on the BJP's rise are Jaffrelot, Christophe. 1998. *The Hindu Nationalist Movement in India.* New York: Columbia University Press; Hansen, Thomas Blom. 1999. *The Saffron Wave: Democracy and Hindu Nationalism in Modern India.* New Jersey: Princeton University Press.
18 Some of the important works on RSS include Anderson, Walter and Damle, Shridhar. 2019. *RSS: A View to the Inside.* New Delhi: Penguin; Anderson, Walter and Damle, Shridhar. 2019. *Brotherhood in Saffron: Rashtriya Swayam Sevak Sangh and Hindu Revivalism.* New Delhi: Penguin; Mukhopadhya, Nilanjan. 2019. *RSS: Icons of the Indian Right.* New Delhi: Tranquebar; Noorani, AG. 2019. *RSS: A Menace to India.* New Dellhi: Leftword Books.
19 See 'Introduction' of Rehman, Mujibur. 2018. (Ed.) *Rise of Saffron Power: Reflections on Indian Politics.* New Delhi: Routledge.
20 See Sinha, Shakti. 2020. *Vajpayee: Man, Method, and Legacy: They Years*

that Changed India. New Delhi: Penguin. Ullekh, NP. 2018. *Untold Vajpayee: Politician and Paradox.* New Delhi: Penguin; Chaudhury, Abhishek. 2023. *Vajpayee: The Ascent of the Hindu Right, 1924-1977.* New Delhi: Picador.

21 Mukhopadyaya, Nilanjan. 2023. *Narendra Modi: The Man, The Times.* New Delhi: Westland.

22 Godse, Nathuram. 2019 (3rd edition). *Why I Assassinated Mahatma Gandhi.* New Delhi: Hindu Sahitya Sadan, Book Publishers and Distributors.

23 Many fiercely argued that the BJP cannot enter south India, which has been a widely accepted wisdom among secularists since the heydays of the Ayodhya movement. After the BJP formed the government in Karnataka in 2008, and the myth exploded. Even today, there are many secularists who believe that the BJP is not going beyond Karnataka, but the BJP is working hard to mobilize Southern voters.

24 For the life of Deve Gowda and his political career, see the biography, Srinivasaraju, Sugata. 2021. *Furrows in a Field: The Unexplored Life of HD Deve Gowda.* New Delhi: Vintage.

25 Gujral, IK. 2011. *Matters of Discretion: An Autobiography.* New Delhi: Hay House.

26 For an elaborate discussion on this, see Rehman, Mujibur. (Ed.). 2018. *Rise of Saffron Power: Reflections on Indian Politics.* New Delhi: Routledge. Also see, Sardesai, Rajdeep. 2014. *The Election that Changed India.* New Delhi: Penguin.

27 Among the several books on the rise of the BJP for a comprehensive analysis, see, Jaffrelot, Christophe. 1998. *The Hindu Nationalist Movement in India.* New York: Columbia University Press.

28 Its predecessor Bhartiya Jana Sangh (BJS) set up in 1950 by Shyama Prasad Mukherjee was merged with the anti-Emergency coalition in 1975 and lost its identity. Indeed, the strand of Hindu majoritarianism always existed since the early days of the Indian Republic. For a detailed discussion on the BJS see, Graham, Bruce. 2007. *Hindu Nationalism and Indian Politics: The Origins and Development of Bhartiya Jana Sangh.* Cambridge: Cambridge University Press.

29 Shok is a Hindi word—its English meaning is mourning.

30 Bhattacharya, DP. 2014. 'BJP gains in polls after every riot says Yale study.' Available at: http://www.economictimes.com (accessed on 8 June 2020).

31 It was published in the *Quarterly Journal of Political Science* (QJPS) and was presented in 2015 at the American Political Science Association.

32 Saigal, Sonam. 2023. 'Reservation for Muslims is against Constitution, says Amit Shah.' Available at: http://www.thehindu.com (accessed on 10 February 2024).

33 *The Times of India.* 2023. 'Muslims must abandon "boisterous rhetoric of supremacy": Mohan Bhagwat.' 10 January 2023 Available at: http://www.thetimesofindia.indiatimes.com (accessed on 10 June 2023).

34 See, Bilgrami, Akeel. 2022. 'Foreword' in *Inheriting Gandhi: Influences, Activisms.* Edited by Satishchandra Kumar, Kanchana Mahadevan, Meher Bhoot, Rajesh Kharat. New Delhi: Speaking Tiger and the University of Mumbai. Pp. 18-19.

35 See, 'Introduction' in Rehman, Mujibur. 2018. (Ed). *Rise of Saffron Power: Reflections on Indian Politics.* New Delhi: Routledge Publications.

36 For details see, Advani, LK. 2008. *My Country, My Life.* New Delhi: Rupa Publications.

37 See Mujibur Rehman, Shaikh. 2019. 'Cleaning up the Kashmir Mess.' Available at: http://www.thehindu.com (accessed on 10 February 2024).

38 For a thoughtful analysis of Ayodhya judgement, see, Khurshid, Salman. 2021. *Sunrise over Ayodhya: Nationhood in Our Times.* New Delhi: Vintage.

39 See, 'Uniform Civil Code being Implemented through states, say BJP chief Nadda.' *The Hindu.* 8 November 2022.

40 See, Mujibur Rehman, Shaikh. 2023. 'A Model Lab for Secular Governance.' Available at: http://www.thehindu.com (accessed on 10 February 2023).

41 Kumar, Devesh. 2024. 'Uttarakhand Assembly passes the UCC Bill; becomes India's first state to implement Uniform Civil Code.' Available at: http://www.livemint.com (accessed on 10 February 2024).

42 Adeny, Katharine and Saez, Lawrence. 2005. *Coalition Politics and Hindu Nationalism.* London: Routledge.

43 For a comprehensive analysis, Rehman, Mujibur. (Ed.). 2018. *Rise of Saffron Power: Reflections on Indian Politics.* New Delhi: Routledge Publications.

44 Guha, Ramachandra. 2020. '3 traits of Modi that have cost India dearly.' Available at: http://www.ndtv.com (accessed on 12 June 2020).

45 See the chapter, 'Targetting Minorities' in Jaffrelot, Christophe. 2019. *Modi's India: Hindu Nationalism and Rise of Ethnic Democracy.* Princeton: Princeton University Press. Pp. 188-210.

46 Some of these leaders include: Sarad Yadav, Biju Patnaik, Mulayam Yadav, VP Singh, Nitish Kumar, Lalu Yadav, Sharad Pawar, Chandrasekhar.

47 See, Thomas, Abraham. 2023. 'Supreme Court calls hate speech

complete menace, cautions Centre, states.' Available at: http://www.hindustantimes.com (accessed on 10 June 2023).

48 There are civil society initiatives against lynching and the most prominent is Harsh Mander led *Karwan-e-Mohabbat*. See the report, Engineer, Tariq. 2017. 'Former IAS officer Harsh Mander decides to go on Karwan E Mohabbat to protest mob lynchings.' Available at: http://www.mumbaimirror.indiatimes.com (accessed on 12 June 2020).

49 DY Chandrachud became Chief Justice of India's Supreme Court on 9 November 2022.

50 See the report, Rajagopal, Krishnadas. 2018. 'SC asks Parliament to bring in the special law against lynching.' Available at: http://www.thehindu.com (accessed on 12 June 2020).

51 Building the Ram Temple in Ayodhya has been a long-standing core agenda of the Hindu Right from the early days of the Republic. For the history of this dispute and how the whole process evolved over the years, see, Jha, Krishna and Jha, Dhirendra. (Ed.). 2021. *Ayodhya—The Dark Night—The Secret History of Rama's Appearance in Babri Masjid*. New Delhi: Harper Collins. For a crucial analysis of the political and legal side, see, Khurshid, Salman. 2021. *Sunrise over Ayodhya—Neighbourhoods in Our Times*. New Delhi: Vintage Books. For a political dimension, see also, Rao, PV Narasimha. 2019. *Ayodhya: 6 December 1992*. New Delhi: Penguin.

52 Laski, Harold. 2014. *A Grammer of Politics*. London: Routledge.

53 In this panel discussion, Mr Modi was accompanied by Digvijay Singh and Farooq Abdullah. The direct exchange that took place was mainly between Digvijay Singh and Narendra Modi.

54 Bahujan Samaj Party candidates Afzal Ansari from Ghazipur, Fazalur Rahman from Saharanpur and Danish Ali in Amroha, and Samajwadi Party's Azam Khan from Rampur, Shafique Rehman Barq from Sambhal and ST Hasan from Moradabad made their way to the Lok Sabha.

55 Jammu and Kashmir has sent three Muslim MPs, all from the National Conference; two from Assam and three from Kerala. Mohammed Faizal of the Nationalist Congress Party won the lone seat in Lakshadweep. The Congress' Mohammad Sadique also won the Faridkot seat from Punjab. Indian Union Muslim League (IUML)'s K Navas Kani won from Ramanathapuram in Tamil Nadu. The All India Majlis-e-Itthadul Muslimeen (AMIMIM) has two candidates: party chief Asaduddin Owaisis from Hyderabad and Imtiaz Jaleel from Aurangabad in Maharashtra.

56 Jaffrelot, Christophe. 2018. 'The Dwindling Minority'. Available at: http://www.theindianexpress.com (accessed on 10 February 2024).

57 Gandhi, Rajmohan. 2011. *Patel: A Life.* New Delhi: Navjivan Trust.

58 Quoted in Gandhi, Rajmohan. 2011. *Patel: A Life.* New Delhi: Navjivan Trust.

59 Jayal, Niraja Gopal. 2006. *Representing India: Ethnic Diversity and the Governance of Public Institutions.* New Delhi: Palgrave MacMillan. P. 55.

60 Ibid. P. 53.

61 Khosla, Madhav. 2019. *India's Founding Moment: The Constitution of a Most Surprising Democracy.* Cambridge: Harvard University Press.

62 See Shruti Kapila review titled, 'Indian Constitution isn't saving it from Narendra Modi's assault on rights: the country's founding document has failed its minorities.' 2020. Available at: www.prospectmagazine.co.uk. (accessed on 12 June 2020).

63 See, Chiriankadat, James. 2000. 'Creating a Secular State in a Religious Country: The Debate in Indian Constituent Assembly.' *Commonwealth and Comparative Politics.* 38(2): 4.

64 See the report, Asrar, Shuja. 2018. 'Rahul compares RSS to Muslim Brotherhood: BJP hits back.' Available at: http://www.timesofindia.indiatimes.com. (accessed on 12 June 2020).

65 See the report, Verma, Lalmani. 2018. 'If Muslims are unwanted, then there is no Hindutva: Mohan Bhagwat at RSS event.' Available at: http://www.indianexpress.com (accessed on 12 June 2020).

66 Sen, Amartya. 2020. 'Amartya Sen on the Wire, the Police and The Beyond'. Available at: http://www.thewire.com (accessed on 12 June 2020).

67 Hansen, Thomas Blom's chapter in Jaffrelot and others. (Ed.). 2019. *The Majoritarian State.* New Delhi: Harper India. For a detailed analysis, see Hansen, Thomas Blom. 2021. *The Law of Force: The Violent Heart of Indian Politics.* New Delhi: Aleph Book Company.

68 Jafri, Alishan. 2023. 'Muslim homes, shops bulldozed; over 150 arrested in Nuh in India's Haryana'. Available at: http://www.aljazeera.com (accessed on 20 February 2024).

69 Ali, Arbab. 2024. 'Killed by police bullets: Deadly clash scars Muslims in India's Haldwani'. Available at: http://www.aljazeera.com (accessed on 20 February 2024).

70 See the chapter , 'Rise of Hindutva' in Yagnik, Achyut and Seth, Suchitra. 2005. *The Shaping of Modern Gujarat.* New Delhi: Penguin Books. Pp. 252-275. Also, Dhatiwala, Raheel. 2020. *Keeping the Peace: Spatial Difference In the Hindu-Muslim Violence in Gujarat in 2002.* Cambridge University Press.

71 For a comprehensive analysis of the historical dimensions of caste and social structure in Gujarat, see, Shah, Ghanashyam. 1990. 'Caste sentiments, class formation and dominance in Gujarat' in Frankel, Francine and Rao, MSA. 1990. *Dominance and State Power in Modern India: Decline of a Social Order* (Vol II). New Delhi: Oxford University Press. Pp. 59-114.

72 Yagnik, Achyut and Seth, Suchitra. 2005. *The Shaping of Modern Gujarat: Plurality, Hindutva and Beyond.* New Delhi: Penguin Books. P. 254.

73 Berenschot, Ward. 2011. *Riot Politics: Hindu-Muslim Violence and the Indian State.* New Delhi: Rainlight (Rupa Publications). P. 189.

74 There is a more detailed discussion on 2002 riot in chapter three in the volume titled *Violence Against Muslims.*

75 O Sullivan, Michael. 2023. *No Birds Passage: A History of Gujarati Muslim Business Communities: 1800-1975.* Cambridge: Harvard University Press.

76 Hasan, Zoya. 1990. 'Power and Mobilization: Patterns of Resilience and Change in Uttar Pradesh Politics.' In Frankel, Francine and Rao, MSA. *Dominance and State Power in Modern India: Decline of a Social Order.* (Vol II). New Delhi: Oxford University Press. 133-203.

77 Pai, Sudha and Kumar, Sajjan. 2023. *Maya, Modi, and Azad: Dalit Politics In the Time of Hindutva.* New Delhi: Harper Collins. Pp. 81-104.

78 Ibid. Pp. 82-83.

79 For a detailed discussion, see Narayan, Badri. 2009. *Fascinating Hindutva: Saffron Politics and Dalit Mobilization.* New Delhi: Sage. P. 8.

80 Rehman, Mujibur.

81 See, Johny, Ritu Maria. 2023. '"Surprised": PM Modi replies as the US reporter questions on Muslim rights in India.' Available at: www.thehindustan times.com (accessed on 15 January 2024).

2

THE CULTURAL AND POLITICAL LIVES OF SOUTH INDIAN MUSLIMS

> 'Everyone knows the southern aromas and flavours; jasmine and coffee, tamarind and coconut, the dosai, idli and appam, and accompaniments that burn the tongue but cannot be resisted. For the eyes and ears, South provides lamps, bells, temples, churches, mosques and shrines, the sounds of its music and the movements of its dances. And the movements and voices, also of its homemakers, fishermen, boatmen, weavers, cobblers and others who toil. Above all, South India today contains hundreds of millions of people, speaking in one or more of several, usually connected, languages, each individual vulnerable and valiant in a unique way, all living in a range of easy or difficult relationships with one another and the world.'
>
> —Rajmohan Gandhi

Muslims are not a monolith is a familiar cliché in academic and popular discussions on Indian Muslims. Curiously though, research available on varied dimensions of socio-economic, cultural or political uniqueness of Muslim communities, factoring in regional affiliations, remains negligible. As Susan Bayly notes, 'The difficulty comes when one seeks to understand Islam as a living system of worship rather than a textual ideal. The ideal says all Muslims are one: the reality is that over many centuries Muslim faith and practice have come to be shaped and modified by dynamic regional cultures and by the changing social and political context in which they have taken root.'[1] Out of all regions of India, the Muslims in the South are considered unique in their political orientations. As Mohammad Mujeeb writes in his magnum opus, *Indian Muslims,* 'The South does not, of course, form a homogenous unit, the Muslims in Mysore and Bangalore being much closer culturally to those of Haidarabad (Hyderabad) than to the Moplahs and Navayats of Kerala, who are geographically much nearer.'[2]

The Ayodhya movement of the late 1980s[3] did not find much traction in South India. However, the movement is the most prominent catalysing factor for the Hindu Right's unprecedented electoral expansion in North India. Also, the impact of India's Partition in the region was largely negligible.[4] Writing on the limited presence of the Hindu Right or the BJP, Rajmohan Gandhi, in his book, *Modern South India,*[5] cites three reasons: 1) Brahmin domination of the Rashtriya Swyamsevak Sangh (RSS) which has opened branches in South since the 1920s; 2) the image of the Jana Sangh (predecessor of the BJP) as 'Hindi/North Indian'; and 3) BJP's inability to connect with India's independence struggle.

In recent years, however, enough empirical evidence points towards radical transformations of these trends signalling tectonic shifts towards a more polarised Southern society around religious identities. As a result, multiple religious Right organisations, both Muslim and Hindu, have become proactive in the region and are making considerable investments in shoring up their social bases and sharpening their political agendas. For instance, the RSS, the most prominent Hindu Right organisation, is holding regular marches in various parts of South India as part of its outreach. The Madras High Court recently permitted the RSS to have its march in Tamil Nadu.[6] The Supreme Court also has cleared it by dismissing the Tamil Nadu government's plea against the RSS march.[7] According to AP Venkatchalapathy, 'In Tamil Nadu itself, Rashtriya Swayam

Sevak Sangh (RSS) front organizations made inroads into Tamil civil society with the active acquiescence of the DMK.'[8] On the other hand, the Popular Front of India (PFI), a conservative political organization (some argue it intended to be a Muslim RSS) was very active in various states till it was banned in February 2023.[9] BJP's Sneha Yatra in Kerala to reach out to Christians and the Prime Minister's Christmas gathering at his residence on 25 December 2023 are part of the BJP's effort to establish its footprint in the South.[10] It is also widely known that the RSS cadre and cadres of various secular organizations such as the Left or the Congress party have engaged in violence against each other rather frequently in parts of Kerala.[11] During the BJP's national executive meeting in Hyderabad, Prime Minister Modi raised the issue of Pasmanda Muslims.[12] Seen from the vantage point of politics of religious polarization, where once India's South appeared as a sharp contrast to its North, it now increasingly appears to be its mirror image.

When the BJP experienced a massive surge in its electoral base in the 1989 parliamentary elections resulting in the rise of its parliamentary strength from 2 in 1984 to 89 in 1989, it did not win a single seat from any of the Southern states (see Table 2.1). The scenario, however, significantly changed during the 2014 and 2019 parliamentary elections. In both the national elections, the party secured seats in Andhra Pradesh, Tamil Nadu, and Karnataka. In Karnataka, it swept the 2019 elections with 25 out of 27 parliamentary seats, and in 2014 it had won 17 seats. What we see is the expansion of BJP's electoral base in a big way in Karnataka but in small strides in Andhra Pradesh and Tamil Nadu. In Kerala, it managed to win only one seat in the Assembly and is yet to open an account in Parliament.

TABLE 2.1 BJP's Performance in South in 1989 Elections

State	Candidates Contested	Candidates Won	Candidates Secured 2nd Position	Candidates Secured More Than 10% Vote
Andhra Pradesh	2	0	2	2
Karnataka	5	0	1	3
Tamil Nadu	3	0	0	0
Kerala	20	0	0	0

The electoral rewards that led to the BJP's significant rise in the 1989 elections in North were attributed to a well-organized Ayodhya campaign led by its leader LK Advani.[13] This has inspired an influential body of scholarship claiming that though the BJP was able to profit electorally in the North owing to its Ayodhya strategy, it won't work in Southern states because the South is immune to politics of polarization around the Ayodhya campaign. And this reasoning continues to dominate as an explanatory variable even today. This is echoed in senior political scientist James Chiriyankandath's analysis in his essay, 'Yes, But Not in South'.[14] According to Chiriyankandath[15]:

> The Peninsular South with its Dravidian languages has long been distinguished by social and cultural differences from the north, west, and east of India despite sharing common Indian civilization and heritage. Historically, the Hindu empires and kingdoms of the South maintained their independence until the relatively late Mughul period with the far South—the South of what is now Tamil Nadu as well as Kerala—never coming under the dominion of Mughals or their Muslim offshoots. Visible in the landscape of towns and cities in the South that contrasts with the Islamic architectural styles that predominate in many of their counterparts in the North, the background may be what has given its politics less of the fraught communal (i.e. Hindu-Muslim) edge evident in the Hindi-speaking states and in both Western and Eastern India. It has been an important factor in limiting the appeal of Hindu nationalism, shading into chauvinism, espoused by the BJP and Rashtriya Swayamsevak Sangh (RSS) Sangha Parivar (associational family) to which it belongs.

In the Telangana Assembly election held in 2023, the Congress Party was able to wrest back power from the regional party, Bharat Rashtra Samithi (BRS) winning 64 seats and a vote share of 39.40 per cent.[16] The BJP, though the party had won five parliamentary seats in 2019 with a vote share of 19.65 per cent, is now reduced to 13.9 per cent votes in the 2023 Assembly elections indicating significant decline in its vote share. During this round of Assembly elections, the BJP won other major states: in Madya Pradesh, it won 163 Assembly seats out of 230 seats; in Rajasthan, it won 115 Assembly seats out of 199 seats; and in Chhattisgarh, it won 54 Assembly seats out of 90 seats.[17] But the BJP's failure to win Telangana suggests everyone is not swayed by the BJP. For details see Table 2.17 in this chapter.

TABLE 2.2 BJP Parliamentary Election Results in 2014

State	*Candidates Contested*	*Candidates Won*	*Candidates Secured 2nd Position*	*Candidates Secured More Than 10% Vote*
Andhra Pradesh	12	3	3	12
Karnataka	28	17	8	27
Tamil Nadu	9	1	3	8
Kerala	18	0	1	9

TABLE 2.3 BJP Parliamentary Election Results in 2019

State	*Candidates Contested*	*Candidates Won*	*Candidates Secured 2nd Position*	*Candidates Secured More Than 10% Vote*
Andhra Pradesh	24	0	0	0
Telangana	17	5	2	12
Karnataka	27	25	2	27
Tamil Nadu	5	0	5	5
Kerala	15	0	1	12

The Muslim population in the South Indian states is considerable and Table 2.4 provides the details based on the 2011 census.[18] Among the active Muslim political organizations in the Muslim community are All India Muslim Union League (AIMUL), All India Majlis-e-

Ittehadul Muslimeen (AIMIM), and the Social Democratic Party of India (SDPI). Some analysis of their history and role could help us understand this complex story a little better.

TABLE 2.4 Muslim Population in South (2011 Census)

States in South	*Muslim Population (in %)*	*Share in Total Muslims in India (%)*	*Muslim Population*
Kerala	26.6	5.2	8,873,472
Karnataka	12.9	4.6	7,893,065
Andhra Pradesh	9.6	4.7	8,082,412
Tamil Nadu	5.9	2.5	4,229,479

Karnataka is among the first and only Southern states that gave an electoral majority to the BJP and the party formed a government in 2008. It remains the only state that could be considered the Hindu Right's Southern bastion despite its massive electoral loss in the 2023 Assembly elections, particularly because it continues to retain its vote share at around 36 per cent—almost identical to its vote share in previous Assembly elections. (See Table 2.13 for details about the BJP in Karnataka). Furthermore, the BJP has been proactively working in the other Southern states at different levels, at times in collaboration with other regional political parties. For instance, it was closely working with the All India Dravida Munetra Kazagham (AIDMK) in Tamil Nadu and there are speculations that the BJP would stitch alliances with Jana Sena(JS) and Telugu Desam Party (TDP) in Andhra Pradesh as well as in Telangana.[19] In Karnataka, the BJP has stitched an alliance with JD(S), which may help improve its electoral performance in future elections compared to its decision to contest alone.[20]

Islam in South India and the Nature of Muslim Politics

The landscape of India's South bears a strong footprint of Islamic institutions and sites such as mosques, madrasas, Khanaqahs (teaching hospices) etc. Also, there are Muslim holy places ranging from wayside shrines to dargahs/tomb shrines. Without a doubt, they represent Muslim religious life and also carry tremendous significance for non-Muslim populations, particularly Hindus. According to Susan Bayly, 'The richness of the region's Muslim religious landscape is conveyed in a large number of locally-produced pilgrimage manuals, biographical texts, devotional poems, descriptive listings of shrines and holy places which are still being produced in the larger Muslim population centres. South Indian scholar-devotees have been compiling these texts for many centuries, and the tradition of Sufi writing is still particularly lively in localities such as Madras (present-day Chennai), Trichy, Nagore, Vellore and Kayalpatanam.'[21]

The most crucial factor in the spread of Islam in South India was the influence of Sufi traditions that contributed to the transmission of Islamic teaching. There are also *qalandars* (or faqirs) and *mazdhubs* (Muslim mystics) who played their part in the spread of Islam. Scholars argue that Islam gained roots in the South well before the waves of invasion from Central Asia that gave rise to the medieval Muslim sultanates of North India.[22] Arab traders settled along the Coromandel coast as early as the eighth/ninth century and began to play a major role in the global textile trade business.[23] In a chapter titled 'The Southern Challenge' in his book, *India After Gandhi*, Ramchandra Guha writes, 'The first Muslims were a product of trade with the Arabs and go back to at least to the eighth century.'[24] Evidence of the early settlement of Muslims in the region is the presence of mosques in the hinterland which are from the earlier times of Muslim settlement. The Abdullah Ibn Muhammad in Trichy is one such example. This well-built little structure stands about a mile from a complex known as Trichy Rock. The mosque in its architecture resembles the locality's eighth and ninth century rock-cut cave temples.[25] An Arabic inscription dated CE 733-4 is carved in the mosque indicating that it was built by one of the Arab traders in the early medieval period. In the South's hinterland, Islam probably took root in the 13th to 14th century CE. In inland south India, too, trade and sufi tradition worked in tandem and moved forward in a harmonious fashion.

Pirs and saints, who are part of the Sufi tradition, played a key role in spreading Islam. These pirs have been the bridge between Muslims and other religious groups such as Hindus. Interestingly, the impact of South India's expanding Sufi cult tradition was not intended to bring forth a purist version of Islamisation of belief and lifestyle. Both Hindus and Muslims have worshipped at the shrines of Pirs. Most dargahs sponsor healing and exorcism rites and in Tamil Muslim tombs life crisis ceremonies are performed in a manner identical to that practised in Hindu temples. Among others, rites such as infant tonsuring are also conducted in a manner identical to local Hindu customs. This event is marked by distributing alms to Brahmans. In the Muslim tradition, the child's cut hair is weighed and the same weight in silver is given to Muslim *fakirs* by the parents. The local Hindu and Muslim traditions have invariably shaped each other. For instance, in Tamil Nadu, Allah was and still is referred to as Allah Swami.[26] Over many centuries the Muslims of Tamil Nadu have evolved a common pattern of belief and worship. Furthermore, in pre-colonial Tami Nadu, there were no divisions between purist and syncretic Muslims. No such divisions play any part in the lives of the region's Muslim population even today. (Bayly 2004, Fakhri 2008).

SM Abdul Khader Fakhri in his book, *Dravidian Sahibs and Brahmin Maulanas,*[27] presents crucial insights into the social stratification and evolution of Muslim identity in Tamil Nadu. Like Muslims of other regions, language, class, and religious doctrine formed the basis of their division, though most spoke or used the Tamil language. Some of them also spoke Urdu, particularly in northern parts of Tamil Nadu, including Madras City, Chengalpattu, North Arcot, South Arcot, Salem, and Tiruchirapalli.

Considering that local Muslims are drawn from the local Hindu society, the relationship with their castes continued. Muslims enjoyed a unique relationship with three non-Muslim castes in Tiruchirapalli, and these castes include the Kammalans, the Tottiyans, and the Pallans. They refer to each other in such a way that a relationship is recognized as if there is a kinship, some sort of evidence of a blood relationship. Muslims and Kammalans called each other *mani*, meaning paternal uncle, Pallans as grandson and granddaughter, and in turn were called grandfather by them, and Tottiyans and Muslims addressed one another as *maman* or maternal uncle. This kind of social relationship obliterated religious boundaries in Tamil Nadu.[28] This is one of the reasons why there are such wonderful social relationships between Hindus and Muslims in South India (Fakhri, 2008).

It does not imply there were no Hindu-Muslim conflicts or riots. According to JBP More, there were riots in the early 1930s. He claims that of the 30 or more riots he had studied, more than 20 occurred around the place of worship or during festivals or religious or caste processions. Not just Hindu-Muslim conflicts, but also conflicts with other social and religious groups. He writes, 'Further, it should be noted that this period witnessed not only Hindu-Muslim friction but also Muslim-Christian, Muslim-untouchable, Muslim-Nadar, and untouchable-caste Hindus frictions.'[29] What is significant is that scholars such as JBP More and others concur with the claim that the Hindu-Muslim conflict was never as bad as it was in North India. I suggest here that with the further penetration of the Hindu Right ideology, it is a matter of time before the South and North will look similar.

According to Mr Fakhri, there are three major social groups: 1) Tamil Muslims are Tamil speakers (henceforth Tamil Muslims); 2) Urdu speakers (henceforth the Dakhnis); and 3) a third and a new sociological category of the Tamil Dakhnis, who share the history of both the earlier groups. Among the scholars, there are differences of opinion on how to classify Muslims of Tamil Nadu based on where they come from, their profession or language etc. Susan Bayly limits the distinction between Marakkayars and Labbais.

But Mr Fakhri identifies Rowthers together with Marakkayars and Labbais. Other scholars such as Mattison Mines, Frank Fenselow, and Kenneth Macpherson offer different kinds of descriptions of Muslims of Tamil society. I have chosen to discuss the division made by Fakhri because this appears to be sufficient to present a general sense of social stratification working among Muslims in Tamil Nadu. Like all divided societies, such divisions have political implications. At the same time, there is some truth to the observations by Susan Bayly, when she writes, 'For all its distinctions of rank and ethnicity, however, the Muslim population of Tamil Nadu has never been truly fragmented. Cutting across all the divisions of Shafi'I and Hanafi's maraikkayar, and non-maraikkayar, elite and "convert" Muslim, there was still a single distinctive religious tradition which formed throughout virtually the whole of the Tamil country.'[30]

Tamil Muslims

It is widely acknowledged that Arab traders brought Islam to Tamil Nadu and married local Tamil women. Their mixed-race children were the first Tamil Muslims. These Muslims were further subdivided into Marakkayars and Rowthers.

The Marakkayar word was extracted from the Arabic word, *markab* (boat), and the Tamil *rayar* (king)—ruler of the maritime trade. The Marakkayar resided on the coast and were involved in foreign trade. They also followed the Shafi school of Islamic jurisprudence. It was and still is an endogamous body. They maintained close ties to Arab centres of trade and pilgrimage. According to Susan Bayly, 'It was through these dominant Muslim trading lineages that the region's rulers gained access to this world of dynamic international trade.'[31]

The Rowther term, on the other hand, was associated with horses, either with Muslims as traders or cavalry. Muslims were horse traders, who imported Arab horses for trade with the Cholas, the Pandyas, and the Pallavas.[32] The Rowthers were found in areas such as Madurai, Thanjavur, Ramanathapuram, and Tirunelveli. It is the Hanafi school of Islamic jurisprudence that they follow.

Labbai is a term extracted from the Arabic *Labbaik*, which means 'Here I Am'.[33] These people were stigmatized by the Marakkayars. Professionally Labbais are mostly coastal fishermen, pearl divers, weavers, petty traders, etc. The British colonial census used the term to signify all Tamil-speaking Muslims so that it could help distinguish them from Urdu speakers. The colonial British government considered Labbai to be of a relatively low rank compared to the Dakhni. In their appointments for the post of Kazis, the colonial British government appointed Muslims with command over Persian and Urdu languages who received preference over those who were proficient in Tamil and Arabic. The Marakkayar claim that knowledge of Arabic is virtually non-existent among the Labbais. The Labbais, for Marakayars, are 'converted' people who deviated from 'proper' Islamic customs. This was evident in their practice of murai marriage alliance—that is marriage to father's sister's daughter—similar to the practice of many Hindu caste groups in Tamil Nadu (Fakhri 2008, Bayly 2004).

What is equally interesting is the deep connections between particular groups of Muslims and certain Hindu castes. The Rowthers were believed to be Maravar converts, the Tarakanar, and the Marakkayar were Iluvan converts and Paravar converts respectively. Although they changed their religion, they maintained their linguistic and cultural ties with the larger Tamil population over generations.[34] Furthermore, the Marakkayars all belong to the Shafi madhab (School of Quranic Law) and its affiliation tends to reflect connections with Arabia, while Labbais are part of Hanafi's school where scholarship is oriented towards central Asia and the Iranian plateau. The Marakkayars take this affiliation with Shafi as evidence of their superior status.[35] By the early 18th century towns such as Kilakkarai, Nagore, Kayalpatanam, and Adirampatanam were known throughout the Indian Ocean trading region for their wealth and religious institutions. Several dargahs, mosques, madrasas, and Sufi Khanaqahs in these Marakkayars towns go back to the 15th and 16th centuries.[36]

Dakhni Muslims

Derived from the word Deccani, a region of South India, Dakhni Muslims are Urdu speakers settled in Tamil Nadu.[37] According to Susan Bayly, '[M]any of the Muslims of Tamil Nadu who describe themselves as Dakhnis claim to be descended from soldiers, officials, and literary men in service to the Muslim ruling houses in Deccan. When the Mughals overran Bijapur and the other Deccani kingdoms at the end of the seventeenth century, a large number of these Muslims migrated to other parts of India, including the south.'[38] The Dakhnis introduced Islamic religious and linguistic traditions (deeply influenced by the customs of north Indian Muslims) to Tamil Nadu. They were divided into Shia and Sunni sects, but in the South, there is no such conflict which is often seen between these two sects in North India. Their relationship is relatively peaceful. These two groups have separate institutions such as mosques, seminaries, theologies, government kazis etc. (Fakhri 2008, Bayly, 2004).

According to Fakhri,[39] Dakhnis advent could have been around the invasion of the Bahmani Sultans in the 16th century. In the northern parts of Tamil Nadu where they settled, recorded a significant rise in the Muslim population and here the Muslims are small in number. Dakhni Muslim itself is a broad category covering different groups such as Navayats, Syeds, Sheikhs and Pathans.

Tamil and Dahkni Muslim groups have their respective social structures and kinship patterns. They shared a Sufi tradition and common space. By the late 19th century, Dakhnis were the first in South India to take the plunge into the Deoband and Aligarh movements. They were also the first to join the bar, the teaching profession, and the bureaucracy. Out of these came the proponents of pan-Indian Islam. By the early 20th century, some Tamil Muslims joined the Dahkni elite and were attracted to the ideology of pan-Indian Islam (Fakhri 2008, Bayly, 2004).

The Dakhni Muslim elite reminded the British of their experience of the Urdu Muslim elite of North India. It was commented on the census of 1921 that, 'If adherence to Hindustani is taken as the criterion of true Northern descent, the Pathans, Sheikhs and Syeds are much more truly direct descendants of invaders than the Labbais, of whom 91% speak Tamil and only 3 % Hindustani.'[40]

Tamil Dakhnis

Another category that came up in Tamil Nadu is called Tamil Dakhnis.[41] It emerged in the early 20th century. Famine and inter-caste conflict are the main reasons for the emergence of this category of Muslims. This migration brought Tamil Muslims into a region already populated by Dakhnis. Dakhni Urdu culture now increasingly influenced Tamil Muslims in their customs and traditions, languages and politics. Dakhni Urdu Muslims never accepted them as 'pure Muslims'. Indeed, Dakhnis often alluded to them as Urdu Labbais.

Tamil Dakhnis made considerable investments in education. The emphasis was on building institutions for traditional religious teaching as well as Western education. Several madrassas such as the Baqiath-us-Salehath (Vellore), Jamalia (Madras), Latheefia (Vellore), and Jamia Darussalam (Ambur) were established in the late 19th and 20th centuries. According to Fakhri, among the most significant aspects of the development of traditional education in Tamil Nadu was that the ulamas were not against the idea of Western education in English. Several prominent Muslim leaders like Mohammad Ismail, Basheer Ahmed Sayeed, Yakub Hasan, P Khalilluah, NM Anwar, Raza Khan, and others helped to establish schools and colleges for Muslims in South India. They were themselves the products of major institutions of Western education in Madras, such as Law College, Madras Presidency College, and in some cases, even the Anglo-Mohammadan Oriental College in Aligarh. Though the educational infrastructure for Muslims expanded rapidly during this period, a majority of common Muslims did not benefit (Fakhri 2008, Bayle, 2004).

One of the worrying aspects of this discussion is this status consciousness among these three categories of Muslims, especially Dakhni Muslims and Marakkayars—and their sense of superiority, which is fundamentally against the egalitarian spirit of Islam. It is also important to know that Islam did not spread in the South the way it did in Bengal or Punjab. And also, there are other implications with Muslim rule in the South. As Dharma Kumar observes, 'For instance, when the low castes converted to Islam, they may have become less willing to accept old conditions of de facto bondage, even without any legal change in their status.'[42] This could be the reason why, she further argues, 'their Hindu masters would have tried to prevent their conversion.'[43] It is worth mentioning here most of Madras Presidency came under Muslim rulers, Tipu Sultan, the Nizam of Hyderabad, or the Nawab of Arcot.

Party Politics in South India

Considerable transformations in party politics in the South have occurred since the early days of the Republic. They impacted the discourse about Muslims and their issues. At least four particular trends could be recognized in the evolution of the party system in South India.

First of all, how the Dravidian movement has contributed to the political discourses on Muslims in the South through its inclusive language. Some of the parties that believed in Dravidian ideology have carried historical legacies and their positions about Muslim issues are shaped accordingly. This is especially true about the Dravidian parties such as DMK and AIDMK.[44]

Secondly, how the major national parties such as the Congress, the Left,[45] and now the BJP have shaped the party system in South and Muslim discourses, though their role and contributions varied from state to state. The CPI(M) is a dominant player in Kerala,[46] and the Congress party is a player in various states such as Kerala, Karnataka, Telangana, and Andra Pradesh. The BJP has a solid base in Karnataka and is working actively to extend its base in the other states of South India.

Thirdly, like other parts of India, there are regional parties playing their part in shaping Muslim discourses and Muslim politics—for instance, Telugu Desam Party (TDP) and Jagan Reddy led YSR

Congress party in Andra Pradesh[47] or K Chandrasekhar Rao's (KCR) Bharat Rashtra Samiti (BSR) in Telangana. Interestingly, each of these regional parties is a dynastic party with no internal party democracy.

And last but not least, how identity-based parties, particularly Muslim identity-based parties are contributing to the formation of Muslim discourses. In South India, the two prominent traditional parties are the Indian Union Muslim League (IUML)[48] and Hyderabad-based AIMIM.[49] Both have deep connections with Muslim history. The PFI, banned by the Indian government in September 2022, is another key player in Muslim politics, though on its own it did not play any direct part in electoral politics. It helped to build the SDPI which participates in electoral politics, particularly in Karnataka and Kerala.

Several small organizations representing various Muslim and Hindu causes have come up over the years in various states in the region. Some of them are in the form of political parties. For instance, the Welfare Party of India, founded by Jamaat-e-Islami on 18 April 2011, has been trying to find a foothold among Kerala Muslims. The party remains on the margins of Kerala Muslim politics and has chosen to shy away from electoral politics, including the 2019 parliamentary elections. Besides, smaller formations such as the Tamil Nadu Towheed Jammat (TNTJ), were in alliance with the AIADMK but its influence in Tamil Nadu politics is limited. It is a cadre-based party and its Muslim voters are solidly supporting the Dravidian parties.

Jamaat-e-Islami is a reformist organization that became active in Kerala in the 1950s. It is committed to advancing the goals of political Islam laid down by its founder, Abdul A'la Maududi. By establishing mosques, madrasas, educational institutions, and orphanages, the Jamaat-e-Islami has influenced the formation of Muslim identities, and, by extension, has its contribution to Muslim politics (Santosh and Visakh, 2020).

South India seemingly has a vibrant multi-party electoral democracy and fierce competition among these parties is shaping the evolving contours of competitive democratic politics among Muslims. In this political environment, the BJP is increasingly becoming a more active player. The party is seeking to expand its footprints beyond Karnataka, where the party formed its first government, and has strengthened its potential as an alternative with its alliance with JD(S).

What made a difference in the Southern party system compared to the North or the rest of India is the way the Dravidian movement framed Muslim identity and formulated their issues in the larger context of Dravidian identities. It was in Tamil Nadu that the impact of this movement has been most enduring.

Dravidian Movement and the Muslim Question

The crucial aspect of Muslim politics in the South is how the Dravidian movement has shaped the political discourse on Muslims and the place of Muslim identity in South Indian politics. The movement is choreographed by the contributions of multiple parties with similar objectives—such as the Justice Party, the Self Respect movement, the Dravid Kazhagam (DK), the Dravida Munetra Kazhagam (DMK), and the Anaitha Indiya Anna Dravida Munnetra Kazhagam or All India Anna Dravidian Progressive Federation (AIADMK). They are all inspired by anti-Brahminic ideologies to varied degrees.[50]

Established in 1916, the Justice Party (JP) was led by a small group of elites such as Vellas, Mudaliars, landlords, and professionals. The creation of a new political vocabulary of non-Brahminism is its signature contribution. With the arrival of EV Ramasamy (popularly known as Periyar) as its leader in 1918, the movement went through rapid expansion and he went on to merge it with the Self-Respect movement in 1944 and formed the Dravida Kazhagam (DK). According to Dagmar Hellman-Rajanayagam, 'It was he (Pariyar) who in the 1940s took the name Dravidian as the name of the movement: Triravijak Kajakam—the combination of Justice Party (JP) and his self-respect movement (Suya Mariyadai Iyakkam).'[51] According to the same author, the term Dravidian has been in usage since the Middle Ages as a Sanskrit term denoting the South and is not a European invention. But the European scholarship is mainly responsible for the juxtaposition of 'Aryan' and 'Dravidian' as antonymns.[52]

The Dravidian movement's main political goal was to bring together Tamil Muslims within its fold which it did by focussing on caste and language. In the view of the movement, Muslims of the region were simply Dravidians and a segment of the Tamil-speaking population. The Tamil terms such as jati, kulam, and inam are frequently deployed in the ideological advancement of the Dravidian movement to convey the meaning of caste and community.

The role and contribution of EV Ramaswamy or Periyar[53] is crucial to make sense of how Muslims are perceived in South India. Noted historian AR Venkatchalapathy sums up the significance of Periyar in the following words in an essay titled, 'Periyar: Prophet from the South'[54] borrowing the usage of the Prophet for Periyar from VS Naipaul, 'A curious paradox, however, marks Periyar's name and fame. In Tamil Nadu, he is an icon for most of the political parties even if they are sold out on his radical ideology. His statues dot the landscape, with a rather combative slogan engraved on the pedestal.

There is no god, there is no god at all.
He who invented god is a fool.
He who propagates god is a scoundrel.
He who worships god is a savage.'[55]

Periyar created a particular political language for Muslim identity in the South in the wider political discourse of the Dravidian movement, a language that owned the Muslims. His political goal was to emancipate oppressed social groups such as Dalits, women and the poor, for which he realized the need to obliterate the boundaries among various oppressed groups. Crucially, Periyar was able to recognize the caste character of India's anti-colonial movement led by the Congress party, with which he was associated in the beginning. He found the Congress party exclusionary and indifferent to the conditions and concerns of India's marginalized groups, particularly

Dalits. This convinced him to quit the Congress party, and was also why he remained its fierce critic till his last breath.

On the other hand, Periyar looked at Islam as an emancipatory religion, especially from caste oppression. He even suggested that mass conversion to Islam by Dalits would benefit subordinate social groups.

When Mohammed Ali Jinnah[56] and the Muslim League were keen to strengthen their separate homeland movement and reached out to various political forces for solidarity, they did not find the task very easy in South India. Periyar had made such a strong case for Tamil Muslims as Dravidians that Jinnah found himself on the back foot. Nonetheless, what bound these two stalwarts together is their resistance to the Congress party and its politics. They came together on an anti-Congress platform to seek separate states for each other: Periyar for Dravid Nadu and Jinnah for Pakistan. In December 1938, the first Dravid Nadu resolution was passed under Periyar's leadership—two years before the famous Lahore resolution in 1940. For Periyar, the Muslim League was the 'complete symbol of self-respect for Muslims.'[57] In April 1941, the 28th annual session of the all-India Muslim League was presided over by Jinnah in Madras. While addressing Tamil Muslims, Jinnah said, 'In this land of ours, there is another nation Dravidistan... I shall do all I can to establish Dravidistan and we Muslims will stretch our hand of friendship and live with you on lines of equality, justice and fair play.'[58]

All along, Periyar was convinced that Tamil Muslims were and ought to remain integral to the vision of a Dravidian/Tamil nation and it was his politics, ideology, and vision that forced Jinnah to bow and realise that he would not be able to force the two-nation theory on Periyar. It is no surprise that few Tamil Muslims migrated to Pakistan after 1947.

Despite the negligible impact of Partition, discrimination against Muslims in Tamil Nadu was quite visible.[59] Though several Muslims played a vital role in the Congress, there was no representation of Muslims in the Congress Cabinet from 1946 to 1962. In 1962, when

Kamraj was in his third term, Abdul Majeed was inducted into the cabinet of the Madras state. Congress also did not nominate any member to the Legislative Council during this period, but it was the DMK that was able to send one member to it. When Karunanidhi[60] succeeded Kamraj, he continued his legacy of secular politics. It was the Karunanidhi government that declared Prophet Mohammed's birthday as a government holiday and some Muslims were included in the backward class category so that they could avail the benefits of reservations.

However, the politics of the AIADMK led by MGR was quite different from that of the DMK.[61] When Jayalalithaa took over the party, she took part in the *shilanyas* for the construction of the Ram temple at Ayodhya. It needs to be noted that the DMK went into alliance with the BJP also. However, there are various interpretations of this alliance and its implications for secular polity, particularly Muslim issues. During the Gujarat riot in 2002, the DMK had no reaction or position except Kanimozhi's condemnation. As a party, it was silent. As Venkatchalapahty puts it, 'The DMK's alliance with the BJP was a blot on Karunanidhi's secular record.'[62]

The Indian Union of Muslim League (IUML) in South

Once Mountbatten's Partition plan was accepted and Pakistan was created, Jinnah embraced a 'moth-eaten' Pakistan—with considerable uneasiness, he did not look at South India at all, and left the Muslims in the South at the mercy of their fate, whatever it was. However, there were efforts to revive the Muslim League again in India. This party which was seen as the main campaign vehicle for Partition finally found some support in the South, particularly in Kerala, where it continues to exist and has a marginal presence in Tamil Nadu and Karnataka. The party had no appeal left in the North after Partition.

The Indian Union of Muslim League (IUML) was established on 10 March 1948 and became a full-fledged party in 1951.[63] The party's evolution has a deep connection with local politics, particularly with the Mappilas, which is crucial to recall to make sense of the unique nature of Muslim politics in South. One of the key figures in the setting up of the Muslim League was KM Setthi Sahib (1899-1962). Setthi Sahib played a crucial role in the Madras conference held in March 1948 to formulate the objectives and programmes of IUML. Setthi was a leader of Muslim Aikya Sanghom, which means Organization of Muslim Unity which was formed in 1922 at Canganore (Kodungallur). This was the first organized effort to spread the message of education and reform among the Mapillas of Kerala. The Aikya Sanghom had annual conferences at various Mapilla centres from 1922 to 1934. Mr Setthi was also an active member of the Congress and was a member of the Cochin Assembly in 1928 and 1931. However, owing to internal issues, particularly whether Muslims should participate in political activities, the Aikya Sanghom had become quite weak. In 1934 the Aikya Sanghom merged into another organization, the Kerala Muslim Majlis.

However, the question of whether Muslims should participate in political activities continued to be a part of the debate which took place in the Muslim Club of Tellichery, in which Mr Setthi played a prominent role. The Muslim Club launched a newspaper called *Chandrika.* This also later became the newspaper of the Muslim League. During this period, Mr Setthi shifted his allegiance from the Congress to the Muslim League (ML) and along with him brought many influential Mappilas to the League. In 1937, a unit of the Muslim League was set up formally in the Malabar district (north Kerala). Interestingly, the Muslim League that became popular supported Pakistan and even demanded a Moplastan. After India's Partition in 1947, there was a suggestion to the Muslim League to stop political activities or function as a political party. Setthi Sahib and Muhammad Ismail Sahib resisted the idea of disbanding the Muslim League, and the party was re-established in 1948. It is important to underline here that Mr Ismail Sahib was a fiery Congressman before he joined the League. As one biographer puts it, 'When Muslim Leaguers were afraid to call themselves Muslim Leaguers, and when lukewarm adherents of the party were running with the hare and hunting with the hound, Ismail Sahib was the solitary Muslim Leaguer in India, and for some time, the Muslim League was a one–man show.'[64]

While some look at the Indian Union of Muslim League as a continuation of the Muslim League that was set up in 1906, it was its deep connection with Mappila movements and local Muslim politics of Kerala that helped the Muslim League to have a life of its own in South India, particularly in Kerala. The Muslim League negotiated with the intra-community politics with considerable pragmatism to champion the cause of Muslims to deal with post-Partition challenges. To counter the excessive Mujahid influence in the party, the Muslim league brought to its supreme leadership the members of Hadrami Sayyid families like Abdurrahiman Bafaki Tangal, PSMA Pookaya Thangal, and Panakkad Mumhamedali Shihab Thangal who enjoyed tremendous credibility among Sunnis. The Thangal descendants of Prophet Mohammad enjoy considerable spiritual authority, which helped the party deal with internal conflicts as well as various forms of ideological competition that the community was confronting on a day-to-day basis.

The party effectively took on the political leadership of a seemingly undivided community that was going through high levels of modernization owing to the spread of mass education and large-scale Gulf migration for employment opportunities, etc.

At this juncture it is worth recalling Mohammad Ismail, who also served in the Constituent Assembly, appealed to all Muslims in the Madras province to observe Independence Day and join hands with the Congress and other friends in the celebration. He declared, 'Musalmans of Hindustan must realize that the new Indian flag is no longer a party flag as it has been accepted as the national flag of Indian Union with the consent of all parties in the Constituent Assembly. It is therefore only right that we Muslims living in the Union should henceforth regard it as our flag and respect it. We are not joining the Independence Day celebrations in any spirit of compulsion but as free citizens of a free Indian Union.'[65]

TABLE 2.5 IUML in Kerala Assembly (1960 to 2021)

Election Year	*Total seats*	*Candidates contested*	*Candidates Won*	*Vote percentage*
1960	114	12	11	4.96
1965	133	16	06	3.83
1967	133	15	14	6.75
1970	133	20	11	7.56
1977	140	16	13	6.66
1980	140	21	14	7.18
1982	140	18	14	6.17
1987	140	23	15	7.73
1991	140	22	19	7.37
1996	140	22	13	7.19
2001	140	21	16	7.59
2006	140	21	07	7.30
2011	140	23	20	7.92
2016	140	23	18	7.40
2021	140	25	15	8.27

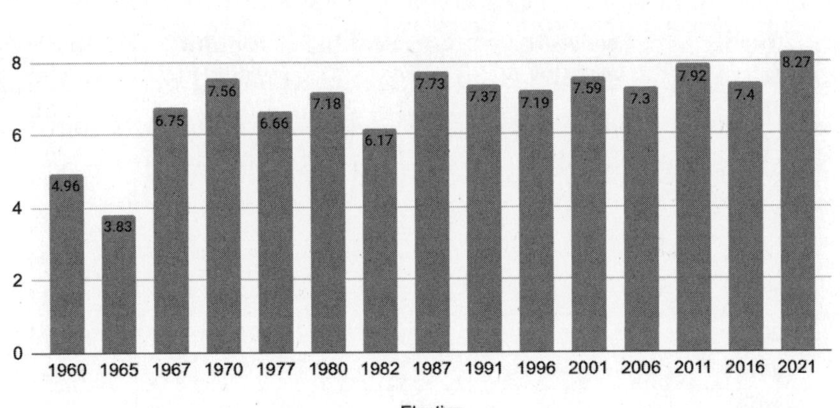

But the party has not managed to find its feet in any other Southern States or any state outside South. Kerala remains its bastion. In 2019, it fielded 14 candidates in Andra Pradesh, and all of them forfeited deposits in their constituencies. In Tamil Nadu, it has fielded candidates in several Assembly elections. Only in 2016, did the party win a seat, and the vote share was always less than one per cent in any election it had participated in since independence. In Karnataka, it has fielded candidates in various elections such as 1989, 2004, 2008, and 2015, but its overall vote share was always less than 0.5 per cent. Only Kerala has its presence and in the 2021 Assembly election, it has 8.27 per cent, which is its highest so far.

All India Majlis-e-Ittehadul Muslimeen (AIMIM)

Apart from IUML, AIMIM has been playing a prominent role in Hyderabad and has become visible at a pan-Indian level under the leadership of Asaduddin Owaisi. Mr Owaisi has been elected to Parliament since 2004 continuously and is its star leader. Table 2.6 offers the details of its parliamentary profile. It had its biggest vote share in 1989, which was 2.1 per cent, but it is now down to 0.73 per cent but has two seats in Parliament including that of Mr Owaisi.

TABLE 2.6 AIMIM Parliamentary Elections in Andra Pradesh

Year	*Candidates Contested*	*Candidates Won*	*Forfeited Deposits(FD)*	*Vote Share in %*
1989	5	1	4	2.1
1991	1	1	0	1.78
1996	2	1	1	1.12
1998	1	1	0	1.52
1999	1	1	0	1.34
2004	2	1	1	1.17
2009	1	1	0	0.73
2014	5	1	4	1.43
2019	2	2	0	0.73

In the post-Shahabuddin[66] era of Muslim politics, Mr Owaisi is perhaps the most visible Muslim politician in the media and public debate. The Party originated during the Nizam's Hyderabad but gradually became part of India's national politics with its position on issues like Shah Bano and Babri Masjid. Over the past few years, Asaduddin Owaisi has begun reacting and responding to every significant Muslim issue that has caught the national attention.

During colonial rule in 1926, the party was founded as the Majlis-e-Ittehadul Muslimeen (MIM),[67] as a Muslim organization to support the Nizams who ruled Hyderabad. A key figure was Qasim Razvi, who first headed the MIM's militia, called Razakkars and later the MIM itself. At the time of Partition, the Nizam, with the MIM's support, chose to defy the new Indian government's attempt to incorporate Hyderabad into its territory. The Razakkars went on a rampage and targeted the Hindu majority and also the communists and Muslims who were in favour of Hyderabad's merger with India. This violence provoked the Indian state which responded by sending military. This operation, called 'Police Action' led to reprisals and violence against Muslims. A government report estimated the loss of lives between 27,000 to 40,000. MIM's headquarters, Darus Salam, was seized and converted into a fire station. There are other estimates, which put the number from 50,000 to as high as 200,000.

The police action which was supposed to take on Razakkars turned out to be unleashed against Muslims who paid a heavy price. Commenting on this police action, AG Noorani wrote a chapter titled 'The Massacre of Muslims' in his book, *The Destruction of Hyderabad.*[68] Mr Noorani said the deceptively titled 'Police Action' was much more than the conquest of a rebel state governed by a megalomaniac under the influence of thugs. According to him, the so-called police action was indeed an attempt at 'the annihilation of a certain way of life, swiftly and almost completely. It's small consolation that something of it still survives.'[69]

The most poignant description of what the police action unleashed was narrated by Wilfred Cantwell Smith, in a journal article titled

'Hyderabad: The Muslim Tragedy'. According to Smith, 'In some areas, all the men were stood in a line, and done to death. Of the total Muslim community in Hyderabad, it would seem that somewhere between one in ten and one in five of the adult males may have lost their lives in those few days. In addition to killing, there was widespread rape, arson, looting, and expropriation.'[70]

In 1957, Razvi was released from jail. He was given two days to leave for Pakistan and many of the MIM leaders had already left for Pakistan. Before his departure, Razvi wanted to hand over the leadership of the MIM to anyone willing to take over. Abdul Wahid Owaisi, grandfather of Asaduddin Owaisi, a young barrister then, decided to take over. It was Abdul Wahid Owaisi who renamed the party All India Majlis Ittehadul Muslimeen (AIMIM) and brought changes by showing the party's allegiance to the Indian Constitution. The party gradually became proactive in electoral politics and began taking part in Parliament to municipal elections with varied degrees of success.

And then the party moved to the hands of Salahuddin, son of Abdul Wahid and father of Asaduddin Owaisi. After spending a few terms in the State Assembly, in 1984 he got elected to Parliament from the Hyderabad constituency. Since the late 1980s, the Ayodhya movement and politics of polarization followed, which helped the AIMIM to be assertive and deepen its social base. Among others, he also served as the Chairman of the Babri Masjid Action Committee, which was a breakaway group. Rival factions also accused Salahuddin of being hand in glove with the Congress party, which they argued was the reason behind his silence on the Babri Masjid demolition.

In 2006, Salahuddin passed away. Ever since, his eldest son Asaduddin Owaisi became the undisputed leader of the party and is actively assisted by two of his brothers. Under his leadership, the party has developed national ambitions and has been able to open an account in the assemblies of Maharashtra and Bihar. Some commentators consider this expansion a perpetuation of old-fashioned divisive politics that might have deep repercussions on India's secular politics. According to Taylor Sherman, 'The revival of the MIM was greeted with much consternation across India, with Urdu papers in Hyderabad and Maulana Azad condemning the move.'[71] Some would like to have similar views about the present state of the AIMIM.

TABLE 2.7 AIMIM in Andhra Pradesh Assembly (1951 to 2019)

Election Year	*Total seats*	*Candidates Contested*	*Candidates Won*	*Forfeited deposits*	*Vote Share(%)*
1989	294	35	4	28	1.99
1994	294	20	1	15	0.70
1999	294	5	4	0	1.08
2004	294	7	4	2	1.05
2009	294	8	7	1	0.83
2014	294	35	7	25	1.52

TABLE 2.8 AIMIM in Telengana (2018 and 2023)

Election Year	*Total seats*	*Candidates fielded*	*Candidates Won*	*Forfeited deposits*	*Vote Share(%)*
2018	119	8	7	0	2.71
2023	119	9	7	2	2.22

So far as the Assembly elections are concerned, its main bastion has been the Hyderabad area. It has had seven MLAs since 2009 in old Andhra Pradesh and now in present-day Telangana. It is argued by scholars that the 2023 Assembly election in Telangana that was won by the Congress was because Muslim voters voted *en masse* for the Congress party though the Congress party was accused of backstabbing the Muslim community by Asaduddin Owaisi. It means Muslim votes were divided between AIMIM and the Congress. It also means AIMIM does not have a monopoly over Muslim votes in the Hyderabad area. It is also suggested that Mr Asaduddin Owaisi is spared of any agency raid owing to his scathing attack on the Congress. In the South, its electoral strength is reflected only in Andhra Pradesh and now in Telangana, which can be studied in Tables 2.7 and 2.8.

But both the IUML and AIMIM have strong connections with Muslim history. They have evolved over the years as political parties. The changed political environment also created new political conditions, giving rise to new political and electoral strategies, particularly alliance-making. The rise of aggressive Hindutva mobilization in the 1990s that has posed a substantial threat to the secular institutions in the country has highly influenced the nature of Muslim politics in South India and shaped these evolving conditions. Besides IUML and AIMIM, there are other political formations as well, for instance, the Social Democratic Party of India (SDPI).

Social Democratic Party of India (SDPI)

The Social Democratic Party of India (SDPI) was formed on 18 October 2009. But its roots could be traced to the political churning of the early 1990s, a period of a new crisis in Muslim society in India including the South. Indian Muslims were confronting unprecedented challenges owing to the aggressive nature of the Ayodhya movement that led to the demolition of Babri Masjid on 6 December 1992. The National Development Front (NDF) was formed in Kozhikode by a group of Muslims in 1993, in the aftermath of the Babri Masjid demolition. In 2006, the NDF became the Popular Front of India (PFI) with the merging of a few more organizations such as the Karnataka Forum of Dignity (KFD) that was set up in coastal Karnataka in the aftermath of the Surathkal Riots in 1998, and Manitha Neethi Pasaria (Forum for Human Justice) which was founded in Tamil Nadu in 2001. The PFI adopted a new constitution on 26 January 2010. The NDF constitution, published in January 1997, and the new Constitution of the PFI are strikingly similar in their secular tone.[72]

The SDPI was formed as the political organ of the PFI in New Delhi. The SDPI claims its presence in more than 26 states, with active organizations in 15 states. The party has the stated objective of 'advancement and uniform development of all the citizenry including Muslims, Dalits and Backward Classes and Adivasis' (SDPI 2018). As a political platform, it welcomes the Muslim-Dalit-OBC alliance.

On the other hand, the PFI looked at itself as a movement 'towards achieving socio-economic, cultural and political empowerment of the downtrodden and the deprived'—with membership open to all citizens over the age of 15 (PFI 2010).[73] It has a women's wing called the National Women's Front and the student wing is called the Campus Front of India. It also has several feeder organizations such as Rehab Foundation, an organization committed to social service whose campaigns include scholarship distribution, disaster relief programs and other related activities. Other organizations such as the Islamic Learning Centres like the Markazul Hidaya (Centre of Guidance), Sathyasarani (Path of Truth) Educational and Charitable Trust, Media Research and Development Foundation, and regional news platforms such as Thejas (Glow). Among others, PFI also organizes public campaigns on issues involving Palestine, Iraq, and other parts of the world (Santosh and Dayal, 2021).

However, the growth of the PFI's organizational network has not translated to the SDPI's electoral fortunes. In Kerala, the vote share declined from 1.5 per cent in the 2014 parliamentary elections to 0.4 per cent in 2019. In Kerala, Dalit participation in SDPI is minimal—except for a few Dalit leaders who have official positions, there is very little Dalit mass participation. In Kerala, the SDPI bagged 51 seats in the 2015 local elections, and over 100 seats in 2020 making considerable inroads into the social base of IUML. From the point of view of electoral politics, SDPI is a marginal player, and 'the politics and ideology of PFI firmly revolve around its bete noire, the Hindutva organizations.'[74]

While carefully avoiding any identification as a Muslim organization or a political party ideologically drawn towards Islam, the PFI-SDPI combine has been all about secular assertions. The absence of any reference to Islamic identity or Muslim politics in the official discourses of the NDF/PFI marked a significant departure from the traditional Muslim political or cultural organizations like the Muslim League, which identified itself with Islam and its community of believers. The PFI's official position is that Islam is a minority religion similar to other minorities and Dalits in India who collectively require protection from the Hindutva onslaught.

In Karnataka, the SDPI could not make inroads in either Parliamentary or Assembly elections (for details see Table 2.12). It had fielded candidates in Kerala, Tamil Nadu, and Andhra Pradesh, but has failed miserably and most of the candidates have forfeited deposits. For details see Table 2.9, Table 2.10, and Table 2.11. But SDPI's success in local elections has been impressive. In the 2015 local elections in Karnataka, the SDPI won 70 of the 372 seats contested—most of which were in coastal Karnataka, and in 2020, it won 225 seats.

TABLE 2.9 SDPI in Kerala Assembly (2011 to 2021)

Election Year	*Total seats*	*Candidates contested*	*Candidates won*	*Forfeited deposits*	*Vote share in %*
2011	140	80	0	80	0.91
2016	140	88	0	88	0.61
2021	140	40	0	40	0.36

TABLE 2.10 SDPI in Tamil Nadu Assembly (2011 to 2021)

Election Year	*Total seats*	*Candidates contested*	*Candidates Won*	*Forfeited deposits*	*Vote share in (%)*
2011	234	5	0	5	0.05
2016	234	29	0	28	0.15
2021	234	6	0	6	0.06

TABLE 2.11 SDPI in Andhra Pradesh Assembly (2014 and 2019)

Election Year	*Total seats*	*Candidates contested*	*Candidates won*	*Forfeited deposits*	*Vote Share in (%)*
2014	294	3	0	3	0.02
2019	175	2	0	2	0.02

TABLE 2.12 SDPI in Karnataka Assembly (2013 to 2023)

Election Year	*Total seat*	*Candidates contested*	*Candidates Won*	*Forfeited Deposits*	*Vote share in %*
2013	224	23	0	22	0.31
2018	223	3	0	2	0.12
2023	224	16	0	15	0.23

Popular Front of India (PFI)

Popular Front of India (PFI) was banned by the government in 2022 but it was active in various parts of India for several years. It, as some argue, wanted to be for Muslims what RSS has been for the Hindus in India. Its goal was to create a political platform for Muslims. SDPI is a result of the PFI's initiative in the hope it could become a party for Muslims the way the BJP has been for Hindus. No such evidence has emerged from the SDPI's electoral interventions in any state thus far.

PFI had multiple founding objectives. One of the main was to prepare Muslims to fight the political battle. Another goal was to generate legal awareness among Muslims and provide legal support to Muslim victims. In October 2019, the PFI organized a legal workshop in various districts of Assam to legally empower Muslims in the region. This legal activism included legal and financial assistance in high-profile cases. The Hadiya case of 2017 is a prominent example. The PFI spent close to 10 lakh rupees on this case to fight for the rights of Hadiya, who converted to Islam and married a Muslim youth. It also fought legal battles for communal victims of mob lynchings. As of June 2018, the PFI claims to have given legal support to more than 1,300 cases all over the country. Besides, various state and district units of the PFI have filed over a thousand defamation cases against various news organizations for spreading hate news.

In coastal Karnataka, the PFI was engaged in various kinds of religious and political violence, moral vigilantism, and the practice of exclusivist and radical Islamist politics. Several Hindu Right organizations have also been active in this region. They include Sri Ram Sene (Army of Lord Rama), Bajrang Dal (Brigade of Lord Hanuman), Hindu Jagran Vedike (Hindu Vigilance Forum), Hindu Jagruta Samithi (Committee of Hindu Awakening), and so on. These groups have been consistently using the bogey of love jihad, cow vigilantism, moral policing of inter-religious relationships, controversies of conversions, and desecration of religious places to unleash violence and protect Hindu culture.

According to a report prepared by Communal Harmony Forum, a Mangalore-based organization, there were about 1088 incidents of communal violence that took place in the region between 2010 to 2018. There is a similarity in the modus operandi of both the Hindu Right organizations and the PFI. One-third of the incidents of moral vigilantism that took place in coastal Karnataka between 2013 and 2015 were carried out by Muslim vigilantes. Despite secular posturing, the PFI has been involved in campaigns related to Islamic issues. It actively mobilizes against Hijab-based discrimination.

PFI's secular credentials were not recognized by other organizations in Kerala. For instance, the Muslim League dubbed the PFI as a Muslim communal outfit promoting militancy among youths. They pointed out that regardless of the Constitution of the PFI saying otherwise, membership is open only to Muslims. The organization is influenced by Islamist political ideals and Salafi theological orientations. Though PFI refutes these allegations, there is enough evidence on the ground to support these concerns. For instance, according to police investigations, those involved in the attack of a college professor in Thodupuzha, TJ Joseph,[75] on 4 July 2010 for setting up a question paper that allegedly contained derogatory remarks on Prophet Muhammad were PFI activists. However, the PFI distanced itself from this violence. Furthermore, the Kerala Police and NIA filed several reports accusing the organization of having terror links and resorting to violence.

SDPI, on the other hand, gives membership to everybody irrespective of religious affiliations. On 25 August 2017, the SDPI's National President, A Sayeed, at a national campaign against lynchings by cow protection vigilantes in several parts of India said, 'Muslims and Dalits must acknowledge that their security is now in their own hands. They have come out with free hands and free minds to take over the mission of self-protection. Nobody else will come to protect them.'

The SDPI presents itself as a political party of the oppressed communities such as Muslims, Other Backward Classes (OBCs), and

Dalits. Office bearers of the SDPI Kerala State Committee include members from the Dalit and OBC communities, though no major Dalit organization in the state extended support to the SDPI in Kerala. The party has organized several political agitations in Kerala.

SDPI has been fighting in all elections since its inception. It has made an impact on the traditional bastions of the Muslim League. The SDPI secured more than 50 seats across the state in the local body elections in 2015. In alliance with the Samajwadi Party (SP), the SDPI contested more than 90 seats in the 2016 Kerala assembly elections, making its presence felt in several constituencies.

The PFI started a nationwide campaign in support of Hadiya,[76] a new convert to Islam, where other organizations were reluctant to intervene. Around 3,000 PFI activists marched to the Kerala High Court in Ernakulam chanting Takbir. The demonstration turned violent and clashed with the police. If the results of the 2023 Assembly elections in Karnataka are anything to go by, Muslim voters in the South, as is in the North or elsewhere, voted for a party that could defeat BJP, which is why they voted *en masse* for the Congress that went on the win the election in 2023 in Karnataka, Telangana, etc.

Hindu Right in its Southern Bastion: Karnataka[77]

Considered as a bastion of Hindu Right, Karnataka is increasingly seen as the laboratory of Hindutva. How Muslim issues are raised and debated or politically contested here would show the possible pattern that the South might take once the Hindu Right begins to electorally expand in the region, for which it is making sincere efforts at various levels.

Karnataka is the first and only southern state that has been governed by the BJP. Although the BJP formed its first government in 2008, it emerged as the second-largest party in 1994, having a few more seats than the Congress. However, the ideological campaign of the Hindu Right has been going on for several decades in Karnataka, particularly in coastal Karnataka, which is nearly 320 km long. On 13 May 2023, the BJP was defeated by the Congress in the state elections but retained its vote share of 36 per cent which indicates a strong social base that the Party has built up over the years[78]. Table 2.13 contains the details of the BJP's performance in elections.

TABLE 2.13 BJP in Karnataka Assembly (1980 to 2023)

Election Year	*Total seats*	*Candidates Contested*	*Candidates Won*	*Forfeited Deposits*	*Vote Share in %*
1983	224	110	18	71	7.93
1985	224	116	2	99	3.88
1989	224	118	4	101	4.14
1994	224	223	40	135	16.99
1999	224	149	44	37	20.69
2004	224	198	79	42	28.33
2008	224	224	110	31	33.86
2013	224	223	40	110	19.89
2018	223	223	104	36	36.22
2023	224	224	66	31	36.

It was in the coastal belt of Karnataka where the Hindu Right has been able to play its politics of polarization rather successfully, reaping tremendous electoral benefits. It was in Karnataka's Udupi town in 1985 that a 'Dharm Sansad' (religious parliament) called for the opening of the disputed Babri Masjid.[79] Karnataka does not fit the stereotype of backwardness, unemployment and illiteracy often associated with a bigoted society.[80] The state has one of the lowest unemployment rates in the country, a higher-than-national-average literacy rate, and boasts of Bengaluru, the Silicon Valley of Asia, as its capital.[81]

Even coastal Karnataka is not considered significantly underdeveloped. On the face of it, the region is urban, multicultural, multilingual, and wealthy. Since the 1980s Bengaluru's thriving IT industry has attracted talent from across the country. Global software giants and almost half of Indian unicorns have offices there. With the first pubs in India, high-rise corporate offices, and gated apartments for the city's upper middle class, Bengaluru is as cosmopolitan as it gets. Meanwhile, a parallel project to 'unify' Hindus divided by castes also continued in Karnataka.

Scholars working on this issue claim that Hindu Right organizations such as RSS have been infiltrating schools, colleges, media, and local neighbourhoods with one clear message: 'Hindu Navella Ondu', or 'Hindus Are One' in Kannada for decades. The local media, for example, refers to Muslims and Christians as 'anya Bharatiya' (the other Indians) or 'anya komu' (the other religion). They do not even mention 'Muslim' because it is assumed that both the reporter and the readers are Hindu, and the 'other community' is Muslim. Sugata Srinivasaraju, biographer of HD Deve Gowda, India's former Prime Minister from Karnataka, recalls how the BJP's efforts with its saffron family to start a movement in Karnataka to reclaim a Sufi shrine at Baba Budangiri Hills in Chikmagalur provoked Mr Deve Gowda to react on 2 December 1998. HN Ananth Kumar, a prominent BJP leader wanted to make it 'Ayodhya of the South'. The plan was to convert this syncretic place as Dattatreya Peetha or the seat of Dattatreya, an incarnation of Brahma, Vishnu and Shiva, the trinity of Hindu Gods.[82]

In coastal Karnataka, however, Muslims form about 24 per cent of the population. The Muslims of coastal Karnataka are locally known as the Byari community. It translates to trade or business in the local Tulu dialect. They are known to have lived in this region for more than a thousand years. The community benefited from the opening up of the Gulf economies to foreign workforces in the 1970s. They own businesses such as malls, hospitals, constructions, and educational institutions in the region. The prosperity of the Byari community also caused rivalry with other trading communities, mainly the Konkanis and the Gowd Saraswat Brahmins, the two dominant Hindu castes in the region.

In recent months, at least three religiously motivated murders in coastal Karnataka, including two Muslim men and a member of the BJP's youth wing took place. Responding to the Hindu man's murder, the BJP chief minister of Karnataka said he would implement a 'Yogi model' in the state, referring to his counterpart in Uttar Pradesh, Yogi Adityanath.[83] Another Karnataka minister was even more direct and said the southern state would 'go five steps ahead of Uttar Pradesh' and was ready to even carry out extrajudicial killings of the accused.[84] In various parts of Karnataka, the work of Jackie Assayag's *At the Confluence of Two Rivers: Muslims and Hindus in South India* argues that over much of recorded history, Hindus and Muslims lived side by side without much friction. In everyday life, co-existence was often more visible than conflict. Their economic life was one of interdependence, with Hindu shopkeepers servicing Muslim clients and vice versa.[85]

Two political developments in the 1970s helped the RSS. First, a popular movement against the imposition of Emergency by the Congress government in 1975 was spearheaded by the RSS, which used the anger against the then-ruling party to push the Hindutva agenda. Second, the land reforms enacted by the Congress further antagonised the dominant Hindu caste groups whose lands were taken and redistributed to people from the less privileged castes. Moreover, sustained social engineering even brought the lower castes closer to the RSS than the Congress. 'But the RSS worked on their social inclusion and they have become the stormtroopers of Hindutva who create terror in the society. For a community with little identity, being called a Hindu and given space and responsibility by the upper castes has meant largely unquestioned devotion to the Hindutva project.'[86]

The BJP has created majoritarian conditions in the state. The state has also banned cow slaughter,[87] introduced an anti-conversion law[88] that makes interfaith marriages a matter of legal scrutiny, the ban on hijab in schools, etc. Many BJP politicians have called for a boycott of Muslim businesses. One of the earliest signs of a more aggressive Hindutva was seen in this region in 2009 when a group of young women in a pub in Mangalore were beaten up for violating 'Indian values' by dozens of activists belonging to a far-right Hindu group, called the Sri Ram Sene.[89] It remains to be seen how the new Congress government is going to address these issues in diluting the majoritarian governance culture and creating space for secular governance. Even after nearly a year, the secular Congress government has not shown the spine to take the BJP as evidenced by its decision to remain silent on the banning of the Bajrang Dal organization which was its agenda according to its election manifesto in the 2023 Assembly elections. It is this ambivalence in the Congress party about secularism that is one of the reasons for its dramatic decline.

TABLE 2.14 BJP in Kerala Assembly (1980 to 2023)

Election Year	*Total seats*	*Candidates contested*	*Candidates Won*	*Forfeited Deposits*	*Vote Share in %*
1980 {JNP+JNP(S)}	140	29+4=33	5+0=5	4+4=8	7.63+0.08=7.71
1982	140	69	0	67	2.75
1987	140	116	0	113	5.56
1991	140	137	0	135	4.76
1996	140	127	0	124	5.48
2001	140	123	0	121	5.02
2006	140	136	0	133	4.75
2011	140	138	0	133	6.03
2016	140	98	1	62	10.53
2021	140	115	0	84	11.3

TABLE 2.15 BJP in Tamil Nadu Assembly (1980 to 2023)

Election Year	*Total seats*	*Candidates Contested*	*Candidates Won*	*Forfeited Deposits*	*Vote share in %*
1980	234	10	0	10	0.07
1984	234	15	0	14	0.25
1989	234	31	0	30	0.35
1991	234	99	0	95	1.70
1996	234	143	1	137	1.81
2001	234	21	4	0	3.19
2006	234	225	0	221	2.02
2011	234	204	0	198	2.22
2016	234	188	0	180	2.84
2021	234	20	4	0	2.62

TABLE 2.16 BJP in Andhra Pradesh Assembly (1980 to 2023)

Election Year	*Total seats*	*Candidates Contested*	*Candidates Won*	*Forfeited deposits*	*Vote Share in %*
1983	294	80	3	62	2.76
1985	294	10	8	0	1.62
1989	294	12	5	0	1.78
1994	294	280	3	266	3.89
1999	294	24	12	0	3.67
2004	294	27	2	4	2.63
2009	294	271	2	263	2.84
2014	294	58	9	28	4.13
2019	175	173	0	173	0.84

TABLE 2.17 BJP in Telangana Assembly (2018 and 2023)

Election Year	*Total seats*	*Candidates contested*	*Candidates Won*	*Forfeited deposits*	*Vote Share in percentage*
2018	119	117	1	102	6.98
2023	119	111	8	66	13.9

On the Backwardness of South Indian Muslims

According to some scholars and commentators, there is a distinct trend concerning backwardness for South Indian Muslims which is not an extension of either North India or the rest of India. This is partly owing to the distinct nature of inclusivity that Muslims in South India experience, particularly in the history of identity politics as encapsulated in the Dravidian movement. Research on this theme also has revealed interesting insights not just about Muslims but also with regard to Dalits—another form of affirmation of inclusive politics leading to inclusive development strategies. There are valuable insights to this end in the research published by A Kalaiyarasan and M Vijayabaskar in the book, *The Dravidian Model.*[90] In its chapter titled, 'Conceptualising Power in Caste Society' it recognizes the contributions of Dravidian mobilization against upper-caste hegemony and its vision of social justice, which broadly created a policy environment for an inclusive intervention that also benefitted minorities, particularly Muslims. The authors further argue, and rightly so, that the Dravidian ideology 'was rooted in the high modern with a strong faith in the ability of modernization of the productive domain to diffuse and undermine social hierarchies.'[91]

However, this Dravidian movement and its impact was not uniform in the South and caste dominance in other states such as Karnataka did result in a less inclusive society, according to some research. We learn this from a comparative study undertaken by Narayan Lakshman whose results are published in the book, *Patrons of the Poor: Caste Politics and Policy Making in India.*[92] In this research, the author recognizes the role of caste dominance and notes, 'There is a significant possibility of an analytical link between the patterns of caste dominance in a society and the policy orientation of the political leadership in that context.'[93] While these are broad results regarding the overall policy environment, there are interesting specifics also about Muslims in South India.

During the preparation of the Sachar Report, it was brought to notice that the affirmative action policies in these states predate India's independence. The recent controversy regarding the Muslim quota of four per cent and the attempt to abolish it by the BJP needs to be seen in the wider context of the history of affirmative politics in Karnataka. The attempt by the Bommai government and the BJP's national leadership to present this reservation as part of appeasement politics is part of their strategy of perpetuating the politics of polarization. Amit Shah, during the 2023 Assembly election campaign, defended scrapping the four per cent reservation of Muslims in Karnataka as he said that the party does not believe in religion-based reservation.[94] The truth is that it is not part of religion-based reservation as it has been made out to be in public debate by the BJP.

In Karnataka and Kerala, Muslims are considered backward classes without their creamy layer and have been given exclusive quotas. The reservation practice began during colonial times. In the erstwhile princely Mysore state, as early as 1874, affirmative action policy began when a government decision was taken to reserve 80 per cent of the posts in police departments for the non-Brahmins, Muslims, and Indian Christians. In Kerala, as early as 1936, in the princely state of Travancore and Cochin, and in Malabar even in 1921, reservation policies were initiated for under-represented communities for religious minorities such as Muslims and Christians. They were also fixed for caste groups such as the Ezhavas.

Once Mysore became part of Karnataka as part of the re-organization in post-independent India, Muslims and Christians were declared as backward classes. In 1960, on the recommendation of the Nagan Gowda Committee, the category of backward classes was divided into backward (28 per cent) and more backward (22 per cent). Together with the SC/ST quota, the size of the quota increased to 60 per cent. But then the Supreme Court set a ceiling of 50 per cent in the reservations.

It is reported in the Sachar Report (2006) that Muslims as a whole continued to be considered backward communities. The State classified Backward Classes into three categories: (a) Most backward, (B) More backward, (c) Backward. All Muslims whose income is less than two lakh per annum have been declared backward and placed exclusively in one of the sub-categories of 'More backward' with four per cent of seats set aside for them. This is how the four per cent reservation came to practice. According to the information shared by the state governments to the Sachar Committee, this policy has a positive impact on the Muslim share in the state government services. The number of seats Muslims get in professional courses like medicine, dental, and engineering has also increased to a considerable extent. Between 1996 to 2002, 436 Muslim students were able to secure seats in medicine, 258 in dental, and 3486 in engineering courses.[95]

In the state of Kerala, the reservation policy was introduced in 1952. According to this policy, the quantum of reservation was fixed at 45 per cent including 10 per cent for SCs and STs. The beneficiaries included the Ezhavas, Kammalas, the Nadars (Hindu and Christian), other Hindu backward castes, and SC and OBC converts to Christianity. In 1956, when the state was reorganized, the quota for backward classes was enhanced to 40 per cent. Later the scheme was modified to introduce sub-quotas for major backward groups. A separate Muslim share was fixed at 10 per cent which later rose to 12 per cent. At present the reservation system in Kerala is as follows: Backward classes: 40 per cent (Ezhavas 14 per cent, Muslims 12 per cent, Latin Catholics 4 per cent, Nadars 2 per cent, Christians converts from SCs 1 per cent, Deeravas 1 per cent), OBCs: 3 per cent, Viswakarmas: 3 per cent, SCs and STs: 10 per cent.[96]

Besides the Kerala and Karnataka model of reservation, the state of Tamil Nadu has its model of reservations for Muslims. Unlike Kerala and Karnataka, Muslims as a distinct group are not eligible for reservation, yet most of the Muslim biradaris are included either in the backward or in the most backward list. The state government has done away with reservation on the grounds of religion, yet nearly 95 per cent of Muslims have been included within the fold of backward classes.

Indeed, there is a history of this process of reservation for Muslims in Kerala. The educationally backward Muslims were given special treatment vide a resolution dated 29 July 1872. It was later extended to the 'aborigines' and low-caste Hindus. As the Brahmins were grossly overrepresented in high-salary jobs, a government order (1972) introduced compartmental reservations whereby the non-Brahmins were to have 42 per cent of the posts available and 17 per cent for the Muslims.[97]

Post-1947, the reservation was extended to only the constitutionally recognized deprived categories, such as SCs and STs and the Backward Classes. A separate quota for Muslims was also withdrawn. However, various communities among Muslims considered backwards were included in the list of backward classes. The Sattanathan Commission (1970) endorsed the 1951 categorisation; it identified 105 castes/communities as backward, and recommended 31 per cent reservation, whereas 18 per cent was left for the SCs and STs. Tamil-speaking Muslim groups, such as Labbais, Deccan Muslims, and others were included in the backward list. In 1980, the 31 per cent quota for backward classes was raised to 50 per cent taking the total to 68 per cent. This is how reservations for Muslims evolved in South India.

Following the recommendation of the Ambasankar Commission (1982), the backward classes were split into Backward Classes (BCs), Most Backward Classes (MBCs), and De-notified Communities. The quantum of reservations currently is 69 per cent, far beyond the Supreme Court limit of 50 per cent. The Tamil Nadu Backward Classes, Scheduled Castes and Scheduled Tribes (Reservation of Seats in Educational Institutions and Appointments or Posts in the Services under the State) Act, 1993, were included in the 9th Schedule through the 76th amendment of the Constitution.

Given this history, it could be argued that affirmative action policy might have contributed to the improved socio-economic conditions of Muslims in the South. There are, however, other studies that provide further insights into this debate. According to new research, the conditions of Muslim backwardness in the South have also been affected post-2014, as is typically the case in the North.

Conclusion

Generally, it is invariably argued that India's South is a distinct region with inherent heterogeneity. Nevertheless, some general conclusions could be made about the region—particularly about Muslims, their politics and their behaviour—in the context of the rise of the Hindu Right.

As it became clear during the Assembly election campaign in 2023 in Karnataka, the Hindu Right is hell-bent on playing the politics of polarization as frequently as possible regardless of the fact whether it works or not. Given that the BJP was able to retain its vote share in Karnataka from the previous Assembly election in 2018, roughly 36 per cent, it could be argued that electoral defeat is in no way an ideological defeat for the BJP. As Suhas Palshikar notes, 'Opponents of Hindutva often use the term "laboratory of Hindutva". Karnataka was supposed to be one such. There is not one laboratory; in every state, efforts to lure Hindus away from their traditional faith and make them hate-filled anti-minority crowds have been going on.'[98] With its new alliance with JD(S), the party of former Prime Minister, HD Deve Gowda, there is a fair chance the Hindu Right will expand its social base and vote share.

Looking at competing political trends, there are signs of tremendous competition between the politics of inclusion and exclusion in India's South. As the Hindu Right invests more and more energy and resources, there is a growing anxiety among religious minorities, particularly Muslims. But this anxiety and fear find expression in two different directions. In one way, the community begins to close ranks and move closer to secular formations. This is the case in Karnataka in 2023 in which Muslims chose to abandon Muslim political parties such as the SDPI and secular parties such as JD(S) led by Deve Gowda. Instead, Muslim voters chose to move towards the Congress to give it a resounding majority which now runs the government. The reason seems to be mainly that the Congress alone could take on the BJP. Without a doubt, the consolidation of secular politics and Muslims' solidarity for such politics occurs simultaneously. This seems to be the case with the results of the Telangana Assembly elections in 2023 as well in which the Congress party has profited again. This has happened despite Asaduddin Owaisi's AIMIM being a traditional player and contender of Muslim voters. On the other hand, there are also signs of Muslim alienation, which in past years found expression in the growth of the PFI, though the community chose not to offer it electoral backing. Broadly, the community still favours secular politics and helps contribute to the resistance of majoritarianism through its secular voting commitment.

Muslims in North India experienced the Partition of 1947 but in South India, no such effort towards separatism found support in the 1940s. However, the politics of the Ayodhya movement have generated unprecedented anxiety, and the rise of majoritarianism presents a completely different context, leading to new formations such as PFI or SDPI. While the BJP is trying to make its footprints in the South—in some areas on its own and other areas in partnership with other political parties—growing propaganda and assertion are going to accompany the process. And this propaganda is vicious and often built on false history, facts, or premises. Issues like the Hijab, Tipu Sultan, and the Uniform Civil Code (UCC), and propaganda films such as *The Kerala Story* continue to contribute to the politics of religious polarization and create conditions parallel to what we witness in North India. But the difference is that in the South, there is still a very indigenous form of resistance to Hindu majoritarianism or Hindutva politics by a combination of factors arising from secular populism, the Dravidian movement, left-wing politics etc. As is evident in various forms of electoral responses, Muslims in the South continue to navigate this increasingly difficult terrain by siding with secular forces, and they do realise that it is in their unity that Hindu majoritarianism could be contained. Through its ability to extract benefits from affirmative action policies and growing global opportunities, particularly in the Middle East, the Muslim community in South India is also able to deal with its economic fortune better than its counterparts in North or any other part of India.

What are the possible trends we could witness in the coming years? The trends could be as follows: a) further aggressive propaganda of various anti-minority stereotypes by the Hindu Right, b) abuse of history for purposes of polarization, c) the possibility of growing small-scale violence of the kind that is seen widely in the North or West, particularly in Maharashtra recently. All of these and more would undermine the unique secular and tolerant culture of the South, and at the same time, these will further secular solidarity and resistance to Hindu majoritarianism setting a new momentum for the ideological struggle between the Hindu Right and the South's inclusive social and cultural landscape. In a nutshell, the future of Muslims in South India mainly hinges on the ability of a new political class to preserve the rich legacy of Periyar.[99] Therefore, the expansion of the Hindu Right to the inner veins of Southern society implies there is a mortal threat to secular modern thinking that respects the core values of humanity.

Notes

1 Bayly, Susan. 2004. *Saints, Goddesses, and Kings: Muslims and Christians in South Indian Society, 1700-1900.* Cambridge: Cambridge University Press. P. 73.

2 Mujeeb, Mohammad. 2017 (first published in 1967). *Indian Muslims.* New Delhi: Munshiram Manoharlal Publishers Pvt. Ltd. P. 18.

3 For an incisive analysis of Ayodhya movement and related issues, see Gopal, Sarvepalli. 1992. *Anatomy of a Confrontation: Ayodhya and Rise of Communal Politics in India.* London: Zed Books. Rao, P V Narasimha. 2019. *Ayodhya: 6 December.* New Delhi: Penguin. Singh, Valay. 2018. *Ayodhya: City of Faith, City of Discord.* New Delhi: Aleph Book Company.

4 See, More, JBP. 1997. *The Political Evolution of Muslims in Tamil Nadu and Madras, 1930-1947.* New Delhi: Orient Blackswan. Also see Fakhri, SM Abdul Khader. 2008. *Dravidian Sahibs and Brahmin Maulanas: The Politics of the Muslims of Tamil Nadu, 1930-1967.* New Delhi: Manohar. Also see, Jalal, Ayesha. 1994. *The Sole Spokesman: Jinnah, the Muslim League, and the Demand for Pakistan.* Cambridge: Cambridge University Press.

5 Gandhi, Rajmohan. 2018. *Modern South India: A History of the 17th Century to our Times.* New Delhi: Aleph book Company. P. 437.

6 See, 'Madras HC gives nod for RSS route march.' Available at: http://www.timesofindia.com 11 February 2023 (accessed on on 20 February 2023).

7 See, 'Supreme Court clears RSS March, dismisses Tamil Nadu government's appeal.' Available at: http://www.ndtv.com April 11 2023 (accessed on 12 March 2023).

8 See, Venkatachalapathy, AP. 2018. *Tamil Characters: Personalities, Politics, and Culture.* New Delhi: Pan Macmillan. P. 47. This is an observation made when the author discusses the DMK-BJP alliance and its implications for Tamil Nadu. Both parties had alliance from 1999-2004. See, 'How Karunanidhi joined hands with BJP before 1999 general elections, then parted ways five years later'. http://www.thehindustantimes.com 8 August 2018 (accessed on 20 January, 2024).

9 *The Times of India.* 2023. 'PFI Banned in India: Centre Declares Unlawful.' (retrieved on 20 Feb 2023).

10 Verma, Lalmani. 2023. 'PM's interaction, Christmas message, Home visits: BJP pushes on with Christian outreach.' Available at: http://www.Indianexpress.com (accessed on 24 January 2024). Also, see Rehman,

Mujibur. 2024. 'Once upon a time, there was a functioning Indian Democracy.' http://www.reset.org (accessed on 1 February 2024).

11 *India Today*. 'RSS worker dies of heart attack in Kerala's Kannur after clash with the CPI(M) cadres.' 25 Jul 2022 (accessed on 12 March 2023).

12 See the report by Tripathi, Purnima S. 2022. 'BJP woos Pasmanda Muslims at the behest of Narendra Modi.' Available at: http://www.thehindu.com (accessed on 12 March 2023).

13 See, Jaffrelot, Christophe. 1998. *The Hindu Nationalist Movement in India*. Cambridge: Cambridge University Press; Hansen, Thomas Blom. 1999. *The Saffron Wave: Democracy and Hindu Nationalism in Modern India*. Princeton: Princeton University Press.

14 See, Chiriyankandath, James. 2018. 'Yes, but not in South' in Rehman, Mujibur. 2018 (Ed.) *Rise of Saffron Power: Reflections on Indian Politics*. New Delhi: Routledge. Pp. 44-61.

15 Ibid. Pp. 45-46.

16 See, Nath, Sanstuti and Thirumalai, Nitya. 2023. 'Telangana Election Results 2023: Congress to form first non-BRS govt, Wins 64 seats with 39. 40 % vote share; All Eyes on Revanth Reddy's role.' http://www.news18.com (accessed on 1 February 2024).

17 See, 'India's BJP wins three of four state polls months before national election.' http://www. aljazeera.com 3 December 2023 (accessed on 31 January 2024).

18 India is yet to hold Census 2021.

19 Reddy, Ireddy Srinivas. 2022. 'TDP, BJP, Jana Sena to form alliance in next Telengana Assembly Polls?' Available at: http://www.indianexpress.com (accessed on 1 February 2024).

20 See, Ranjan, Nishant and Jha, Abhishek. 2023. 'How Will BJP-JD(S) Alliance impact Karnataka'. Available at: http:// www. thehindustantimes.com (accessed on 1 February 2024).

21 Susan Bayly. 2004. *Saints, Goddesses, and Kings: Muslims and Christians in South Indian Society, 1700-1900*. Cambridge: Cambridge University Press. P. 104.

22 Fakhri, SM Abdul Khader. 2008. *Dravidian Sahibs and Brahmin Maulanas: The Politics of the Muslims of Tamil Nadu, 1930-1967*. New Delhi: Manohar.

23 See, Bayly, Susan. 2004. 'The Development of Muslim society in Tamil Nadu' in *Saints, Goddesses, and Kings: Muslims and Christians in South Indian Society, 1700-1900*. Cambridge: Cambridge University Press. Pp. 70-103.

24 Guha, Ramachandra. 2007. 'The Southern Challenge' in *India After Gandhi*. New Delhi: Picador. P. 286.
25 Susan Bayly. 2004. *Saints, Goddesses, and Kings: Muslims and Christians in South Indian Society, 1700-1900*. Cambridge: Cambridge University Press. P. 87.
26 For more elaborate discussion on this see, Ibid. Pp. 94-95.
27 See the chapter, 'Muslim Society in Tamil Nadu' in Fakhri, SM Abdul Khader. 2008. *Dravidian Sahibs and Brahmin Maulanas: The Politics of the Muslims of Tamil Nadu, 1930-1967*. New Delhi: Manohar. Pp. 30-44.
28 Ibid. Pp. 33-34.
29 See, More, JBP. 1997. *The Political Evolution of Muslims in Tamilnadu and Madras 1930-1947*. New Delhi: Orient Longman. P. 101.
30 Bayly, Susan. 2004. *Saints, Goddesses, and Kings: Muslims and Christians in South Indian Society, 1700-1900*. Cambridge: Cambridge University Press. Pp. 91-92.
31 Ibid. Pp. 79-80.
32 The history of Muslims revolved around horse trade until the arrival of Europeans. Tamil Muslims who were working with horses came to be identified as Rowthers. With the passage of time, the Rowthers began to change their professions and some either became artisans or traders engaged in the weaving. Some of them also began the export of mats and textiles. For a detailed discussion on this aspect, see Fakhri, SM Abdul Khader. 2008. *Dravidian Sahibs and Brahmin Maulanas: The Politics of the Muslims of Tamil Nadu, 1930-1967*. New Delhi: Manohar. Pp. 30-34.
33 Ibid. P. 32.
34 There are other interesting stories. Take for example, Kilakkarai Marakayar Sitakati (Shaikh Abdul Qudir) a patron of scholars and commissioned in South India's most well known Muslim devotional work by Umaru Pulavar, *Sirappuranum*, a 5000 stanza epic on Prophet's life. See. Fakhri, SM Abdul Khader. 2008. *Dravidian Sahibs and Brahmin Maulanas: The Politics of the Muslims of Tamil Nadu, 1930-1967*. Pp. 30-34.
35 They maintain these divisions by marrying their fellow Shafis from the Malabar coast and Southeast Asia in preference to Tamil speaking Hanafis.
36 The dargah in the town of Karaikkal is believed to contain the remains of *sahabi*, companions of the Prophet; Kayalpatanam contains a series of early masjids including *periyapalli* (a grand mosque) built in AD 1331. See, Susan Bayly. 2004. *Saints, Goddesses, and Kings: Muslims and Christians in South Indian Society, 1700-1900*. Cambridge: Cambridge University Press. P. 81.

37 For a detailed discussion on Dakhni Muslims, see. Fakhri, SM Abdul Khader. 2008. *Dravidian Sahibs and Brahmin Maulanas: The Politics of the Muslims of Tamil Nadu, 1930-1967*. Pp. 34-37.

38 See, Bayly, Susan. 2004. *Saints, Goddesses, and Kings: Muslims and Christians in South Indian Society, 1700-1900*. Cambridge: Cambridge University Press. Pp. 96-97.

39 See Fakhri. SM Abdul Khader. 2008. *Dravidian Sahibs and Brahmin Maulanas: The Politics of the Muslims of Tamil Nadu, 1930-1967*. Pp. 34-37.

40 Ibid. P. 37.

41 Ibid. Pp. 37-41.

42 Kumar, Dharma. 2023. *Land and Caste in South India*. New Delhi: Manohar. P. 9. The book was first published by Cambridge University Press in 1965. Also, see, 'Dharma Kumar: An Intellectual Portrait' in Guha Ramachandra. 2016. *Democrats and Dissenters*. New Delhi: Penguin Random House. Pp. 239-257.

43 Ibid. P. 9.

44 For a historical analysis of Dravidian movement, see Washbrook, David. 1989. 'Caste Class Dominance in Modern Tamil Nadu'. In MSA Rao amd Francine Frankel (Eds.). *Dominance and State Power in Modern India: Decline of a Social Order*. Vol 10. New Delhi: Oxford University Press. Pp. 204-264.

45 Mannathukkaren, Nissim. 2022. *Communism, Subaltern Studies and Postcolonial Theory: The Left in South India*. New Delhi: Routledge.

46 For an understanding of Left and Congress competitive politics in Kerala, see 'The Southern Challenge' in *India After Gandhi* by Guha, Ramachandra. New Delhi: Picador. Pp. 281-300.

47 For a historical analysis of Andhra Pradesh, see Reddy, G Ram. 1989. 'The Politics of Accommodation: Caste, Class, and Dominance in Andra Pradesh'. In MSA Rao and Francine Frankel. (Eds.). *Dominance and State Power in Modern India: Decline of a Social Order*. Vol 10. New Delhi: Oxford University Press. Pp. 204-264.

48 For an insightful analysis of IUML see, Santosh, R and Visakh, MS. 2020. 'Muslim League in Kerala: Exploring the Question of Being Secular.' *Economic and Political Weekly*. Vol LV. No. 7. Pp. 50-57.

49 See, Bajpai, Rochana and Farooqui, Adnan. 2018. 'Non-extremist outbidding: Muslim Leadership in Majoritarian India.' *Nationalism and Ethnic Politics*. 24(3). Pp. 276-298.

50 For a brief but very insightful analysis of non-Brahmin movement, see

Venkatachalapathy, A. 2018. 'Non-Brahmin Movement: A Hundred Years' in *Tamil Characters: Personalities, Politics and Culture.* New Delhi: Pan MacMillan. Pp. 223-228.

51 See, Hellmann-Rajanayagam, Dagmar. 2006. 'Is there a Tamil Race' in *The Concept of Race in South Asia.* Ed. Peter Robb. New Delhi: Oxford University Press. Pp. 137-148.

52 Ibid. P. 132.

53 For a definitive analysis of Periyar, see, Diehl, Anita. 1978. *Periyar E.V. Ramaswami: A Study of the Influence of a Personality in Contemporary South India.* The University of Michigan: BI publication.

54 Venkatachalapathy, AR. 2018. 'Periyar: Prophet from the South' in *Tamil Characters: Personalities, Politics and Culture.* New Delhi: Pan MacMillan. Pp. 3-13.

55 Ibid. P. 3.

56 Several biographies of Mohammad Ali Jinnah have been written. Some of the recent ones include, Ahmed, Ishtiaq. 2020. *Jinnah: His Successes, Failures and Role in History.* New Delhi: Penguin. Also, see More, JB P. 2019. *Muhammad Ali Jinnah: A Journey from India to Pakistan.* New Delhi: Niyogi Books.

57 See Fakhri, SM Abdul Khader. 2008. Ch. 2. 'Islam and Dravidianism.' *Dravidian Sahibs and Brahmin Maulanas: The Politics of the Muslims of Tamil Nadu, 1930-1967.* New Delhi: Manohar. Pp. 45-102.

58 Ibid. P. 84.

59 Anwar, S. 2018. *Muslims and the Dravidian Movement. Seminar* (708). This is a special issue on Dravidianism. Also, see, Sriramchandran, Ravindran. 2018. *Pluralization of Political Identity.* Seminar (208). August.

60 For a definitive biography and Karunanidhi's larger role, see Vaasanthi. 2020. *Karunanidhi: The Definitive Biography.* New Delhi: Juggernaut.

61 For insightful analysis see, Chatterjee, Partha. 2020. *I Am the People—Reflections on Popular Sovereignity Today.* New York: Columbia University Press.

62 See, Venkatchalapahy, AR. 2018. 'M Karunanidhi: Political Artist' in, *Tamil Characters: Personalities, Politics and Culture.* New Delhi: Pan MacMillan. P. 47.

63 For a detailed analysis of the evolution of the Indian Union Muslim League, see Gangadharan, M. 1995. 'Emergence of the Muslim League in Kerala: A Historical Inquiry.' In Asghar Ali Engineer. (Ed). *Kerala Muslims: A Historical Perspective.* New Delhi: Ajanta Publications. Pp. 207-217.

64 See, Jalal, Zakariah. 1960. *Meet Mohamed Ismail.* Madras: Mani Vilakku Book House. P. 5.

65 Originally quoted in Moore, JBP. 1997. *The Political Evolution of Muslims in Tamilnadu and Madras: 1930-1947.* New Delhi. Orient Longman. P. 204. It is also worth mentioning that Periyar declared 15 August 1947, the day of India's independence, as a 'Day of Sorrow' (*thukka nal*) for the Dravidians and asked his followers to observe it as a day of mourning. P. 205.

66 I am referring to Sayed Shahabuddin, former diplomat turned politician who served many terms in Parliament and was active in Muslims issues like Shah Bano and Babri Masjid.

67 For the larger context of history and politics of the time, see Sherman, Taylor C. 2015. *Muslim Belonging in Secular India*: Negotiating Citizenship in Postcolonial Hyderabad. Cambridge: Cambridge University Press.

68 Noorani, AG. 2019. *The Destruction of Hyderabad.* New Delhi: Tulika Books.

69 Ibid. Noorani. P. 246.

70 Ibid.

71 Sherman, Taylor C. 2022. *Nehru's India: A History in Seven Myths.* Princeton: Princeton University Press. P. 71.

72 Santosh, R and Dayal, Paleri. 2021. 'Crisis of Secularism and the Changing Contours of Minority Politics in India: Lessons from the analysis of a Muslim Political Organization.' *Asian Survey.* 61(6): 1-29.

73 Ibid.

74 Ibid. P. 12.

75 TJ Joseph has provided chilling accounts of his attack in his autobiography, *Attupokatha Ormaka.* The book has won the Kerala Sahitya Academy Award.

76 See, 'Recalling the case of Kerala's Hadiya, whose religious conversion led to SC judgement, NIA probe.' Avaialble at http://www.indianexpres.com (accessed on 10 December 2023).

77 For a rich historical analysis of Karnataka politics and history, see, Manor, James. 1989. 'Caste, Class and Dominance in a Cohesive Society.' In *Dominance and State Power in Modern India: Decline of a Social Order* (Vol 1.) Edited by Frankel, Francine R and Rao, MSA. New Delhi: Oxford University Press. Pp. 46-132.

78 See, Rodrigues, Valerian. 2023. 'The Karnataka Election, the Ideological Contestations.' http://thehindu.com (accessed on 4 February 2024).; Palshikar, Suhas. 2023. 'A Victory, A Defeat & A Question.' http://www.

indianexpress.com (accessed on 4 February 2024).; Ashutosh Varshney. 'What the outcome in Karnataka will achieve—and what it will not.' http://www.indianexpress.com (accessed on 4 February 2024).

79 For a comprehensive understanding of Ayodhya dispute see, Khurshid, Salman. 2021. *Sunrise Over Ayodhya.* New Delhi: Penguin Random House.

80 Dhingra, Sanya. 2022. 'Why Coastal Karnataka is Southern India's Hindutva Laboratory.' Available at http://www.aljazeera.com (accessed on 4 February 2024).

81 Karnataka Development Report 2007. The Planning Commission, Government of India, New Delhi.

82 Srinivasaraju, Sugata. 2021. *Furrows in a Field: The Unexplored Life of H. D. Deve Gowda.* New Delhi: Vintage Publishers. P. 435.

83 '"Yogi Model" will be implemented in Karnataka if situation demands: CM Bommai.' Available at http://www.timesofindia.com 28 July 2022 (accessed on 4 February 2024).

84 MS, Shreeja. 2022. 'Will be 5 times ahead of UP, even for encounter: Karnataka Minister.' http://www.ndtv.com (accessed on 4 February 2024).

85 For a closer examination of this thesis, see Guha, Ramchandra. 2023. 'How the BJP Benefits from Stoking Religious divisions in Karnataka.' http://www.scroll.in (accessed on 15 May 2023).

86 Dhingra, Sanya. 2022. 'Why Coastal Karnataka is Southern India's Hindutva Laboratory.' http://www.aljazeera.com (accessed on 4 February 2024).

87 Sayeed, Vikhar Ahmed. 2021. 'Karnataka Cattle Slaughter Ban: An Act of Bias.' http://www.frontline.thehindu.com (accessed on 12 January 2023).

88 Sayeed, Vikhar Ahmed. 2022.'Karnataka Legislative Assembly Passes Anti-Conversion Bill Amid Criticism.' http://www.frontline.thehindu.com (accessed on 12 January 2023).

89 Jha, Dhirendra K. 2017. *Shadow Armies: Fringe Organizations and Foot soldiers of Hindutva.* New Delhi: Juggernaut. It is noteworthy that Sriram Sene chief, Pramod Muthalik, lost the Assembly election in 2023 which he fought from Karkal and secured only 4508 votes. See the report, Rohmetra, Amogh. 2023. 'Sri Ram Sene Chief Pramod Muthalik loses in Karnataka's Karkal. Incumbent BJP MLA emerges winner.' http://wwwtheprint.in (accessed on 18 May 2023).

90 A, Kalaiyarasan. and M, Vijayabaskar. 2021. *The Dravidian Model:*

Interpreting the Political Economy of Tamil Nadu. New Delhi: Cambridge University Press.

91 A, Kalaiyarasan. A and M, Vijayabaskar. 2021. *The Dravidian Model: Interpreting the Political Economy of Tamil Nadu.* New Delhi: Cambridge University Press.

92 Lakshman, Narayan. 2011. *Patrons of the Poor: Caste Politics and Policymaking In India.* New Delhi: Oxford University Press.

93 Ibid. P. 228.

94 'Amit Shah Defends Scrapping 4 % reservation for Muslims in Karnataka.' 25 April 2023. New Delhi. http://www.thehindu.com (accessed on 4 February 2024).

95 See Sachar Report (2006) particularly Chapter 10, 'The Muslim OBCs and the Affirmative Action.' Pp. 189-216.

96 Ibid.

97 Ibid.

98 Palshikar, Suhas. 2023. 'A Victory, a Defeat & A Question.' Available at http://www.indianexpress.com (accessed on 4 February 2024).

99 For a nuanced understanding of the legacy of Periyar, see, Pandian, MSS. 2020. *The Strangeness of Tamilnadu.* New Delhi: Permanent Black.

3

VIOLENCE AGAINST MUSLIMS AND THE IDEA OF 'BANALITY OF VIOLENCE'

> 'The nationalist leaders had always feared the potential for violence and disorder in Indian society. Gandhi's non-violence was not something that simply arose out of an indigenous tradition of peace and spirituality, but rather was a tactic which acknowledged the enormous potential for violence which existed in a highly fragmented and culturally heterogenous society.'
>
> —Paul Brass, *The Politics of India Since Independence*

Lynching, riots, and bulldozer justice constitute the triangle that represents the modern structure of violence against Indian Muslims. Situated at the heart of this violent triangle, the Indian Muslim stares at the state for protection—often without any hope. Sadly, the Indian state remains either indifferent or mostly complicit with the political forces that unleash anti-Muslim violence. To paraphrase German philosopher, Hanna Arendt, India has arrived at a new moment that could be most accurately described as 'banality of violence.'

Without a doubt, riots are the most widely known and oldest form of violence against Muslims. Indeed, it predates the Hindu Right's electoral dominance in modern Indian politics. The complicity of organized as well as unorganized Hindu Right groups could be found even during colonial times, particularly when riots were triggered owing to issues such as cow slaughter or incidents related to places of worship (like music, or processions, etc.). Some new forms of violence against Muslims include lynching and bulldozer justice. What is striking, however, is that the nature of riots and how they are dealt with (such as standard operating procedures or compensations to victims, or setting up judicial committees for investigation, etc.) have gone through radical change or have fallen into the 'not necessary category' of governance under the Hindu Right regimes in present India.

The violence we witness these days is qualitatively different from what has been studied under the rubric of riots or ethnic violence in earlier times. Muslims are the sole targets of this new era of violence. The fact is, even if there is no ongoing violence in a locality or region, Muslims still feel they are living in an environment of violence around them. For instance, a WhatsApp message is circulated in the form of an advisory by some private citizens saying Muslims should not travel in trains or buses in North India around the time of the inauguration on 22 January 2024 or what is called *Pran Pratistha* of a newly-built Ram Mandir in Ayodhya. This fear is palpable in cities, towns, *kasbas*, or villages in regions where lynching or bulldozer justice has taken place. Steve I. Wilkinson, has explained the cause of riots as follows, 'Ethnic riots far from being relatively spontaneous eruptions of anger, are often planned by politicians for a clear electoral purpose.'[1] This argument by Wilkinson could be valid in some instances, but riots have become far too endemic and abrupt. And its motivational factor is not limited to purely electoral purposes. That is why conventional definitions or explanations of riots or any other form, say, *pogrom* or *genocide,* fail to capture this dimension of a new environment and its potential. One needs to take into account the new linkages between society, political parties, vigilante groups, and the state in perpetuating violence against Muslims. By no means is it true that non-Muslims do not pay the price, but Muslims most definitely pay a disproportionately higher price and often as its singular target. In any case, enough research suggests that Muslims have been paying a disproportionate price in riots long before even the BJP came into existence in 1980. What is different is the multi-dimensional nature of the price, say demolitions owing to bulldozer justice in Nuh, Haryana violence in 2023 or the Mira Road, Mumbai violence in January 2024.

Furthermore, viewing the violence against Muslims as an aberration or viewing it as something that started sometime around the 1920s as the political project of Hindutva began to take shape could be deeply misleading. The place of violence in Indian body polity has a long history that predates not just the advent of so-called Muslim rule but even the arrival of Islam in this land. Therefore, we need to see the present phase of violence more in the continuum of the history of violence that Indian society has inflicted for hundreds of years on its women, on former untouchables/Dalits, on its poor, or various other religious minorities, such as the Buddhists. It is thus no exaggeration to argue that violence as Neera Chandhoke puts it, has been in our bones.[2] This violence has unfolded in various domains such as political, social, cultural, etc. and is often legitimized in the name of customs, traditions, so on and so forth. Only by seeing it as a continuum, will there be clarity in our understanding of these forms of violence against Muslims. It will also help us to make sense of why there is so little protest or uproar against this violence in modern India or why it receives silent approval from the majority of its citizens.

We learn from Upinder Singh's research in great detail how violence was prominently present in ancient India.[3] The loud and persistent claim that India achieved its freedom from British colonialism by the Gandhian method of non-violence has made us intellectually complacent. It has generated a false image of our history. It has further encouraged us not to look deeper into the pervasive presence of violence in our society and history. Indians are so carried away in blaming colonialism for everything wrong in society that they have forgotten to recognize their flaws, which existed much before the arrival of British colonialism. Indeed, Ambedkar has brought attention to some aspects of such violence in Indian society through his writings. A conversation between Gandhi and Ambedkar in their first meeting during the time of the second session of the Round Table Conference is very instructive in this regard.[4]

The conversation is as follows:

> **Ambedkar**: Gandhiji, I have no homeland.
>
> **Gandhiji** (taken aback and cutting him short): You have got a homeland, and from the reports that have reached me of your work at the Round Table Conference, I know you are a patriot of sterling worth.
>
> **Ambedkar**: You say I have got a homeland but still I repeat that I am without it. How can I call this land my homeland and this religion my own wherein we are treated worse than cats and dogs, wherein we cannot get water to drink? No self-respecting Untouchable worth the name will be proud of this land.[5]

If we put all of these together in perspective, we will be less amazed by these new forms of violence against Muslims.

Put simply, violence either in Indian society or against Muslims, is not new. What is new is its methods, its technology, and its justifications. Muslims are seemingly on a priority list now because they, as a targeted group, serve as an incentive in the expansion and consolidation of the Hindu Right's political power. A comparative analysis of selected riots will provide insights into new ways of how majoritarian ideology has transformed state intervention prior to, during, and after riots.

Lynching

While lynching has been quite a known category of violence against African-Americans in America, its emergence in India is rather new. Not surprisingly there is a considerable amount of scholarship on lynching in America, but not in India as it is still an evolving phenomenon. According to Ersula J Ore, 'Lynching has been a constitutive performance of American civic identity since the eighteenth century when its debut as a punitive response to British

Tories during the American Revolution set the stage for its later development as a violent rhetoric of American citizenship.'[6] Zia Us Salam's *Lynching Files* is one of the few early books available on the subject of the Indian experience of lynching that began hitting headlines rather frequently after the lynching of Mohammad Akhlaq in 2015. A majority of lynchings of Muslims have taken place on the suspicion of cow slaughter, which is why people involved in these crimes are also known as cow vigilantes. Since the Indian state is yet to classify it as a separate crime, there is no official data on it.[7]

According to a report published in *Firstpost* in March 2018 in response to a question posed in the Lok Sabha regarding lynching, the home ministry did furnish some data on mob lynching collected by the States. Between 2014 and 3 March 2018, 45 persons were killed in 40 cases of mob lynching. According to the Home Ministry Report, 217 persons were arrested in these related cases. The motives that were attributed to these lynching cases include cow vigilantism, rumours of child lifting, and communal and caste hatred. Interestingly, states such as Bihar, Chhattisgarh, Goa, Karnataka, Madhya Pradesh, Manipur, Odisha, Sikkim, Uttarakhand, West Bengal, Andaman and Nicobar Islands, Dadra and Nagar Haveli, Delhi, and Puducherry did not share any data. According to this report based on two databases prepared by INDIASPEND, 80 cases were recorded and 41 deaths were due to lynching, and it does not include caste or communal violence.[8] According to INDIASPEND again, 86 attacks fueled by the suspicion of cow slaughter or beef consumption have been reported in English media in various states since 2010. Roughly, 98 per cent of these cases took place post-May 2014. At least 33 persons were killed, 29 or 88 per cent of whom were Muslims. The data in Table 3.1 below shows that lynching of Muslims is not limited to only BJP-ruled states. It suggests that Muslim vigilantism is widespread.

TABLE 3.1 Major Cases of Lynching of Muslims in India

Date	*Name*	*State*	*Remarks*	*Government at the State*	*Source (accessed on 4 February 2024)*
28 Sep 2015	Mohd Akhlaq	Uttar Pradesh	Beaten to death by his own village mob over suspicion of beef consumption.	Samajwadi Party (SP)	*The Hindu.* Available at: https://www.thehindu.com/specials/in-depth/The-Dadri-lynching-how-events-unfolded/article60291071.ece
9 Oct 2015	Zahid Ahmad Bhatt	Jammu and Kashmir	His truck, ferrying cow carcasses, was attacked with petrol bombs.	People's Democratic Party (PDP)	*The Times of India.* Available at: https://timesofindia.indiatimes.com/blogs/gray-areas/kashmir-is-sitting-on-powder-keg-again/
15 Oct 2015	Noman	Himachal Pradesh	Lynched to death in suspicion of 'smuggling' cows in Sarahan.	Bhartiya Janta Party (BJP)	*The Hindu.* Available at: https://www.thehindu.com/news/national/other-states/lynching-of-up-man-himachal-police-book-case/article7771060.ece
17 March 2016	Mazlum Ansar (Father), Imteyaz Khan (13, Son)	Jharkhand	A minor boy and a Muslim man were found hanging from a tree after being lynched by a mob.	Bhartiya Janta Party (BJP)	*Hindustan Times.* Available at: https://www.hindustantimes.com/ranchi/eight-sentenced-to-life-imprisonment-for-lynching-cattle-herders-in-jharkhand/story-zmbZoHrI5QUOtEoogFBWKL.html
11 May 2016	Kaushik Purkait	West Bengal	By a mob who mistook him to be a member of a gang which was involved in smuggling cattle. Beaten to death.	All India Trinamool Congress (AITC)	*The Times of India.* Available at: https://timesofindia.indiatimes.com/city/kolkata/tmc-man-accused-of-lynching-youth-arrested/articleshow/52234915.cms

1 April 2017	Pehlu Khan	Rajasthan	Pehlu Khan and four others were attacked by a mob of self-appointed cow vigilantes.	Bhartiya Janta Party (BJP)	*Citizens for Justice and Peace.* Available at: https://cjp.org.in/lynching-timeline/
30 April 2017	Riazuddin Ali	Assam	Alleged theft of cows.	Bhartiya Janta Party (BJP)	*India Today.* Available at: https://www.indiatoday.in/india/story/assam-cow-vigilantism-two-killed-bjp-lynching-974450-2017-05-01
22 June 2017	Junaid	Haryana	Muslim teen died of multiple stab wounds after he and his brothers were attacked on a train.	Bhartiya Janta Party (BJP)	*Citizens for Justice and Peace.* Available at: https://cjp.org.in/lynching-timeline/
27 August 2017	Anwar Hussain and Hafizul Sheikh	West Bengal	Lynched by a mob, which dragged them out of a pick-up van carrying cows.	All India Trinamool Congress (AITC)	*Citizens for Justice and Peace.* Available at:https://cjp.org.in/lynching-timeline/
17 May 2018	Siraj	Madhya Pradesh	He was beaten to death after a mob attacked alleging that he was involved in slaughtering a bull.	Bhartiya Janta Party (BJP)	*Citizens for Justice and Peace.* Available at: https://cjp.org.in/lynching-timeline/
18 June 2018	Qasim	Uttar Pradesh	Lynched in Hapur on suspicions of cattle theft.	Bhartiya Janta Party (BJP)	*Citizens for Justice and Peace.* Available at: https://cjp.org.in/lynching-timeline/

17 June 2019	Tabrez Ansari	Jharkhand	A mob accused him of theft, tied him to a pole, forced him to chant "Jai Shri Ram" and beat him through the night.	Jharkhand Mukti Morcha (JMM)—Alliance with Indian National Congress	*The Hindu.* Available at: https://www.thehindu.com/news/national other-states/tabrez-ansari-lynching-case-jharkhand-cour sentences-10-accused-to-ten-years-of-rigorous-imprisonme article67045516.ece

In September 2015, the lynching of Mohammad Akhlaq in Dadri, Uttar Pradesh, captured global attention. Subsequently, cases were reported from other states in India such as Jharkhand, Rajasthan, Haryana, Himachal Pradesh, Karnataka, and others. India's Supreme Court took cognizance of the gravity of the crime and its implications and asked the government of India to come out with a separate law on lynching. 'We think it appropriate to recommend to the legislature, that is, the Parliament, to create a separate offence for lynching and provide adequate punishment for the same. We have said so as a special law in this field would instil a sense of fear for the law amongst the people who involve themselves in such kinds of activities. There can be no trace of doubt that fear of law and veneration for the command of law constitute the foundation of a civilized society,' the Supreme Court observed in August 2018.[9] After remaining silent on this suggestion of the Supreme Court, the Narendra Modi government has come out with a proposal for a law on lynching in 2023.[10] It took more than four years for the Indian government to pay heed to Supreme Court's recommendation, which speaks volumes about the intent and how seriously the issue of anti-Muslim violence is taken in our society. No major opposition party made an uproar on this negligence.

What Is a Riot?

The term riot, as Paul Brass writes, 'has historically meant a disorderly action that constitutes a direct assault upon or represents a danger to established authority. Even when riots are directed against groups other than the state, they are often considered assaults upon the state's order or groups entitled to state protection.'[11] Scholars who study riots have often debated over their nature and gravity. They also deploy various alternative terminologies such as pogroms or genocide to explain this violence. In the use of such terminologies as an alternative to riots, scholars often have focused on the role of the state, particularly the depth of its complicity in targeting Muslims or other communities such as Sikhs in the 1984 riots.

It is instructive to pay attention to why Ashutosh Varshney described the Gujarat riots as the first pogrom in modern India.[12] In a column titled, 'Gujarat 2002 was independent India's first full-blooded pogrom. Delhi 1984 was a semi-pogrom' in *The Print* on 26 February 2020, Varshney explained his claim as follows, 'In later essays, I used the term "semi-pogrom" for Delhi 1984 while noting that Gujarat 2002 was a "purer form of the pogrom". In Delhi 1984, (a) the state looked on while mobs killed Sikhs, but (b) there was no ideological element in it (Congress did not have an anti-Sikh ideology). In Gujarat 2002, both (a) and (b) were present. The ideology, of course, was anti-Muslim.'[13] The Gujarat government at the time, Varshney further explained, did not make a distinction between Muslim citizens and Muslim criminals. This failure of distinction continued to be seen in post-riot situations and such trends are visible in the interventions by many Hindu Right regimes in other parts of India.

The concept of 'pogroms' first came to be deployed in describing riots against Jews in the 19th and early 20th centuries in Russia. It is now widely used in explaining state-supported and state-instigated riots against a minority ethnic group.[14]

History of Riots in India

In modern India, a riot invariably implies a Hindu-Muslim riot. It remains the most dominant form of violence against Muslims. Also, there are riots in modern India that are not between Hindus and Muslims. For instance, the anti-Sikh riots in 1984,[15] and the anti-

Christian riots in Kandhamal[16] in 2008 in Odisha. But the Hindu-Muslim riots have been more frequent in modern India and their frequency has risen dramatically under the Hindu Right regimes. On riots, evidence of early occurrence can be found in the writings of Ibn Batuta, a 14th-century traveller to India.[17] Chris Bayly presents a detailed analysis of what he calls the pre-history of communalism in an essay he wrote on religious conflict covering the period from 1700-1860.[18]

Riots have erupted at different points of time during the colonial and post-colonial periods owing to various reasons. As early as 1886, Delhi and Etawah witnessed religious riots. There were riots in Prabhas Patan in 1888 and Dera Ghazi Khan in 1889. A chain of Hindu-Muslim riots took place in Palakkad in the Madras Presidency in 1891. Also, communal riots took place in Ballia, Bareilly, Bahraich, Banaras, and Azamgarh in North India and Rangoon in 1893, and also in Bombay and Prabhas Patan.[19] According to Sumit Sarkar, 'In the industrial suburbs of Calcutta, the first recorded riot took place in May 1891, followed by disturbances at Titagarh and Garden Reach during Bakr-e-id in 1896 and the large scale Talla riot in north Calcutta in 1897.'[20] In his study on communal riots in Bengal 1905-1947, Suranjan Das draws our attention to the complex interplay of various factors often causing riots, ranging from political economy to class mobilization, to the colonial state's nefarious roles, etc. For instance, 'the 1906-07 Mymensingh riot had a strong class basis of Muslim peasantry's attack on their Hindu economic superior.'[21] Likewise, what triggered the Calcutta riot of September 1918 was a passage in an Anglo-Indian newspaper that Muslims found disrespectful. Then it took the shape of a Muslim assault on the symbols of colonial oppression. According to Das,[22] the participants were from the lower social order and this remained a feature for all riots in Calcutta till the 1940s. The issue of playing music in front of a Mosque was the main factor behind the riots that broke out in Calcutta, Pabna, and Dacca in 1926.

Political movements such as the Khilafat movement and Muslim separatist politics or Pakistan movement also contributed to the making of many riots in pre-partition India. Various riots that took place during the colonial period—say, the Dacca riot of May 1930, the Kishoreganj violence of July 1930 and the Dacca violence in 1941—resulted from the interplay of various forms of organized and unorganized politics. However, each had its distinct strands. We also learn from the research by Sandria B Frietag[23] that in 1893 riots were triggered by cow-protection issues spread in the countryside from village to village, though conventionally riots that erupt in villages remain isolated. The key point is that Hindu-Muslim riots were not a uniform phenomenon in colonial India, and their causes and context varied. This is not any different in the post-colonial period. The riots India is witnessing today under the Hindu Right regime are outcomes of different factors, and their consequences or impact on the Muslim community or Indian society also varies. Also, there is a consensus among scholars that riots in North India are far more frequent than they have been in South India.

To illustrate this further, in post-colonial India riots are often triggered by ordinary incidents as well as owing to larger political phenomena. For instance, riots that followed the Partition of India in 1947 were mainly associated with the unruly, unorganized movements of angry and helpless people of various faiths from both sides, India and Pakistan. Likewise, a series of riots that rocked India in 1990 was owing to the Rath Yatra of the BJP leader, LK Advani, from Somnath to Ayodhya, or the riots that erupted after the demolition of the Babri-Masjid on 6 December 1992. In other words, there are riots connected with high politics such as Partition, Ayodhya movement, or Babri Masjid demolition and there are riots owing to micro-incidents as was the case with Muzaffarnagar 2013 or Nuh in 2023. Paul Brass describes the riots that erupt owing to high politics as 'wave riots', and they are not unique to India but occur in other parts of the world as well. Such waves were seen in the racial riots in America post-World War I and World War II. There are other examples also, say, for instance, pogroms against Jews in 14th-century Spain and 19th-century Russia.[24]

Post-1947, India's secular constitution is committed to saving the lives and properties of people of all religions; hence riots, in this particular sense of failure, are living evidence of the failure of the Indian constitution, and a blot on democracy.

After the demolition of the Babri Masjid on 6 December 1992, Prime Minister PV Narasimha Rao dismissed the governments of four BJP-ruled States—Uttar Pradesh, Madhya Pradesh, Rajasthan, and Himachal Pradesh. An argument was made against the dismissal of the BJP state governments by stating that the BJP provided riot-free regimes in these states, therefore, the party is more secular. The so-called secular parties failed to prevent riots during their rule, explained the argument, and thus were less caring towards Muslims who suffered a great deal owing to riots. This argument that the Hindu Right regimes have an impressive record of riot-free governance and are good for Muslims or minorities continues to be made even today with greater force. The Nuh violence in Haryana in 2023, a BJP-ruled state does not support this claim. In April 2023, Chief Minister Yogi Adityanath made a similar claim that his state Uttar Pradesh has been riot-free since 2017. According to the latest National Crime Record Bureau Data, Uttar Pradesh saw 35,040 cases of rioting during 2017-21, which refutes the claim by the Uttar Pradesh Chief Minister. Although 5,302 riots were reported in 2021 itself, it has reduced by 41 per cent from 8,990 in 2017. In the past five years, the number of people who fell victim to these riots also dipped by 49 per cent to 5,846 in 2021.[25] However, the claim that Uttar Pradesh is riot-free is not factually correct according to government reports.

During the Karnataka Assembly elections campaign in April 2023, Home Minister Amit Shah warned at a rally in Belagavi that if the Congress came to power, there would be riots, implying that there were no riots under the BJP rule. In Maharashtra, a state governed by a BJP coalition since April 2023, there have been multiple incidents of riots in places like Kolhapur, Mumbai, Sambhajinagar, Jalgaon, Akola, and Ahmednagar. In the majority of instances, a pattern emerges—with the presence of a temple or a mosque, a social

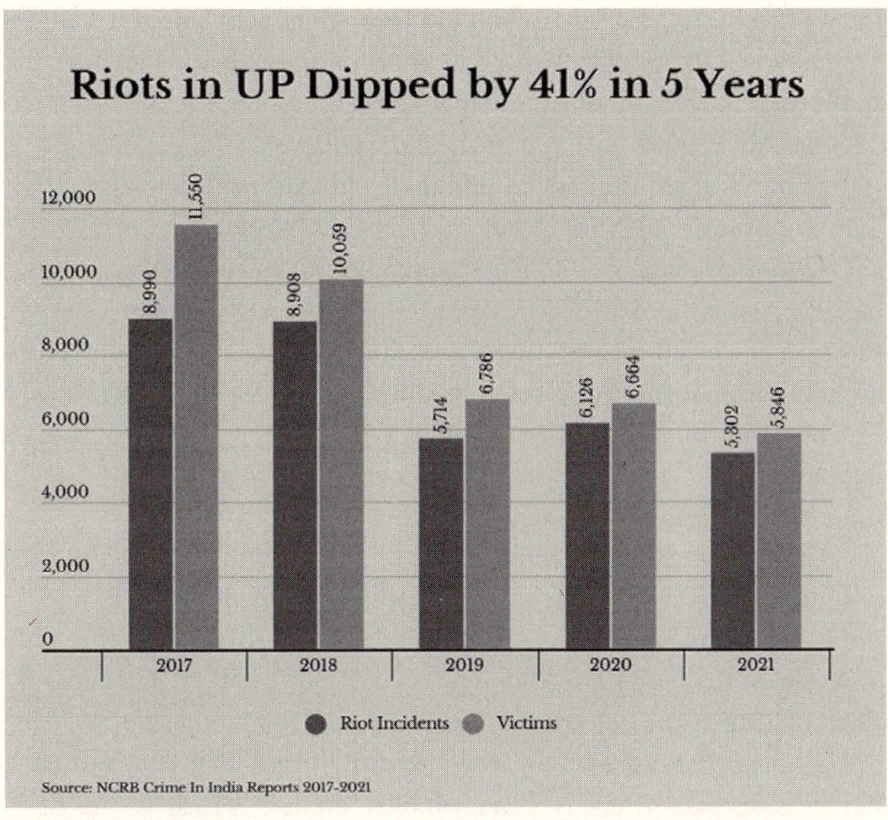

(Reproduced from the report by Dubey, Divyani. 2022. 'Fact Check: Were there no riots in Uttar Pradesh in the past five years, as Adityanath claims?' Available at: http://wwwscroll.in (accessed on 4 February 2024)

media post, and processions—establishing a circle of reason resulting in this otherwise spontaneous-looking riot. The Nuh violence of 2023 in Haryana, a state again governed by the BJP, also presents a similar pattern representing an identical circle of reason. Clearly, there is no direct relationship between riot-free regimes and the BJP's governance; instead there is plenty of evidence in the opposite direction. Research by Amrita Basu, which I have mentioned earlier presents a comprehensive case for a causal link between Hindutva ideology and anti-Muslim riots.[26]

It is believed riots occur owing to the presence of communalism in the minds of people of various faiths say, Hindus and Muslims.

In my volume, *Communalism in Post-Colonial India: Changing Contours,*[27] I have elaborated on four points: firstly, I claim that the forms of communalism have changed in recent years, compared to what they used to be, say in the 1940s or 1950s; secondly, a riot is no longer limited to Hindus and Muslims because other communities are also involved, say, the Hindu-Sikh riots in 1984 or anti-Christian riots in 2008 in Kandhamal, Odisha; thirdly, political parties, media, and other institutions are playing a greater role in promoting communalism now; and, finally, riots continue to erupt in post-colonial India because the state has neo-colonial tendencies. However, in the Hindu Right's political discourse, communalism is a legitimate or even a desirable phenomenon because it is an inherent ingredient of Hindu nationalism.

Analysis of a few selected cases of riots might provide us with potential clues about the changing nature of violence and its impact on Indian Muslims. Case studies included here are: 1) the Nuh violence of 2023, 2) the Delhi riots of 2020, 3) the Muzaffarnagar riots of 2013, and 4) the Gujarat riots of 2002. These riots took place under the watch of various non-BJP and BJP governments, but in each case, there is a majoritarian context which is crucial to delineate its uniqueness. While the BJP was running the government in the Gujarat riots 2002 and Nuh riots 2023, in the case of the Delhi riots 2020, the state was governed by the Arvind Kejriwal-led Aam Aadmi Party (AAP). For the Muzaffarnagar riots in 2013, the state of Uttar Pradesh was ruled by the Akhilesh Yadav-led Samajwadi Party, but it came under the BJP rule in 2017 with Yogi Adityanath as its chief minister. Out of all these, only the Gujarat riots 2002 received sustained global attention. The riots took place at a time when Gujarat and New Delhi were both governed by the BJP. Prime Minister Atal Bihari Vajpayee was heading the National Democratic Association (NDA) coalition (1998-2004) in New Delhi at the time of the riot. According to a report in *The Indian Express,* 'Some political observers even attributed the unexpected defeat of Atal Bihari Vajpayee in the 2004 Lok Sabha elections to the Gujarat riots. Vajpayee told a television channel that 'the impact of the Gujarat riots was felt nationwide...Modi should have been removed after the incident.' However, Advani called Modi a victim of a vilification campaign over the Gujarat riots.[28] If the Gujarat riot of 2002 had such an adverse impact on the electoral outcome, how could we explain the massive continued electoral success of Narendra Modi in all these years not just in Parliamentary elections, like 2014 or 2019, but also in various state elections both in Gujarat which he won in 2002, 2007, and 2012, and outside where he often led the BJP's campaign? In my view, establishing a causal connection between the Gujarat 2002 and the BJP's defeat is not convincing at all. Furthermore, in the wider context of the BJP's continued electoral success, such a claim requires more careful examination though it is politically pleasant for secularists to make such a causal link.

Nuh Riot (July-August 2023)

Nuh is a Muslim-majority district in the Indian state of Haryana. At the time of the riot, it was ruled by the BJP with Manohar Lal Khattar as its chief minister. On 31 July 2023, Vishwa Hindu Parishad (VHP) organized a procession in Nuh town. There was a pelting of stones at the procession by the locals who were presumed to be Muslims. Two police officials were killed and 15 others were injured. More than 2500 women and children were rescued from the Shiva Temple in Nuh town, according to the state's Home Minister, Anil Vij. The provocation that led to the pelting of stones was an objectionable video posted on social media by a Bajrang Dal activist in Ballabhgarh. Also, there were reports that Monu Manesar, a cow vigilante, was going to take part in the VHP-organized procession. Mr Manesar was booked in the case of the murder of two Muslim men whose charred bodies were found in the Bhiwani district.

Violence erupted in Nuh but did not remain confined to Nuh alone. It spread to Gurgaon and other parts of Haryana. Around midnight, a mob attacked the Anjuman Jama Masjid in Sector 57 of Gurugram. Imam Mohammad Saad, 26, was killed in this attack and a staff member, Khursheed, sustained injuries.[29] Interestingly, the Hindu Right groups were targeting this Masjid for some time and the matter was taken to the Supreme Court. Only a few weeks before this violence, the Honorable Supreme Court had passed the order regarding the Masjid. Since 2020, there have been regular protests by various Hindu Right groups against Muslims offering Friday prayer in designated public places that had the desired impact owing to the Hindu Right regime asking the administration to withdraw designated places and ban namaaz. This is also known as the Gurgaon Namaaz controversy, about which I discuss in detail in the 'Conclusion' section of this book. Indeed, this violence was not abrupt and has deeper roots, which is why the ideological context and movements are crucial to our analysis.

Muslims of Nuh district are also known as Meo Muslims. This Muslim-majority district falls under the Mewat region which is comprised of districts such as the Nuh, Palwal, Faridabad, and Gurgaon districts of Haryana, the Alwar, and Bharatpur districts of Rajasthan, and a few areas of western UP, including Mathura. The Meos follow syncretic traditions.[30] This community has a typical religio-cultural identity which combines the worship of cows with Islamic practices of namaaz. According to Shail Mayaram, the multi-religiosity of Meo Muslims is owing to the fact that while embracing Islam mainly under the influence of a certain Sufi pir, they retained their traditional Hindu practices. Meo Muslims celebrate Hindu festivals like Diwali, Holi, and Teej together with Islamic festivals like Eid, and Bakri-Eid.

Some discussion on the local history of the region will be helpful to understand the context better. Mewat was one of 15 subahs (provinces) during the reign of Mughal Emperor Akbar. Meos were initially not Muslims and they embraced Islam during the 12th to 17th centuries. According to one school of thought, mainly represented by PW Powett, Meos were originally a tribe, most probably Meenas. In the 'District Gazetteer of Ulwur (1878)', Powett referred to a ballad of Dariya Khan/Meo, who was married to, separated from, and again remarried to Sisbadani, a tribal woman belonging to the Meena community. Powett further suggested the presence of common surnames among Meos and Meenas, and similar nomenclatures.

During the 1920s and also around Partition, the Meos underwent a transformation under the influence of the Tablighi Jamaat movement started by Muhammad Ilyas al-Kandhlawi. The Tablighis taught them various Islamic rituals such as namaaz, keeping a beard, and the recitation of the Holy Quran. During Partition, a genocide against the Meos was carried out by the Alwar and Bharatpur states. The Tablighi Jamaat came out with an explanation that the violence was a manifestation of Allah's anger, for being 'bad Muslims', according to Shail Mayaram, a scholar who has conducted pioneering research on Meo Muslims.[31]

Since 1947, the religious identity in the Mewat region has been defined by the discourse of Sunni Islam but their 'Hindu' cultural practices continue to be part of their lives. The Meos also continue to follow the Hindu system of recording ancestry known as the gotra. At their weddings, they would celebrate the song about the marriage of Mahadev and their descent from Krishna. Even today, Meos continue to practice *ghur savari*. According to this custom, the groom will arrive on a horse. Despite such strong similarities between the Meo Muslim culture with local Hindu culture, the otherness of Muslim Meo remains, which is the reason for the violence. After the violence, a Mahapanchayat was held in Tigra village, which gave a call for the boycott of Muslims and their businesses.[32] There was also the decision by the government of Haryana to run bulldozers over the homes of people, mostly Muslims.[33] More than 1208 structures were destroyed of local Muslims, which led to the *suo motto* cognizance by the Honorable High Court of Panjab, Haryana, and Chandigarh. The court passed an order to stop bulldozer action and asked the Haryana government to offer an explanation for its action of bulldozer justice. According to a report in the *Hindustan Times,* people whose property was demolished were neither given any notice nor prior information. This demolition drive took place for five days in 11 towns and hamlets of Nuh district—what is widely known as bulldozer justice.[34] *The Times of India* published a report titled 'Ethnic cleansing by the state? HC halts Haryana's Nuh demolitions'.[35] The report alluded to the ethnic cleansing of Muslims. 'The issue also arises whether the buildings belonging to a particular community are being brought down under the guise of law and order problem and an exercise of ethnic cleansing is being conducted by the state. We are of the considered opinion that the Constitution of India protects the citizens of this country and no demolition as such can be done without following the procedure prescribed in law,' Justice Sandwalia observed.[36]

According to a report by the *BBC*, in Nuh officials gave contradictory answers about the reason for demolitions. District Magistrate Dhirendra Khadgata told the *BBC Hindi* channel that only illegal buildings were being razed. Some government officials said only those homes from where stones were pelted were demolished. Many in Nuh had the documents to prove their buildings were not illegal and the Haryana government neither gave them any notice nor time to remove their belongings. In an interview with *BBC*, Madan Lokur, former justice of India's Supreme Court reacted as follows, 'How can the State club everybody and put them in one basket, regardless of the facts, without ascertaining the truth and go on a demolition spree? In situations like this, collective punishment is anathema to the rule of law and constitutional rights, regardless of religion.'[37] The key phrase that Justice Lokur has used is *collective punishment*. Not just in Nuh, but in nearly all instances of bulldozer justice practised mainly by the Hindu right regimes, the underlying goal seems to be the *collective punishment of the Muslim community*.

The most significant part of this violence is the story of bulldozer justice. Haryana is not the state where the bulldozer was first used. It was first deployed in Uttar Pradesh not by a BJP government but by the Akhilesh Yadav-led Samajwadi government, which has greater credibility as a secular government. When relief camps after the Muzaffarnagar Riots in 2013 became a source of controversy owing to mismanagement, the UP government wanted to shut them down forcibly. That is when they used bulldozers to demolish tents so that the survivors would leave and the camps could be declared closed. It was meant to show that the issues of riot victims were addressed on the eve of Assembly elections in 2017.

But this bulldozer justice is more strongly associated with the Uttar Pradesh Chief Minister, Yogi Adityanath. According to Badri Narayan, 'The Yogi Adityanath government has reinvented the bulldozer in Uttar Pradesh. It was always a terrifying instrument that represented demolition—*dhwast, vinash*. But now it is a political symbol—this has reframed and reshaped its use and meaning. It is no longer just an instrument for building or road construction. It is an instrument of State administration.'[38] The use of bulldozers by the Yogi government was so extensive that he was referred to as bulldozer baba!

Sadly, this bulldozer justice has inspired other state governments, mainly ruled by the BJP. In Assam, it was used quite frequently. In January 2023, a report appeared in media titled, 'Bulldozers in action as eviction drive begins in Assam reserve forest.'[39] This happened in Laxmipur district of Assam. Guwahati High Court, however, declared this approach illegal.[40] In April 2022, after the Khargone communal riot, even Shiv Raj Singh Chouhan used bulldozers to demolish 16 houses, and 29 shops, across four locations in the town.[41] One of the first things that Madhya Pradesh's new chief minister, Mohan Yadav, did after his government was formed in 2023 was that he passed an order to check illegal buying and selling of fish, meat etc. As a part of it, 10 meat shops were demolished in Bhopal and on the same day, the government razed the homes of three men accused of attacking a BJP worker.[42] Therefore, bulldozer justice that we saw in Nuh violence is rather a widely used template of the Hindu Right regimes—mainly intended to target Muslims, deny them access to justice, and send a message to the community that an instant collective punishment will follow if a member of the community is believed to be part of any misdemeanour. This is more a case for Muslims to be viewed as subjects of the Hindu Right regime rather than citizens with rights of the Indian state. The story is still unfolding.

Delhi Riot (2020)

Rather unexpectedly, a Hindu-Muslim riot broke out in Delhi mainly in its northeastern district in late February 2020. By all accounts, the riot had strong features of an anti-Muslim riot. It lasted more than three days, from 23 February to 26 February. Sporadic violence was witnessed in some areas on February 27 as well. According to a report prepared by the Delhi Minorities Commission (DMC), 53 persons were killed, 250 people were injured, thousands of people were rendered homeless, and the loss of property in various neighbourhoods was immense. New Delhi, being the capital city of India, has the highest concentration of security forces in the country, outside of Kashmir, and yet the riot not only broke out but lasted for several days.

At least three particular contexts are to be borne in mind for making an objective assessment of the Delhi Riot 2020, its cause and implications. Firstly, the national anti-Citizenship Amendment Act (CAA) protest of which Delhi's Shaheen Bagh was the epicentre; second, campaign rhetoric and the results of the Delhi Assembly elections held on 8 February 2020. It was the Aam Admi Party (AAP) that won the election despite the high voltage campaign by the BJP which created a fresh context for violence, and, finally, the visit of American president Donald Trump.[43]

Indian Parliament held a special debate on the Delhi Riot 2020 on 11 and 12 March 2020. Amit Shah, India's Home Minister, lauded the role of Delhi police for bringing peace to the city,[6] although the police failure was widely deplored in the media and even by the Delhi High Court.[7] The Home Minister also claimed that the riot was a 'conspiracy and pre-planned.' Indeed, it is the police complicity that led to such a massive loss of lives and property according to various fact-finding reports and media, but the BJP government is reluctant to recognize this obvious fact.[44]

At the time of the riot, the State was ruled by Chief Minister Arvind Kejriwal led-AAP, but the country was governed by the BJP led by Prime Minister Narendra Modi. Considered to be a secular political party, the AAP enjoyed overwhelming support of Muslim votes and has a few Muslim MLAs. But because of the party's rather ambivalent approach towards the Shaheen Bagh movement, many Muslim and secular voters were disillusioned with AAP. While Delhi is an independent state, the chief minister or the state government do not have power over its law and order machinery, which falls directly under India's Home Ministry and was therefore under the Narendra Modi government. Had the law and order been with the AAP, the riot might not have happened or been prevented easily, some argue. Even though the BJP has three MLAs in the present Delhi Assembly, it has a strong organization and substantial support base reflected in its 39 per cent vote share, which is its biggest since 1993 when it won the state election with a 48 per cent vote share.[45] The BJP was in power at the Municipal Corporation of Delhi (MCD) for 15 years but lost in 2022 to the AAP. Here again, it saw a rise in its vote share by 3 per cent.[46] This shows the strong organizational and popular social base the BJP party and the Hindu Right enjoy in Delhi.

One of the largest and oldest cities in South Asia, Delhi has served as the capital of the Mughal Empire as well as of the British Empire for hundreds of years. It also has a long history of violence. Rajmohan Gandhi in *Revenge and Reconciliation*[47] has a fascinating account of why and how New Delhi has witnessed such bloody violence time and again. In modern times, even when India's first Prime Minister Jawaharlal Nehru was in charge, small riots broke out, with small-scale violence in Old Delhi or the Walled City. But only in November 1966 and May 1974, there were riots in which more than five people were killed. Furthermore, the anti-Sikh pogrom in 1984 after the assassination of Prime Minister Indira Gandhi has been a subject of frequent discussion for a long time.[48] But the major anti-Muslim riot that took place in recent years was after the demolition of the Babri Masjid in December 1992 in the Seelampur area of Delhi. According to a report in *The Los Angeles Times* published on 12 December 1992, 'The Seelampur district of northeast Delhi, a crowded middle-class community of Hindus and Muslims, was a war zone for most of the night and all day Friday as rampaging crowds of rock-throwing youths torched scores of homes and shops, burned at least one man and two children alive, hacked others with swords and fought police in pitched street battles. Residents said most of the victims were Muslims.'

The Delhi riot of February 2020 was a large-scale one and spread to several parts of Delhi's northeastern neighbourhoods. According to the data presented in *Frontline*, the majority of victims were Muslims.[49] In this list of 53 people, four were not identified, 36 were Muslims, and 13 were Hindus. The reason for their deaths was gunshot injuries or physical assault. In terms of loss of property and other related damages, the targeting of Muslims became more apparent. According to a fact-finding report set up by the Delhi Minorities Commission (DMC):

> The violence followed an organized and systematic pattern. Different mobs numbering anywhere between 100-1000 people, chanting common slogans like "Jai Shri Ram", and even "Har Har Modi", "Modiji Kaat Do In Mullon Ko" (Modi, cut these Muslims into pieces), "Aaj Tumhe Azadi Denge" (today we will give you freedom), selectively attacked Muslim individual houses, shops, vehicles, mosques, and other property.[50]

The report further stated in its findings that 'the attacks were selectively towards the Muslim population. In some instances, victims were asked to show their ID cards, and then targeted based on their faith.'[51] Muslims were, it is apparent, disproportionately targeted in this riot.

Northeastern Delhi is one of the eleven districts of the National Capital of Territory (NCT). The region is a mixed neighbourhood and borders the Yamuna River on the West, Ghaziabad on the North and East, East Delhi to the South, and North Delhi to the West across the Yamuna. Based on the 2011 Census, Hindus are 68.22 per cent,

Muslims are 29.34 per cent, and Christians are 0.41 per cent in these districts. Its eight Assembly constituency seats include Seemapuri, Gokulpuri, Ghonda, Seelampur, Rohtash Nagar, Babarpur, Karwal Nagar, and Mustafabad. Out of this, Muslim-majority constituencies are Seelampur, Ghonda, Babarpur, and Mustafabad. Just before this riot, a highly polarized election campaign across religious lines had taken place in these constituencies during the 2022 Assembly elections, which constitutes a crucial background to the violence as well.

On 15 January 2020, a peaceful sit-in protest took place, mainly by women in the Jaffrabad-Seelampur area, prior to the Delhi Assembly election held on 8 February 2020. The AAP won for the third consecutive term, winning 62 out of 70 seats of the Delhi Assembly. Despite running a highly polarized campaign, the BJP managed to garner a meagre eight seats. The Delhi violence was preceded by some provocative speeches given by BJP leaders in different parts of Delhi. On 27 January 2020, India's Home Minister urged Delhi voters to vote for the BJP so that the protestors of Shaheen Bagh would feel the current. On 11 February 2020, Delhi's Chief Minister Arvind Kejriwal said in his speech at his oath-taking ceremony that his victory was a result of his work on development. The days of dirty politics around religion or caste were over, claimed Kejriwal, but by the last week of February, Delhi witnessed another major anti-Muslim riot.

Though several BJP leaders made provocative speeches, Kapil Mishra's[52] speech on 23 February 2020 is widely considered the trigger that led to the riot. Within hours of Kapil Mishra's speech, violence broke out and spread like wildfire in various localities of Northeast Delhi such as Shiv Vihar, Khajuri Khas, Chand Bagh, Gokulpuri, Maujpur, Karawal Nagar, Jaffrabad, Mustafabad, Ashok Nagar, Bhagirathi Vihar, Bhajan Pura, and Kardam Puri. The official number of deaths recorded is 53, with at least 250 injured, and an unknown number of missing persons. The violence led to massive loss of property owing to looting and arson, attacks on homes, shops, and other businesses. In addition, several places of worship as well as a graveyard were desecrated.[53]

According to the Delhi Minorities Commissions (DMC) Report, perpetrators were armed with lathis, iron rods, tear gas bombs, cylinders, and firearms. The most disturbing aspect of the report is the role of the Delhi police. Testimonies suggest how the patrolling police ignored requests for help saying that they had no order to assist. In multiple testimonies, First Information Reports (FIRs) were either delayed or not acted upon. According to the DMC Report, 'police were complicit and abetted the attacks. Where police did attack, victims state that police stopped their colleagues when they attempted to disperse the crowd (do not stop them). In others, they explicitly gave go-ahead to perpetrators to continue with their rampage (do what you want).'[54]

Another dimension of the violence has been in the manner in which women were targeted. According to the report, hijabs and burqas of Muslim women were pulled off. It needs to be noted that Muslim women have led the anti-CAA protest not just in Shaheen Bagh but also in the Chand Bagh area, where they were attacked by male police officers and mobs.[55]

Whenever a Hindu-Muslim riot, or any riot for that matter, occurs in India, a commission of enquiry headed by a retired judge of a High Court or Supreme Court is set up for its investigation. Sadly, the reports of such Commissions in past riots have rarely been taken seriously by previous governments. For instance, recommendations of the Sri Krishna Commission of the Mumbai riots 1992-1993 are yet to be implemented. In another example, the Justice Naidu Commission that was set up to inquire into the anti-Christian violence in Kandhamal, Odisha, in 2008 is yet to be tabled in the Odisha State Assembly. Some of these lacunae in the follow-up processes of various Hindu-Muslim riots have made the Indian state vulnerable to riots and their consequences. In the case of the Delhi riot, there is no demand for a Commission of Inquiry either by the BJP government at the Centre or the AAP government at the State. Some activists and retired bureaucrats asked for an inquiry according to the Commission of Inquiry Act of 1952, by appointing sitting/retired judges of the higher judiciary.[56] No such step was taken by the Modi government. No effort was made by the AAP government for judicial investigation, which suggests such a riot was not taken seriously by either of the governments in the state or at the centre.

In the parliament debate on the Delhi riot, some of the prominent Parliament members who took part include Adhir Ranjan Chaudhury of the Congress, Asaduddin Owaisi of the AIMIM, Hyderabad, Danish Ali of the BSP, and Meenakshi Lekhi of the BJP.[57] But the government's response was articulated by India's Home Minister Amit Shah. The Home Minister argued that the killing of more than 76 per cent of the people in the riots had taken place in Congress-ruled states. He further lauded the role of the police that brought peace to four per cent area of Delhi where 13 per cent of its population lived. Terming the violence a conspiracy, the Home Minister said that material from ISIS has been found and numerous social media accounts have been shut. In his description of further action taken by the police, he also shared the news of the arrest of the people responsible for killing Head Constable Ratan Lal and Ankit Saxena. The Modi government is moving ahead on the investigation in a speedy manner, Shah told Rajya Sabha.[58] However, skepticism was expressed about the probe as noted journalist Ashish Khetan wrote that the Modi government was appointing lawyers of its choice to investigate the Delhi riots.[59] To conclude, the Delhi riot is a typical example of how a riot is dealt with under the Hindu Right regime. Neither the Chief Minister nor the Prime Minister visited the victims or the neighbourhoods.

Muzaffarnagar Riot (2013)

In August-September 2013, a Hindu-Muslim riot broke out in the districts of Muzaffarnagar and Shamli in Uttar Pradesh. Uttar Pradesh at the time was ruled by the SP, led by Akhilesh Yadav as its chief minister (2012-2017), and New Delhi central government was run by Dr Manmohan Singh's United Progressive Alliance (2004-2014). The BJP was not in power in either the state or at the centre. But it came to power in Uttar Pradesh in 2017, four years after the riot, and at the Centre in 2014, just a year after the riot broke out. Some argue that the riot created the required polarizing atmosphere that helped the BJP to win more votes. I would suggest there are more convincing reasons for the massive victory that Narendra Modi achieved in 2014 than the Muzaffarnagar riot.

After the riot, a committee of inquiry headed by Justice Bishnu Sahai was set up by the Samajwadi government to examine the factors that led to the riot. According to the Sahai Commission Report (2016),[60] 62 lives were lost and 60,000 people were displaced in Muzaffarnagar and Shamli.[61] However, independent reports prepared by civil society organizations present a higher number of deaths and loss of property.[62] The 700-page Justice Sahai Commission Report together with a 14-page Action Taken Report (ATR) was presented to the Uttar Pradesh Assembly by the Akhilesh Yadav government on 6 March 2016. According to the report, the major reasons for the riot are as follows:

a) failure to arrest 14 Muslim youths involved in the killing of Sachin, brother of the Hindu girl who was the target of 'eve-teasing', and Sachin's friend Gaurav;
b) poor local intelligence;
c) transfer of the Muzaffarnagar District Magistrate and Superintendent of Police (SP) causing an administrative vacuum which let the violence to spiral out of control.

The report further recommended a departmental enquiry against Prabol Pratap Singh, local police in charge of intelligence gathering. He was blamed for failing to guess the exact turnout at the 7 September *maha panchayat* held at Nagla-Mandaur, not very far from Muzaffarnagar town.[63] Mr Singh estimated a 15,000-20,000 crowd, but the turnout roughly was around 50,000-60,000 people. Setting up an inquiry commission in India after a riot is a routine matter and it often takes years to complete the report—often delayed owing to frequent requests for extensions. Surprisingly, Justice Sahai's commission took only three years. Set up in 2013, the Commission submitted its report in 2016—just one year before the Assembly election in 2017. The report provided a clean chit to the Akhilesh Yadav government perhaps to help the SP government so that it could enter the 2017 Assembly election armed with the clean chit from the Sahai commission. The massive victory of the Modi-led BJP in the parliamentary election in 2014 in Uttar Pradesh[64] had made all the efforts by the SP inconsequential.[65]

During the Muzaffarnagar riot in 2013, Chief Minister Akhilesh Yadav himself was in charge of the Home Ministry under whose auspices the police department works. Mr Yadav as Home Minister should have been the first person to be indicted by the Sahai Commission for his failure to contain violence. However, the Sahai Commission chose not to mention the Home Ministry. According to Sudha Pai:

> Their [Muslims] support enabled the SP to win elections, particularly to obtain a majority in 2012. However, there is much anguish within the Muslim community following the Muzaffarnagar riots that the SP failed to prevent or help rehabilitate the riot-affected. Statements of the old guard regarding the amount and nature of compensation and the relief camps were particularly controversial.[66]

The BJP swept the 2017 Assembly election and formed the government with Yogi Adityanath as its Chief Minister, whose appointment surprised even many BJP sympathizers and commentators.[67] According to Devesh Kapur:

> The appointment of Adityanath thus seems to indicate that the BJP will employ anti-Muslim animus in its effort to consolidate Hindu votes in the 2019 national elections. But that strategy is clearly at odds with Modi's rhetorical focus on economic development. One of the likely consequences of Adityanath's promotion—and

> the negative signal it sends to India's largest religious minority—is that economic development will suffer.[68]

Muzaffarnagar is located in the western part of India's largest state, Uttar Pradesh.[69] According to the Census 2011, Hindus are 79.73 per cent, Muslims are 19.26 per cent, Christians are 0.18 per cent, Sikhs are 0.32 per cent, Buddhists are 0.01 per cent, and other religions are 0.01 per cent.[70] Described as the sugar bowl of India, Muzaffarnagar's economy is based on agriculture. Sugarcane is one of its major products.

What is striking is that there was a growing number of communal incidents in Uttar Pradesh—particularly after the Akhilesh Yadav-led Samajwadi Party formed the government in 2012.[71] The state registered the highest number of communal incidents in 2013 in the entire country. In a Parliament discussion in 2014, the Home Ministry, under the Dr Manmohan Singh government, shared 247 incidents in 2013 and 118 incidents in 2012 of communal violence, and an overall rise of about 30 per cent at the national level in 2013.[72] According to the Home Ministry Report, 133 people died and 2,229 people were injured in 2013, and 94 deaths and 2,117 injuries occured in 2012 in the communal violence. Besides Uttar Pradesh, Bihar and Gujarat also saw a rise in communal violence.[73]

The 2013 Muzaffarnagar violence was triggered by an 'eve-teasing' incident. In Kawal village, a Jat girl (a Hindu) was reportedly 'eve teased' and harassed by Shahnawaz, a Muslim boy. Her brother Sachin, and his friend Gaurav confronted Shahnawaz over this issue. All three of them—Shahnawaz, Sachin, and Gaurav—were killed. Instead of turning to Indian law, the local political leadership of both the Hindu and Muslim communities chose to politicize it as a Hindu-Muslim conflict. Two major meetings took place, hosted by Muslim and Hindu leaders, respectively. On 30 August 2013, after the *Jumma* (Friday prayer) the first meeting of Muslim leaders took place. According to the *Hindustan Times* (New Delhi) report, 'Thousands gathered at Meenakshi Chowk immediately after Friday namaaz and BSP MP Qadir Rana, MLA Jameel Ahmad, former MP

Saeedujjama, his son Salman Saeed, and BSP leader Noor Saleem Rana reportedly gave provocative speeches.'[74] On 7 September 2013, another gathering by the Hindu community in violation of section 144 of the CrPC was held at Nagla-Mandaur, 20 kilometres away from Muzaffarnagar town. [75]

Those who attended the 7 September Maha Panchayat at Nagla-Mandaur came from western UP, Haryana, and Delhi. Provoked by the speeches given by their leaders in this Maha Panchayat, and armed with swords, axes, and lathis, these people attacked Muslim villages on their way back. In February 2016, Umesh Mallick, a BJP executive committee member,[76] attributed the BJP's victory in Uttar Pradesh in the 2014 parliamentary election to the Muzaffarnagar riots. According to Mallick, 'The embers [of the riots] led to the victory of Modi in Uttar Pradesh.'[77] This statement was made in the presence of a local Member of Parliament (MP), Sanjeev Baliyan, an accused in the 2013 violence, and a member of Modi's Cabinet. Mr Mallick further said that it was all planned in jail where Balyan was detained as a preventive step. The 2014 electoral outcome suggests that the results of this polarization profited the BJP.[78] Rewards continued for the BJP. In the 2017 Assembly election, the party won 312 of 384 seats it contested in the 403-member Assembly in Uttar Pradesh. In my view, while this riot did help politically, it is NOT the only reason for the BJP's victory in the 2014 parliamentary election.

In Uttar Pradesh, Hindu-Muslim polarization witnessed a dramatic rise during the Ayodhya movement in the late 1980s. After the initial rise in the BJP's electoral fortune owing to the Ayodhya movement, it began declining during the 1990s onwards. The BJP's decline was caused by several reasons. Mandalization of politics in Uttar Pradesh,[79] and the rise of caste-based parties like the BSP set up by Kanshi Ram,[80] and the SP set up by Mulayam Yadav are some of the factors that contributed to the BJP's decline. Some scholars, for example, Rajni Kothari, argue that this division around caste lines in Indian politics contributed to the secularization of the polity.[81] The Hindutva juggernaut owing to this development was stopped in

Uttar Pradesh and also in India, but the 2014 election results proved it decisively wrong.

Before the Ayodhya movement in the 1980s, the politics in this region of Uttar Pradesh was dominated by Chaudhury Charan Singh. Mr Singh was the Chief Minister for two terms and also served briefly in 1979 as Prime Minister after the fall of the Moraraji Desai government.[82] He had stitched together a coalition consisting of Muslims, Ahirs (Yadav), Jats, Gujjars, and Rajputs, also described as MAJGAR.[83] The post-Charan Singh period in Uttar Pradesh politics saw new political formations. The SP core voter base was formed by Yadavs; while most Gujjars and Rajputs moved towards the BJP, some also moved towards the SP. The remnants of Charan Singh's party led by his son, Ajit Singh, enjoyed the loyalty of Muslims and Jats, but the Muzaffarnagar violence disturbed it.

The BJP was desperate to win Uttar Pradesh back after its severe decline in post-Mandal politics in the 1990s. Eager to attract Jat votes, the BJP adopted a strategy to polarize the situation between Muslims and Jats/Hindus. With time, the Jat-Muslim issue was politicized to fit into a larger Hindu-Muslim conflict. This trend was noticed by various political parties, who were opposed to the BJP's politics of polarization. According to Sitaram Yechury, the CPI(M) leader, the Muzaffarnagar riot was the perfect background to anoint Modi as a PM hopeful.[84] Manmohan Singh echoed the sentiment at the National Integration Council (NIC) meeting on 14 March 2014.[85]

Unfortunately, the Akhilesh Yadav-led government (2012-2017) had ignored various reports submitted by the intelligence agencies before the violence suggesting that the situation in the region could explode. This government faced harsh observations from the Supreme Court on the issues relating to services to the relief camps and rehabilitation of victims. According to a report, a Supreme Court bench led by the then Chief Justice P Sathasivam, observed, 'More than a month ago, we passed a detailed order that all the necessary materials should be made available to the inmates of relief camps, especially children and women. Despite our order, such things are still happening. We read it in the newspapers and the parliament has also taken up the issue of children's death. We want to ascertain if it is correct.'[86] Worse, it bulldozed and closed camps down, forcing the victims to fend for themselves. These actions were from a party that claims to be pro-minority and secular.

On 24 September 2013, a Special Investigation Team (SIT) was established. In all, 567 riot-related cases were lodged and the FIRs were filed. In the end, in most cases, witnesses turned hostile. According to a victim, 'Despite lodging complaints several times at Fugana and Buhari police stations, no one came to help us. People on behalf of the accused approached us and even threatened us with dire consequences. We are a poor family. There is no one to take care of the family if anything happens to me. We did what we thought was correct.'[87]

In 2014, the Narendra Modi-led BJP assumed power. Prime Minister Modi has remained largely silent on Muzaffarnagar violence. He chose not to visit the violence-affected areas. Many consider the massive victory of the BJP in the 2017 Assembly election a vote for Modi. Both the campaigns in 2014 and 2017 presented Modi with the opportunity to address the conditions of victims of the Muzaffarnagar riot, but he chose to ignore it. He alluded to the Muzaffarnagar riots only to attack Rahul Gandhi during the 2014 election campaign since Rahul Gandhi had said that Pakistan's intelligence agency (ISI) was working to brainwash young Muslim victims and recruit them for terror activities.[88] He accused Rahul Gandhi of tarnishing the image of the Muslim community and later attacked Mulayam Singh Yadav for failing to help the victims.[89] Ironically, Sanjeev Baliyan, one of the accused in the Muzaffarnagar violence was appointed by Modi in his cabinet. The Yogi Adityanath government made efforts to withdraw cases against the BJP leaders who were accused as perpetrators of violence against Muslims.[90] Many consider the failure on the part of the state to punish the perpetrators a failure of India's criminal justice system.

Gujarat Riot (2002)

In the history of riots in modern India, the Gujarat riot of 2002 stands out for its enormous transformative impact on Indian politics. The controversies and public debates around the Gujarat riot have shaped Narendra Modi's rise and his contribution to the deepening of Hindutva and expansion of the Hindu Right's social base all over India. Perhaps no other riot has defined the trajectory of the Hindu Rashtra project the way this riot has. This is evident in the BJP's victory led by Narendra Modi in India's two major parliamentary elections, 2014 and 2019.

Considered the first televised riot in India, the Gujarat riot of 2002 and the name of Narendra Modi are so deeply intertwined that no other Indian politician has ever been identified with a riot in such a manner. Other riots, such as the 1984 anti-Sikh riot took place under Prime Minister Rajiv Gandhi and there are similarities between the two.[91] But, there was no global uproar against Rajiv Gandhi as was the case with Mr Narendra Modi.[92] In June 2022, the Supreme Court of India gave a clean chit to Prime Minister Narendra Modi for any culpability associated with the Gujarat riot of 2002, dismissing an appeal made by Zakia Jafri, widow of Ehsan Jafri.[93] Mrs Jafri wanted a 'larger conspiracy' in riots to be probed into, against the Prime Minister and 63 others, including officials and politicians.

From an ideological viewpoint, the Gujarat riot of 2002 is a paradigmatic case representing religious fault lines of Indian secularism. While secular critics of Narendra Modi viewed the riot as evidence of his commitment to Hindu Right politics, his supporters looked at it more as evidence of him being a champion of Hindutva ideology, who showed Muslims their place. According to Ashutosh Varshney, 'In the Gujarat government's eyes, Muslims are disloyal and deserve to be treated harshly, regardless of whether all Muslims were involved in, or supported, the torching of the train at Godhra. No distinction needs to be made between Muslim criminals and innocent Muslim citizens. And the most powerful civil society organizations—the VHP and RSS—are also of the same view. Instead of civil society resisting the state, or the state resisting marauding civic groups like the VHP, there was a coincidence between the two in March 2002. It is this coincidence that created the ideal conditions for a pogrom.'[94]

During the Partition of India in 1947, Gujarat, unlike Bengal or Punjab, did not witness any major riot or violence.[95] Migration of Muslims from Gujarat to Pakistan was not significant at all. Only 2.2 per cent of the migrants who moved to Pakistan were from Gujarat and the city of Bombay. Out of these, 75 per cent went to Karachi owing to their business connections.[96]

However, frequent riots between Hindus and Muslims began taking place after 1947. Gujarat had the highest per capita rate of deaths due to Hindu-Muslim riots: 117 per million of the urban population during the period between 1950 and 1995. In a riot in Ahmedabad in 1969 large-scale Hindu-Muslim violence was witnessed for the first time, claiming 600 lives in five days. An argument over cows disrupting a Muslim religious procession was the trigger for the riot.[97] What further contributed to the deepening of the hate campaign in Gujarat is the pre-colonial Gujarati literature which attributed the decline of Gujarat's cultural ethos and knowledge of Muslim rule. The works of poets like Narmad and Dalpatram gave birth to the idea of Gujarati 'asmita' or pride and Swadesh or independence. In other words, there are various dimensions to the evolution of majoritarianism in Gujarat. Revati Laul's account in *Anatomy of Hate* presents vivid accounts of the depth of prejudices and how they affected victims of both religions during the riot.[98]

Ethnic violence in Gujarat has a political context. And the context is the changing strategy of mobilization around caste and religion in the state's electoral politics. The Gujarat riot of 2002 needs to be seen in this context, defined by an ongoing religious polarization at the time, which subsequently became the national strategy for the Hindu Right. Ever since such a strategy of religious polarization has been seen as the way to go in both the state and Parliamentary elections.

Like most Indian states, the Congress party was the dominant political party in the early years of Gujarat. The party during the 1970s was able to establish a working coalition of caste and religion known as KHAM: Kashtriyas (a political alliance of upper-caste Rajputs and lower-caste Kolis), Harijans (Scheduled Castes), Adivasis (Scheduled Tribes), and Muslims. In response, the Hindu Right, particularly the BJP during the 1980s, began organizing Rath Yatras—first the Gangajal or Ekatamata Yatra in 1983, and then the Ram-Janki Dharma Yatra in 1989 as its alternative way of political mobilization. The key objective was to bring together various caste groups to build a broader Hindu political case with an electoral goal of having a wider electoral reach than KHAM. From the point of view of the nine per cent Muslim population of Gujarat, this strategy by the BJP was undoubtedly exclusivist. But it also used upper caste Hindus as its anchor for the expansion of the Hindu Right's social base across caste groups.[99]

However, according to Achyut Yagnik and Suchitra Seth, the rise of Hindu nationalism in Gujarat in the 1980s created a new context for inter-community relations and the composite culture of Gujarat. One striking aspect of the Gujarat riot was its direct connection with the Ayodhya movement of the late 1980s.[100] In 1990, Advani's Rath Yatra began in the city of Somnath in Gujarat which is seen as a major turning point in BJP's electoral fortune. Narendra Modi played a key role in this Yatra, though a relatively unknown figure in India's national politics at the time. This yatra caused riots in many parts of the country and ended with the arrest of Mr LK Advani by then Bihar Chief Minister, Lalu Prasad Yadav. This arrest led to the collapse of the coalition government of Prime Minister VP Singh in New Delhi, which was running with the support of the BJP. The Ayodhya movement triggered around 300 instances of Hindu-Muslim violence across India and in the end, the demolition of the Babri Masjid on 6 December 1992. Between September 1990 and January 1993, more than 500 people were killed in Gujarat.[101] In 1990, LK Advani's Rath Yatra sparked riots that left 220 dead in the state. In 1992, after the demolition, close to 325 people were killed in Gujarat, mostly Muslims.[102]

The immediate factor that led to the Gujarat riot in 2002 was the Godhra tragedy. On 27 February 2002, the VHP[103] came out with a plan to begin the construction of the Ram Temple in Ayodhya and appealed to the Kar Sevaks to join them. From various parts of India, including Gujarat, thousands of Kar Sevaks joined. Out of these Kar Sevaks, 2000 men returned to Ahmedabad by boarding the Sabarmati Express which caught fire near Godhra on 27 February 2002. Fifty-seven passengers died who were Hindus, including 25 women and 14 children, travelling on this train at the time.[104] These Kar Sevaks throughout their journey were chanting slogans. One Muslim family did not chant Jai Sri Ram and was asked to get off the train. A Muslim shopkeeper was asked to shout 'Jai Sri Ram' in Godhra station and was assaulted. The Kar Sevaks also attacked a Muslim woman with her two daughters. The train was stopped at a neighbourhood inhabited by Ghanchis after some time. Vendors mostly came from this community. Roughly, 500 to 2000 people surrounded and attacked the coach with stones and torches. Coach No. S6 caught fire, killing 57 Kar Sevaks and their families.[105] Although different sources quote different numbers of people who gathered and attacked the train, the Godhra incident was the trigger for the large-scale riot that followed.

The state authorities offered varied and multiple explanations for the Godhra incident. And the subsequent measures that the state government took helped inflame the passion and did not help in de-escalation.

The burned bodies of kar sevaks were brought to Ahmedabad for post-mortem on the same evening and the arrival of dead bodies was shown on television. A bandh was followed by the VHP and the BJP on the following day leading to Hindu backlash against Muslims in the state. The riot broke out and it began to spread to different corners of Gujarat. Cities such as Gandhinagar, Vadodara, and Sabarkantha were affected by the violence in Godhra and Ahmedabad. The riot also spread to rural regions. Some rural districts including Panchmahals, Mehsana, Kheda, Junagarh, Banaskhantha, Patan, Anand, and Narmada were also impacted by the riot. Other districts such as Bharuch, Rajkot, and Surat were not spared either. On 28 February alone, 248 Muslims were killed and the violence continued across the state. The reports of sporadic killings continued until December of that year. One of the most repeated slogans was, '*Muslai ne gaam ma thi kado*' (Run the Muslims out of the village). The spread of riots to rural areas was a prominent feature of the Gujarat riot in 2002 (Jaffrelot, 2003).

According to the 2001 census, 42 per cent of Muslims lived in rural areas in Gujarat. Even districts such as Mehsana and Gandhinagar with only a 6.6 per cent and 2.9 per cent Muslim population were targetted. These attackers were divided into three different groups: 1) todwalla (those who were destroyers); lootwalla (those who were looting); baadwavalla (those who were burning). In the district of Sabarkantha, in all 2161 houses, 1461 shops, 71 workshops, and 38 hotels were looted.[106] Forty-five places of worship were attacked and destroyed. Close to 1200 villages were impacted by the riot—mainly in districts such as Bharuch, Bhavnagar, Vadodara, Panhmahals, Mehsana, and Sabarkanataha.[107]

In this riot, members of STs in the eastern part of Gujarat were also mobilized in thousands to participate in violence against Muslims and their property.[108] In the first five days of the riot alone, the state had incurred economic losses worth US $500 million[109] and 2,50,000 people, largely Muslims, were displaced from urban and rural areas, with many living in makeshift relief camps.[110]

According to a report by Human Rights Watch (HRW), Muslims who called the police were told, 'We have no orders to save you.' Many Hindu nationalist organizations took part in the carnage. A report by the Forensic Science Laboratory in Gujarat in 2002 refuted the claim that the train was set alight from outside.[111] In 2004, the Ministry of Railways of India stated in a report that the fire was accidental.[112] As many as 125,000 refugees were in the camps at the height of violence. There was a general complaint of the state being biased and most assistance came from the civil society organizations run by Muslims.[113]

There was evidence of police complicity in the Gujarat riot in 2002. In the early days of March 2002 in Ahmedabad, former general of the Indian army, Zameer Uddin Shah, recalled having to face a 'parochial, partial "police force and home guards battalions" that were actual participants in riots.'[114] In the aftermath, moreover, the police failed to properly investigate and persecute. Since then, the Supreme Court of India ordered the police to review and reopen 2000 cases of violence that they had closed. Even as violence continued, the BJP called for early elections, and the Governor of Gujarat dissolved the Legislative Assembly on 19 July 2002. Elections were held in December 2002. The election campaign was dominated by slogans like 'Alis, Malis and Jamalis'—obvious Muslim names. The campaign was extremely polarized and it helped the BJP to return to power in the state in the December elections, winning 127 out of 182 seats. Since then the election campaigns have been polarized in Gujarat and later the same model was applied by the BJP at the Centre and in other states (Jaffrelot 2003).

Violence and Kashmiri Muslims

Any discussion on violence against Muslims in India needs to reflect on the violence against Kashmiri Muslims, who have suffered the worst kind long before the Hindu Right had tasted political power in New Delhi. They continue to do so. While it is true that removal of the Article 370[115] has been a key ideological agenda of the Hindu Right, its campaign was largely carried forward outside the power structure by the Hindu Right. By undertaking its removal, the Modi government fulfilled its key ideological agenda. But violence against Kashmiri Muslims has a unique context to it, which is South Asia's volatile geopolitics, and the role of Pakistan and the imperial legacy in the dispute between India and Pakistan. On the one hand, there was violence against Kashmiri Pandits,[116] whose cause was largely neglected by secular parties and thus it became a Hindu Right project. Indian state's response, which led to unprecedented human rights violations against Kashmiri Muslims, has been described by some as collateral damage. A large bulk of this violence was caused by the Indian state run by secular parties. One may consider the role of Jagmohan as governor, the Vajpayee government from 1998-2004, and then the Narendra Modi regime as part of the narrative of what the Hindu Right has done to Kashmiri Muslims.

Leaving aside these periods under Hindu Right leadership, the rest of the period since independence, the state was governed by secular regimes of one or another kind. It includes the period under Prime Minister Rajiv Gandhi, VP Singh, PV Narasimha Rao, and then Dr Manmohan Singh. After Dr Manmohan Singh took over in 2004, there was a discussion to address the Kashmir situation and Mr Abid Hussain, a senior bureaucrat was approached to head the committee which he turned down. In a discussion with me, he shared the reason for his reluctance to head a committee as follows, 'No one is serious.' Dilip Padgaonkar, a senior journalist, confided to me the lack of commitment by the Dr Manmohan Singh government to implement the recommendations of the interlocuter's report prepared after 2010.[117] There is some truth to the allegation that India's secular political elites did not take the task seriously in addressing vexed issues like Kashmir. As Jairam Ramesh once said, the Kashmir governance was basically left to the deep state. While the removal of Article 370 has received judicial approval[118] it is not very clear as yet how the Hindu Right regime is going to address the Kashmir issue as a subject of even basic electoral democracy. As Table 3.1 on electoral data shows, there is a growing foothold of the BJP inside the state and its vote share has risen enormously in 2014 and 2019 parliamentary elections. Will similar vote share of the BJP be the case with the Assembly elections? Will the party be able to govern on its own in Kashmir in the future? It remains a million-dollar question. Considering that the media reports and information are controlled so heavily, it is difficult to reflect. As things stand, New Delhi's approach to Kashmir has radically changed.

TABLE 3.1 BJP's Parliamentary Elections performance (Jammu and Kashmir)

Year	*Total no. of Seats*	*Candidates Contested*	*Candidates Won*	*2nd Position*	*Party Vote Share (%)*
1980	6	-	-	-	-
1984	6	-	-	-	-
1989	6	2	0	0	7.15
1991*	6	-	-	-	-
1996	6	5	1	1	19.04
1998	6	6	2	0	28.64
1999	6	6	2	0	31.56
2004	6	6	0	2	23.04
2009	6	4	0	2	18.61
2014	6	6	3	0	32.65
2019	6	6	3	0	46.675

**Elections not held in 1991.*

TABLE 3.2 BJP's Assembly Elections Performance (Jammu and Kashmir)

Year	*Total no. of Seats*	*Candidates Contested*	*Candidates Won*	*2nd Position*	*Party Vote Share (%)*
1983	76	27	0	6	3.19
1987	76	29	2	6	5.10
1996	87	53	8	8	12.13
2002	87	58	1	9	8.57
2008	87	64	11	13	12.45
2014	87	75	25	7	22.98

Should the violence against Kashmiri Muslims be seen or equated as violence against Indian Muslims? In some sense it is. But it is also a fact that some Kashmiri Muslims always looked at themselves as Muslims of a special kind or *nasal*. When a section of Kashmiri Muslims asked for Azadi or freedom from India, it also meant freedom from Indian Muslims. The relationship between the two has been rather tricky. For instance, Indian Muslims have nothing to do with the suffering that was inflicted or continues to be inflicted against Kashmiri Pandits. This was a result of Muslim militancy, mainly connected with Pakistan's patronage of various local militant wings in Kashmir. The spiral of violence has also presented a special challenge for Indian secularists—particularly those of Hindu heritage. Some of them are found to be reluctant to speak for Kashmiri Pandits as they fear they may be accused of being anti-Muslim. By and large, in India's ideological discourse, a secularist found it a challenge to take a stand against violence on Kashmiri Pandits as well as innocent Kashmiri Muslims with equal measure. It is this ambivalence that has created some legitimacy for the Hindu Right to make a forceful intervention, especially for Kashmiri Pandits, though substantive results on this front, particularly the return of Pandits or their rehabilitation, continue to face stiff challenges and the larger goal of peace remain, elusive.

Whatever unfolds in Kashmir will have repercussions for Indian Muslims particularly because the Hindu Right will use it in its narrative to legitimize its arguments against Indian Muslims and their loyalty. The violence that the average Kashmiri has suffered is enormous and multi-dimensional.[119] Some are asking if there will be Kashmirization of the Indian Muslim issue. And the question has some relevance.

Conclusion

Various shapes and forms of violence against Muslims need to be seen as part of the continuum of violence that Indian society has unleashed on its own people for a very long time. That is why it would be misleading to see anti-Muslim violence as a mere aberration or something that could be tackled by law alone. The fact is that Indian Muslims are only a new target group of violent machines that have been integral to Indian society. The dominant social group that has been behind the violence against Dalits for centuries is also the key perpetrator of violence against Muslims. It needs to be underlined that no scientific study suggests Muslims have anything to do with the violence against Dalits in India. Some sections of Muslims may nurture some form of prejudices against Dalits but there is no research that indicates Muslim involvement in violence against Dalits in an organized fashion. If there are examples, it could be merely individual cases. However, it does not involve the community in general. Prejudices against Dalits do not carry any sanction from the Muslim community at all. That is why it is crucial to ask why a particular dominant social group that has been practising violence against Dalits is also carrying out similar violence against Muslims. What does it tell us about the history and place of violence in Indian society? And what challenge does it pose to address the violence? Clearly, mere stringent laws have not proved to be enough in the case of Dalits. Likewise, mere laws to deal with violence against Muslims might not work.

Moreover, there are indeed certain particularities of this new form of violence against Muslims. Given that the Gujarat 2002 riot received so much national and global attention, the then Modi government in Gujarat and the BJP as a political party had to engage in considerable firefighting both at home and abroad. Currently, there has been a shift in the strategy of Hindu Right forces. Research by Sudha Pai and Sajjan Kumar[120] presents insights into this new trend. Based on their extensive fieldwork in east and west UP, they have argued why antagonism between Hindus and Muslims is so violent, and how the social fabric and agrarian nature of the political economy have become vulnerable to sustained assault by the Hindu Right. According to the authors, Hindu Right organizations seek to create and sustain constant, low-key communal tension. These tensions are frequent, small, low-intensity incidents that arise out of petty everyday issues intending to keep the communal pot boiling. We see a similar pattern in most parts of India where Muslims live whether it is Maharashtra or West Bengal or any other state. In my view, this is a significant shift in the strategy of politics of religious polarization and contributes to an environment of violence in which Muslims live these days not just in Uttar Pradesh but nearly all states ruled by the BJP.

While the evolving majoritarian polity is a major contextual factor for the new types of riots that are more savage and organized, the evidence of communal state behavior has a long history. For instance, the custodial killings of more than forty innocent Muslim youth in Hashimpura on 22 May 1987, by Uttar Pradesh's Provincial Armed Constabulary (PAC) of the 41st Battalion is a prominent example of a communalized state. It was an example of a modern-day Jallianwala Bagh or worse. In Jallianwala, the crowd had gathered to take part in a political protest; here these innocent youths were simply picked up from neighbouring villages for no reason except deep-seated prejudices of the PAC's 41st battalion led by Platoon Commander Surender Pal Singh. They chose young Muslim men from a crowd of roughly 500 people. Loaded into an official truck with the number plate URU 1352, these people were driven to a nearby water canal, shot one by one, and thrown into a canal. Twenty-eight years later, on 21 March 2015, a court verdict led to all the accused being released. Vibhuti N Rai, who was serving as the Superintendent of Police (SP) of the district at the time conducted an early investigation and wrote a book.[121] Again, this particular example is suggestive of the continuous nature of violence that Indian society unleashes—especially its deep-seated prejudices against Muslims.

India's majoritarian state has also adopted new ways to deal with violence in which Muslims find justice elusive. Firstly, often an attempt is made to present victims as perpetrators—for instance, the Kasganj riot (2015) in Uttar Pradesh.[122] Secondly, reconciliation in post-riot situations between supposedly warring communities (in this case, Hindus and Muslims) is barely attempted. For instance, in earlier times, there would be efforts to set up a peace committee and persuade people to look at the bigger picture of peaceful living, etc. Instead, the communities are encouraged to live away from each other so that they remain an enduring source of politics of religious polarization. Both tendencies have deep implications for the Muslim psyche and their identities.[123] For instance, after the Muzaffarnagar riot in 2013 even prominent leaders of the Samajwadi Party advised victims and survivors to accept compensation, move out of their native villages, withdraw legal cases, and settle down in newly built faraway colonies.[124] Such initiatives are meant to institutionalize the Hindu-Muslim prejudices towards each other—and create a new society to show that they cannot live together in a village or kasba. And finally, as the case of Nuh violence suggests, the state approach to violence against Muslims is more of a collective punishment of which bulldozer justice is an integral part.

While India is still governed by a secular constitution, the political system has changed and has become what I would like to call a 'saffron system.'[125] Under these new majoritarian conditions, the prospect of violence against Muslims not only remains, but state complicity becomes normal, confirming the fear that the state is increasingly going against Muslims.

Notes

1 Wilkinson, Steve I. 2004. *Votes and Violence: Electoral Competition and Ethnic Riots in India.* New Delhi: Cambridge University Press. P. 1.
2 Chandhoke, Neera. 2021. *Violence in Our Bones: Mapping the Deadly Fault Lines in Indian Society.* New Delhi: Aleph.
3 Singh, Upinder. 2021. *Political Violence in Ancient India.* Cambridge: Harvard University Press.
4 For a contextual analysis of this conversation see, Omvedt, Gail. 2017. *Ambedkar: Towards an Enlightened India.* New Delhi: Penguin.
5 See Ambedkar, BR. 2020 (first published in 1979). 'I have no homeland' Dr *Babasaheb Ambedkar: Writings and Speeches: Dr BR Ambedkar and his Egalitarian Revolution Struggle for Human* Rights. Vol 17, Part 1. New Delhi: Dr Ambedkar Foundation. Ministry of Social Justice and Empowerment. Government of India. P. 53.
6 See, Ore, Ersula. J. 2019. *Lynching: Violence, Rhetoric and American Identity.* Jackson: University of Mississippi Press. P. 14.
7 Sandhu, Kamaljeet. 2022. 'Have no data on mob lynchings, govt says in Parliament.' Available at: http://www.indiatoday.in (accessed on 5 February 2024).
8 Saldanha, Alison. 2018. 'BJP govt tells parliament no data available on mob lynching; fact checks show this isn't entirely true.' Available at: http:// www.firstpostpost.com (accessed on 4 February 2024).
9 Quoted in the report, Sheriff M, Kaunain M. 2023. 'Lynching and hate crime murder in penal code: punishment 7 years to death.' Available at: http:// www.indianexpress.com. (accessed on 4 February 2024).
10 Ibid.
11 Brass, Paul. 1998. *Theft of An Idol: Text and Context in the Representation of Collective Violence.* Calcutta: Seagull Press.
12 Varshney, Ashutosh. 2020. 'Gujarat 2002 was independent India's first full-blooded pogrom. Delhi 1984 was a semi-pogrom.' Available at: http://www.theprint.in (accessed on 8 August 2020).
13 Ibid.
14 Brass, Paul. 1998. *Theft of An Idol: Text and Context in the Representation of Collective Violence.* Calcutta: Seagull Press. P.11.
15 Mukhopadhya, Nilanjan. 2023. *Sikhs: The Untold Agony of 1984.* New Delhi: Westland.
16 See Rehman, Mujibur. 2016. 'Politics of Anti-Christian Violence in Kandhamal' in *Communalism in postcolonial India: Changing Contours.* Edited by Mujibur Rehman. New Delhi: Routledge Publications.
17 Quoted in Jaffrelot, Christophe. 2003. 'Communal riots in Gujarat: The

State at Risk?' Working Paper, No. 17. Heidelberg Papers in South Asian and Comparative Politics. University of Heidelberg, Germany.

18 Bayly, Chris. 1985. 'The Pre-History of Communalism? Religious Conflict in India 1700-1860.' *Modern Asian Studies.* 19(2).

19 See, Yagnik, Achyut and Seth, Sucharita. 2005. *The Shaping of Modern Gujarat: Plurality, Hindutva and Beyond.* New Delhi: Penguin Books.

20 See, Sarkar, Sumit. 2014. *Modern India: 1885-1947.* New Delhi: Pearson. P. 52.

21 Das, Suranjan. 1991. *Communal Riots in Bengal, 1905- 1947.* New Delhi: Oxford University Press. P. 4.

22 Ibid. P. 5.

23 Freitag, Sandria B. 1989. *Collective Action and Community: Public Arenas and the Emergence of Communalism in North India.* Berkeley: California University Press.

24 For a detailed comparative analysis, see Brass, Paul. 1998. *Theft of An Idol: Text and Context in the Representation of Collective Violence.* Calcutta: Seagull Press.

25 Dubey, Divyani. 2022. 'Fact Check: Where there no riots in Uttar Pradesh in the past five years, as Adityanath claims?' Available at: http://wwwscroll.in (accessed on 4 February 2024).

26 Basu, Amrita. 2015. *Violent Conjunctures in Democratic India.* New Delhi: Cambridge University Press.

27 See, Mujibur Rehman. 2018. *Communalism in postcolonial India: Changing Contours.* New Delhi: Routledge.

28 See the report, Mathew, Liz. 2020. 'Explained: The Intertwined Journeys of Narendra Modi and the temple in Ayodhya.' Available at: http://www.Indianexpress.com (accessed on 8 August 2020).

29 See the report, 'Haryana Violence| Imam Killed in attack on Gurugram Mosque; Haryana CM says 5 dead in communal violence'. Available at: http://www.thehindu.com (accessed on 20 December 2023).

30 Siwach, Sukhbir. 2023. 'Nuh Violence: Who Are Mewat's Meo Muslims?' Available at: http://www.indianexpress.com (accessed on 20 December 2023).

31 Ibid.

32 Tewari, Samridhi. 2023. 'Calls for an economic boycott are crushing us, say Muslim traders.' Available at: http://www.thehindu.com (accessed on 4 February 2024).

33 Mateen, Zoya and Pasha, Dilnawaz. 2023. 'Nuh violence: Is bulldozer punishment trampling justice in India?' Avaialble at: http:// www.bbc.com (accessed on 4 February 2024).

34 Dhankar, Leena. 2023. 'Nuh Violence: 1,208 structures razed by Haryana govt, mostly of 1 community.' Avaialble at: http://www.thehindustantimes.com (accessed on 20 December 2023).

35 See, Sura, Ajay. 2023. 'Ethnic Cleansing By the State? HC halts Haryana's Nuh demolitions.' Available at: http://www.thetimesofindia.com (accessed on 20 December 2023).

36 Ibid.

37 Ibid.

38 See, Narayan, Badri. 2022. 'Why 'Bulldozer Baba' Yogi Adityanath keeps using the machine for law and order.' Available at: http://www.theprint.com (accessed on 5 December 2023).

39 Choudhury, Ratnadip. 2023. 'Bulldozers in Action As Eviction Drive Begins in Assam Reserve forest.' Available at: http://www.ndtv.com (accessed on 4 February 2024).

40 Jaiswal, Umanand. 2023. 'Setback to Assam bulldozer raj trial run.' Available at: http://www.telegraphindia.com (accessed on 5 January 2023).

41 See the report, 'Decode Politics: Back in Madhya Pradesh, the history of Bulldozer Politics in Hindi Heartland.'Available at: http://www.indianexpress.com. 15 Dec 2023 (accessed on 5 Jan 2024).

42 Singh, Ravish Pal. 2023. 'Video: Bulldozer action on house of man who attacked BJP worker in Madhya Pradesh.' Available at: http://www.indiatoday.in (accessed on 5 January 2024).

43 See the report, Peterson, Hannah Ellis. 2020. 'Delhi rocked by deadly protests during Donald Trump's India visit.' Available at: http://www.theguardian.com (accessed on 8 August 2020).

44 See, 'Reports of Delhi Fact Finding Committee on North-East Delhi Riots of February 2020.' Delhi Minorities Commission, Govt of NCT of Delhi. New Delhi.

45 Dutta, Prabhash K. 2020. 'Despite biggest mandate in 27 years, BJP beaten squarely in Delhi election.' Available at: http://www.indiatoday.in (accessed on 25 December 2023).

46 See, *PTI*. 2020. 'MCD Election Results 2022: Even in Defeat, BJP's vote share rises by 3 Per Cent.' Available at: http://www.timesofindia.com. (accessed on 25 December 2023).

47 Gandhi, Rajmohan. 2000. *Revenge and Reconciliation: Understanding South Asian History*. New Delhi: Penguin Random House.

48 Mukhopadhya, Nilanjan. 2023. *Sikhs: The Untold Agony of 1984*. New Delhi: Westland.

49 See reports on Delhi Riot in the *Frontline*. 27 March 2020. Pp. 4-48.

50 See the Report on Delhi Riots. Delhi Comminssion for Minortiies, Government of Delhi. P. 100.

51 Ibid.

52 Kapil Mishra was an AAP party MLA in New Delhi Assembly before he joined the BJP.

53 Some of the places of worship include: Chand Masjid, Ashok Nagar; Masjid Farooqi and Jamiatul Huda Madarsa, Brijpuri; Jannati Masjid, and Madarsatul Uloom Madarsa in Gokulpuri; Sayeed Chand Baba(Baba Shaikh) Mazar, Bhajanpura; Qubaristan, Jyoti Colony; Fatima Masjid and Madarsa Mahmudia in Khajuri Khas; Masjid and Madarsa Abdullah Bukhari, Tyre Market, Gokulpuri; Masjid Umar Farooq, Ghonda; Madina Masjid, Auliya Masjid, and Tayyeba Masjid in Shiv Vihar; Allah Wali Masjid, Bhagat Singh Colony; Masjid Maula Baksh in Ashok Nagar, Gokulpuri; and Madarsa Tayyibul Uloom, Ashok Nagar (Shahdara).

54 Delhi Minority Commission Report. P. 102.

55 See, Khan, Aiman and Jaya, Arpita. 2020. 'Burkhas, All "Markers of Muslimness" Targeted, Report Details Women's Plight in Delhi Riots.' Available at: http://www.thewire.in (accessed on 22 July 2020).

56 See the report, 'Delhi Riots: 72 concerned citizens, including former bureaucrats, write to President seeking Probe.' 2020. Available at: http://www.newsclick.in (accessed on 10 August 2020).

57 See, Tiwary, Deeptiman. 2020. 'Delhi riots debate: Police complicit… hate speech fanned flames, Oppn slams govt.' Available at: http://www.indianexpress.com (accessed on 10 August 2020).

58 See, 'Parliament Highlights: 1922 Delhi Rioters Identified, Shah in Rajya Sabha.' Available at: http://www.business-standard.com. 12 March 2020 (accessed on 20 July 2020).

59 See, Khetan, Ashish. 2020. 'Delhi Riots: Is the Center Importing the "Gujarat Model" to Subvert Prosecution.' Available at: http://www.thewire.in (accessed on 10 August 2020).

60 An inquiry commission was set up under the chairmanship of Justice Vishnu Sahai, a former judge of Allahabad High Court.

61 Muzaffarnagar and neighbouring district Shamli were affected by the riot, though it is widely known as Muzaffarnagar violence as it began there.

62 See the report, Mishra, Ish, Rao, Mohan, Singh, Pragya, and Bajpai, Vikas. 2014. 'Fact Finding Report: Independent Inquiry In Muzaffarnagar Riots.' Available at: http://www.epw.in vol 49, Issue no 2. (accessed on 10 August 2020).

63 This *Maha Panchayat* was called by various affiliates of Hindu Right organizations, which included local leaders of the BJP.

64 See, Pai, Sudha and Kumar, Avinash. 2018. 'Understanding the BJP's victory in Uttar Pradesh' in Rehman, Mujibur. (Ed). 2018. *Rise of Saffron Power: Reflections on Indian Politics.* New Delhi: Routledge. Pp. 111-129.

65 For an analysis of 2017 elections, see Rehman, Mujibur. 2018. 'An inquiry into the causes and consequences of the saffron whirlwind that swept Uttar Pradesh in 2017 Assembly election' in Rehman, Mujibur. (Ed). *Rise of Saffron Power: Reflections on Indian Politics.* New Delhi: Routledge. Pp. 368-383.

66 Pai, Sudha. 2016. 'Who is Samajwadi Party?' Available at: http://www.indianexpress.com (accessed on 8 August 2020)

67 For an account of his life, see, Santanu Gupta. 2017. *The Monk Who Became a Chief Minister,* New Delhi: Bloomsbury.

68 See, Kapur, Devesh. 2017. 'Muslim anxieties and India's future'. Available at: http://www.project-syndicate.org (accessed on 10 August 2020).

69 Narendra Modi's decision to contest from Varanasi in 2014 election and retain the constituency as opposed to Vadodara, Gujarat, where he won as well. It indicates the importance of Uttar Pradesh in national politics. In the past, several Indian Prime Ministers such as Jawaharlal Nehru, Indira Gandhi, Rajiv Gandhi, Charan Singh, VP Singh, and Atal Bihari Vajpayee, were elected from Uttar Pradesh. The state sends 80 members to the 543-member Lok Sabha, the largest number among the states. In 2000, it was split into two states: Uttarakhand and Uttar Pradesh; but the impact of the politics of Uttar Pradesh on India's national polity remains as it used to be prior to its division.

70 See, 'Uttar Pradesh Religious Census 2011.' Available at: http://www.census2011.co.in (accessed on 10 August 2020).

71 Samajwadi Party (SP) was founded by Mulayam Yadav in 1990. After they won the election in 2012, Akhilesh Yadav, his son, took over as the Chief Minister for the first time.

72 See, 'Communal incidents up 30% in 2013,UP tops the list.' *The Indian Express,* 5 February 2014 (accessed on 10 August 2020).

73 According to the federal nature of the government, the Central government has various means through which it communicates its intentions or concerns. One of the ways it does this is by sending an advisory. In this role, the Centre broadly shares its concerns and the states enjoy flexibility to devise means to address this concern depending on its own understanding and resources at its disposal.

74 Singh, Rajesh Kumar and Raju, S. 2013. 'Muzaffarnagar Reports: FIR against politicians for hate speeches.' Available at: http://www.hindustantimes.com (accessed on 10 August 2020).

75 Bhatt, Virendra Nath. 2013. 'What led to Muzaffarnagar Riots.' Available at: http://www.tehelka.com (accessed on 10 August 2020).

76 He was a member of State BJP executive committee in 2016.

77 Bhardwaj, Ashutosh. 2016. 'Embers from Muzaffarnagar made Narendra Modi PM, says BJP leader.' Available at: http://www.indianexpress.com (accessed on 10 August 2020).

78 'UP Riots: BJP to capitalise on vote polarization.' Available at: http://www.business-standard.com. 17 September 2013 (accessed on 10 August 2020).

79 Jaffrelot, Christophe and Kumar, Sanjay. 2009. *Rise of the Plebians? The Changing Face of the Indian Legislative Assemblies.* New Delhi: Routledge.

80 For a nuanced understanding of Kanshi Ram and his contribution to Indian politics, see, Narayan, Badri. 2014. *Kanshi Ram: Leader of Dalits.* New Delhi: Viking.

81 Kothari, Rajni. 1994. 'Rise of Dalits and the Renewed Debate on Caste,' *Economic and Political Weekly* . Vol 29, Issue No 26.

82 For a well-researched biography of Charan Singh, see, Brass, Paul. 2014. *An Indian Political Life: Charan Singh and the Congress.* New Delhi: Oxford University Press.

83 See, Ashraf, Ajaz. 2013. 'Meltdown of the MAJGAR alliance.' Available at: http://www.thehindu.com (accessed on 10 August 2020).

84 'Riots perfect background to anoint Modi as PM hopeful: CPI(M).' The *Indian Express.* 20 September 2013 (accessed on 10 August 2020).

85 'PM addresses NIC meeting, Says Communal Riot Is a Challenge to Democracy,' *The Indian Express.* 14 March 2014 (accessed on 10 August 2020).

86 See the report. Anand, Utkarsh. 2013. 'Muzaffarnagar riots: SC orders UP to prevent further death of children in relief camps.' Available at: http://www.indianexpress.com (accessed on 10 August 2020).

87 Sahu, Manish. 2016. '2013 Muzaffarnagar Riots: 4 acquitted in a gangrape case after victim, family turn hostile. Husband says, we were threatened.' Available at: http://www.indianexpress.com (accessed on 10 August 2020). There were 16 people who were alleged to be a part of the gangrape, all from Fugana village.

88 Singh, Rashpal and Datta, Saikat. 2013. 'Youth in Muzaffarnagar contacted by ISI: officials deny Rahul's Claim.' Available at: http://www.hindustantimes.com (accessed on 10 August 2020).

89 PTI. 'Narendra Modi refers to Muzaffarnagar riots to attack Mulayam Singh Yadav, says he failed victims.' 2014. Available at: http://www.indianexpress.com (accessed on 10 August 2020).

90 'Uttar Pradesh Considers withdrawing Muzaffarnagar Riot Cases.' 2018. Available at: http://www.indianexpress.com (accessed on 10 August 2020).

91 In public debate the BJP always alluded to 1984 as a parallel counter example to Gujarat 2002.

92 See a report, 'Visa Row: A Tremulous Modi-US story.' 2014. Available at: http://www.thehindustantimes.com (accessed on 8 August 2020).

93 See, Singh, Darpan. 2022. 'Gujarat riots clean chit to PM: Two decades of legal battle and what's next'. Available at: http://www.indiatoday.in (accessed on 4 January 2023).

94 Varshney, Ashutosh. 2020. 'Gujarat 2002 was independent India's first full-blooded pogrom. Delhi 1984 was a semi-pogrom.' Available at: http://www.theprint.in (accessed on 8 August 2020).

95 See, Pandey, Gyanendra. 2001. *Remembering Partition: Violence, Nationalism and History In India*. Cambridge: Cambridge University Press; Also see Butalia, Urvashi. 2017. *The Other Side of Violence: Voices from the Partition of India*. New Delhi: Penguin.

96 Yagnick, Achyut and Seth, Suchitra. 2005. *The Shaping of Modern Gujarat*. New Delhi: Penguin. P. 225.

97 Ibid.

98 See Laul, Revati. 2018. *Anatomy of Hate*. New Delhi: Context (An Imprint of Westland).

99 See, Dattiwala, Raheel. 2019. *Keeping the Peace*. Cambridge: Cambridge University Press.

100 See, Gopal, Sarvepalli. (Ed.). 1992. *Anatomy of a Confrontation: Ayodhya and Rise of Communal Politics in India*. London: Zed books.

101 Varshney, Ashutosh and Wilkinson, Steven. 2006. 'Varshney-Wilkinson Dataset on the Hindu- Muslim Violence in India, 1950-1995.' Inter-University Consortium for Political and Social Research (Distributor). Ann Arbor. MI: 17 February.

102 See Jaffrelot, Christophe. 2003. 'Communal Riots: The State at Risk? Working Paper'. 17 July. South Asian Institute, Department of Political Science, University of Heidelberg, Germany.

103 For an authoritative account of the VHP, see Katju, Manjari. 2010. *Vishwa Hindu Parishad and Indian Politics*. New Delhi: Orient Blackswan.

104 Vardarajan, Siddharth. (Ed.). 2002. *Gujarat: The Making of a Tragedy*.

New Delhi: Penguin. This volume presents a comprehensive account of the politics that led to the Gujarat riot and its aftermath.

105 Jaffrelot, Christophe. 2003. 'Communal Riots: The State at Risk? Working Paper'. 17 July. South Asian Institute, Department of Political Science, University of Heidelberg, Germany.

106 Bhatia, Bela. 'A step back in Sabarkantha' Available at: www.india-seminar.com. 513. May 2002 (accessed on 25 January 2024). This is a special issue titled, *A Society Under Seige: A Symposium on the breakdown of civil society in Gujarat.*

107 Jaffrelot, Christophe. 2003. 'Communal Riots: The State at Risk? Working Paper'. 17 July. South Asian Institute, Department of Political Science, University of Heidelberg, Germany. Also see, Gupta, Dipankar .'Limits of Tolerance: Prospects of Secularism in India after Gujarat.' *Economic and Political Weekly* 37(46)4615-4620.

108 See, Devy, Ganesh. 'Tribal Voice and Violence' Available at: www.india-seminar.com. 513. May 2002 (accessed on 25 January 2024). This is a special issue with a title, 'A Society Under Seige: A Symposium on the breakdown of civil society in Gujarat'

109 See, Spodek, Howard. 2011. *Ahmedabad: Shock City of 20th Century India.* Bloomington: Indiana University Press.

110 This is according to the report prepared by the Department of State, USA.

111 See the report in the *Outlook*, 22 November 2002.

112 See the analysis, Bidwai, Praful. 'Who Lit the Fire?' 2005. Avaialble at: http://www.frontline.thehindu.com. (accessed on 10 August 2020).

113 For detailed analysis of what happened during the riot and afterwards, see Mander, Harsh. 2020. *Between Memory and Forgetting.* New Delhi: Yoda Press.

114 See the report, 'Indian Army does not like being committed to civilian operations, they are our own people.' Available at: www.theprint.in. 13 October 2018 (accessed on 10 August 2020).

115 For an incisive analysis of the origins and significance of the Article 370, see Noorani, AG. 2015. *Article 370: A Constitutional History of Jammu and Kashmir.* New Delhi: Oxford University Press.

116 For a detailed account on this theme, see Pandita, Rahul. 2017. *Our Moon Has Blood Clots: The Exodus of the Kashmiri Pandits.* New Delhi: Penguin.

117 For a detailed discussion on the interlocuter's report and related issues see, Kumar, Radha. 2018. *Paradise at War: A definitive yet accessible study of perhaps the most troubled state in India.* New Delhi: Aleph Book Company.

118 See, Bhakto, Ananda. 2023. 'Jammu and Kashmir: Supreme Court upholds abrogation of Article 370 in landmark decision.' Available at: http://www.frontline.thehindu.com (accessed on 4 February 2024).

119 For a comprehensive analysis of multi-dimensional nature of this issue before and after the abrogation of Article 370, see, Jalal, Ayesha and Bose, Sugato. 2020. *Kashmir and the Future of South Asia.* New Delhi: Routledge Publications.

120 See Pai, Sudha and Kumar, Sajjan. 2018. *Everyday Communalism: Riots in Contemporary Uttar Pradesh.* New Delhi: Oxford University Press.

121 This book has now become an invaluable source of our history, not just on Hindu-Muslim relations; but also of the Indian state's conduct that appears to be worse than the colonial state in this case. See Rai, Vibhuti. 2016. *Hashimpura 22 May: The Forgotten Custodial Killings.* New Delhi: Penguin.

122 This is not limited to riots. Widespread evidence of this tendency is seen in cases of multiple lynching that have been going on since 2015.

123 For various elements of the relationship between identities and violence, see Sen, Amartya. 2006. *Identity and Violence: The Illusion of Destiny.* New York: Allen Lane.

124 For an analysis of the lives in such colonies by the survivors and victims of Muzaffarnagar riot, see, Mander, Harsh, Chaudhury, Akram Akhtar, Eqbal, Zafar, and Bose, Rajanya. 2016. *Living Apart: Communal Violence and Forced Displacement in Muzaffarnagar and Shamli.* New Delhi: Yoda Press.

125 See Rehman, Mujibur. 2018. 'Introduction' in Rehman, Mujibur. (Ed.). 2018. *Rise of Saffron Power: Reflections on Indian Politics.* New Delhi: Routledge.

4

INDIAN MUSLIM WOMEN: WHICH WAY NOW?

'Condemnation of Islam's treatment of women has united conservative Catholics and nostalgic Stalinists, neoliberals and social democrats. This rare point of unity among philosophers and politicians more often found at each other's throats does not, however, grow from a profound moment of Western cultural consensus.'

—Anne Norton, *On the Muslim Question*

The story of India's Muslim women is cast mainly as a story of perpetual suffering—worse than the conditions of the community itself. In the supposedly secular era of modern India, before the electoral prominence of the BJP in national politics, say till the late 1980s, the Indian state was seen in collusion with the forces of Islamic patriarchy to keep Muslim women entangled in the spiralling web of oppression and suffering. The most prominent instance of this version of the suffering of Muslim women became apparent during the passage of the Shah Bano Bill in 1986. Rajiv Gandhi was the Prime Minister of India at that time.[1] In the current era of Hindu majoritarianism, however, Muslim women continue to grapple with various genres of domination, exploitation, and violence. The Hindu Right views Muslim women as victims of Islamic practices and Islam as a religion equipped with regressive attributes. While the Hindu Right or any such school of thought may have its own Islamophobic biases, other possible reasons might have led to such general formulations on Muslim women . For instance, the implication of the over-arching context of the Western colonial project. The Western colonial project has had a profound impact on our world. It has influenced our society's power dynamics, culture, and language. Its implications are far-reaching and can still be felt today. Leila Ahmed's book, *Women and Gender in Islam: Historical Roots of a Modern Debate* provides valuable insights into the historical roots and contemporary discourse surrounding issues of gender and women's rights within the Islamic context. She writes, 'Colonial feminism, or feminism as used against other cultures in the service of colonialism, was shaped into a variety of similar constructs, each tailored to fit the particular culture that was the immediate target of domination—India, the Islamic world, and sub-Saharan Africa. Concerning the Islamic world, regarded as an enemy (indeed as the enemy) since the Crusades, colonialism—as I have already suggested—had a rich vein of bigotry and misinformation to draw on.'[2]

Therefore, the Indian debate on the women question is not entirely disconnected from the colonial legacy, though I intend to focus here on post-colonial India, specifically in the context of secularism and the Hindu majoritarianism debate.

Having confronted dual pressures—from Islamic patriarchy and the Indian state—often in conjunction, Indian Muslim women are facing terrifying challenges emanating from the Hindu Right's fast-expanding political muscle in various regions in India. Also, growing claims by political observers—mainly sympathetic to the BJP—that Indian Muslim women constitute a new social base for the BJP are made regularly.[3] This, according to some, is due to the Narendra Modi government's decision to abolish the Triple Talaq Practice (TTP) in 2019. There is no solid empirical evidence available to this claim that Muslim women form a solid electoral base for the Hindu Right.

The national debate triggered by college-going Muslim girls' determination to wear hijab, defying the uniform code in colleges in Karnataka in 2021 is a prominent example of a new set of challenges that Muslim women are confronting in modern India.[4] This hijab episode is also another key instance of the Hindu Right's ability to convert a local issue into a national one as part of its strategy of politics of religious polarization. It further reveals its objective to present a portrait of Indian Muslims constantly at odds with modernity and gender freedom. The Narendra Modi government passed a historic women's reservation bill in the Indian Parliament in September 2023, with no provision for Muslim women to benefit from its quota.[5] Therefore, the question of the Hindu Rights position concerning Muslim women and their welfare presents considerable concerns.

My analysis of Indian Muslim women and their relationship with Hindu Right will mainly veer around two key issues: the Triple Talaq issue and the hijab controversy. As part of contextual analysis, some interrogation of the relationship between women and Islam will help steer clear of the general misunderstanding about the place of women in Islam. A strong perception—both in India as well as in the West—prevails that Islamic patriarchy is more rigid and hostile to gender equity as opposed to other religions. This view has gathered greater legitimacy in the wake of the Taliban's return to Afghanistan resulting from an ill-considered decision by American President Joe Biden.[6] The undoing of gains on gender freedom made during the US-led coalition of Afghanistan is argued to be one of the most pricey and painful costs that the American withdrawal has caused.[7] Even before the Afghanistan problem, the non-Muslim world, especially the West, looked at Islam as a religion in dire need of reform to offer a rightful place to Muslim women.

Several scholars are deeply concerned with the Western stereotypes of Islam and its treatment of women. In an important book titled, *Do Muslim Women Need Saving?*, Lila Abu Lughod, an anthropologist at Columbia University, has argued that after the attacks of 11 September 2001, the image of the oppressed Muslim women became one of the motivating factors for Western missions to rescue them from their cultures.[8] This perspective, which Lughod expands upon, has formed the basis for Western intervention across the Middle East and other regions. Commenting on the West's harsh view on Islam's treatment of Muslim women, Carl W. Ernst, a leading American scholar on Islam observed that, 'English women did not have full property rights until the Married Women's Property Acts of 1870 and 1882, yet under Islamic Law, Muslim women have been guaranteed inheritance and property rights since the seventh century.'[9]

For a long time, scholars from various disciplines have sought to elucidate the position of women in Islam in an impressive array of books. Their works often draw on particular case studies from different countries. Among the scholarship on this theme of Islam and women, engaging with the writings and analyses of two prominent scholars, Fatima Mernissi and Amin Wadud, will be immensely useful. Fatima Mernissi's *Women and Islam: An Historical and Theological Enquiry*[10] has demonstrated that Muslim women's conditions are not as bad as it is presented by the West according to Islamic sources and history. Likewise, Amina Wadud in a chapter titled, 'Rights and Roles of Women: Some Perspectives' in her widely acclaimed book, *Quran and Woman; Rereading the Sacred Text from a Woman's Perspective,* sheds valuable insights into the question of why Islam is misconstrued from the point of view of gender rights. In urging readers to pay attention to various aspects of context in their interpretation of the Quran, Wadud notes, 'Hermeneutics of any text must confront three different aspects to support its conclusions.'[11] She further elaborates, '1) The context in which the text was written (in the case of Quran, in which it was revealed); 2) the grammatical composition of the text (how it says what it says); and 3) the whole text, its *Weltanschauung,* or worldview' provides the framework for the analysis of a text. She concludes that variation in the eventual argument is a reflection of the variation of interpretations in the analysis of contexts. She then goes on to scrutinize various terms such as *Faddala, Darajah,* and various verses to arrive at the following conclusions on the view that the Quran presents: '1) there is no inherent value placed on man and woman. There is no arbitrary, pre-ordained, and eternal system of hierarchy, 2) the Qur'an does not strictly delineate the roles of women and the roles of men to such an extent as to propose only a single possibility for each gender.'[12]

There is another dimension to this debate over the relationship between Islam and women, which Nilüfer Göle captures in the following words: 'The existence of oppression by the community and of religious conservatism cannot be denied: but neither can we deny that Islam is becoming a point of personal and collective attraction for those who are experiencing secular modernity.'[13] Therefore, it is necessary to examine various dimensions of these concerns not only in the West but also in the Indian context.

Some Aspects of the Debate over Muslim Women

In India, Islamic patriarchy has been a subject of prime attention since the Shah Bano debate[14] in the mid-eighties, particularly among liberals as well as the Hindu Right for different reasons. The Hindu Right has consistently campaigned over the Shah Bano issue describing it as part of 'Muslim appeasement politics' and 'vote bank' politics, almost interchangeably. These two phrases are deployed by the Hindu Right against anything concerning Muslim issues in India including the Triple Talaq Bill or the Uniform Civil Code debate, etc.

Besides, there are additional issues crucial for comprehending the challenges faced by Muslim women. While the Sachar Committee Report[15] has made the most powerful intervention at the policy level since Independence, the Committee did not have a single Muslim woman as a member unfortunately.[16] But the report included a chapter on Muslim women. The report provides valuable insights on the standing of Muslim women compared to women of other religious or social groups. According to this report, the work participation rate (hereafter WPR) for Muslim women are much lower compared to upper-caste Hindu households where there may be socio-cultural constraints to women's work.[17] In India, 44 per cent of women in the prime age group of 15-64 years, participate in the workforce, compared to 85 per cent of men. On average, the WPR for Muslim women is approximately 25 per cent. In rural areas, around 70 per cent of Hindu women participate in the workforce, compared to only about 29 per cent of Muslim women. Even the upper caste Hindu women in rural areas have a higher participation rate which stands at 43 per cent. The lower participation of Muslim women in rural areas is partly explained by the fact that Muslim households (hence women) are less likely to be engaged in agriculture. The WPRs for Muslims in urban areas are even lower presumably because work opportunities for women within the household are very limited. Such opportunities may be somewhat higher in rural areas with ownership (though limited) of land, making participation of Muslim women somewhat higher in these areas.

One of the reasons for the lower participation rate of Muslim women may be higher dependency rates which may be attributed to the relatively higher share of the younger population in the community, resulting in women staying at home. According to the report,[18] the Muslim population is much younger than the total population. While 23 per cent of the total population is below 10 years of age (that is, in the age range 0-9 years), 27 per cent of the Muslim population falls in the range. Further, in the age group of 10-14 years, there is an excess of two percentage points for Muslims. This is a situation of large young-age dependency. However, both the general population and Muslim population have a low percentage of elderly people. Thus, the old age dependency is not very high. What implication does the young age dependency have on the aggregate WPRs? Age-specific WPRs show that participation rates are lower for Muslims in almost all the age groups for males and females, both in rural and urban areas. Therefore, young age dependency does not seem to be driving lower the WPRs among Muslims.

On the subject of education, valuable observations could also be found in the Sachar Report.[19] The Census provides the most commonly used estimate of literacy in India, with a literacy rate of approximately 65 per cent. Literacy levels are expectedly higher for males (75.3 per cent) than females (53.7 per cent). Literacy levels are higher in urban areas (79.9 per cent) compared to rural areas (58.7 per cent). This gap of approximately 20 per cent between urban and rural areas, as well as across genders, has persisted in Indian society over the last two decades despite the rise in literacy levels.

The low literacy level of Muslims, SCs, and STs is well documented in social science research. In the mid-sixties, literacy levels of these groups were low and far lower than that of 'All Others'. In many states, the position of SCs and STs was worse than that of the Muslims. The literacy rate among Muslims in 2001 was 59.1 per cent. This is far below the national average (65.1 per cent). In urban areas, Muslims have a 11 per cent lower literacy rate compared to the national average of 81.1 per cent, while the literacy rate of the 'All Others' category is 15 per cent higher than the national average. Although the levels of literacy in rural areas is 52.7 per cent, the gap between the compared categories is also narrower. It is important to note that literacy rate for SCs and STs in both urban and rural India remains low. Although the literacy levels of 64 per cent and 68 per cent amongst the male SCs/STs and Muslims, respectively, are not low, they are far below the level for 'All Others', which is 81 per cent. However, Muslim women with a literacy level of 50 per cent have been able to keep up with women of other communities and are much ahead of the SC/ST women in rural India.

The data that the Sachar Report has shown on various issues such as work participation or education are unlikely to witness positive trends for Muslims in the wider context of the governance under Hindu Right regimes either at the federal or state level. Indeed, there is research that has shown negative trends.[20]

Politics of Triple Talaq Bill (TTB) and the Hindu Right

Seen primarily as anti-minority/anti-Muslim, the majoritarian Hindutva ideology is understood to be implicitly directed against

Muslim women. However, the Narendra Modi government's decision to pass the Triple Talaq Bill (TTB) in July 2019, overturning the controversial Shah Bano Bill[21] that the Rajiv Gandhi government had enacted in 1986 has brought a fresh twist to the debate over the relationship between Muslim women and the Hindu Right. Several non-Congress regimes that governed New Delhi since the days of the Shah Bano case chose to remain indifferent. These regimes include the NDA coalition government led by then Prime Minister Atal Bihari Vajpayee, which was in power from 1998 to 2004. These regimes and their supporting partners left no opportunity to blame Rajiv Gandhi's government for the Shah Bano Bill and its complicity, particularly with Muslim conservatives or its clergy class.

The Modi government has taken a proactive interest in this issue since the early days of its government that came into existence in 2014. It was able to pass the Bill eventually in 2019. Despite the apparent overlap of goals on the issue of Muslim women's emancipation by the Modi government and various stripes of secularists and feminists, the secularists and progressive liberal groups remain deeply intrigued by the Hindu Right's rather feminist spin on its majoritarian goals.

How could a Hindu Right government whose foundational ideology has been so anti-Muslim be a savior of Muslim women?

What does it imply for the future of India's Muslim women?

While the issue of gender equality among Indian Muslims has a longer history, an attempt to analyze the politics of the late 1980s, specifically the tenure of the Rajiv Gandhi government, would present valuable perspectives. It is the period when the Muslim Women (Protection of Rights on Divorce Act) 1986 (also known as the Shah Bano Bill) was passed. The Rajiv Gandhi government's decision to pass the Shah Bano Bill was viewed by secularists and feminists alike as an abject surrender to Muslim clergy and conservatives who sought to perpetuate Islamic patriarchy. For them, this was agonizing because Prime Minister Rajiv Gandhi was perceived to be a modern man. On the personal front, Mr Gandhi had an inter-religious marriage, and his wife Sonia Gandhi emerged as a dominant political player in the post-Rajiv era of Indian politics.[22] According to Mani Shakar Aiyer, a close confidant of the late Rajiv Gandhi, there are two reasons why Mr Gandhi chose to disregard the Court judgement. One was the overwhelming support for Muslim Personal Law among Muslim MPs barring Arif Mohammad Khan,[23] then in the Congress party, and Saifuddin Chowdhury of the CPI(M) and a meeting with young students of Aligarh Muslim University organized by Salman Khurshid[24] at his house.[25]

For the Hindu Right, the passage of the Shah Bano Bill was another sterling concession granted to the Muslim community, driven by vote bank politics. This Bill further legitimized the Hindu Right's age-old allegation that the Muslim community seeks to have separate laws for itself, thus showing unwillingness for its integration into India's mainstream. Various political and civil society groups representing the Hindu Right ideology have left no stone unturned to weaponize the Shah Bano Bill to make an ideological case against secularism and minority rights at every opportunity ever since.

The Shah Bano controversy that dominated Indian politics during the late 1980s has deep ramifications on the evolving ideological debate over secularism and the rights of Muslims in India.[26] According to Zoya Hasan, 'This one piece of legislation which allowed Muslim Personal Law to prevail in the reversal of court decision ruined his (Rajiv Gandhi's) reputation for modernity and progressiveness, and the move inflamed Hindu sentiments.'[27] The key protagonist was Shah Bano, a 62-year-old Muslim woman from Madhya Pradesh. She was divorced by her lawyer husband, Mohammed Ahmad Khan, in April 1978. Mr Khan had a law degree from Bahrain and was practicing in the Supreme Court and High Court. The two were married in 1932 and had five children. Because Shah Bano had no source of income of her own, she filed a claim for maintenance in Court under Section 123 of the Code of Criminal Procedure 1973 after her husband decided to give her divorce (talaq).[28] According to Indian law, a husband has a legal obligation to offer maintenance to his wife during the marriage and after, in case the woman cannot fend for herself. Mr Khan, however, challenged the claim by invoking the Muslim Personal Law (MPL) according to which the husband is obliged to pay only during the *iddat,*[29] (the period of waiting after the divorce that follows the dissolution of marriage) but not beyond.

The All-India Muslim Personal Law Board (AIMPLB), the most powerful entity committed to protecting Muslim personal law, stood by Shah Bano's husband, Mr Khan. The AIMPLB argued that the honourable Court would violate the Muslim Personal Law (Shariat) Application Act 1937 if its verdict favours alimony for Shah Bano after the *iddat* period. According to the Act, the AIMPLB argued that the court's decisions on matters of divorce, maintenance, and other family issues have to be based on Shariat. When the case finally moved to the Supreme Court, then Chief Justice YV Chandrachud passed an order in 1985. While upholding the Madhya Pradesh High Court's decision, which had instructed maintenance to Shah Bano to be given under CrPC 1973 as applicable to all Indian citizens regardless of their religion, India's Supreme Court further increased the maintenance sum as well.

In his decision, Justice YV Chandrachud noted, 'Section 125 was enacted to provide a quick and summary remedy to a class of persons who are unable to maintain themselves. What difference would it then make as to what the religion professed by the neglected wife, child or parent? Neglect by a person of sufficient means to maintain these and the inability of these persons to maintain themselves are the objective criteria that determine the applicability of section 125. Such provisions, which are essential of a prophylactic nature, cut across the barriers of religion. The liability imposed by section 125 to maintain close relatives who are indigent is founded upon the individual's obligation to society to prevent vagrancy and destitution. That is the moral edict of the law and morality cannot be clubbed with religion.'

According to the Muslim Women (Protection on Divorce Act) 1986 passed by the Rajiv Gandhi government, if a woman wasn't able to provide for herself, the magistrate had the power to direct the WAQF Board to provide the aggrieved woman's means of sustenance for her and her dependent children. Shah Bano's lawyer, Danial Latifi, had challenged the Act's constitutional validity.[30] The apex court, though upholding the validity of the new law, announced that the liability can't be restricted to the period of *iddat*. But the Shah Bano Act left Muslim women without the protection that women of other faiths had under Indian law.

Regardless of how we view the Bill, the fact remains, as Ruth Verma Williams writes, that the Rajiv Gandhi government intervention proved to be a critical inflection point in the definition of Muslim identity in India in ways that played into the hands of Hindu nationalism, and especially their political party, the Bhartiya Janata Party.[31] While secularists and feminists sought to change the Shah Bano Act so that Muslim women could enjoy equality of law like women of other religions, which the Modi government's Triple Talaq Bill (TTB), 2019, has restored, they continue to have doubts about Modi government's real intent. What has further provoked leaders of secular parties and activists of various stripes is the provision of criminalization of instant triple talaq in the Modi government's TTB. Any husband pronouncing triple talaq—whether spoken, written, or electronic—can be punished with a fine and three-year jail term as per the law. Furthermore, arrests can be made without a warrant, and bail is given only at the discretion of a magistrate. Also, the law applies retrospectively back to September 2018, meaning earlier transgressions can now be filed with the police.

The Narendra Modi government's law was framed two years after the Supreme Court's verdict that declared talaq-e-biddat unconstitutional in 2017.[32] The government enacted the law because it realized that the verdict would not make any difference without a law. According to Mukhtar Abbas Naqvi, the then Minister for Minority Affairs in the Modi government, there was an 82 per cent decline in triple talaq cases since the law was enacted.[33] Political leaders from the Opposition see the political foul play at work and they argue that the government's real objective has been to harass Muslim men and discipline the community.

The fact that the Bill was cleared in the third attempt demonstrates the Narendra Modi government's commitment to the Bill. During the first two attempts, the Bill was passed by the Lok Sabha but failed to pass in the Rajya Sabha. However, during the third attempt in the Lok Sabha, the Bill successfully passed with 302 members voting in favour and 78 members voting against it.[34] In the Rajya Sabha, the Bill was passed with 99 votes in favour and 84 against.[35] This victory in the Rajya Sabha was possible owing to cooperation offered by several secular parties. For instance, parties such as AIDMK, BSP, Janata Dal(U), and Telangana Rashtriya Samiti (TRS) were not present in the House, and the absentee in the NDA ranks was made up of the absentees from the Congress, SP, Telugu Desam Party (TDP), YSR Congress party (YSRCP), and Rashtriya Janata Dal (RJD) benches. According to the then Law Minister, Ravi Shankar Prasad, 200 cases were still reported after the Supreme Court declared talaq-e-biddat illegal.[36] Former Union Minister and a Congress leader, Shashi Tharoor, announced that he was not opposed to the Bill as such but was against a particular component of the bill which conflates civil and criminal laws. Describing it as a textbook example of class legislation, Mr Tharoor further argued that the Bill was discriminatory because it was directed towards the Muslim community. Since abandoning wives is not a practice unique to the Muslim community, Mr Tharoor called for a law universally applicable to all in the case of abandoning wives. Mr Asaduddin Owaisi,[37] President of the AIMIM, is a prominent Muslim voice in Indian politics today who articulated his dissent by pointing out the double standard in the Hindu Right ideology. According to Owaisi, the BJP, on the one hand, stands for equality between Muslim women and men, but has a different standard for Hindu women, apparent by its opposition to the rights of Hindu women to enter the Sabarimala temple in Kerala.[38] Citing a violation of Article 26, Mr Owaisi stated that women should have the right to leave a marriage as well. 'Will the husband give maintenance from jail?' he questioned. 'Why should the woman remain married to the husband who's in jail? The bill proposes a three-year jail term for husbands, which goes against the criminal jurisprudence. You put a condition that if a husband gives a woman a divorce, then the amount of meher will go to the woman. Marriage is a contract. This is not a "janam janam ka saath hai". This life is enough. Muslims are not homogenous in India,' added Owaisi.[39] He further highlighted shortcomings in the TTB as it stipulates a three-year jail term for guilty Muslim men while non-Muslim men get only one year of jail term for a similar offense.

The Modi government on its own added certain safeguards to the Bill such as adding a provision for bail for the accused during trial, which was approved by the Cabinet on 29 August 2018. While making Triple Talaq a non-bailable offense as per the Bill, an accused can approach a magistrate even before trial to seek bail. In a non-bailable offense, bail cannot be granted by the police at the police station itself. A provision was added to allow the magistrate to grant bail after hearing the wife. According to a newspaper report, many Muslim women expressed gratitude to Prime Minister Modi for the passage of the TTB in New Delhi organized at the residence of Vijay Goel as well as at the Delhi BJP office at Pant Marg, New Delhi.[40]

The Modi government has been taking credit for the bill. However, various secular organizations and individuals have contributed significantly to the campaign against the Shah Bano Bill since the late 1980s. In 2016-17, two Muslim women groups facilitated the abolition of talaq-e-biddat by acting as co-petitioners in the court case. One was Bebaak Collective, a prominent women's campaign alliance led by Hasina Khan.[41] The other was Bhartiya Muslim Mahila Andolan (BMMA)[42] set up in 2007, a grassroots organization of Muslim women. Both organizations demanded the abolition of talaq-e-biddat. In response to the court ruling that declared it illegal, the position of both the organizations concerning the new Women's Bill has been different.[43] Bebaak Collective criticized the bill saying that this law would make women vulnerable in other ways owing to its criminalization provisions. Thus the law is not pro-women but anti-minority. The Bebaak Collective cited several flaws in various drafts of the Bill. One of them was published in the *Leaftlet* on 8 March 2019.[44]

However, BMMA has been supportive of the law. Because the BMMA has been campaigning for the codification of Muslim Personal Law (MPL).[45] The Triple Talaq is a step forward in that direction. One of its founders, Zakia Soman,[46] explained in an interview about BMMA's position saying that all women-centric laws in India such as dowry or bigamy have jail terms. According to Soman, 'The purpose of any law is justice and not mere punishment to erring party. However, criminalization cannot be the reason to throw the baby out with the bath water.'[47] Therefore, criminalization provisions in the bill is good for implementation, according to her. Those who are critical of the criminalization component of the bill are concerned about men. 'Why are they so concerned for men? Especially those who did nothing for women,' she questions.[48] The BMMA sought to persuade Dr Manmohan Singh's government to initiate the codification of Muslim personal law, but their campaign was treated indifferently by the so-called secular leadership. Zakia Soman wrote to Prime Minister Modi to take steps to bring about the reform. The founders of BMMA did offer recommendations to the Modi government when it first came out with a draft for the bill and some of their recommendations were accepted. The BMMA leaders point out that talaq-e-biddat is criminalized in more than 20 Muslim-majority countries.

The BMMA leaders argue their position is based on their work at the grassroots level of offering legal guidance to victims. Since triple talaq was declared invalid, victims have approached the BMMA for help. Some husbands have continued the practice of Shariah laws regardless of the bill and vulnerable wives can hardly confront them. There are reports in the media about continued violation of the Court judgement.

On the Debate over India's Uniform Civil Code (UCC)

The position on whether India should have a Uniform Civil Code (UCC) by the Hindu Right and Muslim conservatives has been contested from the very beginning. But by unraveling various layers of this debate, we can make sense of how the debate over women, more specifically, Muslim women, took place since Independence. On the one hand, the Hindu Right has always been enthusiastic about the UCC and India's conservative Muslim clergy has been determined to oppose it. The latter has been deeply suspicious of the UCC because it believes it would undermine the MPL and run down community identity beyond recognition. Indeed, the institution of the AIMPLAB came into existence primarily to protect and preserve Muslim personal laws. A report in *India Today* shed light on the perspectives of the AIMPLB on the UCC. According to this report, 'All India Muslim Personal Law Board (AIMPLB) has termed it as unconstitutional and anti-minority. According to AIMPLB general secretary Hazrat Maulana Khalid Saifullah Rahmani, personal laws were made for minority groups as per their wishes under the fundamental rights in the Constitution and these must be continued. He said that this has helped to maintain unity and trust between majority and minority communities in the nation and has not caused any harm. Mohammad Suleman, the founding member of the All India Muslim Personal Law Board, alleged that the issue of the Uniform Civil Code had been brought up to divert attention from real issues and called the BJP government's policies divisive.'[49]

The clamour for the UCC has grown in recent years, particularly among the BJP leaders in various states such as Uttar Pradesh,[50] Madhya Pradesh, Uttarakhand, Assam, etc. The Uttarakhand government had set up an expert committee to draft the UCC, according to Pushkar Singh Dhami, the state's BJP chief.[51] A five-member panel headed by retired Supreme Court judge, Justice Ranjana Desai, has completed a draft report on the implementation in Uttarakhand.[52] If adopted, Uttarakhand will become the first Indian state to implement UCC. Goa also has UCC, but it was implemented during Portuguese rule.

During the deliberations in the Constituent Assembly—it was decided that India would have a UCC. While Article 44 of the Indian Constitution had the provision for a UCC, Articles 25 to 29 guaranteed religious freedom to communities.[53] While this was a constitutional position, the overall public perception was not consistent with what was promised in the Constitution. No serious initiative was taken to frame the UCC after India's independence, though there was a passage of the Hindu Code and later on laws for Parsis, Christians, and Muslims—the two other major religious communities were allowed to have their laws, and these laws on which personal laws were built had a pre-1947 history. They were constantly evolving but not necessarily in favour of women.

Even during colonial days, different laws were required for different religious communities in their personal and family affairs. However, by comparison with the laws applying to other communities, Muslim personal laws in India were never codified systematically. According to Noorjahan, one of the founders of a leading Muslim women's organization, BMMA, 'By 2037, it will be a century of depriving the Muslim community of a codified law. We have been getting bits and pieces—Dissolution of Muslim Marriages Act 1939; Shah Bano Muslim Women (Protection on Divorce Act) 1986; and now Triple Talaq. Hindus, Christians, Parsis, and all religions have had their personal laws codified. But each time we raise issues, we are told that the "time is not right" or "Why are you bringing in religion?" or "Why do you need separate laws?"; so, the Muslim woman should not raise her issues?'[54]

While MPL and its forerunner, Anglo Muhammadan Law, are sometimes talked about as a coherent body of law shaped by legal digests and case precedents, there is little in Muslim law that parallels the statutory acts that already determine the family laws of Hindu, Christians, and other citizens. Even the few direct legislative interventions into Muslim personal laws before and after 1947 have been more notable for what they omit rather than include. For example, the Shariat Application Act (SAA) of 1937, while confirming that Muslims were subject to Shariah Laws in their personal and family matters, specified almost nothing about the content of these stipulations nor about the legal bodies authorized to adjudicate them.

Even the Dissolution of the Muslim Marriages Act (DMMA) has only codified the nine grounds on which a woman can file for divorce, for example, a husband's absence, neglect, or cruelty. It is silent about issues arising from divorce, like post-divorce maintenance, meher (bridal dowry), marital property, or child custody; nor does it change anything about forms of male-initiated divorce. While discussions for government intervention in Muslim personal laws have been going on for decades, India's supposedly secular political class across the board has been exempting these laws from legislative interference (Agnes, 1995, Jones, 2020).

Unlike in India, the framing of full or partial family law codes has been the major legal trajectory elsewhere in various Muslim countries over the last century. Following the Ottoman Law of Family Rights (1917) which created an early template for a codified family law, several prominent Arab governments have successfully tried to codify Islamic laws soon after their independence in the 1950s. Personal status codes were created by the governments of the newly independent Jordan (1951), Syria (1953), Tunisia (1957), Morocco (1958), Iraq (1959), and many others. These codifications were meant to foster social stability, enhance national cohesion, and promote the state's modernizing agenda. The 1961 Family Laws Ordinance of Pakistan was inspired by laws enacted in Arab countries. After the creation of Bangladesh in 1971, this law was retained by Bangladesh.[55]

For instance, there was the Dissolution of Muslim Marriage Act of 1939 governing the divorce of Muslim women that has remained unchanged with no provision for custody of children or maintenance. In the case of the Christian community, there is the Indian Divorce Act promulgated by the British in 1869 which applied to foreigners and native Christians. Most feminists look at it mainly as anti-women. Its objective was to facilitate the smooth functioning of the colonial regime. Currently, it is applied to Indian Christians, referred to as Native Christians in the Act. Under Section 10 of the Act, while a man can get a divorce on the grounds of adultery, a Christian woman has to prove an additional ground such as cruelty or desertion. There were women's organizations including Christian women's organizations that have been campaigning for change. Unfortunately, there is no response.

Generally speaking, though favourable change has occurred in the global and domestic conditions, no significant effort was made in India to pursue the UCC. There is at present a conducive ambience for the codification owing to many factors such as 1) models of codified law in the wider Islamic world; 2) codification of the Hindu family law; 3) weight of significant support from the Muslim community, etc.

According to Justin Jones,[56] some of the reasons why no effort was made for legislative interventions are as follows: Firstly, the Constituent Assembly first turned its attention to Hindu religious personal laws owing to the assumption that regulating the family unit of the majority community was the priority for the postcolonial projects of nation-building and socio-economic regulation.

Secondly, political need for community accommodation after Partition called for a strong emphasis upon the language of minorities, including their distinct personal laws, rather than upon more assimilationist forms of civil integration.

Thirdly, there remained an impression among lawmakers—inherited from the colonial era—that Muslims were attached to their religious personal laws and unwilling to accept any government interference in community regulations.

Fourthly, the acrimony surrounding the Hindu Code Bill debates in the early 1950s, in which Hindu community, caste, and women groups clashed heavily on many issues instilled fatigue among politicians and diminished their willingness to follow the codification of Hindu personal laws with a similar effort for Muslim ones.

While all these factors that Justin Jones has laid out are valid, in my view the key problem lies in the way India's secular politics and its minority politics evolved—particularly the inability of Nehruvian secular politics to give space or voice to Muslim liberals to lead the

Muslim community. Invariably, it is the clergy and conservatives who were seen as the representatives of Indian Muslims, and their opposition to MPL is interpreted by secular regimes as the opposition of the community as well. Rajiv Gandhi's conduct during the Shah Bano controversy is a classic case of how Muslim liberals were let down by an otherwise modern man who was blinded by what the BJP called 'vote bank politics'.

Why Uniform Civil Code?

Part of the reason is: the Hindu Right believes that Muslims are enjoying undue advantage by acquiring separate legal space in the name of MPL in a Hindu-majority country. With the passage of the Hindu Code Bill, the Hindu Right also believes the gender issue has been resolved for Hindus. A thoughtful analysis of reasons and their contexts on this issue is provided by Farrah Ahmed in her book, *Religious Freedom Under Personal Law System.*[57] Among others, a few reasons why this has been pursued with such determination for so long are: a) to correct gender-based problems; b) to end religious communalism; c) to bring about national unity. It needs to be recalled here that the BJP in its vision document (2004) notes, 'The BJP views the Uniform Civil Code (UCC) primarily as an instrument to promote gender justice.'[58] Though the BJP did say in this vision document to generate a social and political consensus before the enactment of the UCC in India.

This issue, addressing the need and merit of India aspiring to have a UCC, has attracted considerable attention among scholars with no connection to Hindu Right politics. Noted scholar Marc Gallanter has thoughtful arguments on this issue. Mr Gallanter articulates his view while engaging with DE Smith who was convinced that India must have a UCC.[59] While evaluating various arguments for the UCC, particularly, 'national integration and modernization of state,' Gallanter presents his argument as follows, 'Presumably national integration does not justify or require the obliteration of all differences. But if diversity of beliefs is a good thing, deserving of protection, why not a diversity of marriage laws based on these beliefs?'[60] In my view, while these debates are interesting, the key question is whether women's right to equality and dignity is preserved by such processes. Therefore, the argument about whether the diversity of laws regarding marriage should be welcomed or not should be determined by the fact that whether such laws grant the equality that women deserve. In other words, neither diversity nor uniformity should be glorified as such and their relevance needs to be judged by their contribution to women's equality.

As stated earlier, the reason why the Hindu Right seems so committed to the UCC is because it believes this issue has been sorted for Hindus with the passage of the Hindu Code Bill. So, why not for Muslims? According to the noted lawyer and feminist, Flavia Agnes,[61] there were several loopholes in the Hindu Code Bill, and none of these anti-women biases in the Hindu code received publicity, and remained hidden in statute books and legal manuals. The women's movement did not rally around litigations challenging these anti-women biases in its campaign for a uniform secular code. Consequently, the movement contributed to the fiction by the Hindu fundamentalists that the Hindu code is a perfect family code. And that it should be extended to other religious communities to 'liberate' women. The women's movement could not thus allay the fears of Muslim women or women of other minorities that the Hindu code would be imposed upon them in the name of the UCC.

Some of the sexist biases that Agnes has pointed out are as follows: 1) The Hinduization of the Special Marriage Act is an example, which happened during the changes made to the Special Marriage Act of 1954. According to this ammendment, if two Hindus are married under the Special Marriage Act then the secular code which granted equal rights to men and women—the Indian Succession Act of 1925—would not apply to them. And parties would continue to be governed by the Hindu Succession Act which ensured male coparcenary rights.

2) This amendment was both anti-women and anti-minority. It

sought to protect the property interests of a Hindu man who married any woman within the broad Hindu fold, by not depriving him of his coparcenary rights. Since the concept of coparcenary (through which a male at birth becomes a partner in the ancestral property; a woman can never be a coparcener) per se is anti-women, this ammendment was de facto against women's rights. It further served as a deterrent for a Hindu male wishing to marry a woman from the minority religious communities because then he could be penalized and made to forfeit his rights to ancestral property.

3) The procedure of solemnizing Hindu marriages remained Brahminical. At another level, the code validated customary rituals and ceremonies. It permitted non-registration of marriages, which gave the man the right to practice polygamy as he enjoyed the freedom to declare which of his marriages was a real marriage where rituals were performed. When the man refuses to validate a marriage, the woman loses her right to maintenance. Additionally, she has to face humiliation and social stigma as a mistress. In criminal proceedings for bigamy under Section 494 of the Indian Penal Code (IPC), years of litigation fail to end in a conviction for the errant man because courts have adopted a rigid view that only *saptapadi* and *vivahnama* are valid marriage ceremonies. If in the second marriage it cannot be established that these ceremonies have taken place, the Courts will hold the second marriage to be invalid even if the couple has been living as husband and wife and the community has accepted the marriage.

4) The constitution of coparcenary concepts within the Hindu Succession Act denied equal property rights, and also, the right to the ancestral home and property to women. Daughters had equal rights only in the self-earned property of their fathers. This provision made it easy for men to turn their self-earned property into joint property rights. It is widely known that Hindu revivalists were opposed to the idea of property rights for women. Some states such as Tamil Nadu, Andhra Pradesh, and Karnataka have amended their laws to address discrimination against women, but this has not been the case across India.

5) According to the Hindu Adoption and Maintenance Act, a Hindu wife can neither adopt nor give up her child in adoption. The father remains the natural guardian of the child (under the Hindu Guardianship and Adoption Act). Based on the strong desire to control women's sexuality, the law continued its distinction between legitimate and illegitimate children. It made mothers natural guardians of illegitimate children, absolving the fathers of any moral responsibility towards the child.

On the Politics of Muslim Personal Law (MPL)

Several institutions have contributed to the discourses over the politics of personal law as well as politics of the UCC in India. In the post-Shah Bano period, there has been a significant rise of women's organizations that have taken a position on gender equity despite variations in their ideologies. Regardless of varied ideologies, they were able to create a positive environment that has generated sensitivity towards Muslim women's causes.[62] To a great extent, Prime Minister Modi's attempt to push the TTB profited from the positive environment that such campaigns by these organizations had already created since the days of the Shah Bano Bill, much before the arrival of Narendra Modi as India's Prime Minister in 2014.

Barring the women's rights organizations, the most powerful institutional player in this domain is the AIMPLB. It is identical to a pressure group. Though it has a large network of ulemas, it has no formal authority to determine rulings on the implementation of MPL. But it has the potential to mobilize for its cause, which it did during the Shah Bano case—and also later, though not as successfully as it did during the Rajiv Gandhi period. The Hindu Right power structure chose to ignore it.

The Board gained tremendous national importance when it decided to oppose the Supreme Court verdict declaring it as against MPL in 1985-1986. It pressurised the Rajiv Gandhi government to pass the Shah Bano Bill that overturned the Court verdict. In addition, the Board was critical of family planning laws or what was known as a sterilisation program during the Emergency[63] that caused massive alienation of Muslim voters from the Congress party. It has further played a prominent role in fighting the case for Babri Masjid, though it was eventually lost, and the verdict is widely criticized.[64] The role of the AIMPLB was not limited just to working for the preservation of MPL but participating in many other issues that concern Muslims.[65]

The AIMPLB was set up in 1973 at the initiative of Muhammad Taiyab, who was then serving as Muhtamim of the Deoband madarsa. When HR Gokhale as India's Home Minister tabled an Adoption Bill in Parliament which was not consistent with Muslim religious laws on guardianship, it raised fear among Muslim clergies. They looked at it as a precursor to the UCC. A small meeting took place in Deoband followed by a larger congregation in Mumbai on 27-28 December 1972, giving birth to the AIMPLB in Hyderabad four months later. The fear of the UCC, and in the process, the preservation of MPL was the founding reason for the AIMPLB.

According to the website,[66] the Board's objectives are:

1. To take effective steps to protect the Muslim Personal Law in India and for the retention, and implementation of the Shariat Act;
2. To strive for the annulment of all such Laws, passed by or on the anvil in any State Legislature or Parliament, and such judgments by courts of Law which may directly or indirectly amount to interference in or run parallel to the Muslim Personal Law or, in the alternative, to see that the Muslims are exempted from the ambit of such legislations;
3. To promote awareness among Muslims about the Laws and teachings of, and rights conferred and duties cast by *Shariah* in the sphere of their family and social life, and to publish and disseminate literature for that purpose;
4. To publish and popularize the personal Laws of Muslims as laid down by Shariah and to prepare a comprehensive framework for their implementation on and observance by the Muslims;

5. To set up an 'Action Committee' as and when needed, for safeguarding the Muslim Personal Law through which organized countrywide campaign is taken up in order to implement decisions of the Board;
6. To promote good-will, fraternity, and the feeling of mutual co-operation among all sects and schools of thought among Muslims, and to generate the spirit of unity and co-ordination among them for the common goal of safeguarding the Muslim Personal Law;
7. To scrutinise the 'Mohammedan Law' as now in force in India, in the light of *Shariah,* and to arrange for an analytical study of the different schools of Islamic jurisprudence while keeping in view the new issues and to search for their proper solution based on the Quran and *Sunnah,* sticking to the principles of *Shariah* under the guidance of those well-versed in Shariah and Islamic jurisprudence;
8. To set up delegations and study teams; organize conferences, seminars, symposia, public meetings and undertake tours and to publish and disseminate suitable literature, as and when needed, to bring out newspapers, periodicals, and newsletters and to perform all other acts as may be necessary, for achieving the aims and objectives of the Board in general.

In recent years, the Board has published tracts and booklets on several issues, mainly in Urdu. These are mostly literature meant to advise Muslims on a wide range of family-related issues such as marriage, divorce, the preparation of wills, or procedures of inheritance. It also has material meant to enlighten local ulemas, imams, and muftis issuing standardised Friday Khutba (sermons).

Clearly, the Board has been committed to the role and rights of women in which it has attempted to regulate Muslim women's behaviour, determining their duties, and advising on their marital, financial, or custodial rights. There have been, however, some shifts in recent years. This is partly owing to the pressure it felt due to the public debate on Shah Bano's issue. While working on the preservation of MPL it could not deny the need for reform within the community on gender issues, which led to some effort towards codification. To address the allegation against the board that was a male body, it opened up membership for women.

The Board has attempted partial codification of the MPL in India. In 1989 a council affiliated with the AIMPLB known as the Fiqui Academy was founded by Mujahid-al-Islam Qasimi. He became its President. The academy mainly worked on marriage and divorce laws. This led to the preparation of a standardized *nikahnama* (contract of marriage) by the AIMPLB in 1999-2000. The most effective outcome of the codification project was the publication of a large volume, *Mammu a Qawanen I Islami* (A Compendium of Islamic Laws). This is based on the sources from the legal works of Abdul Hari Firangi Mahali, Ashraf Ali Thanawai, and Aziz Ur Rehman. According to Justin Jones, its purpose is to assist people dealing with the law and influence decision-making in various bodies such as offices of qazis, Shariat courts, local panchayats, and baradari. These are the individuals and institutions that deal with a large number of marriage-related cases or issues.

While the passage of the Shah Bano Bill did indicate the victory of the AIMPLB and Muslim conservatives, there were parallel efforts by various Muslim organizations to challenge this in the hope of altering this course of history and to force the Indian state to concede on the issue of gender equality to Muslim women. In 2000, the AIMPLB was expanded and places reserved for women was increased, but women only represented 12 per cent of its membership. Even if they voted as a block, they could not influence the outcome or promote the women's cause. Most of these women, some argue, go by what their male partners advise, thus serving as agents of Islamic patriarchy. Some of them, according to Sylvia Vatuk,[67] had taken strong pro-women positions, but they were of little consequence in the end. This line of criticism led to the setting up a parallel organization called All India Muslim Women's Personal Board (AIMWPB).

In March 2005 the AIMWPLB was established. In the first

meeting, there were 35 women. They represented major sects and schools of Islamic jurisprudence, including a few Hindus. At the end of February 2005 they called for a Mahila Adalat (women's court) in which 166 cases of unilateral divorce and atrocities related to dowry were registered. The AIMPLB, as expected, questioned the women's scholarly credentials, and raised concerns over their political motives. These women were devout Muslims. Many were willing to be governed entirely by Muslim law in the domain of family related issues. But they were not willing to embrace what was told to them by the AIMPLB or any other male clerical organization what the law consists of according to Islam. They claimed that over the centuries Islamic laws had been subjected to patriarchal interpretations, which had resulted in the denial of the women-friendly rights given to them originally by the Holy Quran.

While we witnessed the changing roles of the AIMPLB, becoming more and more sensitive towards the role of women, they are still seen as a patriarchal body. On the other hand, the political environment in India has been transformed with the rise of various Muslim women-led civil society groups. Many of them often seek to address women's issues within the framework of Islam.

In India, there are many Muslim women's organizations that have been asking for reform in MPL—justifying their demands for gender equity with religious arguments. They are alluding to the arguments in the Quran instead of reasonings of the Indian Constitution or universal human rights. In the Middle East, similar Muslim women's movements have gathered momentum since the 1990s, particularly in countries such as Egypt and Iran, under the banner of Islamic feminism. With this, the women are seeking to reclaim their Islam 'through a re-reading of the Quran and early Islamic history' which has been subjected to both Islamist patriarchal distortions and Western stereotypes of Islam as backward.[68]

In India, unlike in the Middle East, Muslim women do not face an authoritarian Islamic state. Until recently, they faced a male religious establishment, and are interested in using Quranic sources to bring changes from within. Islamic feminist movements in India are small in number and are not very organized. They are usually simply groups and individuals—mainly operating as non-governmental organizations (NGOs) with small staffs in cities such as Lucknow, Hyderabad, Calicut, etc. There are also women's wings of organizations like the Tablighi Jama'at (TJ) or Jamat-at-I Islami Hind (JIH).

Muslim women's rights activists assert they are to read the Quran for themselves and present women-friendly interpretations. In thus insisting on going back to the foundational Islamic texts for guidance, they are reclaiming the right to *ijtihad*. These women point out that the MPL was created during the colonial period and reject the notion that the MPL was divinely given.

As stated earlier, several organizations have come up and they do have varied perspectives and ways of operation to advance their ways of understanding of Muslim women's rights. One of the oldest and largest Muslim-led women's NGO is the Mumbai-based Awaaz-e-Niswaan (AeN), founded in 1987.[69] Several other Muslim women's networks operating in these areas are the Muslim Women Forum (MWF) in Delhi and the Federation of Muslim Women of Bangalore (FEMWOB). All India Muslim Women's Rights Network (MWRN) is the longest and most successful network. It was started in 1999 in Mumbai by leaders from Women's Research and Action (WRAG) and AeN. These organizations are trying to develop a dialogue on women's issues among themselves.[70]

Among the prominent organizations that have played a key role in championing Muslim women's issues in recent years is BMMA that was set up in 2007. In 2014, the BMMA[71] published the Muslim Family Law Act, which is an attempt to codify MPL as has been the case with many Muslim countries such as Morocco, Tunisia, Turkey, Egypt, Jordan, Bangladesh, Pakistan, etc. In 2015, the BMMA conducted a national survey on the question of codification of family law in which it claimed that close to 83 per cent of women respondents believed that codification would help to protect women's rights.

In 2016, the BMMA's conveners filed a public interest litigation (PIL) application to the Supreme Court seeking abolition of talaq-e-biddat.[72] This led to the Supreme Court passing the judgement in 2017, and making the practice unconstitutional and legally invalid. The BMMA supported the government's attempts to legislate upon the court's decision. A bill on this issue was passed in July 2019, also called the TTB. As a result, the Muslim Women (Protection of Rights on Marriage) Bill has finally been enacted, rendering talaq-e-biddat both legally invalid and a criminal offence.[73]

Politics of the Hijab Debate in India

The 2021-2022 hijab controversy that unfolded in Karnataka presents another opportunity to examine the Hindu Right approach towards Muslim women issues. At the global level, this debate has been going on for quite some time. In 2010, French President Nicolas Sarkozy ordered the French government to prepare legislation paving the way for a complete ban on the full Islamic veil. In 2016, British Prime Minister David Cameron said that he would back institutions with 'sensible rules' over Muslims wearing full-face veils. This provoked journalist Mariam Khan to publish a volume, *It's Not About the Burqa* (2019), in which several prominent women voices from various walks of life articulated their challenges and relationship with Islam, the West, and their societies.[74] In 2019, British Prime Minister Boris Johnson received severe criticism for the use of Islamophobic language against Muslim women who wear burqas. On the other side, there have been massive protests by Muslim women against Iranian state policy, which enforces the hijab.[75] As Leila Ahmed notes, such practices of Islam concerning women became a crucial part of Western narratives of Otherness as well as the 'inferiority of Islam.'[76] The global debate is influenced by four interrelated questions: Should Muslim women have the right to exercise their choice to wear the hijab/veil? What is the provision in Islam on gender freedom? Should the state have the authority to make a law for them? In case of a clash between state policy and Islamic provisions, which should prevail?

In the post-Shah Bano and post-Triple Talaq era in India, the hijab debate has become the most prominent national debate over the other issues of Muslim women and their rights. The Karnataka High Court has passed the verdict that the hijab is not an essential part of religion. A three-member bench of Karnataka High Court led by Chief Justice Ritu Raj Awasthi observed that, 'We are of the considered opinion that wearing of hijab by Muslim women does not form a part of essential religious practice in the Islamic faith.' The Court upheld the 5 February 2022 Basavraj Bommai government order which banned 'clothes that were against law and order' and said it did not violate constitutional provisions. When the matter reached the Supreme Court, the Court gave a split verdict in October 2022. In this two-judge bench, Justice Hemant Gupta said that the Karnataka government is empowered to enforce the uniform mandate. But Justice Sudhansu Dhulia said wearing a hijab should be a matter of choice for a Muslim girl and there cannot be any restriction against it.[77]

Scholarly debate that was triggered by this controversy interpreted the court's decisions in varied ways. According to noted legal theorist, Upendra Baxi, 'The entire future of the Indian judicial process is being put at stake in the "Faith vs Constitution" controversy. The primary task of constitutional politics is to transmute a partisan controversy into a reasoned public debate. Allegations of "judicial overreach" greet any adjudicative "reasonable accommodation", especially when it engages the constitutional right to education under Article 21-A.'[78]

Baxi further argued that the Karnataka High Court (KHC) advanced the doctrine of 'qualified public space' in the hijab case which is not usually witnessed in the critical discourse engaging with the essential practice of religion or the rights to dignity, culture, and privacy. The Karnataka High Court allows wearing hijab on the school campus or other public spaces while disallowing hijab in classrooms. This judicial feat, however, according to Baxi, is marred by disallowing even a 'hijab of structure and colour that suit the prescribed dress code.' The KHC is determined to prevent 'non-uniformity in the matter of uniforms' and an undesirable sense of 'social separateness'.

Several other scholars have commented on this verdict as well as controversy which forms part of my discussion here. Indian Muslim women have been wearing hijab or burqa for ages but the timing of the controversy only confirms the aggressive posture of Hindu majoritarianism. The changed political conditions shaped by Hindutva politics have not only triggered this debate but have altered its tone and tenor.

The Karnataka Hijab controversy began in the Government Pre-University College for Girls in Udupi town where students were not allowed to attend classes wearing hijab. It passed a guideline on 1 July 2021 prescribing a uniform code. On 28 December 2021, six students reported that since September they were not allowed to attend classes citing hijabs. A student protest followed on 31 December 2021. The college prevented hijab-wearing students from attending classes for 15 days before the protest. The students filed a writ petition in the Karnataka High Court. They also approached the National Human Rights Commission (NHRC). This development took a political turn. A group of boys at the Government Pre-University College in Kundapur went to college wearing saffron shawls representing Hindutva ideology in protest against the Muslim girls wearing hijab. Both hijab-wearing girls and saffron-wearing boys were barred from the college. Another twist took place when some students from the IDSG Government First Grade College arrived wearing blue shawls chanting Jai Bhim slogans and supported the decision of Muslim girls to wear hijab. The Jai Bhim slogans and blue shawls were reflective of Ambedkarite ideology.

These developments led to protests accompanied by violence and stone-pelting in various parts of Karnataka, and outside. There were law and order issues in many areas in Karnataka including Udupi, Bengaluru, Shivamogga, and Dakshina Kannada etc. And schools and colleges were shut down.

According to the then Primary and Secondary Education Minister of Karnataka, BC Nagesh, rules framed under the Karnataka

Educational Act 2013 and 2018 empowered educational institutions to frame policies regarding uniforms in schools and pre-university colleges. Though uniform is not mandatory in colleges, college development committees headed by local MLAs were insisting on banning the hijab. In Karnataka, most of these development committees are headed by MLAs affiliated with the BJP or Hindutva ideology. The political leadership associated with Hindutva ideology is opposed to the hijab, which is otherwise allowed despite uniform rules in various colleges until the controversy erupted.

The Karnataka High Court verdict received mixed responses from politicians of various ideological spectrums. As expected, Prahlad Joshi, Union Minister of the Parliamentary Affairs ministry under the Narendra Modi government, welcomed the verdict, 'I appeal to everyone that the state and country have to go forward... everyone has to maintain peace by accepting the order. The basic work of students is to study. So leaving all this aside they should study and be united.'[79] On the other hand, Mehbooba Mufti and Omar Abdullah, both former Chief Ministers of Jammu and Kashmir expressed deep disappointment over verdict.[80] 'On one hand, we talk about empowering women yet we are denying them the right to a simple choice. It isn't just about religion but the freedom to choose,' Mufti tweeted.

Commenting on the Karnataka High Court judgement, noted legal scholar Faizan Mustafa,[81] wrote that in declaring hijab not an essential religious practice of Islam, the judges did not refer whatsoever to the acceptance of the review of the Sabarimala judgement (2018) and framing of seven questions by the seven-judge bench of the Supreme Court. The Sabarimala review (2020) clearly shows that the Supreme Court itself is in doubt about the correctness of the essentiality doctrine. It further raises questions if the courts should assume the role of the clergy. The most crucial point that Mustafa highlights is his discussion of the Supreme Court verdict on Shirur Mutt's (1954) case. In this case, the Supreme Court held that the term 'religion' in Article 25 covers all rituals and practices that are 'integral' to religion. In this manner, the judiciary took it upon itself to determine what is integral—and what is not—to religion. According to Mustafa, in doing so, it implicitly rejected the 'assertion test' of the United States, 'whereby a [plaintiff] could just assert that a particular practice was a religious practice' and courts would not probe it any further. Furthermore, it should be seen in the context of a Supreme Court verdict in Gandhi vs. the State of Bombay (1954), where the Court said that no outside authority has any right to say that these are the essential parts of religion. Therefore, it is not open to the secular authority of the state to restrict or prohibit them in any manner they like. According to the Karnataka High Court judgement, the hijab is not an essential Islamic practice because there is no punishment for not having a hijab. Interestingly, adultery and homosexuality are to be considered haram (prohibited) as there are severe punishments for them under Islam. The verdict, according to Mustafa, is a setback to the liberty model of administration as it says fundamental rights have relative content, and their efficacy hinges upon the circumstances in which they are sought to be exercised.

Other scholars—particularly women scholars and feminists—have their spin on the controversy as well as the verdict. According to Sonalde Desai, a scholar at the University of Maryland, USA,[82] 'Education serves as the most indispensable resource for women to take on gender-related oppression. In any religious community whether Muslims or Hindus, data suggests that education contributes to the reduction of practice of purdah or ghunghat.' She further adds that about 67 per cent of women with less than a Class V education practice ghunghat or purdah compared to 38 per cent of college-educated women. Asking for the removal of hijab to obtain an education, according to her, is like putting the cart before the horse. In secondary education, based on the National Statistical Office estimation, gross attendance ratio for Muslim women is 43 per cent whereas it is 63 per cent for all Indian women. Her analysis seems to be in line with Judge Dhulia's argument that if the choice for Muslim girls to wear hijab was not given then it would stand in her way of education. Professor Desai is pursuing the same line of reasoning. She argues that the institutional rules in colleges should be doing all it can to encourage participation among Muslim girls rather than placing obstacles.

There are other areas where data shows disparity between Hindu and Muslim students. For instance, the data from the India Human Development Survey (IHUD), conducted by the National Council of Applied Economic Research (NCEAR) and the University of Maryland, USA, demonstrates significant inequalities in learning outcomes among various social groups. It was found that while 68 per cent of upper-caste children aged 8-11 can read a short paragraph, the proportion is barely 47 per cent for Muslim children. These inequalities are likely to aggravate by not allowing Muslim girls to wear hijab and will lead them to staying away from schools or colleges. For the Hindu Right political leadership, uniform seems to be an ultimate priority and if this leads girls staying away from higher education so be it.

Other women scholars have a different take on the subject. I will discuss very interesting perspectives from the writings of Ambreen Agha and Zakia Soman. According to Ambreen Agha,[83] if the state policy shows prejudice against hijab-wearing girls, it will perpetuate historical disadvantage against them resulting in the community's disempowerment. Viewing of the hijab as a sign of increasing Arabization and an instrument of oppression is a disregard for alternative Muslim history. To view the practice of veiling with prejudice, she further argues, is nothing short of robbing the faith of its alternative histories and an expression of Islamophobia. The women's rights movement, with and without the hijab, is a legitimate part of the larger political struggle for dignity and integrity in both contemporary Muslim majority and non-Muslim majority societies, like India. According to Zakia Soman[84] all girls must be in school, with or without hijab. The main focus of society as well as the state should be on enabling greater access to girls' education including higher education.

The veil debate is not limited to India. Within India, it is confined to Karnataka for the time being. But there is a Western dimension to it, which precedes the Karnataka story. Nilüfer Göle's writing on this subject in the wider context of the Western debate is reflected in the following words: 'In other terms, we have to adjust our perception of the veil and women who wear it and who seek, not without peril, to transform its symbolic meaning. If the recognition of the personal and bodily aspect of the veil is the problem, that is because it presupposes at least in the context of political pluralism, of the existence of a feminine agency, of the personal decisions made by women.'[85] She further adds, 'Every debate on the veil encounters this blind spot: every criticism of the veil is based on a denial of the Muslim woman's agency and consequently on the denunciation of the Muslim man, masculine entourage, Islamic governments, or community pressures.'[86] She elaborates on this and argues that it represents a double subjection of women, by religion as well as masculine power. This criticism, though correct, is incomplete. There is a considerable resonance in this interpretation of the Karnataka controversy.

Conclusion

With the increasing domination of the BJP and fast expansion of various Hindu Right organizations into various regions of India, one wonders how these developments would shape the destiny of Muslim women. There is little hope of any positive change towards Muslim women. There are loud claims that the TTB has shaken up Islamic patriarchy, emancipated Muslim women, and made them ever-loyal to Prime Minister Narendra Modi and the BJP. If there is sincerity in the intent behind the bill pertaining to Muslim women, then the Hindu Right regimes and organizations should have continued with further interventions in society to make Muslim women safe, which sadly is not the case. As Nazima Parveen puts it, 'In this media driven popular discourse, the existence of Muslim women as agency—a decisive and informed decision maker—is completely missing. For Muslim women, this condition has created a dilemma to either be morally and politically obliged to assert her Muslim identity and reject the law in total or to rejoice it while bearing the blame for destruction of families and fall into the perceived trap against Muslims in India.'[87]

Also, no robust empirical evidence exists to support that Muslim women have emerged as a distinct social base for Mr Modi and the BJP. It is naïve to argue that Muslim women are a sociological or religious group entirely detached from the Muslim community and their political behaviour could be independent of violence or discrimination against the Muslim community generally. Muslim women are rooted in the family structure and have multiple roles like mother, sister, wife, etc. So, without Muslim women, there is no Muslim community. Their views about politics, governance, and community are also shaped by close sociological interaction with male counterparts who could be a father, a brother, a son, a husband, or a mentor. On the hijab controversy, the Hindu Right outlook became more apparent.

There are further developments such as bulldozer justice, love jihad, cow vigilantism, lynchings, so on and so forth—and they have cumulatively contributed to the rising tide of Islamophobia in the country. Enough empirical evidence exists to indicate the dramatic growth of Islamophobia that has encouraged Muslim women to look at the Hindu Right more as a lingering threat to their safety and security. There are further trends to indicate that the overall majoritarian outlook is based on an anti-minority/anti-Muslim ideology, creating a climate of fear and hate at various levels of polity. Muslim women are as vulnerable as Muslim men, and the idea that some Muslim women would in their appreciation of the Triple Talaq Bill disregard violence unleashed on their male members or Muslim community only reflects how poor the understanding of attitude formation in a society is. What has been intriguing about the debate is that there is no effort or appreciation for academic debate over these issues. For instance, Fatima Mernissi informs that the veil originated in Islam 'not to put a barrier between a man and woman, but between two men.'[88] As Azizah Y Al-Hibri puts it, 'Why is it oppressive to wear a head scarf but liberating to wear a miniskirt? The crux of the explanation lies in the assumptions each side makes about the women involved and their ability to make choices.'[89]

At no point it is suggested here that there are no issues or challenges with Muslim women in society. By all accounts, India is a patriarchal society, and Muslim women, like other women, face multidimensional challenges concerning dignity and equality quite regularly. Gail Minault writes, even in the past reformers such as Sayyid Ahmad Khan of Aligarh (1817-98), Maulana Ashraf Ali Thanavi of Deoband (1864-1943), Sayiid Mumtaz Ali of Lahore (1860-1935) recognized the need for improvement of the status of Muslim women.[90] Some of their views might not live up to modern feminist standards and might have some patriarchal elements. But the Hindu Right's concerns are not driven by modern feminist standards either and it contains its brand of Islamophobic elements.

The Hindutva movement, which shapes various strands of Islamophobia, is an ideological movement, and it invents its own facts and forecloses any further conversation on the subject. In a nutshell, Muslim women today stand at a crossroads like other religious minorities in India. They are fearful and vulnerable. Well-established studies have shown that in any form of societal or state violence, it is the women who are its worst victims. The evolving majoritarian polity presents a similar threat to Muslim women—and consequently they are more vulnerable to violence and discrimination than ever before. In a widely read work, Jacquline Rose has pointed out a particular nature of violence, which is, violence as a form of entitlement.[91] This is the most dangerous part of the evolution of Hindu majoritarian politics today, of which Muslim women might be its direct and most immediate victims.With interventions like the TTB, the Hindu Right may claim that it is liberating Muslim women from Islamic patriarchy, but in reality, it is reconfiguring patriarchy.[92] By the overall violence, the majoritarian polity results in creating fresh intricate layers of fear and insecurity in homes, neighbourhoods, and society in general and patriarchy thus finds a new lease of life.

Notes

1 Rajiv Gandhi served as India's Prime Minister from 1984-1989. Mr Gandhi reluctantly entered politics in 1980 after his younger brother Sanjay Gandhi died in a plane crash in New Delhi. He was assassinated on 21 May 1991 by a Liberation Tigers of Tamil Eelam (LTTE) suicide bomber in Sripurumbudur, Tamil Nadu, at the age of 46.

2 Ahmed, Leila. 2021 (first published in 1992). *Women and Gender in Islam: Historical Roots of a Modern Debate.* New Haven: Yale University Press. P. 151. For a better understanding of how colonialism survived and consolidated as well as its various implications also see, Elkins, Caroline. 2022. *Legacy of Violence: A History of British Empire.* London: Penguin Random House. Wilson, Jon. 2017. *India Conquered.* New Delhi: Simon and Schuster. Chandra, Bipan. 1981. *Nationalism and Colonialism in Modern India.* New Delhi: Orient Blackswan. Tharoor, Shashi. 2016. *An Era of Darkness: The British Empire in India.* New Delhi: Aleph Book Company.

3 See the report, Pandey, Manish Chandra. 2023. 'Women's Reservation: Over One Lakh Muslim Women from Uttar Pradesh to Send Thank you letters to Modi'. Available at http://www.hindustantimes.com (accessed on 10 November 2023).

4 Sabarwal, Harshit. 2022. 'Karnataka Hijab Row: The Controversy Explained.' Available at: http://www.thehindustantimes.com (accessed on 26 July 2022).

5 Phukan, Sandeep. 2023. 'Lok Sabha Passes Historic Women's Reservation Bill. Available at http://www. thehindu.com (accessed on 10 November 2023). For a detailed study of women in the Indian Parliament, see Rai, Shirin and Spary, Carole. 2018. *Performing Representation: Women Members in Indian Parliament.* New Delhi: Oxford University Press.

6 See, 'Women's rights under threat in Taliban run Afghanistan.' Available at: www.chathamhouse.org. 10 June 2022 (accessed on 26 July 2022).

7 See, Limaye, Yogita. 2023. 'Five Key Moments in Crushing of Afghan women's rights.' Available at http://www.bbc.com. (accessed on 10 December 2023).

8 Lughod, Lila Abu. 2015. *Do Muslim Women Need Saving?* Cambridge: Harvard University Press.

9 See, Ernst, Carl W. 2004. *Rethinking Islam in the Contemporary World.* Edinburg: Edinburgh University Press. P. 27.

10 See, 'The Muslim and The Time' in Mernissi, Fatima. 2004 (first published in 1987). *Women and Islam: An Historical and Theological Enquiry.* New Delhi: Women Unlimited. Pp. 15-24.

11 Wadud, Amina. 1999. *Quran and Woman: Rereading the Sacred Text from a Woman's Perspective.* New York: Oxford University Press. P. 62.

12 Ibid. P. 63.

13 Gule, Nilufer. 2011. *The Lure of Fundamentalism and the Allure of Cosmopolitism.* Princeton: Markus Wiener Publishers.

14 The Shah Bano case inspired considerable scholarship from various disciplines. A few important publications are Engineer, Asghar Ali. 1987. *The Shah Bano Controversy.* New Delhi: Sangam Books; for a better understanding of the Shah Bano case and its implications for secularism, see Baxi, Upendra. 2007. 'Sitting Secularism in a Uniform Civil Code: A Riddle Wrapped Inside an Enigma' in Anuradha D Needham and Rajeswari Sunder Rajan. (Ed.). *The Crisis of Secularism in India.* New Delhi: Permanent Black; Ghosh, Partho. 2021. *The Politics of Personal Law in South Asia: Identity, Nationalism, and the Uniform Civil Code.* New Delhi: Routledge; Kapur, Ratna and Cossman, Brenda. 1996. *Subversive Sites: Feminist Engagements With Law in India.* New Delhi: Sage; Ahmed, Farrah. 2016. *Religious Freedom Under Personal Law System.* New Delhi: Oxford University Press. Williams, Rina Verma. 2006. *Postcolonial Politics and Personal Laws: Colonial Legal Legacies and the Indian State.* New Delhi: Oxford University Press. Philips, Amali. 2011. 'Sharia and Shah Bano: Multiculturalism and Women's Rights'. Anthropologica. Vol 53. No 21. Pp. 275-290.

15 Ever since the publication of the Sachar Report (2006) there are several critical writings on its content and recommendations. See, Jodhka, Surinder. 2007. 'Perceptions and Receptions: Sachar Committee and the Secular Left' in *Economic and Political Weekly,* 42(29), 2996-2999; Wilkinson, Steve. 2007. 'A Comment On the Analysis In Sachar Report' in *Economic and Political Weekly,* 42(29); Robinson, Rowena. 2007. 'Indian Muslims: The Varied Dimensions' in *Economic and Political Weekly,* 42(29).

16 In his Foreword to the Report, Justice Sachar sought to explain how the Committee tried to address this complaint by holding interactions and meetings with women's groups and women activists, etc. Apparently, the Committee held one day meeting in July 2006 exclusively from all over India. See, Sachar Report. 2006. Government of India. P. XIII. In my view, this does not compensate for the deliberate exclusion of a Muslim woman or gender experts in the Committee, particularly when there are so many accomplished women scholars in the country.

17 See, Chapter 5 titled, 'Economy and Employment: Situating Muslims' in Sachar Report (2006). Govt of India: New Delhi. Pp. 87-122.

18 See, Chapter 3 titled, 'Population Size, Distribution and Health Conditions of Muslims' in Sachar Report (2006), Govt of India: New Delhi. Pp. 27-47.

19 See, Chapter 4 titled, 'Educational Conditions of Muslims' in Sachar Report (2006), Government of India. Pp. 49-86.

20 See, Kalaiyasaran, A. Unpublished MS. 'Indian Muslims: Educational (IM) Mobility and Emerging Deprivations'.

21 The Shah Bano case inspired various types of scholarships from different disciplines. A few important works are as follows: Engineer, Asghar Ali. 1987. *The Shah Bano Controversy.* New Delhi: Sangam Books; for a deeper understanding of the Shah Bano case and its implications for secularism, see Baxi, Upendra. 2007. 'Sitting Secularism in a Uniform Civil Code: A Riddle Wrapped Inside an Enigma' in Anuradha D Needham and Rajeswari Sunder Rajan (Eds.). *The Crisis of Secularism in India.* New Delhi: Permanent Black; Partho Ghosh. 2021. *The Politics of Personal Law in South Asia: Identity, Nationalism, and the Uniform Civil Code.* New Delhi: Routledge; Ratna Kapur and Brenda Crossman. 1996. *Subversive Sites: Feminist Engagements With Law in India.* New Delhi: Sage; Farrah Ahmad. 2016. *Religious Freedom Under Personal Law System.* New Delhi: Oxford University Press. Williams, Rina Verma. 2006. *Postcolonial Politics and Personal Laws: Colonial Legal Legacies and the Indian State.* New Delhi: Oxford University Press. Philips, Amali. 2011. *Sharia and Shah Bano: Multiculturalism and Women's Rights.* Anthropologica. Vol 53. No 21. Pp. 275-290.

22 Among the myriad explanations for why Rajiv Gandhi made a U-turn on his position on the Shah Bano Bill, two recent books have shed interesting light on this issue. Dixit, Sheila. 2018. *Citizen's Delhi: My Time, My Life.* New Delhi: Bloomsbury. Also, see, Habibullah, Wajahat. 2020. *My Years with Rajiv: Triumph and Tragedy.* New Delhi: Westland. Aslo, Aiyer, Mani Shankar. 2024. *The Rajiv I Knew.* New Delhi: Juggernaut.

23 Mr Arif Mohammad Khan, a member of Rajiv Gandhi's cabinet, became a hero for liberals and feminists for taking a firm stand in favour of women equality and Supreme Court judgement, and also resigned from the Cabinet on this issue. Mr Khan later joined the Bhartiya Janata Party (BJP) and currently serves as the Governor in the state of Kerala appointed by the Narendra Modi government since 6 September 2019.

24 Salman Khurshid is a senior Congress politician and served as minister in various Congress Cabinets.

25 For a detailed discussion on this see, Aiyer, Mani Shankar. 2024. *The Rajiv I Knew.* New Delhi: Juggernaut. Pp. 49-66.

26 See, *Indian Express*. 2017. 'What is Shah Bano Case?' Available at: http://www.indianexpress.com. 23 August 2017 (accessed on 15 April 2021).

27 See. Hasan, Zoya. 2014. *Congress After Indira: Policy, Power, Political Change (1984-2009)*. New Delhi: Oxford University Press.

28 According to Siddiqua Ahmed, daughter of Shah Bano, 'My mother was a simple woman but circumstances made her tough. She was so angry with my father that she warned him, Wakil saab, if I go to Court, you will never be able to wear your black coat again.' He lost the case and never wore the coat again. See Ghatwai, Milind. 2016. 'Revisiting Shah Bano's family, 31 years later: My mother got threats after SC (Supreme Court) order, but stuck to stand.' Available at: http://www.indian express.com (accessed on 20 January 2024).

29 *Iddat* is the waiting period a woman must observe after the death of her husband or divorce before she can marry another man. The length of the *iddat* period is circumstantial. The period is usually three months after either of the two instances. In case the woman is pregnant, the period carries on until childbirth.

30 For an analysis of this case, see, 'Daniel Latifi v. Union of India-A Complete Analysis,' Available at: http://www.thelawmatics.in (accessed on 15 July 2022).

31 See, Williams, Ruth Verma. 2012. 'Making minorities identities: Gender, State, Muslim Personal Law.' Minority Studies. (Ed.) Rowena Robinson. New Delhi: Oxford University Press. P. 90.

32 See the report, 'In Landmark verdict, instant Triple Talaq declared illegal by the SC, parliament asked to make law in six months.' Available at: www.indiatoday.in. 22 August 2017 (accessed on 31 January 2022).

33 'About 82 per cent decline in Triple Talaq Cases Since law enacted by Modi government: Muktar Abbas Naqvi.' Available at: www.economictimes.indiatimes.com. 22 July 2020.

34 See, 'Lok Sabha passes Bill banning triple talaq amid JD(U) and opposition protests.' Available at: www.livemint.com. 26 July 2019 (accessed on 31 January 2022).

35 See, 'In big win, the government swings Rajya Sabha Vote to clear Triple Talaq Bill.' Available at: www.timesofindia 31 July 2019 (accessed on 31 January 2022).

36 'Fresh Triple Talaq Bill introduced in Lok Sabha, Opposition Members Protest.' Available at: www.economictimes.indiatimes.com. 21 June 2019 (accessed on 31 January 2022).

37 See, 'Introducing a law won't eradicate social evil: Owaisi opposed triple

talaq bill in LS.' Available at: www.indianexpress.com. 25 July 2019 (accessed on 31 January 2022).

38 The Sabrimala Sree Dharma Sastha Temple is a famous temple dedicated to Lord Ayyappa in Kerala. In 1990, a ban on the entry of women of menstruating age between 10 to 50 years was sought, which Kerala High Court imposed in its order S Mahendran vs The Secretary, Travancore (1993). In 2018, the Supreme Court overturned the Kerala High Court Order and allowed entry of women irrespective of age into the Sabrimala Temple. The Supreme Court said in its order that the restriction violated the fundamental right of freedom of religion as per Article 25 of the Constitution. For a detailed analysis of this case see, Jamal, Ayesha. 2020. 'Sabrimala Verdict: A Watershed Moment in the History of Affirmative Action.' Available at: http://www.theleaftlet.in (accessed on 10 November 2023).

39 Ibid.

40 'Muslim women Thank PM Modi on Passage of Triple Talaq Bill' Available at: www.timesofindia.indiatimes.com. 31 July 2019 (accessed on 31 January, 2022).

41 Bebaak Collective is led by Hasina Khan. For a good understanding of Bebaak Collective's profile and its activities, see, 'In Conversation With Bebaak Collective: Talking About Muslim Women's Issues.' Available at: www.feminisminindia.com. 30 May 2017 (accessed on 30 January 2022). Among others, at its national convention in Delhi in 2016, *Musalman Aurotan Ki Awaz: Sadak Se Sansad Tak*, drew considerable attention.

42 On contributions of BMMA, see Jones, Justin. 2020. 'Acting Upon Our Religion: Muslim Women's movements and the remodeling of Islamic Practice in India.' *Modern Asian Studies*. Cambridge: Cambridge University Press. Pp. 1-35.

43 See. 'Complete Charade: Activists, Civil Socity Groups condemn Triple Talaq Bill'. Available at: www.thewire.in. 31 July 2019 (accessed on 27 January 2024).

44 See, 'Stop the Criminalization of Triple Talaq: Bebaak Collective.' Available at: www.theleaflet.in 8 March 2019 (accessed on 31 January 2022).

45 For a detailed discussion, see Soman, Zakia and Niaz, Dr Noorjehan Safia. 2020. *Indian Muslim Women's Movement: for Gender Justice and Equal Citizenship*. Chennai: Notion Press.

46 Interview with Zakia Soman on 29 January 2024.

47 Ibid.

48 Ibid.

49 'BJP says Uniform Civil Code (UCC) benefit all after Muslim Personal Board calls it unconstitutional.' Available at: www.indiatoday.on 27 April 2022 (accessed on 23 May 2022).

50 See, 'UP government working to implement the Uniform Civil Code: Deputy CM KP Mourya.' Available at: www.hindustantimes.com 24 April 2022 (accessed on 23 May 2022).

51 See 'Uttarakhand Cabinet Gives Nod To Set Up a Committee To Draft Uniform Civil Code.' Available at: www.apblive.com 14 April 2022 (accessed on 23 May 2022).

52 Singh, Kautilya. 'Uttarakhand government plans special assembly session to introduce UCC Bill.' Available at: www.timesofindia.indiatimes.com. 12 November 2023 (accessed on 10 December, 2023).

53 See, Bajpai, Rochana. 2016. *Debating Difference: Group Rights and Liberal Democracy in India.* New Delhi: Oxford University Press.

54 See Kohli, Namita. 2022. 'I can see the pitfalls of supporting practices such as hijab: Noorjehan Safia Niaz.' *The Hindu.* (accessed on 10 March 2022).

55 For a comparative analysis, see Khurshid, Salman. 2018. 'Reforms in Islamic States' in *Triple Talaq: Examining Faith.* New Delhi: Oxford University Press. Pp. 109-122.

56 Jones, Justine. 2010. 'Signs of Churning: Muslim Personal Law and Public Contestation in Twenty-first Century India.' *Modern Asian Studies* (44). Cambridge University Press. Pp. 175-200.

57 See Ahmed, Farrah. 2016. 'Introduction' in *Religious Freedom Under Personal Law System.* New Delhi: Oxford. Pp. 1-17.

58 Vision Document 2004. www.library.bjp.org. (accessed on 20 January 2024). Though the party was alluding to consensus building, such a thing is not seen in its effort to pass the Triple Talaq Bill .

59 Gallanter, Marc. 1999. 'Secularism in India: The Early Debate' in *Secularism and Its Critics.* edited by Bhargava, Rajeev. New Delhi: Oxford University Press. 234-267.

60 Ibid. P. 248.

61 See the chapter by Flavia Agnes in 'Women and the Hindu Right' edited by Butalia, Urvashi and Sarkar, Tanika. 1995. Kali for Women. Also, see the chapter by Agnes, Flavia in Flavia Agnes, Sudhir Chandra, and Monmayee Basu. (Ed.). 2003. *Women and Law in India.* New Delhi: Oxford University Press.

62 For an analysis of this aspect, see Patel, Razia. 2009. 'Indian Muslim

Women, Politics of Muslim Personal Law and Struggle for Life with Dignity and Justice.' *Economic and Political Weekly*. Vol 44. Pp. 44-48.

63 See Mehta, Vinod. 2015. *The Sanjay Story*. New Delhi: Harper Collins. Also, see Jaffrelot, Christophe and Pratinav, Anil. 2021. *India's First Dictatorship: The Emergency, 1975-1977*. New Delhi: Harper Collins.

64 See Mukhopadhyay, Nilanjan. 2021. *The Demolition and The Verdict: Ayodhya and The Project to Reconfigure India*. New Delhi: Speaking Tiger.

65 With fresh litigations over the Masjid-Mandir issue in Varanasi, Mathura, and elsewhere, it is likely the AIMPLB is going to play a further role in Muslim community affairs.

66 See, www.alimplb.in (accessed on 6 February 2024).

67 Vatuk, Slyvia. 2016. 'Islamic Feminism in India: Muslim Women Activists and Reform of Muslim Personal Law' in *Marriage and Its Discontents: Women, Islam, and Law in India*. New Delhi: Women Unlimited. Pp. 154-195.

68 Ibid.

69 See, Vatuk. P. 160.

70 For a detailed analysis of women network, see, Kirmani, Nida. 2009. 'Claiming their Space: Muslim Women-Led Networks and the Women's Movement in India.' *Journal of International Women's Studies*, Vol 11. Issue 1. Pp. 72-85.

71 In Englsih, BMMA means Indian Muslim Women's Movement.

72 A form of instant Islamic divorce by which a husband can unilaterally repudiate a wife.

73 For a critical analysis of various feminist positions see, Faziya, Ummul. 2021. 'From Shah Bano to Shayara Bano (1985-2017): Changing feminist positions on the politics of Muslim Personal Law, Women's Rights, Minority Rights in India.' *Journal of Muslim Minority Affairs*, Vol 41. No 1. 122-140.

74 See my review of this volume titled, *Its Not About Burqua*, published in *The Hindustan Times* on 25 June 2020. The book lays bare various shades of Islamophobia. Its contributors include journalists, writers, and activists. Some of the names are Mona Eltahawy, Coco Khan, Sufiya Ahmed, Nafisa Bakkar, Saima Mir, Yassmin Abdel-Magied.

75 Motamedi, Mazier. 2023. 'Iranian women post images without hijabs despite crackdown.' Available at: http://www.aljazeera.com (accessed on 24 January 2024); For a more detailed analysis, see Al Talei, Rafiah Al, Bazoobandi, Sara, and Khorrami, Nima. 2022. 'Hijab in Iran: From Religious to Political Symbol'. Available at: http://www.carnegieendowment.org. (accessed on 24 January 2024).

76 Ahmed, Leila. 2021. *Women and Gender in Islam: Historical Roots of a Modern Debate.* New Haven: Yale University Press.

77 See, Anand, Utkarsh. 2022. 'Karnataka Hijab Ban Case: Supreme Court delivers Split Verdict'. Available at: http://www.thehindustantimes.com (Accessed on 20 January 2024).

78 Baxi, Upendra. 'The hijab case and the struggle for the right to be and remain different.' *The Indian Express.* 7 April 2022.

79 See, 'Prahlad Joshi welcomes Karnataka HC verdict on Hijab, appeals for peace.' Available at: www.deccanchronicle.com. 15 March 2022 (accessed on 15 July 2022).

80 See, Karthikeyan, Suchitra. 'Right to Choose Not Upheld: Mehbooba Mufti and Omar Abdullah disappointed by Karnataka HC Verdict on Hijab Row.' Available at: http://www.republicworld.com (accessed on 15 July 2022).

81 Mustafa, Faizan. 'The problem with the Karnataka HC's hijab ruling.' Available at: http://www.indianexpress.com (accessed on 15 July 2022)

82 Desai, Sonalde. 2022. 'The Hijab Hurdle'. *The Indian Express,* 26 February.

83 Agha, Ambreen. 2022. 'Hijab verdict will only push Muslim women further to the margins.' Available at: http://www.indianexpress.com (accessed on 15 July 2022).

84 Soman, Zakia. 'Uniform cannot be more important than education.' www.indianexpress.com. 18 March 2022 (accessed on 15 July 2022).

85 Göle, Nilüfer. 2011. *Islam in Europe: The Lure of Fundamentalism and the Allure of Cosmopolitanism.* Princeton: Markus Wiener Publishing Inc.

86 Ibid. P. 146.

87 Parveen, Nazima. 'Muslim Personal Law and Triple Talaq: Claims and Counter Claims and Media Discourse.' *Rethinking Muslim Personal Law.* 2022. Routledge India.

88 See Mernissi, Fatima. 2004. 'The Hijab or the Veil 'in her book, *Women, and Islam: An Historical and Theological Enquiry*. New Delhi: Kali for Women.

89 Al-Habiri, Azizah Y. 'Is Western Patriarchal Feminism Good for Third World/Minority Women' in *Is Multiculturalism Bad For Women*? Susan Moller Okin with respondents. Edited by Joshua Cohen, Mathew Howard, and Martha Nussbaum. New Jersey: Princeton University Press. P. 46.

90 See, Minault, Gail. 2009. 'Women, Legal Reform, and Muslim Identity' in *Gender, Language and Learning: Essays in Indo-Muslim Cultural History.* Ranikhet: Permanent Black. Besides Muslim women are also into religious learning that is on rise. For this aspect, see Sanyal, Usha. 2020. *Scholars of*

Faith: South Asian Muslim Women and Embodiment of Religious Knowledge. New Delhi: Oxford University Press.

91 Rose, Jacqueline. 2021. *On Violence and On Violence Against Women.* Faber: London.

92 There are many ways patriarchy gets reconstituted or finds new forms. For some of its facets during colonial times, see, Sangari, Kumkum and Vaid, Sudesh. 2003. *Recasting Women: Essays in Colonial History.* New Delhi: Zubaan.

5

SHAHEEN BAGH AND THE FUTURE OF INDIA'S CITIZENSHIP DEBATE

'If we don't raise our voice, if we don't come out of our houses, how will the government know that we have an issue?'

—Bilkis Dadi of Shaheen Bagh, in an interview to *The Wire*

For some, Shaheen Bagh is dead. For others, it is alive and kicking—at least in thoughts, in memories, and imagination. And there is politics in thoughts, in memories and imagination. Shaheen Bagh is the protest movement that unleashed fresh air in a country that was feeling acutely suffocated by the unprecedented domination of the Hindu Right—a movement that spawned multiple protests with signature slogans and unified goals all over India. It helped India's beleaguered national media, which was increasingly behaving like just another organ of the Indian state, to finally resurrect itself with a voice and begin reporting with some courage and clarity. Opposition political parties also found new courage to take on the all-powerful Narendra Modi government on this issue. For progressive scholars and various stripes of secularists, Shaheen Bagh has left behind an enduring legacy of a protest movement that challenged stereotypes regarding Muslim women, and aspirations for equal citizenship for people regardless of their class, creed, and gender. Some even drew a parallel with the Khilafat movement.[1] The Shaheen Bagh protest site was closed off due to the countrywide Covid-19 lockdown. Many believed that the movement would resurface once the countrywide shutdown was over. That has not happened and seems unlikely. That is because India's increasingly Hindu majoritarian state has acquired new teeth to pre-empt such political movements by means which historian Caroline Elkes calls 'legal lawlessness'.[2] Scholars, researchers, and journalists from various parts of the world are still curious about it. They visit the site to learn more firsthand and seek out people who were part of it. Books and scientific essays have already been written and more are going to follow.

I visited the protest site multiple times. Once with the award-winning writer Amit Chaudhuri.[3] We took an electric auto-rickshaw from Jamia Millia University where he was invited to deliver the Ahmed Ali Memorial Lecture in February 2020. Based on the lecture, Amit Chaudhuri wrote a book titled, *On Being Indian* (2023). During the short auto ride of roughly 20 minutes through the crowded lanes of New Delhi's Okhla area, Mr Chaudhuri told me the neighbourhood resembles parts of Dacca. This comparison perhaps suggests the un-partitionable nature of South Asian lives and ways of living. And how neighbourhoods of cities, small towns, *kasbas,* and villages, remain mirror images of each other in all three countries: India, Pakistan, and Bangladesh. Despite boundaries, different flags, and national anthems, South Asian society has largely remained the same internally. Mr Chaudhuri's concluding note in *On Being Indian* says, 'The anti-CAA protests are testament to the possibility not just of an aim being realized, but of a universal transformation, and putting to use the country's long history of thought for democracy in a way not seen even during the freedom movement. It happened—and it now allows us to realign how we live and what we know.'[4] Shaheen Bagh's contribution to the ongoing citizenship debate in India is significant and we need to know its history and context.

The citizenship issue stands out as the most prominent one among all the issues that define the direction of the political future of Indian Muslims in contemporary times. That is because only the kind of rights (such as legal, fundamental, etc.) that are enshrined in the constitution will determine the nature of their association with the modern Indian state as well as society. More specifically, their relationships with other citizens, particularly citizens of other faiths, say, of the Hindu majority, are determined by virtue of these rights, hence their dignity too depends on it. Consequently, the character of Indian society, whether it is inclusive or exclusive, is further determined based on how citizenship is defined for minorities such as Muslims.

Are they equal or second-class citizens?

Or something more degrading?

This subject of citizenship—particularly concerning Muslims—has become a raging debate in the country today with the passage of the Citizenship Amendment Act (CAA) in December 2019. And the protests against the CAA 2019 have received widespread global attention.[5] According to Nirja Jayal Gopal, former Vice President of the American Political Science Association (2011-12), 'Though the Citizenship Amendment Bill ostensibly relates only to migrants seeking the legal status of citizenship, this is not just about migrants. The threat, rhetorical or otherwise, of a nationwide NRC (National Register of Citizens) shows that the fig leaf of illegal immigration is being used to bring the citizenship of all Muslim citizens into question.'[6] She further asserts in her book, *Citizenship Imperiled: India's Fragile Democracy,* 'For Muslims, their legal status as citizens threatened to become a function of their religious identity.'[7] Without a doubt, Indian Muslims as a community were never as vulnerable, fearful, and anxious as they are these days. A deep sense of despondency has begun to be seen in their thinking. By participating in large numbers in the nationwide anti-CAA protests, they have revealed that they are worried about their future. The announcement by Home Minister Amit Shah that the CAA will implemented before Lok Sabha only indicates how committed the BJP government is on this issue considered exclusionary not just by minorities such as Muslims and secularists, but also multi-culturalists worldwide.[8]

Writing on citizenship, Ornit Shani has argued that India has been able to contain many underlying conflicts by pursuing multiple conceptions of citizenships.[9] However, this new citizenship act has potentially disrupted the multiple conceptions of citizenship.

No one perhaps has sensed the Muslim community's concern more than the Prime Minister, who remarked that the protestors could be identified by their clothes in an election rally during the Jharkhand Assembly elections in December 2019, only a few days after the passage of the CAA, 2019.[10] In a jointly authored Op-ed in *The New York Times* titled, 'We are witnessing a Rediscovery of India's Republic,' on 27 December 2019, Rohit De and Surabhi Ranganathan wrote, 'The CAA offers an accelerated pathway to citizenship for Hindu, Sikh, Zoroastrian, Buddhist and Christian migrants from Pakistan, Bangladesh and Afghanistan but excludes Muslims. It effectively creates a hierarchical system of citizenship determined by an individual's religion, reminiscent of Myanmar's 1982 Citizenship Law, which privileged citizenship for "indigenous races," excluded the Rohingya and paved the ground for the genocidal violence against them.'

Between December 9-12, the CAA 2019 was fiercely debated in both the Lok Sabha and the Rajya Sabha. The Bill was introduced by India's Home Minister, Amit Shah. Curiously, Prime Minister Narendra Modi was not present on either of these occasions because he was away campaigning for the Jharkhand Assembly elections, where he addressed 11 rallies.[11] His party lost the election showing the limits of electoral value of not only Prime Minister Narendra Modi's campaign power but also of national issues in state elections.[12]

In both houses of the Parliament, however, Amit Shah made a powerful case with arguments about why Muslims from neighbouring countries such as Pakistan, Afghanistan, and Bangladesh should NOT be included in the amended Act. According to Mr Shah, Muslims are not a religious minority in these Muslim majority nations, hence disqualified. According to the CAA 2019, six major religious groups such as Hindus, Sikhs, Jains, Buddhists, Parsis, and Christians from

Pakistan, Afghanistan, and Bangladesh who migrated to India before 31 December 2014, and have lived in India for five years are deemed eligible for citizenship, but Muslims are excluded.

In its Bill form, the CAA was first introduced in India's Lower House (Lok Sabha). It was passed eventually after a nine-hour debate with 311 votes in favour and 80 votes against. Amit Shah, who introduced the Bill argued, 'If minorities are getting persecuted in neighbouring countries, we cannot be mute spectators. We have to ensure their safety and dignity.'[13] Blaming the Congress for dividing the country, Mr Shah further argued, 'We will have to differentiate between intruders and refugees. The Citizenship Amendment bill does not discriminate against anyone and does not snatch anyone's rights.'[14] Shah further backed his claim by saying that the Bill was part of the BJP's election manifesto in 2014 and 2019 and he was right in these claims. Asaduddin Owaisi of AIMIM[15] from Hyderabad tore a copy of the bill and called it an insult to India's freedom fighters. 'The bill is against the Constitution. It is a conspiracy to make Muslims stateless,'[16] Owaisi said. The discussions in both houses of the Parliament took place in a highly charged atmosphere and tempers flared.

A few points, however, need to be kept in mind for a sober assessment of this vexed issue. India's first Citizenship Act was passed in 1955 based on a very well-informed debate in the Constituent Assembly at the time. However, multiple modifications have occurred since, resulting in various Acts till this latest one, the CAA 2019. In this process of evolution, India has moved from Jus soli to Jus sanguinis—descent-based citizenship. Against this larger background, Amit Shah's allusion to Partition and its connection to citizenship is not entirely off the mark. What is disputed among scholars is Shah's claim that the Congress alone is to be blamed for Partition.[17] It is worth pondering over the observations that Joya Chatterji has made in her book, *Shadows at Noon,* 'Partition is often thought of as a physical process, a massive earthquake that sent different segments of the subcontinent hurtling apart in different directions. Because India and Pakistan (and later Bangladesh) evolved differently in certain important aspects, and because the chatter about these differences has been so loud, the facts of their shared predicament in the early years of nation-building have been all but drowned out.'[18]

The painful truth is that Partition as is increasingly realized has created more problems than solutions for the people of the subcontinent. In no other area has it been more impactful than in the domain of citizenship discourse in South Asia. This fresh wave of discussions over citizenship is not going to end soon.

Owing to Partition, resulting in the movement of people on both sides, there was an animated debate in India's Constituent Assembly over citizenship and its criteria in a communally charged environment. In the Indian Constitution, the Articles from 5 to 11 deal with the citizenship issue.[19] But it was Article 7 that dealt with the large numbers of Muslims who first fled during Partition-related violence, but later chose to return. In the deliberation, two words were used: migrant and refugee. Hindus fleeing from Pakistan were identified as refugees and the returning Muslims were identified as migrants. While there was not any overt use of religious identity, it was subtly clear what these phrases meant through the lens of religion. Fortunately, the Constituent Assembly adopted a democratic conception of citizenship instead of embracing 'an idea of racial citizenship'. This is how the Citizenship Act 1955 came about—with the notion of jus soli or citizenship by birth as a statutory basis. Therefore, what the Assembly adopted is described as 'enlightened modern civilised' (CAD, I:424).

In short, India's first Citizenship Act of 1955 was religion-neutral. It is consistent with India's secular foundational structure, an ideology around which the freedom movement was led by the Congress party and other secular allies. In subsequent years, some scholars have argued that this religion-neutral dimension of India's Citizenship Act has moved towards more descent-based citizenship, also called jus sanguinis—dependent on religious identity (Jayal 2019). With the passage of the CAA 2019, this move has been decisive and complete.

Anupama Roy, another scholar consistently engaged on this question, makes a very important point when she writes, 'The changes in citizenship law in India, therefore, must not be seen as points in its historical evolution but in terms of their location in historical time-space.'[20] She further explains the most thoughtful way of reading this evolution needs to look at 'moments punctuated by historical choices and conscious decisions.'[21] Using this guideline, Roy recognizes three decisive moments in the evolution of legal-formal citizenship in India before the passage of the CAA in 2019. According to her, the first moment is marked by the passage of the Citizenship Act of 1955; the second moment is the amendment of the Citizenship Act of 1986 impacted by the Assam Accord; and the third moment is represented by the amendment of the Citizenship Act of 2003 with the inclusion of the Overseas Citizens of India (OCI). I would like to improvise this framework and suggest that India has entered the fourth moment with the CAA of 2019 that has excluded Muslims from neighbouring countries. What is further crucial to recognize is the ideological aspect of political change in India, which is where the context of Hindu Right politics forms a crucial component. We will perhaps understand these changes a little better if we can unravel the complicity of so-called secular regimes in laying out these changes or what is argued to be an evolution of Indian citizenship.

The present Act is not a one-time masterstroke by the BJP, though it would appear so at the surface level. Several modifications took place at different points, creating helpful conditions for the BJP to make a decisive turn towards religion-based citizenship, bringing India closer to its dream ideological project of Hindu Rashtra. The BJP has received considerable assistance through various Acts and decisions of the non-BJP, secular regimes of the past, particularly the Congress. Also, the present debate is deeply entangled with the politics in Assam. Assam Accord plays a crucial part and has helped BJP's ideological agenda, resulting in the exclusion of Muslims.

Some resonance of these aspects were apparent in the debate in both Houses of the Parliament. Given that the BJP does not have a majority in the Rajya Sabha, the Bill could have been stopped there, which in turn could have prevented it from becoming an Act. However, the so-called secular Opposition parties did not take their commitment to secularism seriously, and the BJP not only achieved a legislative victory but fulfilled its key ideological goal.

While some members of the opposition parties argued against Muslim exclusion, at the tactical level, however, adequate efforts were not made to stop the BJP from getting the Bill passed. Their commitment did not move beyond the rhetorical, and efforts were casual and reckless. In the end, they appeared complicit in the process that led to the passage of the Bill. Only after a nationwide protest, they felt emboldened enough to show some courage in their criticisms. In the Lok Sabha, Shashi Tharoor and Manish Tiwari from the Congress party, Supriya Sule from the National Congress Party (NCP), and Abhishek Banerjee from the Trinamool Congress party (TMC) were some of the star speakers from the Opposition. The nine-hour debate in Lok Sabha revolved around three key themes.

- **Rights of minorities in India.** The Opposition said the Bill discriminated against Muslims and linked religion to citizenship. Home Minister Amit Shah responded by saying that the Bill had nothing to do with Muslims and argued, 'This bill is not even 0.001 per cent against Muslims. It is against infiltrators.' He further presented data on the persecution of Hindus and people of minority faiths in Pakistan, Afghanistan, and Bangladesh.
- **Constitutional rights and provisions.** The Opposition alleged that the bill violated the Indian constitution's fundamental rights, especially Article 14 which guarantees equality to all citizens before the law. But Shah justified it as part of the provision allowing for reasonable classification in the Constitution, which his government has met by not legislating in favour of any particular religion or community.
- **The North-East issue.** The Opposition parties argued that the National Register of Citizens (NRC) exercise, aimed at detecting illegal immigrants, had failed. Further, the CAB

> favoured Hindu immigrants, which was the reason for the protests against the Bill all over the country.

The passage of the Bill in the Lok Sabha in which the Modi government enjoys the majority was a foregone conclusion, but it could have been stalled in Rajya Sabha. It was reported that opposition parties, particularly the Congress, the DMK, and the Left parties, had prepared individual drafts of their motion to stop the Bill. The Bill, however, was passed in the Rajya Sabha as well, with 125 votes in favour and 105 votes against it. It received support from friendly parties like AIDMK, while Shiv Sena walked out. P Chidambaram, Anand Sharma, and Kapil Sibal from the Congress, Javed Ali Khan from the Samajwadi Party, K Keshav Rao from Telangana Rashtriya Samithi (TRS), TK Rangarajan from the CPI(M) were the star speakers.[22] Like with other Bills such as the J&K Reorganization Act that demoted the state to a Union Territory[23] and abolished Article 370,[24] and the Triple Talaq Bill (TTB),[25] the ruling party was able to cobble together the support for the Bill and turn it into an Act.

On 12 December 2019, Amit Shah, in his response during the Rajya Sabha debate rather emphatically said, 'The citizenship of Muslims of India has no connection with this Bill. This is a Bill meant to grant citizenship not take it away.' He further said, 'This country will never be Muslim mukta (free of Muslims),' referring to a charge made by Javed Ali Khan, an MP of the Samajwadi Party. Prime Minister Narendra Modi welcomed the passage of the Bill in his Twitter handle from Jharkhand, 'A landmark day for India and our nation's ethos of compassion and brotherhood. This Bill will alleviate the suffering of many who faced persecution for years.'[26] What is, however, debated nationally as well as globally today in this citizenship debate are ideas of brotherhood vastly different from what the Prime Minister meant and how the attempt to selectively end persecution could trigger further persecution and discrimination.

On more than one occasion, Prime Minister Narendra Modi has proudly announced to the world that India is the 'mother of democracy,' on various national and global platforms. At the level of rhetoric, this is understandable. If the idea of citizenship is integral to democracy, there is a lot we need to discuss for self-reflection as people. As Nirja Jayal reminds us rather dispassionately, 'Unlike in Western antiquity, the rubric of citizenship, either as performance or equality, was historically alien to Indian experience. There was no antecedent tradition of citizenship that could be excavated or invoked in the way in which chronicles of a national past were produced in impassioned response to the colonial accusation that Indians lacked history.'[27]

On the Western discourse of citizenship, there is a long history. So far as theories of citizenship are concerned, there are mainly two types: 1) normative theory, and 2) empirical theory. The normative theory mainly addresses the rights and duties that citizens should have, whereas the empirical theories aim to explain how citizens come to acquire such rights and duties.[28] It is in the history of ancient Greece and Rome that the dominant model of citizenship is grounded. The Greek model of citizenship is drawn from the writings of Aristotle—mainly from the political system in Athens and Sparta in the 5th and 6th centuries BC. The key work of Aristotle that is the source of the narrative of citizenship is *The Politics* which was written between 335 and 323 BCE.

Sociologists Stein Rokkan and TH Marshal have advanced our understanding of the modern notion of democratic citizenship through their works. The writings of TH Marshall are widely quoted in the analysis of the citizenship debate. Marshall argued that there are three distinct periods in the evolution of citizenship historically. The 17th to mid-19th century witnessed the consolidation of civil rights required for engagement in socio-economic activities. From the end of the 18th to the 20th century the political right to vote—first by property owners, then by adult males and, finally, by women—became a part of citizenship rights. From the end of the 19th to the mid-20th century, the third period saw the creation of social rights. This theory of TH Marshall has its share of criticism. Critics of TH Marshall's theory have argued that he has set aside the extraneous factors in shaping the evolution of these rights.

Assam Accord and Its Impact on the Citizenship Debate

What has triggered fear among Indian citizens, particularly Muslims, is the Modi government's attempt to link the Citizenship Act with the National Registrar for Citizenship (NRC) which has its roots in Assam politics. Given the Assam experience of NRC, and its countless bureaucratic follies resulting in the exclusion of Muslims and poor people, Muslims have convincing reasons to be fearful of becoming stateless owing to lack of documents.[29] During the parliament debate over the Citizenship Amendment Bill in 2019, Home Minister Amit Shah emphatically said that his government would implement the nationwide NRC[30] as if it were a war cry. There have been statements and counter-statements by both the Home Minister and Prime Minister on this issue on various occasions ever since.

Assam has a long and complex history of immigration from the 19th century onwards. Two scholars, Sanjib Baruah and Sanjoy Hazarika, have extensively written on the politics of Assam, and its implications for India and the region. Sanjib Baruah's *In the Name of Nation: India and Its North East* addresses issues such as migration, settlement, regional geopolitics, and resource extraction.[31] Baruah writes, 'Political tensions around the issue of citizenship of post-Partition migrants have come to a head in Assam with the rise of the BJP—a political formation known both for its strong support of the cause of Partition refugees and for its advocacy of a firm line between Hindu and Muslim unauthorised immigrants. Any Hindu migrant from Pakistan or Bangladesh irrespective of when s/he entered India, it believes, deserves refugee status and to be on the road to citizenship. But Muslims crossing the border into India are illegal immigrants.'

Even during Partition, Assam and its future were part of a heated debate among leaders of Muslim League and Congress owing to its demography.[32] Since 1947 and subsequently for a variety of reasons (such as the Indo-Pak war in 1965 and later Bangladesh liberation war in 1971) there has been massive migration, but otherwise Assam has been a destination for Indians even before from various parts of India, particularly Bengal, Bihar, and other states owing to employment opportunities in tea plantations. Sanjoy Hazarika in his widely read book, *Rites of Passage*, has given a detailed analysis of this dimension of Assam's politics and history of migration.[33]

The passage of the CAA came amidst widespread protests in Assam, which spread like wildfire to other parts of India. The Modi government was caught by surprise, and found itself cornered in a manner it has never experienced since coming to power. The Assam protests grew day by day despite the government's assurances that special measures would be taken under Clause 6 of the 1985 Assam Accord to address the concerns of the agitators. The protests continued unabated and the military had to be deployed on the ground. On 12 December 2020, Prime Minister Modi posted on Twitter: 'I want to assure my brothers and sisters of Assam that they have nothing to worry about after the passing of CAB. I want to assure them—no one can take away your rights, unique identity and beautiful culture. It will continue to flourish and grow. The Central government and I are committed to constitutionally safeguarding the political, linguistic, cultural and land rights of the Assamese people as per the spirit of Clause 6.'[34]

The Clause 6 that Prime Minister Narendra Modi was alluding to is from the Assam Accord of 1985. It addresses the issue of safeguards for the Assamese people. It reads as follows: 'Constitutional, legislative, and administrative safeguards, as may be appropriate shall be provided to protect, preserve, and promote the culture, social, linguistic identity and heritage of the Assamese people.' The major communities, perceived to be migrants in Assam, have expressed concern over the recommendations of the high-powered committee on the implementation of Clause 6 of the Assam Accord of 1985. These communities are of Bengali origin or Bengali-speaking Muslims referred to as Miyas, Bengali Hindus, and the Gurkhas.[35]

On the present Citizenship Act 2019, the key turning point is the Assam Accord 1985, a Memorandum of Settlement signed by the Governments of India and Assam, and leaders of the All Assam

Students' Union (AASU)[36] and the All Assam Gana Sangram Parishad (AAGSP) in New Delhi on August 15 in the same year. Its purpose was to end the violent movement launched in 1979 that lasted six years. Its main goal was to make Assam free of infiltration. The six long years of this historic movement was violent and cost many lives. Eight hundred and sixty people (as submitted by AASU) were killed. The Assam Accord brought closure to a phase of unprecedented violence in the modern history of Assam.[37] And the most disturbing one was the Nellie massacre of 1983.[38]

Though the dialogue between the AASU and AAGSP and the government started under Indira Gandhi's government after it returned to power in 1980, the Accord was signed in 1985 under the Rajiv Gandhi government. Indira Gandhi was assassinated by then. The main issue in the Accord was the 'Foreigners Issue' (Clause 5), and 'Safeguards and Economic Development' (Clauses 6 and 7). There were some 'Other Issues' (Clauses 8-12), and a section on 'Restoration of Normalcy' (Clauses 13 and 14).[39] The Accord led to the amendment that created categories of citizenship and created opportunities for the Hindu Right to manipulate it to move India's citizenship from jus soli (birth-based) to jus sanguinis (descent-based), though gradually.

According to the new rule set up by the Assam Accord 'for purposes of detection and deletion of foreigners, 1.1.1966 shall be the base data and year', and 'all persons who came to Assam before 1.1.1966, including those amongst them whose names appeared on the electoral rolls used in 1967 elections shall be regularised.' It further recognized the presence of foreigners and under Clause 5.8, 'Foreigners who came to Assam on or after March 25 1971, shall continue to be detected, deleted and practical steps shall be taken to expel such foreigners.'[40]

In other words, migrants who arrived before 1966 were accepted as citizens, and those who arrived between 1966-1971 were removed from the electoral rolls. They had to wait 10 years for their renewed application. Those who came post-1971 became illegal immigrants. These categorizations gave a new twist to the debate in the Constituent

Assembly that had settled in favour of inclusive citizenship. An attempt that was made in the Citizenship Act in 1955 to give a progressive spin to the citizenship debate by removing the religious factor found a fresh life in these modifications owing to the Assam Accord. In a way, Partition appeared to be a never-ending source of creating never-ending issues in the region, and the citizenship debate found itself in the whirlpool forever.

Two further amendments of 2004—the Citizenship Act and the other to the Rules under the Act under the Vajpayee government (1998-2004) deepened the religious dimension of the debate. The amendment to the Citizenship Act introduced a religion-based exception. Even if born on Indian soil, it said that a person who had one parent who was an illegal migrant at the time of her or his birth, would not be eligible for citizenship by birth. Most illegal migrants from Bangladesh were Muslims, so Vajpayee's Hindu Right government understood well the implication of this one-parent norm. It had a decisive factor in a person's claim for citizenship—a clever but an important step to undermine the jus soli premise of Indian citizenship. The Hindu Right governments argue that Partition was a result of mass movement so these poor people should be punished owing to their religion, particularly Muslims.

TABLE 5.1 BJP in Parliamentary Elections in Assam (1980-2019)

Year	*Total no. of Seats*	*Candidates Contested*	*Candidates Won*	*Runner up*	*Vote Share (%)*
1984-85	14	2	0	0	0.37
1989*	-	-	-	-	-
1991	14	8	2	1	9.60
1996	14	14	1	1	15.92
1998	14	14	1	8	24.47
1999	14	12	2	8	29.84
2004	14	12	2	4	22.94
2009	14	7	4	2	16.21
2014	14	13	7	4	36.86
2019	14	10	9	1	36.41

**Assam did not go on polls in the 9th Lok Sabha Elections (1989).*

TABLE 5.2 BJP in Assembly Elections in Assam (1980-2019)

Year	*Total no. of Seats*	*Candidates Contested*	*Candidates Won*	*Runner Up*	*Vote Share (%)*
1983	109	-	-	-	-
1985	126	37	0	2	1.07
1991	126	48	10	8	6.55
1996	122	117	4	10	10.41
2001	126	46	8	22	9.35
2006	126	125	10	12	11.98
2011	126	120	5	22	11.47
2016	126	89	60	13	29.51
2021	126	93	60	27	33.21

Illegal migrant issues have been an ideological cause for the Hindu Right—not because they are illegal but because they suspect they are Muslims. Also, because it harbours an imaginary fear of India becoming over-populated with Muslims in the future. The 2014 parliamentary campaign that was mainly run on *vikas* (development) also witnessed migrant issues raised by Modi during his campaign speeches in West Bengal.[41] In 2016 again, in the run-up to the Assembly elections in Assam, the BJP had made an electoral promise to free the state from illegal Bangladeshi migrants and simultaneously promised to give Indian citizenship to all Bangladeshi Hindu immigrants if it won the election.[42]

Table 5.1. and Table 5.2. show the growing electoral dominance of the BJP in Assam. It is now governed by a Chief Minister who was once the leader of the Congress, but his commitment to Hindu Rashtra seems to be greater than other politicians who have grown in Hindu Right organizations. Given this, the prospect of the BJP's future in Assam is very bright and therefore its ability to pass a citizenship bill of its choice is very much going to be there for some years.

Politics of National Registrar of Citizens (NRC)

In the wake of massive protests, both Prime Minister Modi and Home Minister Amit Shah have repeatedly explained that the CAA

2019's exclusion would not directly impact Indian Muslims. The Act, according to them, is meant to offer fresh citizenships but not to snatch them from anyone. Some truth is there in this explanation, but it falls flat when seen with their repeated claims that the national level NRC would follow the introduction of the CAA 2019, which is why the politics of the NRC needs to be understood.

The National Register of Citizens (NRC) is an official record of legal Indian citizens.[43] It contains demographic information about individuals who are eligible as citizens of India as per the Citizenship Act, 1955.[44] First prepared after the 1951 Census of India, it remained dormant till recently. In 2005, Dr Manmohan Singh, the then Prime Minister, chaired a meeting between the New Delhi government, the Assam Government, and the AASU in which it was decided to take steps towards updating the NRC. It was intended to meet the objectives of the Assam Accord of 1985 that the Congress party's former Prime Minister Rajiv Gandhi had signed. Interestingly, Dr Singh, who was also a member of the Rajya Sabha from Assam took a special interest in addressing Assam issues.

However, an NGO called Assam Public Works filed a petition in the Supreme Court asking for the NRC to be updated. In 2014, India's Supreme Court passed an order to update the NRC in all parts of Assam under the Citizenship Act, 1955, and Citizenship Rules, 2003. The process began in 2015. The work continued with considerable challenges but the final NRC was released on 31 August, of the same year in which 1.9 million failed to make the final cut. Surprisingly, many of these were Hindus. This became a matter of concern for the BJP leadership and Hindu Right groups. Protests followed and the home ministry declared that the NRC would be carried out again in Assam. On the watch of the Supreme Court, Assam has served as a laboratory for a potentially dangerous experiment of exclusion of citizens through the NRC.

The NRC results have shown that undocumented nationals may be unfairly denied citizenship owing to a lack of documents. In a poor society with massive illiteracy and often inflicted with many natural disasters such as floods in which people often lose all their belongings and often homes, these laws sound pretty absurd. There were strange cases of exclusion, which also demonstrated bureaucratic unprofessionalism. The cases of such exclusions included 1) the nephew of former Indian president Fakhruddin Ali Ahmed[45] 2) even Syeda Anwara Taimur, the only woman chief minister Assam ever had,[46] and 3) people who have served in the Indian Army or the Border Security Force for decades.[47]

But these absurd exclusions were not the only reason the BJP government was disheartened. The exclusion of Hindus was the main reason, so an attempt has been made to explore ways to accommodate undocumented, excluded Hindus and at the same time continue to have the NRC so that only undocumented Muslims become its sole victims. This is part of what I describe as the 'Muslims No More' agenda of the Hindu Right. This is apparent in the decision by the government to ask the detention centres in Assam to release non-Muslim detainees, who have been forced to seek shelter in the state before 31 December 2014, with expired or without valid documents, according to the minister for home, Nityanand Rai.[48] Undocumented Hindus could, based on their religious identity, be reinstated as citizens when the Citizen Amendment Bill (CAB) becomes law. It is genuine but undocumented Indian nationals belonging to the Muslim faith who would be excluded with no recourse to the CAB. Therefore, the design is well calculated concerning Muslim exclusion. If all goes according to the plan of the Hindu Right regime, the consequence could be what Indrajit Roy claims in the following words, 'The world then would witness the largest crisis of social exclusion, statelessness, and citizenship in history—potentially during the crisis in Europe on the eve of the World War II.'[49]

Another important consequence of this exercise is that while the government is determined to deport, yet it does not have any clue about where to. Bangladesh, apparently the alleged destination, a land seen as the major source of 'illegal migrants' is not on board.[50] Therefore, the plan is to move these stranded human beings to detention centres, causing a large-scale human rights violation. According to a reply by Nityanand Rai, on 2 July 2019, to the Indian Parliament, the Ministry of Home Affairs instructed various state governments since 2009 to establish detention centres to restrict foreign nationals staying illegally so that they are physically available at all times for expeditious repatriation. This instruction has been issued to several states and union territories in 2009, 2012, 2014, and 2018. A detailed manual of a 'model detention centre' is also circulated. Interestingly, Prime Minister Narendra Modi on 22 December 2019, at a Delhi rally said, 'These rumours of detention centres being spread by the Congress and Urban Naxals are completely false... the Muslims of the country are neither being sent to detention centres nor is there a detention centre in India, this is a white lie.'[51] Assam has six detention centres and more to come up soon. And Delhi has three such centres. The Prime Minister's statement is, perhaps, a result of the pressure he was feeling owing to massive protests against the CAA 2019. A country like India with its massive urban-poor population visible to every naked eye, hardly has any decent night shelter homes, as is generally seen in most big cities in the world. And there is no plan for a model night shelter home by any government, even in Delhi, India's national capital. However, the BJP government is keen to pump crores of rupees for Detention Centres to drag already settled people who are looking after themselves out of their homes, deny them their livelihoods, and make them live in those Centres at government cost.

Impact of CAA 2019 on India's Fledging Secularism

At the heart of the debate is the argument that the exclusion of Muslims in India's CAA 2019 has undermined the secular character of our Constitution. The Hindu Right has consistently campaigned against India's secularism even before independence.

The word SECULAR does exist in the Indian Constitution. It was introduced as part of the 42nd Amendment in 1976, during the emergency by the Indira Gandhi government. Since the word was not part of the original Constitution adopted on 26 January 1950, according to the Hindu Right, this later inclusion was politically motivated. Rajnath Singh, India's then Home Minister, brought attention to this matter in a parliament debate over intolerance in November 2015.[52]

Prime Minister Modi remains the first Prime Ministerial candidate of modern India during the 2014 election campaign to unleash ferocious attack on secularism in rally after rally in various parts of India. On 26 March 2014, he warned people how the idea of secularism has kept Indian Muslims poor and backwards at a meeting in Bulandshahar, Uttar Pradesh. Not surprisingly, he has remained consistent on this issue. In Berlin, at a party hosted by the Indian Ambassador on 14 April 2015,[53] he spoke of how India's 'secular fever' has prevented Sanskrit from prospering in modern India. Furthermore, his party, the BJP, has been accused of pursuing an anti-minority/Muslim agenda owing to its commitment to issues such as the abolition of Article 370, the UCC, and the Ram Temple issue in Ayodhya for years.[54] With the removal of Article 370, the inauguration of Ram Mandir on 22 January 2024, and the BJP-run state Uttarakhand, most of its ideological goals are accomplished.

While explaining the present Act, India's Home Minister says that the exclusion of Muslims from these countries is not guided by any religious criteria because the core criteria for inclusion is religious persecution and the law is not anti-Muslim.[55] Since Pakistan, Bangladesh, and Afghanistan are officially Islamic republics, one doesn't expect Muslims to be discriminated against or persecuted in these countries. There is enough scholarship to suggest mere official declaration of a country as an Islamic or secular one does not mean it follows rules or customs accordingly. For instance, even if India is officially a secular country, there are numerous instances of violence against religious minorities such as lynchings in recent years or during riots/pogroms[56] or backwardness as documented in the Sachar Report (2006)[57] or anti-Christian violence in Kandhamal in 2008.[58] A gap between an officially declared objective of a state and realities on the ground often exists.

Furthermore, Ahmadiyas and Rohingyas among Muslims are widely recognized as persecuted people. India's Home Minister cleverly justifies the exclusion of Rohingyas[59] on the ground that since they come via Bangladesh, they cannot be considered for citizenship in India. In other words, Rohingyas' decision to use a Muslim nation as a passage route is a good enough reason for exclusion as given by the Home Minister. Mere passage through Bangladesh does not make Rohingyas Bangladeshi Muslims. These explanations by the Home Minister, also seen as the official explanation, are unfortunate attempts to legitimize discrimination. By abolishing Article 370 and being proactive in the implementation of the Court verdict to build the Ram Temple in recent months, the Modi regime has built a rather robust reputation as a majoritarian regime.

According to noted constitutional scholar, Faizan Mustafa, the CAA is against the constitutional vision for three reasons. Firstly, the classification is not reasonable. Because it does not cover all neighboring countries; secondly, it does not cover all persecuted minorities; and thirdly, it is arbitrary.[60] According to the Indian Constitution, Article 14 empowers any person, citizen or non-citizen, of India residing within its territory the right to equality. Migrants of the Muslim faith who have entered before 31 December 2014 should, according to Article 14, be entitled to citizenship. The provisions of the Act violate Article 14. In addition, Articles 29 and 30 elaborate on the particular nature of minority rights, which is also violated owing to the Act.

However, some legal experts endorse the government's position and argue that the Act is not unconstitutional. Harish Salve, one of India's leading lawyers, supports the Act. In an opinion piece for *The Times of India* on 5 March 2020:

> CAA's avowed objective is to enable conferment of Indian citizenship upon members of minority communities who hail from Afghanistan, Bangladesh and Pakistan. Do we really need proof that minorities are persecuted in these Islamic republics? How can Parliament be faulted for coming to the conclusion that such minorities in the

> three named neighbours need to be protected? Classification on the basis of religion is not per se unconstitutional—it is worth reminding ourselves that our Constitution confers special rights upon members of minority religious communities in India. If the law was broader and allowed members of all religious communities from Pakistan, Bangladesh and Afghanistan to migrate into India, we could as well do away with our borders.[61]

Given these concerns, there are petitions against the Act's constitutional validity in India's Supreme Court. But there is widespread public anger among secular citizens and minorities all over India, and among various global bodies that are calling out the Act's discriminatory premise. The implications of these developments can be interpreted in multiple ways.

TABLE 5.3 BJP in Parliamentary Elections in West Bengal (1980-2019)

Year	*Candidates Contested*	*Candidates Won*	*Runner-up*	*Vote Share (%)*
1989	19	0	0	1.67
1991	42	0	0	11.66
1996	42	0	0	6.88
1998	14	1	10	10.20
1999	13	2	9	11.13
2004	13	0	9	8.06
2009	42	1	0	6.14
2014	42	2	5	17.02
2019	42	18	20	40.64

TABLE 5.4 BJP in Assembly Elections in West Bengal (1980-2019)

Year	*Candidates Contested*	*Candidates Won*	*Runner-up*	*Vote Share (%)*
1982	52	0	1	0.58
1987	57	0	0	0.51
1991	291	0	11	11.34
1996	292	0	1	6.49
2001	266	0	2	5.19

2006	29	0	17	1.93
2011	289	0	1	4.06
2016	291	3	8	10.16
2021	293	77	201	37.97

West Bengal is one of the states that would face challenges about the citizenship issue. In some ways, such challenges could be similar to what has been seen in Assam. But then West Bengal would pose a challenge of its own. The BJP seems to be determined to win over the state, which is necessary to establish domination in India's Eastern region. Given that Bengal has a significant Muslim population, the politics of polarization has started working as reflected in the surge of the BJP's support base, which was 37.97 per cent in the 2021 Assembly election, as shown in Table 5.3, and 40.46 per cent in the 2019 Parliamentary election as shown in Table 5.4.

Writing on West Bengal politics in the late 1980s at the time of Communist rule, Atul Kohli raised three issues to explain what he described as 'Bengali political exceptionalism'.[62] Kohli reflected on this by focusing on three particular issues: the first one is the role of a critical intelligentsia within Bengal, the Bengali *Bhadralok*; the second issue is the 'elite-mass links mediated by structures of caste and class;'[63] and finally, a 'well organized disciplined political party'.[64] The party that is referred to here is the CPI(M), which has become almost a history now. The elite-mass links are also quite weak these days and competition between Mamata Banerjee-led TMC and the BJP is fierce and often violent at the street level. The critical intelligentsia remains a major voice of criticism against Hindutva politics—not just in Bengal or India but globally. The Congress party that was criticized as early as the 1890s as, 'three days fun', 'rich man's club', 'sentimental braggarts', and 'a debating forum for the brown sahibs'[65] has become irrelevant in mass politics ever since Left parties dominated its political landscape and has never managed to revive itself, though Mamata Banerjee began her career from the Congress. There is very little benefit that has come from making Adhir Ranjan

Chaudhury as party's opposition leader in Lok Sabha other than unwarranted controversies for making irresponsible observations.

With the publication of the Sachar Report (2006), it came to light that Muslim conditions in West Bengal are worrisome and there are solid pieces of evidence of under-representation in most sectors under Left rule. Sitaram Yechury, a prominent community leader during a discussion at Jamia Millia Islamia around the time of the publication of the Sachar Report, explained this by saying that there was never any discrimination against Muslims in land reform etc. But the fact is Muslim conditions did not improve and therefore questions are raised regarding the Left brand of secularism. One encouraging development of the Left rule was that Bengal did not witness communal violence which was happening with terrible frequency before Partition.

While the West Bengal was relatively peaceful, the Muslim backwardness remained a concern. In a report titled, *Living Reality of Muslims in West Bengal* (2016), co–produced by Amartya Sen's Pratichi Institute and Association SNAP, it is claimed that 47 per cent Muslims live in rural Bengal and are mostly employed in agricultural and non-agricultural jobs and only one per cent Muslim households are fortunate to have salaried jobs in the private sector. About 80 per cent of Muslim households in rural Bengal earn Rs 5000 as household income per month. This is equal to the cut-off level of income for a family of five for poverty line. The report further says Muslims in Hooghly and Howrah are relatively well off and in districts like North Dinajpur, Jalpaiguri, and Purulia Muslims are extremely poor.[66]

The BJP and other Hindu Right organizations have expressed concerns for illegal migrants from Bangladesh. From this point of view, Bengal politics has become a hotbed of politics of polarization and also there has been secular resistance. The BJP is trying to co-opt Bengal political elites, and building up threats from Muslim majoritarianism to create a new ecosystem that will help the party to win state power. Together with communal violence, the communal narrative has returned to West Bengal that was absent for some decades—particularly under the Left rule.

Legacy of Shaheen Bagh

Among all the protests against the CAA 2019, the protest in Shaheen Bagh, New Delhi, received considerable attention in national and global media. It has now become a historic neighbourhood in New Delhi for hosting a 101-day-long peaceful protest—one of the longest sit-ins in modern Indian history. It began in mid-December 2019, but was suspended in late March 2020, owing to the Modi government's decision to impose a nationwide lockdown to contain the pandemic.[67] Although India has returned to pre-pandemic normal life, the Shaheen Bagh movement has not resumed as yet. It is unlikely to happen as things stand now. Its key goal to stop the CAA/NRC from being implemented has remained unmet and the Modi government has shown no interest in the revision of the CAA 2019 either. In early January 2020, Home Minister Amit Shah made it clear while addressing a rally in Jodhpur that his government wouldn't move even an inch even if the entire opposition united against the CAA.[68] The rally was organized as one of the first awareness programmes in support of the Modi government's new citizenship law.

Whether the protest will be resumed in the future or not, an evaluation of the legacy of the movement's first phase will be a worthwhile exercise because it represents a new political protest culture. For the first time in Indian history, a movement was launched and led by Muslim women showing their unwavering commitment to India's founding constitutional values, such as secularism, equal rights, and human dignity. By doing so, it has further challenged many age-old stereotypes about India's Muslim women, and also about Muslim men who are otherwise known as their women's incorrigible oppressors since time immemorial. A report in the *Huffington Post* put it beautifully in the following words, 'That the protest at Shaheen Bagh will end one day feels like an inevitable pinprick. But what of its legacy? The *daadis* of Shaheen Bagh, who drew a line in the sand, will pass into Delhi's folklore. But what change has their resilience wrought for India's Muslims.'[69]

Despite lasting for more than three months, facing many attempts of disruption including a gun attack,[70] the movement chose to remain politically leaderless. It kept its platform off limits to leaders of political parties to NOT let the movement be identified with or hijacked by any political party. In our recent history, the anti-corruption movement by India Against Corruption (IAC) in 2011 (also known as the Anna Movement) maintained a similar position with regard to political parties, but it had leaders: Arvind Kejriwal, who later became Delhi's Chief Minister, and Anna Hazare, the Gandhian himself. One common point between the two movements is the deep disdain with which each maintained distance from conventional political parties, but in other aspects, they are significantly different.

According to a report by *CNN*, 'Each night, women and children gather in the centre of a tent while men offer their support along the periphery. The women—many of whom are grandmothers, mothers and sisters of students at Jamia Millia Islamia—sing songs and chant slogans of freedom, while speakers on stage discuss the Indian Constitution. Members of the community serve tea and snacks. Then, many of them bunker down for the night on cheap cotton mattresses.'[71]

Sayida Hameed, noted writer and former member of India's Planning Commission, wrote that during her 35 years of working with them, she had never seen such activism by Muslim women. She shared her thoughts in a column titled 'The Brave Women of Shaheen Bagh':

> More than 2,000 women were sitting on the road in the biting cold when we entered the Shaheen Bagh protest site, which had completed its seventh day. Huge crowds of men, young and old, stood all around the women in a circle. From the stage we looked at the crowd, bright lights shone on the stage and audience alike. Posters and placards of Mahatma Gandhi, the Dandi March, and Babasaheb Ambedkar were displayed alongside slogans rejecting the National Register of Citizens and Citizenship (Amendment) Act.[72]

During the evening hours the protest became lively with songs, speeches, and calls for saving India's secular soul. Though professional politicians were not allowed, writers, poets, singers, painters, musicians, actors, lawyers, teachers, doctors, filmmakers, and activists spoke from the platform, sharing their views about the CAA, the value of tolerance, secularism, the right to dissent, etc. Issues of Indian democracy, particularly communalism, caste inequality, exploitation of women, etc. were part of the regular deliberations. Musicians such as Shubha Mudgal,[73] Prateek Kuhad, Anushka Manchanda, Shaswat Bulusu, Sabika Abbas Naqvi, Amir Aziz, and others took part. Noted Carnatic musician TM Krishnan sang Faiz Ahmad Faiz's 'Hum Dekhenge' in four languages at Shaheen Bagh.[74] The idea was of a secular, inclusive nationalism with a fervour for communal harmony and brotherhood, with the national flag flying in front of a poster of the Preamble of the Constitution of India. A makeshift library came up near the protest site for visitors, particularly students, as there were many who not only visited but spent the night there—to educate themselves about Indian democracy and its challenges. There was a gallery with photos of various other protests, including some from the recent police attack on Jamia students in the university library.

The movement received widespread support from different social groups. A group of Sikhs came and spent days with the protest to show solidarity. A report about this was titled 'Sikh Farmers from Punjab Come to Cheer Shaheen Bagh women, cook langar.'[75] DS Bindra, an advocate who practices at the Karkardooma court complex in New Delhi, began a langar (community kitchen) and even sold his flat to raise money for this service. His wife and son also ran langars in other locations of protests in Delhi such as Mustafabad and Khureji. According to a report in the *Frontline*,[76] 'Bindra said the women of Shaheen Bagh "are not mere human beings, they are brave and courageous lionesses." Bindra took care to provide different types of food every day, including dal-chawal, poori-aloo, subzi, kheer and tea. Bindra said once Sikh farmers from different places in Punjab came to participate in the ongoing protest, he thought of starting the langar, which, he says, will continue until the protesters remain there. Bindra said he wanted to highlight the fraternity that exists between

Sikhs and Muslims. His act is to turn the slogan of "Hindu, Muslim, Sikh, Isai *apas mein hai bhai bhai* [we are all one] into a reality." But this exercise has not been easy for him.' Once the police and the local administration disrupted the langar by taking away all the utensils, but he remained committed to his langar. This is evidence of the secular nature of the movement.

The movement's most significant contribution has been that it inspired movements elsewhere in Delhi and the rest of India. New protest sites came up in places such as in Kolkota, Gaya, Chennai, Mumbai, Bengaluru, and other places. According to a report, 'On an average, every day around 20,000-25,000 people come to our protest from morning till night; on Republic Day more than one lakh assembled. On holidays the crowd is particularly strong,' said Asmat. Although there are men present at the protest site, they are there just to provide a protective circle around the women; the protest is conducted by women themselves.[77] A similar protest was staged in Mumbai where women protestors said they would continue protesting as long as the protests continued in Shaheen Bagh. *The Print*, a web portal, reported that Muslim women came up with 'Mumbai Bagh' in solidarity with Delhi's Shaheen Bagh. Likewise, there were protests in Chennai. A report in *The Hindu* appeared with the following title, 'Shaheen Bagh Style anti-CAA protest enters day 3 in Chennai.'[78]

Acclaimed filmmaker Saeed Mirza wrote an article 'Remembering the women of Shaheen Bagh, who showed how poetry can overpower violence and hate' in *Scroll* on 17 March 2020. He noted, 'But what this movement did reveal was that even the stark brutishness of majoritarian democracy could be resisted. Poetry was the answer to ugliness. And that is why this memory is vital.' He further wrote, 'So let me begin this short tale. They were rising to tell the ruling regime that they were as Indian as anybody else and they were tired of trying to prove this fact for the last 73 years.'[79] There are similar observations from other academics.[80]

Mani Shankar Aiyar, one of the few politicians who got the

opportunity to address the Shaheen Bagh protestors listed several points as part of the movement's legacy.[81] According to Aiyar, first, the movement challenged the stereotype of Muslim women. In Aiyar's words, they were not a 'submissive breed, hooded and veiled, non-political.'[82] Second, Muslim women had demonstrated that they could politically be organized. Third, Muslim men were willing to allow their women to play the political role, lead a protest and accept the women's decision to be politically active and lead. Fourth, Muslims were able to assert their Indian identity. In the words of Mr Aiyar, 'There was no call for jihad, no appeal to violence, no attempt to hurt anyone's religious sentiments and no provocation'[83] and finally, Shaheen Bagh, according to Aiyar, 'scored a great political and legislative victory when the Prime Minister backed off, claiming his government had not even discussed the National Population Register (NPR) and the National Register of Citizens (NRC), whereas his home minister had at least nine times on the floor of the house insisted that the Citizenship Amendment Act, the NPR and the NRC were inextricably linked.'[84] Though one is not sure how enduring this victory that Mr Aiyar is claiming would last.

While it is encouraging to record the success of the Shaheen Bagh movement, the fact remains its ability to stop the Bill is acutely limited. The Hindu Right regime remains ideologically committed to the Bill. What is indeed intriguing is that the Shaheen Bagh issue came to the Supreme Court in the context of the blockage of the road for which the Honourable Court appointed three interlocutors: Wajahat Habibullah, Sanjay Hegde, and Sadhana Ramachandran. According to the affidavit by Wajahat Habibullah, the police had barricaded several roads with no connection to the peaceful protests at Shaheen Bagh. He further added, 'Shaheen Bagh stands tall as a firm example of a peaceful, dignified dissent, more so, in the face of various instances of State-sponsored violence on similar dissents across India.'[85]

What is indeed further intriguing is that the Home Minister did show some inclination to meet the protestors but decided not to do so later on. His willingness expressed via media was taken seriously by the protestors—but it did not materialize as they were not allowed to proceed to the Home Minister's house.[86] Whether being leaderless has harmed the movement and staying away from political parties made it a weak and fragmented voice are some of the questions that scholars who intend to evaluate the movement would raise again and again. Without a doubt, whatever its limits, the movement will be remembered as the evidence of growing politicization of Indian Muslims, particularly Muslim women.

Notes

1 Bilgrami, Akeel. 'Two Historic Deeds: The Common Muslim has done that even Gandhi, Nehru, Ambedkar or Azad Could Not.' www.theoutlookindia.com. 9 February 2020 (accessed on 18 Dec 2023).

2 Elkins, Caroline. 2022. *Legacy of Violence: A History of the British Empire.* London: The Bodley Ltd.

3 Amit Chaudhuri is a novelist, poet, essayist and musician.

4 Chaudhuri, Amit. 2023. *On Being Indian.* New Delhi: Westland Books. P. 71.

5 See reports, Petersen, Hannah Ellis. 2020. 'Delhi rocked by deadly protests during Donald Trump's India visit.' Available at: http://www.theguardian.com. (accessed on 8 June 2020). Also see, 'How foreign media covered anti-CAA protests in India' Available at: http://www.deccanherald.com 19 December 2020 (accessed on 8 June 2020).

6 Jayal, Niraja Gopal. 2019. 'Faith Based Citizenship.' Available at: http://www.indianforum.in. (accessed on 5 May 2020).

7 Jayal, Niraja Gopal. 2021. *Citizenship Imperilled: India's Fragile Democracy.* New Delhi: Orient Blackswan. P 3.

8 'CAA will be implemented before Lok Sabha election, says Amit Shah.' Available at: http://www.thehindu.com. 11 February 2024. (accessed on 24 February 2024).

9 See, Shani, Ornit. 2010.' Conceptions of Citizenship in India and the Muslim Question' *Modern Asian Studies. 44(1):145-173.*

10 See the report, 'Those indulging in arson can be identified by their clothes': Narendra Modi on anti-CAA protest. Available at: http://www.economictimes.indiatimes.com 15 December 2019 (accessed on 8 June 2020).

11 See the report, 'pm-modi-to-hold-5-more-rallies-as-bjp-plans-campaign-blitz' www.thehindustantimes. com. 11 December 2019 (accessed on 5 May 2020).

12 See the report, 'Explained: BJP's defeat in Jharkhand shows limits of the Modi centric campaign in state elections.' Available at: www. Indianexpress.com. 24 December 2019 (accessed on 5 May 2020). According to experts, the BJP campaigned mainly on national issues such as abrogation of Article 370, Ram Mandir, and the citizenship issue.

13 See the report, 'citizenship-bill-clears-lok-sabha-after-fierce-rights-debate.' www.the hindustantimes.com. 10 December 2019 (accessed on 8 June 2020).

14 Ibid.

15 For a comprehensive analysis of AIMIM, see, Farooquee, Neyaz. 2019. 'Asaduddin Owaisi and the AIMIM's rough-and-tumble politics'. Available at: http://www.caravanmagazine.in (accessed on 10 June 2020).

16 Ibid.

17 See Jalal, Ayesha. 1994. *The Sole Spokesman, Jinnah and the Demand For Pakistan*. Cambridge University Press; Pandey, Gyanendra. 2001. *Remembering Partition: Violence, Nationalism, and History In India*. Cambridge University Press; Dhulipala, Venkat. 2015. *Creating a New Medina: State Power, Islam, and the Quest for Pakistan in late Colonial North India*. Cambridge University Press.

18 See Chatterji, Joya. 2023. *Shadows at Noon: The South Asian Twentieth Century*. New Delhi: Penguin Random House. P. 85.

19 See Austin, Granville. 2003. *Working in a Democratic Constitution: A History of Indian Experience*. New Delhi: Oxford University Press.

20 See Roy, Anupama. 2016. *Citizenship in India*. New Delhi: Oxford University Press. P. 8.

21 Ibid. P. 9.

22 See the report, Das, Shaswati and Anuja. 2019. 'Citizenship Bill Clears Rajya Sabha Test in Big win for the BJP.' Available at: http://www. livemint.com. (accessed on 20 June 2020).

23 See the report, 'Government Abolishes Article 370, massive opposition uproar in the House.' Available at: www.economictimes.indiatimes.com. 5 August 2019 (accessed on 10 June 2020).

24 See also my interview, 'Kashmir's Crisis Simmers Dangerously: Attention is Needed.' Available at: http://www.usip.org. 29 October 2019 (accessed on 12 June 2020); also, see Rehman, Shaikh Mujibur. 2019. 'Clearing Up Kashmir Mess.' Available at: http://www.thehindu.com (accessed on 12 June 2020).

25 See, Khurshid, Salman. 2018. *Triple Talaq: Examining Faith.* New Delhi:Oxford University Press; Also see, Khalid, Saif. 2017. 'Faizan Mustafa on India's Triple Talaq Ruling.' Available at: http://www.aljazeera.com. (accessed on 12 June 2020).

26 See the twitter handle@PMOIndia

27 See, Jayal, Niraja Gopal. 2013. *Citizenship and Its Discontents: An Indian History.* Harvard University Press. P. 273.

28 For an incisive analysis on this issue, see Bellamy, Richard. 2008. *Citizenship.* Particularly Chapter 2 titled, 'Theories of Citizenship and their History'. Pp. 27-51.

29 See the report, Venkatesan, V. 2019. 'The NRC case: The Supreme Court's role.' Avaialvble at: http://www.thefrontline.com. 11 (accessed on 20 June 2020).

30 See the report, Venkataramakrishnan, Rohan. 2019. 'Who is Linking the Citizenship Act to NRC? Here are five times Amit Shah did so.' Available at: http://www.scroll.in. (accessed on 8 June 2020).

31 Baruah, Sanjib. 2020. *In the Name of Nation: India and Its North East.* Stanford University Press. P. 49.

32 See, Goswami, Priyam. 2012. *The History of Assam: From Yandabo to Partition, 1826-1947.* New Delhi: Orient Blackswan. Also see, Misra, Udayon. 2018. *Burden of History: Assam and the Partition-Unresolved Issues.* New Delhi: Oxford University Press.

33 See Hazarika, Sanjoy. 2000. *Rites of Passage: Border Crossings, Imagined Homelands, India's East and Bangladesh.* New Delhi: Penguin.

34 See the report, 'Explained: What is the Assam Accord that is fueling protests in the state.' Available at: http://www.Indian express.com. 13 December 2019 (accessed on 8 June 2020).

35 See the report, '3 Communities Wary of Clause 6 in 1985 Assam Accord.' Available at: www. thehindu.com. 26 February 2020 (accessed on 8 June 2020).

36 One of the top leaders of the agitation and a signatory to the Accord, Prafulla Kumar Mahanta, went on to become Chief Minister, and the other, Bhrigu Kumar Phukan, a Minister in the state government. The current Deputy Chief Minister, Sarbananda Sonowal is, like Mahanta, a former president of AASU.

37 See Pisharoty, Sangeeta Barooah. 2019. *Assam: The Accord, The Discord.* New Delhi: Penguin.

38 See, Kimura, Makiko. 2013. *The Nellie Massacre of 1983: Agency of Rioters. New Delhi: Sage.*

39 The Home Ministry took the responsibility to implement the Assam Accord. As part of this task, In 1986, a new Department called "Implementation of Assam Accord Department", to implement the various clauses of the Memorandum of Settlement set up by the Government of Assam. According to the Assam government's website, Implementation of Assam Accord Department monitors 'the works implementing under various clauses of the Assam Accord which is executed by different Department(s)/Organization(s) as entrusted by the Government of India as well as the Govt. of Assam'. Ever since, a sea change in the politics of North-east as well as Assam has taken place. Presently Assam is governed by the BJP government.

40 Foreigners who 'came to Assam after 1.1.1966 (inclusive) and up to 24 March 1971 shall be detected under the provisions of The Foreigners Act, 1946, and The Foreigners (Tribunals) Order, 1964'. Their names 'will be deleted from the electoral rolls in force'. 'Such persons will be required to register themselves before the Registration Officers of the respective districts under the provisions of The Registration of Foreigners Act, 1939, and The Registration of Foreigners Rules, 1939'. While, 'On the expiry of a period of ten years following the date of detection, the names of all such persons which have been deleted from the electoral rolls shall be restored'.

41 See Madhav, Ram. 2014. 'Why Modi is Right on the Bangladeshi migrants' issue.' Available at: http://www.rediff.com. (accessed on 20 June 2020). Ram Madhav is presently spokesman of the BJP.

42 See, Tripathi, Vikas, Das, Tamasa and Goswami, Sandhya. 2018. 'National Narrative and Regional Subtext: Understanding the rise of the BJP in Assam.' *Studies in Indian Politics*. 6(1):60-70.

43 As per the Citizenship Act, 1955, every person born in India (a) on or after the 26th day of January 1950, but before the 1st day of July 1987 (b) on or after the 1st day of July 1987, but before the commencement of the Citizenship (Amendment) Act, 2003 and either of whose parents is a citizen of India at the time of his birth (c) on or after the commencement of the Citizenship (Amendment) Act, 2003, where (i) both of his parents are citizens of India, or (ii) one of whose parents is a citizen of India and the other is not an illegal migrant at the time of his birth, shall be a citizen of India by birth.

44 See the report, 'What is NRC : All you need to know about National Register of Citizens.' Available at: http://www.indiatoday.in. 18 December 2019 (accessed on 8 June 2020).

45 See the report, 'NRC Final list: family members of former President Fakhruddin Ali Ahmed again left out.' Available at: http://www.indianexpress.com. 1 September 2019 (accessed on 20 June 2020).

46 See the report, 'Syeda Anowara Taimur, Assam's lone chief minister, fails to find a place in NRC final draft.' Available at: www.thehindu.com. 4 August 2018 (accessed on 20 June 2020).

47 See the report, Singh, Bikash. 2019. 'Retired army officer from Assam declared foreigner, sent to detention camp'. Available at: http://www.economictimes.indiatimes.com. (accessed on 20 June 2020).

48 See the report, Kalita, Prabin. 2020. 'Assam told to free non-Muslims from detention camps: MoS in Lok Sabha.' Available at: http://www.timesofindia.indiatimes.com. (accessed on 20 June 2020).

49 Roy, Indrajit. 2021. 'Reimagining Citizenship: The Politics of India's Amended Citizenship Laws'. *PS: Political Science & Politics.* 54(4):631.

50 See the report, 'On illegal immigrants in Assam, Bangladesh says no relation with us.' Available at: http://www.deccanchronicle.com. 1 August 2018 (accessed on 20 June 2020).

51 See the report, Singh, Vijaita. 2019. 'Since 2009, States asked by the MHA to set up Detention Centres.' Available at: http://www.thehindu.com. (accessed on 5 May 2020).

52 See Rehman, Mujibur. 'Diversity Needs Secularism.' www.thehindu.com. 2 November 2020 (accessed on 5 May 2020).

53 Ibid.

54 Rehman, Mujibur. (Ed.). 2018. *Rise of Saffron Power: Reflections on Indian Politics.* New Delhi: Routledge.

55 See the report 'Citizenship law not anti-Muslim,Can personally clarify on It: Amit Shah.' Available at: http://www.ndtv.com. 14 February 2020 (accessed on 8 June 2020).

56 See, Engineer, Asghar Ali. 2009. *Communal Riots Since Independence.* New Delhi: Shipra Publications.

57 See Sachar Report. 2006. Government of India, New Delhi.

58 Rehman, Mujibur. (Ed.). 2018. 'Anti-Christian violence in Kandhamal, Odisha' in *Communalism in post-colonial India: Changing Contours.* New Delhi: Routledge. Pp. 216-233.

59 See Basu Ray Chaudhury, Sabyasachi and Ranabir Samadar. (Ed.). 2018. *Rohingyas in South Asia: People without a State.* Routledge; also see, Azeem Ibrahim's *The Rohingyas: Inside Myanmar's Hidden Genocide.* New Delhi: Speaking Tiger.

60 Sukumar, CR. 2019. 'Citizenship Law Fails Three Tests of Classification:

Faizan Mustafa, VC, NALSAR, University of Law.' Available at: http://www.economictimes.indiatimes.com. (accessed on 27 May 2020).

61 See Salve, Harish. 2020. 'CAA is Necessary: Why the Many Arguments About Its Being unconstitutional Don't Hold Water.' Available at: http://www.thetimesofindia.indiatimes.com. Also see, Dehadrai, Jai. 2020. 'Why Harish Salve's Defence Of The CAA is Wrong In Law.' http://www.thewire.com (accessed on 8 June 2020).

62 Kohli, Atul. 1990. 'From Elite Activism to Democratic consolidation: The Rise of Reform Communism in West Bengal.' In Frankel, Francine,and Rao, MSA. (eds.) *Dominance and State Power in Modern India: Decline of a Social Order* (vol 11). New Delhi: Oxford University Press. P. 367.

63 Ibid. P. 368

64 Ibid. P. 368

65 For detailed discussion on this, see ibid. Pp 385-403.

66 See details on the report, Das, Madhuparna. 2016. 'Muslims a Poor Lot in West Bengal: Amartya Sen's Report'. Available at: http://www.economictimes.com. (accessed on 10 January 2024).

67 See, 'After a 101-day sit-in, Shaheen Bagh protest cleared due to Coronavirus Lockdown'. Available at: http://www.thewire.in. (accessed on 8 June 2020).

68 See the report, 'Won't move back on inch even if ... ' Amit Shah to Oppn on CAA. Available at: http://www.thehindustantimes.com. 17 August 2020 (accessed on 10 June 2021).

69 See the report, Sharma, Betwa. 2020. 'The Idea of India: A tribute to Shaheen Bagh.' Available at: http://www.huffintonpost.com. (accessed on 10 June 2020).

70 See the report, Ojha, Arvind. 2020. 'Shaheen Bagh Firing: Shooter Shouts Sirf Hinduon Ki Chalegi, detained.' Available at: http://www.indiatoday.in. (accessed on 20 June 2020).

71 See the report, Gupta, Swati, Suri, Manveena and Hollingsworth, Julia. 2020. 'They tried to stifle the voices of our children: meet the women protestors who have been occupying a New Delhi street for a month.' Available at: http://www.cnn.com. (accessed on 9 June 2020).

72 See, Hameed, Syeda. 2019. 'The Brave Women of Shaheen Bagh.' Available at: http://www.thewire.com. (accessed on 8 June 2020).

73 See the report, 'Video of Shubha Mudgal performing at Shaheen Bagh goes viral.' Available at: http://www.indianexpress.com. 5 February 2020 (accessed on 10 June 2020).

74 See the report, 'TM Krishna sings hum dekhenge in four languages at

Shaheen Bagh in Delhi.' Available at: http://www.scroll.in. 8 Feb 2020 (accessed on 9 June 2020).

75 See, Rawat, Gargi. 2020. 'Sikh farmers from Punjab come to cheer Shaheen Bagh women, cook langar.' Available at: http://www.ndtv.com. (accessed on 10 June 2020).

76 See the report, Hamid, Adil. 2020. 'A Lawyer who feeds the protestors in Shaheen Bagh.' Available at: http://www.frontline.thehindu.com. (accessed on 9 June 2020).

77 See the report, Chattopadhyay, Suhrid Sankar. 2020. 'Kolkota's Shaheen Bagh.' Available at: http://www.frontline.the hindu.com. (accessed on 8 June 2020).

78 See the report, Naig, Udhav. 2020. 'Shaheen Bagh style anti-CAA protest enters day 3 in Chennai.' Available at: http://www.inkl.com (accessed on 12 June 2020).

79 See Mirza, Saeed Akhtar. 2020. 'Remembering the women of Shaheen Bagh, who showed how poetry can overpower violence and hate.' Available at: http://www.scroll.in (accessed on 12 June 2020).

80 Dina M. Siddiqi, an anthropologist at New York University, said these women have broken the monopoly that religious men and 'cherry-picked' politicians had when it came to speaking for India's Muslims. 'That is an enormous step forward for women who are Muslim in India. That is terrific. Nobody is going to go back to those men who were not necessarily representative at all,' she said.

81 Aiyar, Mani Shankar. 2020. 'Eight Takeaways from Shaheen Bagh'. Available at: http://www.theweek.in (accessed on 10 February 2024).

82 Ibid.

83 Ibid.

84 Ibid.

85 See, Rajagopal, Krishnadas. 2020. 'Shaheen Bagh interlocutors file report in Supreme Court.' Available at: http://www.thehindu.com. (accessed on 20 June 2020).

86 See the report, 'Shaheen Bagh protestors not allowed to march to Amit Shah's house.' Available at: http://www.thehindu.com. 16 Feb 2020 (accessed on 20 June 2020).

6

THE UNENDING DEBATE ON MUSLIM BACKWARDNESS

> 'On the 26th of January 1950, we are going to enter into a life of contradictions. In politics we will have equality and in social and economic life we will have inequality. In politics we will be recognizing the principle of one man one vote and one vote one value. In our social and economic life, we shall, by reason of our social and economic structure, continue to deny the principle of one man one value. How long shall we continue to live this life of contradictions?'
>
> —BR Ambedkar, Constituent Assemble Debates

For ages, Indian Muslims have been considered backward, not because they wear sherwani, or skullcap, or eat biryani, or enjoy Qawwali. Their failure to earn enough surplus income to maintain a respectable standard of living is the cause of their backwardness. Indian Muslims are economically backward or poor. They are unable to secure well-paid employment or get a break in entrepreneurial strongholds controlled by ethnic networks.[1] Where they manage to break in, they often do well, for instance, the Khans in Bollywood.[2] Not long ago, Azim Premji,[3] was India's richest man and was considered India's 'most generous' billionaire for the second straight year in 2021. In their book, Raghuram G Rajan and Rohit Lamba[4] provide the example of PC Musthafa's (son of a labourer from Wayanad,

Kerala) successful career as an entrepreneur. Indeed, among the numerous inspiring examples, there is the example of Dr APJ Kalam, India's former President, also known as Missile Man. Being from a modest family background, despite enormous hardships, Dr Kalam, emerged as India's iconic scientist and is celebrated as the People's President. Similar examples could be found from various walks of life in the nooks and corners of this vast land. But these are exceptions, not patterns.

There are two distinct points often lost in the popular or academic discussions on Muslim backwardness. Firstly, what is under discussion is *economic backwardness* not cultural backwardness. Indeed, enough anecdotal accounts exist to show that even conservative Hindus who otherwise consider Islam alien to this land and are distrustful of Muslims hold a high opinion about Muslim culture, say, for instance, the richness of the Urdu language. Secondly, what we need to examine is the longstanding *patterns* not exceptions. The general pattern reflects that a majority of Muslims have neither succeeded in education nor in entrepreneurship.

In 2006, when the Sachar Report published its findings, it came to everyone's knowledge—government as well as people at large—that a vast bulk of Indian Muslims live at the edge of destitution. As the modern world's poorest religious minority, Indian Muslims live in a functioning liberal democracy but they neither crowd streets as beggars nor resort to crime; they often work as vendors and rickshaw pullers for meagre earnings, often reported in glorified terms by economists under the *self-employed* category of employment. According to the Sachar Report (2006), more than 12 per cent of Muslims work as vendors, whereas the national average is only eight per cent. *The New York Times* published a report on Sachar Committee findings titled *Report Shows Muslims Near Bottom of Social Ladder*.[5] While the entire world empathized with the shocking data about the abysmal socio-economic conditions of Indian Muslims, the Hindu Right saw it differently. It saw conspiracy and argued it to be another attempt by the Dr Manmohan Singh-led UPA government and its secular coalition to appease Muslims. And all with a narrow aim to advance their 'vote bank' politics. One wonders if the Hindu Right considers the sufferings of Indian Muslims desirable.

Since my analysis is in the wider context of the Hindu Right, it is only appropriate to preface my discussion by sharing the research findings of Christophe Jaffrelot and A Kalaiyasaran presented in a jointly authored paper titled, *Post-Sachar Indian Muslims: Facets of Socio-economic decline.* In this paper, Muslim conditions under most of the socio-economic indicators, they argue, have deteriorated between the years 2005 to 2012. Based on their analysis of the National Sample Survey (NSS) data, they show further marginalization of Muslim youths since 2014. The authors have some caveats regarding the limitations of data, but the overall exercise appears quite comprehensive to arrive at definite conclusions.

Jaffrelot and Kalaiyasaran further claim that post-2014, there is no 'progressive and decisive policy push'[6] to transform the Muslim conditions that existed before 2012. They write emphatically, 'The most alarming aspect is the worsening situation of the Muslim youth in formal education vis-à-vis other social groups.'[7] They put forward two specific factors to explain their findings: firstly, there are limited policy interventions post-2014 to address exacerbating socio-economic conditions of Indian Muslims. Secondly, many state governments abolished positive discrimination measures for Muslims after 2014. Additionally, since Muslims are disproportionately concentrated in the informal sector, policy decisions such as demonetization and Goods and Services Tax (GST) have adversely affected them. The deepening of communal politics manifested in vigilante groups, and campaigns like ghar wapsi, love jihad, and gau rakshaks. This has also adversely affected the confidence and morale of the Muslim community.

FIGURE 6.1 Percentage of Youth Having Graduate Degree and Above for Social Groups (2012-2018)

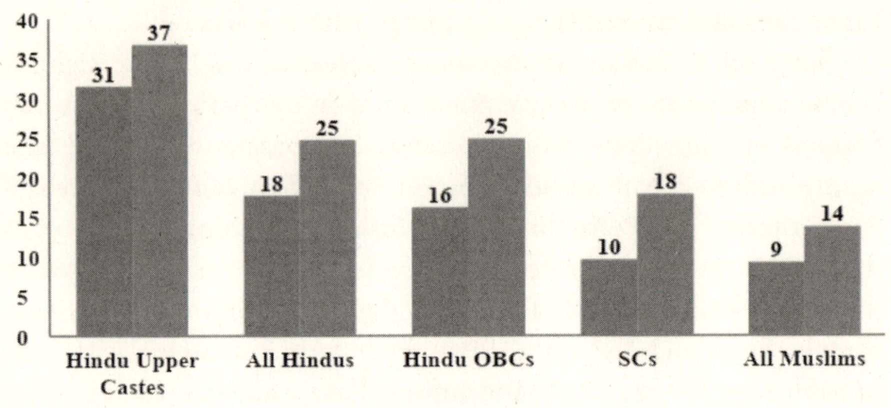

(Source: Christophe Jaffrelot and Kalaiyasaran. 2023. Post Sachar Muslims: Socio- Economic Profile)

As Figure 6.1 shows Muslim youths possessing a graduation degree and above in 2017-18 is 14 per cent as against 18 per cent among Dalits. In the same category, the percentage share for Hindu OBCs is 25 per cent, and for Hindu upper castes is 37 per cent. In 2017-18, the difference between SCs and Muslims was four per cent. Interestingly, in 2011-12, the SC youth was above that of Muslims by one per cent in educational attainment. Furthermore, the gap between Muslims and Hindu OBCs is now 11 per cent and it used to be only seven per cent in 2011-12. It is not hard to surmise from the data presented in the above Figure why Jaffrelot and Kalaiyasaran argue that the educational conditions of Muslim youths have deteriorated.

We need to connect many dots before we make sense of this rather multi-faceted problem called *Muslim backwardness,* which has lasted far too long. Furthermore, the impact of the new politics of the Hindu Right on this perennial problem deserves critical attention.

In an essay I published in 2010, I made the argument that overall accounts of Indian Muslims' relationships with Indian society could be characterized by three particular characteristics: 1) victimhood, 2) violence, and 3) domination.[8] The victimhood dimension is reflected in the perceptions of enduring discrimination that Indian Muslims confront in modern India and the violence part is a result of frequent riots that the community has encountered—even in the heydays of Indian secularism, if there was one! However, the domination aspect of the relationship is revealed in the claim that India was under Muslim rule for hundreds of years. The obvious question then is, how could a vast bulk of a community that governed India for centuries be so poor? Were Muslims also backward or poor during the so-called Muslim rule?[9] A fraction of Muslims certainly were poor even during the so-called Muslim rule—as could be the case with some Hindus or Christians under their respective rules anywhere in the world. For instance, while a fraction of the white population in America could be found to be destitute or poor it won't be similar to the poverty of black people/African Americans that is to be attributed to particular factors rooted in racism or institutionalized discrimination, not merely owing to the flaws of an economic system or failures of a political system.[10] Likewise, Muslim poverty during the so-called Muslim rule and their poverty either in colonial India or modern India are context-specific and demand careful investigation. The electoral dominance of the Hindu Right thus presents a particular context in modern India and how this new context is shaping and likely to shape the Muslim backwardness debate calls for close examination.

Muslim Backwardness Debate After 1857 Mutiny

Analysis of scientific literature on Muslim backwardness would reveal that its nature, depth, and durability has varied from period to period—from colonial times to now—hence the political context holds the key to the investigation. In this chapter, two specific questions are raised:

1. Why has the Muslim community remained so backward despite constitutional provisions against discrimination in modern India?
2. How has the Muslim backwardness debate changed because of the electoral dominance of the Hindu Right?

The subject of Muslim backwardness became a matter of debate during the colonial period, particularly after the 1857 Sepoy mutiny. Having received the fiercest resistance from Muslims during the 1857 revolt, the colonial rulers were keen to understand the rebellious mindset of Indian Muslims.[11] Veer Savarkar, who otherwise wrote multiple volumes portraying Muslims as the enemy community of the Hindus and India, has admired Muslim participation in the mutiny and their valiant role in his book, *The First War of Independence 1857.*[12] Perhaps being inspired by this interpretation by Savarkar, Prime Minister Narendra Modi in his speech in Parliament after the 2019 election results spoke about the way Hindus and Muslims fought against the British in 1857.

The advent of British colonialism not only marked the end of the Mughal rule, it also eclipsed the economic and cultural structure on which Mughal economy operated. Consequently, it devastated the general lives of a vast Muslim population. For instance, the Persian language was superseded in 1837, shutting the doors of employment for many Muslims. Additionally, various new provisions of the law such as the Permanent Settlement of Land Revenue (1793) and the Resumption Proceedings deprived many Muslim families of their livelihood and impacted heavily the economy of the Muslim upper class. At a macro-level, the reorganizing of the political economy of trade resulted in the throwing out of Muslim merchants and business people. A study by Lakshmi Subramanian and Rajat Ray found substantial ship-owning Muslim merchants in 17th century Surat and their oceanic trade with West Asia was favoured by the Mughal regime.[13] However, with the arrival of the British, these Muslim merchants began to lose ground as the English East India Company edged them out.

All in all, Muslims found themselves purged out of the flourishing British colonial economic system. On top of it, many Muslims were reluctant to allow their children to receive an English education, which they suspected to be un-Islamic and a medium for the propagation of Christian ideals. Others believed in the infallibility of the Mughal or

Islamic system, which they hoped might return sooner or later. Henry Bloachmann,[14] an observer of the late 19th century Muslim scene in Bengal, wrote as follows:

> On my rambles in Hoogly district I have invariably met with most educated fathers and most illiterate youths. In the Muhammadan villages, roundabout Pandooah or in the district west of Howrah… I have often been told of the learned men of past generations… where nowadays scarcely an almanack or books of fairy tales are to be met.[15]

Rafiuddin Ahmed in a chapter titled, 'Education, Employment and Social Mobilization' in his book, *The Bengal Muslims 1871-1900,* presents a lucid analysis of Muslim backwardness, and the educational problems and challenges that the colonial system faced, particularly in Bengal during that period. The British policy towards Muslims took a new direction when the so-called Wahhabi trials of 1870-71 brought to the knowledge of the colonial state officials the community's deep disenchantment and suspicion. Prominent officials of the colonial state such as the Viceroy took interest in the well-being of Muslims. According to viceregal notes, Lord Mayo issued his Resolution on Muslim education in 1871 because he wanted to remove 'a cause of disaffection' arising from the Muslims' failure to participate in 'the material advantages which Government education has conferred on the Hindus.'[16]

The publication of WW Hunter's classic, *The Indian Musalmans: Are they Bound in Conscience to Rebel Against the Queen?* is widely considered the first major intellectual articulation of Muslim backwardness. Based on a modest empirical study of Muslims in Bengal, Hunter wrote, 'A great many sections of the Indian population, some 30 million in number, finds itself decaying under the British rule. They complain that they, who but yesterday were conquerors and Governors of the Land, can find no subsistence in it today.'[17] He further noted, 'The truth is that our system of public instruction, which has awakened the Hindus from the sleep of centuries and quickened the inert masses with some noble impulses of a nation, is opposed to the traditions, unsuited to the requirements, and hateful to the religion of the Musalmans.'[18]

Two points in Hunter's study deserve our attention: first, the Indian Muslims' resistance to modernity; and the second is the British response's limitation in addressing Muslim backwardness.[19] It is plausible by replacing *the British system* in the above quote of WW Hunter with *the modern Indian state,* one would be startled to realize nothing much has changed in Muslim conditions despite the end of colonialism and considerable developmental investment by the Indian state after 1947. The widespread perception of discrimination runs deep in the Muslim mind despite the Indian state's constitutional commitment to address backwardness.

According to Raifuddin Ahmad, Hunter's study was focused on Bengal and the problems regarding education among Muslims were mainly a Bengal problem at the time. In other provinces such as West Provinces and Oudh, Muslims were over-represented in comparison to Hindus in colleges and schools. Likewise, the data suggests that in Madras and Bombay, their proportion was reasonable in the education sector. The data in the Punjab also compared favourably against their conditions in Bengal (and Assam).

However, the issue of backwardness was considered a subject of grave concern among the colonial rulers.[20] Bengal was the main example of Muslim backwardness in education. Table 6.2 indicates the proportion of Muslims in various educational institutions in 1874-75:

TABLE 6.2 Muslim Education 1874-5: Bengal Proper[21]

The Unending Debate On Muslim Backwardness	*% Muslim Population*	*% at Schools*	*% Hindu Population*	*% at Schools*
Burdwan	12.8	6.0	85.3	93.5
Rajshahi	61.0	45.0	38.5	54.5
Dacca	59.1	27.0	40.4	73.3

Chittagong	67.4	43.0	29.7	54.5
Presidency	48.2	24.0	50.9	75.0
Total for Bengal Proper	48.8	29.0	50.1	70.1

A particular feature of the Muslim education problem that deserves attention and is not reflected in the Table 6.2 above is: Muslim presence was abnormally low at the higher levels of education. This continues to be the case according to the Sachar Report published in 2006. That, however, does not imply that political context is irrelevant. It matters all the more because the ethical and political obligation of the modern Indian state is far deeper and superior than the British colonial state. In 1875, for example, in the Bengal Presidency, only 5.4 per cent were Muslims of the total number of college students and 93.9 per cent were Hindus. And the story was not different at the secondary school level. In the three Zillah schools of Mymensingh, Comilla, and Barisal, the percentage of Muslim students in 1871 was only 7.4. In the Rajshahi and Chittagong divisions, the relevant percentages were similar. Only at the lower levels of education were the Muslim numbers as high as those of the Hindu community. In Rajshahi, for example, 64 per cent of the primary school children were Muslims in 1874-75; in Dinajpur roughly 63 per cent; in Rangpur 63 per cent; in Bogra about 50 per cent; and in Pabna 44 per cent.[22]

By the mid-19th century, the Muslim upper classes started showing increasing interest in English education. The colonial state initiated measures to address the educational disparity between Muslims and Hindus. Initiated in 1870-71, these measures continued through the 80s and 90s and followed mainly two broad patterns.[23]

Firstly, the colonial state sought to make schools attractive for Muslims to neutralize their prejudices against Western education. These measures included Arabic, Persian, and Urdu languages being made a part of the curriculum in the institutions. Besides, hostels for Muslim students were set up in schools and colleges together with the appointment of Muslim educational officers and teachers, etc. There were scholarships for Muslim students also.

Secondly, measures were taken to bring particularly the maktabs and madrasas under the governance structure of the Education Department. As Nilanjana Paul observes, 'The urban Muslim elites wanted to reconcile and develop an amicable relationship with the British. In this direction, Nawab Bahadur Abdul Latif in Bengal and Syed Ahmad Khan in North India played significant roles in changing the Muslim approach towards the colonizers. According to Syed Ahmad Khan, there were four major reasons for Muslim backwardness: their political traditions, social customs, religious beliefs and poverty.'[24]

At this juncture, we need to reflect on the role of Sir Syed Ahmed Khan to understand what happened to the Muslim backwardness debate during the colonial era. It is widely recognized that Sir Syed established Aligarh Muslim University (AMU). He also made far greater efforts to create a platform for modern education among Muslims, more than just a college or University. His objective was to spread the Aligarh message to Muslims throughout the country. With this larger goal for Muslims in mind, Sir Sayed established the All India Muslim Educational Conference (AIMEC) in 1886. Its goal was to encourage 'the study of Western sciences and literature.'[25] Its annual sessions were held from 1886 to 1945 regularly. Muslim notables, active in education rather than in politics, participated. Between 1905 and 1926, AIMEC appointed full-time agents who travelled for fund collection to various destinations. Grants from the princely states of Bhopal, Hyderabad, and Bahawalpur came for the AIMEC. Among the many goals it set out for itself, it opened a women's school at Aligarh in 1906, and it later became a women's college. The AIMEC promoted various regional associations devoted to Muslim education—for instance, the Anjuman-I-Himayat-i-Islam (AHI) in Lahore. The AIMEC had positive objectives but the task of transforming them into institutions was challenged by the Ulema's opposition to Western learning also. According to Satish Saberwal,[26] Bombay had affluent Muslim merchants in the 19th century but in the 1870s and 1880s, rivalries among them was not of much help.

However, a generation later, AIMEC was able to establish links with Sulaimani Bohra and the Ismaili leadership there. During the pre-partition period, there was a substantial deficit among Indian Muslims' efforts in the domain of institution-building, which continued to be the case in most parts of post-colonial India except in some states in the South, particularly Kerala.

Muslim Backwardness Debate in Post-1947 India

During the 70-odd years of the modern Indian state, a major paradigmatic shift occurred in early 1991-92 when Dr Manmohan Singh as India's finance minister inaugurated the liberalization policy.[27] Consequently, India's development model that was state-led (also called the Nehruvian model because it was devised by India's first Prime Minister Jawaharlal Nehru) was replaced by a market-led strategy. India's liberalization policy continued regardless of the ideologies of coalition groups or political parties which governed India afterwards, marking a new consensus on the ideological debate over economic policy.

Two official reports on the socio-economic conditions of Indians were published since Independence: the first was the Gopal Singh Panel Report[28] submitted to Prime Minister Indira Gandhi in 1983, and the second was the Sachar Report[29] submitted to Dr Manmohan Singh's UPA government in 2006. When the Gopal Singh Panel Report in 1983 was submitted, India was still governed by the Nehruvian model of development, and the Sachar Report was published after more than 15 years of India's liberalization policy.[30] Both reports presented the dismal state of socio-economic conditions of Indian Muslims. Some scholars, such as Bishnu N Mohapatra, have argued that the Sachar Report (2006) is a replication of what Gopal Singh Panel Report (1983) presented.[31] In terms of the thrust of major findings, such a claim is valid, but some key differences exist between the two reports. The Sachar Report is the first official report by the Indian state that focuses exclusively on Indian Muslims, though it contains considerable comparative data with other religions, described as 'socio-religious communities' (SRCs); it also demonstrated under-representation and discrimination against Muslims under riot-free and secular regimes like the Left Front governed West Bengal. Noted Left-wing economist Amiya Kumar Bagchi had hinted at this trend in an essay he wrote in *Economic and Political Weekly* in 1996.[32] Given the overlap in the findings of both the reports, it can be surmised that neither state-led nor market-led models of development has worked for Indian Muslims. What is further striking is the big change in the political and ideological climate in the country that took place between the publication of these two reports.[33] This case is particularly unique to India. Scholars have made forceful arguments that globalization had an adverse effect on the poor in general. The debate between Joseph Stiglitz and Jagdish Bhagwati on the merits and demerits of globalization is useful to look at.[34] Most devastating observations are made by Joseph Stiglitz, who writes, 'The crises that have brought in their wake massive unemployment has, in turn, been followed by longer-term problems of social resolution from urban violence in Latin America to ethnic conflicts in other parts of the world, such as Indonesia.'[35]

The sustained rise of the Hindu Right's electoral power has created fresh political conditions for Muslim backwardness. Thus, any comprehensive examination of the socio-economic backwardness of Indian Muslims should factor in all of these changes that have occurred in the modern Indian state, and the political environment generally. In my opinion, Indian Muslim poverty or backwardness needs to be seen in two broad ways. Firstly, as an integral part of the general backwardness of Indian people, particularly the Indian poor. Sadly, the Indian state, both at the Centre and state level, has failed consistently regardless of the ideological orientation of their regimes over the years. Variations in terms of degree could be identified but overall the failure is spectacular and visible—for instance, in Congress-ruled states, or the Left-ruled states like the Left Front regime in West Bengal or the Hindu Right regime in Gujarat, despite the much-trumpeted Gujarat model. Secondly, there are community-specific factors, which need to be examined to make sense of why Muslim backwardness has been such a lasting phenomenon.

Indian poverty, which is widely recognized in the literature on the subject, is mainly of two kinds: firstly, *economic poverty*; and secondly, *institutionalized poverty*. Like people of other faiths such as Hindus, Christians, or Sikhs, Indian Muslims suffer from both types of poverty. With the formulation of the poverty line by Rath and Dandekar,[36] a far more systematic attempt was made to address economic poverty. Assessments of various anti-poverty programmes have consistently demonstrated that the accomplishment of the Indian state has been modest on this front. Institutionalized poverty is owing to age-old institutions such as caste that have remained the dominant source of discrimination. Indian Muslims have also suffered owing to caste-related factors, which is where discussion on Pasmanda Muslims is important, though egalitarian Islam as a religion does not recognize caste.[37]

Three crucial texts on India's political economy present varying perspectives on the Indian state's accomplishments on the issue of poverty removal and other developmental objectives. Authored by leading economists of distinct ideological persuasions, these three texts are the results of the S Radhakrishnan Memorial Lectures hosted by the University of Oxford, UK, since the early 1980s. They are Pranab Bardhan's *Political Economy of Development In India* (1998), Sukhomoy Chakrabarty's *Development Planning: Indian Experience* (1980), and Jagdish Bhagwati's *India in Transition: Freeing the Economy* (1993). These texts shed valuable insights into the Indian state's approach to address poverty. Broadly, the conclusions of these findings are valid for Indian Muslim situations as well. None of these texts addressed Muslim poverty independently or separately. Muslim poverty has also been neglected in the writings of mainstream scholars writing on India's political economy or development for years. Only after the publication of the Sachar Report was some research undertaken. With the rise of the Hindu Right, particularly after its claim on state power, this interest has substantially reduced.

During the period of Nehruvian development that lasted till the early 1990s, policymaking was mainly dominated by India's Planning Commission. The Commission's understanding of poverty and also of minority issues evolved over the years. The Planning Commission was closed down after the arrival of the Narendra Modi government in 2014, though it had remained a powerful body even during the years of India's liberalization phase, launched in 1991-92.[38] The Commission was adaptive, but its adaptive potential did not convince Prime Minister Modi who perhaps saw it as an appendage of the Nehruvian legacy that needed to be removed as part of the grand objective to make India Congress mukta (Congress-free).

In an op-ed in *The Hindu* in 2017, I made the following observations, 'Nehru and Modi are by far the most ideological Prime Ministers in modern India. Atal Bihari Vajpayee was the first Prime Minister from a Rastriya Swayam Sevak (RSS) background, but he was accommodative, not secular. While Nehru wanted a left-aligned India, Mr Modi is working assiduously to move it towards the Right. The undoing of Nehru is thus a necessary pre-requisite. Federal regimes post Nehru have considerably undone Nehru, consequently creating the conditions for Mr Modi and his fellow travelers to move forward with ease.'[39] Therefore, the decision to replace India's Planning Commission with Niti Ayog needs to be seen in the context of the ongoing ideological struggle between supposedly secular versus the Hindutva elites led by Prime Minister Narendra Modi.

From the point of view of Muslim under-representation as a cause of Muslim backwardness, the composition of the Planning Commission established under Nehru presents an interesting case study. Surprisingly, the Planning Commission did not have a single Muslim as a member during Nehru's tenure as India's Prime Minister. Later, a few Muslims joined the Commission as members, which included AM Khushru, SL Hashim, Abid Hussain, Anwarul Hoda, and Sayida Hameed. Pandit Nehru was aware of Muslim issues very well—particularly its under-representation. In some of his letters to chief ministers, he often recalled the issue of Muslim under-representation. For instance, as early as 1953, Nehru wrote, 'I am distressed to find that position is disadvantageous to them, chiefly to Muslims... In our defense services, there are few Muslims left and in our vast central secretariat there are few Muslims....'[40] His observation in a letter to chief ministers in 1954 was more specific: 'Muslims feel a deep sense of frustrations. They feel services are not open to them in a marked degree, whether defense, police or civil.'[41] And yet, the government organizations, particularly key policy-making bodies such as India's Planning Commission, working under his nose, did not have a single Muslim member! No other Prime Minister was committed to Muslim welfare or building a secular India the way Pandit Nehru was during his time. And yet, Muslim under-representation remained an issue.

Taylor Sherman presents a thoughtful analysis of Nehruvian socialism and its evolution in a chapter titled 'The Myth of Socialism' in her book, *Nehru's India: A History of Seven Myths*. She writes, 'The myth of India's socialism is entwined with the myth of Nehru as the architect of post-colonial India.'[42] She further adds, 'Writing his autobiography while in prison in 1944, Nehru had confessed that studying Marx and Lenin had 'produced a powerful effect' on his earlier self. Skipping through his life, one can easily find material to define him as a socialist.'[43] One way to examine this puzzle is to figure out the relationship between the worldview of socialism and representation or under-representation. Furthermore, there was no direct causal linkage between representation and backwardness in the overall global model of socialism that Nehru was interested in establishing in India. At the same time, Muslim under-representation was pervasive at various levels of the governance structure of the Indian state.

In 1980, Indira Gandhi returned to power in New Delhi after the collapse of the Janata Party government that ousted her in 1977 by launching nationwide anti-emergency protests. The political purpose behind her decision to set up the Gopal Singh Panel report was, among other things, to encourage Muslims to return to the Congress fold.

Many Muslim voters had drifted away during the Emergency owing to coercive family programs that her son Sanjay Gandhi was mainly considered responsible for implementing.[44] This was the first report by the government of India that revealed Muslim backwardness. It was submitted in two volumes to Prime Minister Indira Gandhi in 1983. Since the Congress party had ruled India till then (barring the Emergency period from 1977-1980) Indira Gandhi could not blame anyone. Rafiq Zakaria, a towering intellectual Muslim politician had served as the Member-Secretary of the Committee. Indira Gandhi said to Mr Zakaria that, 'post mortem does not help forget the past. Let us look for the future.'[45] Indian Muslims, according to the report, were educationally worse off than most religious minorities, even compared to Dalits. They are severely under-represented in various services—IAS (3.22 per cent); IPS (2.64 per cent) and IFS (3.14 per cent). These findings about Muslim under-representation reflecting communities' backwardness remained outside the domain of public knowledge because the government of Indira Gandhi (1980-84) and Rajiv Gandhi (1984-89) chose not to present the report in parliament. It remained outside public knowledge for a long time. Eventually, it was the government of VP Singh who chose to present the report in the Parliament. However, the report's major recommendations were rejected.[46]

By the late 1980s, the politics of India was moving gradually towards the Hindu Right. Owing to the growing popularity of the Ayodhya movement,[47] public sentiment against Muslims also started rising rather sharply. In the 1989 parliamentary election, the BJP emerged as a major electoral force with 89 seats in the Parliament, deepening tensions in Hindu-Muslim relations in most parts of India. As part of its propaganda against Muslims, the Hindu Right renewed its age old Muslim appeasement accusation with greater vigor. The Shah Bano Bill (1987) passed by Rajiv Gandhi further lent legitimacy to the appeasement argument. Although Muslims were backward and under-represented in most sectors of the Indian economy, as recorded by the Gopal Singh Panel Report (1983), the Hindutva forces were able to mobilize around the argument of appeasement causing mass resentment against Muslims. Had the report been made public and data about Muslim backwardness available during the late 1980s, there was a fair chance that the politically motivated anti-Muslim campaign could have been considerably neutralized. A healthy public debate over Muslim or minority issues could have undermined the Hindutva campaign against Muslims.

The 1990s saw a massive social and electoral expansion of the Hindu Right. It is a period when the Hindu Right and the BJP became electorally and politically dominant. The BJP emerged as the single largest party in 1996 with 161 seats and the vote share rose to 20.29 per cent. With this transformation in the political arena, the discussion on poverty took a completely new turn. It was believed that the state-led development had not worked for any section of Indian society since the late 1980s. The deep crisis of the Indian economy was manifested in the staggering Balance of Payment (BOP) crisis, which became the background to launch India's much-celebrated liberalization policy in 1991-92.[48] All in all, the Muslim issue was pushed into the background as a policy question but figured prominently as a polarizing subject with the demolition of Babri Masijd in 1992.[49] As Zoya Hasan rightly observes, 'Issues relating to education, health, housing, and employment were rarely ever raised by the Congress and its Muslim interlocutors who found it easier to mobilize the community through identity-related issues.'[50]

Sachar Report and Challenges

On the Muslim backwardness issues, the UPA government led by Dr Manmohan Singh published two reports prepared under the chairmanship of two former judges—one by Justice Rajinder Sachar[51] (popularly known as Sachar Report) and the other by Justice Ranganath Mishra[52] (known as Mishra Commission Report) with considerable overlap in their objectives. These two reports became key to public debate on Muslim issues, particularly on its backwardness puzzle. But it is the Sachar Report that drew worldwide attention and continues to be a reference point despite the Modi regime's deliberate attempt to give it less prominence. The notification for the Sachar Commission by the Prime Minister's office was taken out on 9 March 2005, and the report was submitted in 2006. On the other hand, the notification for the Ranganath Mishra Commission was taken out on 29 October 2004, a few months earlier than the Sachar Report but its report was submitted on 10 May 2007, also a few months later.

The Sachar Report was exclusively on Indian Muslims, which in itself was the first of its kind. Earlier, the Gopal Singh Panel Report (1983) studied religious communities from a comparative perspective. A Muslim-specific report was not only unprecedented but a politically bold decision by the UPA government given that the Hindu Right organizations were by now well-entrenched in India's political system, unlike the early 1980s when the Gopal Singh Panel was given the task to prepare a report. The decision to set up a Sachar Committee was made at a time when the political climate during the NDA regime was increasingly getting polarized across religious lines, and the Hindu-Muslim issue had received a new lease of life. There were debates concerning communication of the educational curriculum, also known as textbook controversy.[53] More importantly, the Gujarat carnage in 2002 was part of national as well as global debate. Though Prime Minister Vajpayee enjoyed a far more moderate image compared to Prime Minister Narendra Modi, these developments caused considerable anxiety among India's religious minorities—particularly Muslims and Christians. Dr Manmohan Singh's government had the support of the Left parties and considered it a matter of priority to intervene to restore the confidence of Muslims in the Indian political system.

Dr Manmohan Singh took an active interest in the setting up of the Sachar Committee and Ranganath Commission. Dr Singh personally persuaded reluctant members to serve on the Committee. For instance, Tahir Mehmood, a member of the Ranganath Commission, was persuaded by Dr Manmohan Singh who was aware that he supported reservation for minorities.[54] He persuaded Tahir Mahmood by saying, 'I am not a lawman. Recommending reservations needs support with legal grounds; that is why I set up this Commission and that is why I nominate you to this commission.'[55] Likewise, Dr Abu Saleh Shariff told me in a conversation how he requested Prime Minister Dr Singh that he would serve the commission only if it was exclusively on Muslims.[56]

It was Dr Manmohan Singh's pro-active interest, I'd like to argue, that led to the formation of the Sachar Committee. Had Dr Singh not been the Prime Minister, one wouldn't be too sure if such a Committee could have ever come into existence. The Congress party's secular politics since the late 1980s or even before, according to some scholars such as Paul Brass, was perceived as seriously compromised.[57] Concerning Muslims, it became quite apparent during the Ayodhya movement that the Congress party was more into a balancing act between supposedly Hindu interests and Muslim interests—hoping that it could remain a catch-all party in an increasingly polarized political environment. What the Congress party could not foresee was the rapidly changing dynamics of the political forces around caste and religion unfolding on the ground—particularly after the Mandal Commission Report. The emergence of political parties such as the BSP or SP presented a sustained threat to the Congress party's old strategies to retain divergent social bases, particularly in Uttar Pradesh.[58] Hence, its ambivalent position caused Muslim voters, particularly in North India, to drift towards emerging parties such as SP and BSP during the late 1980s and 1990s.

Dr Manmohan Singh, as a seasoned policy maker, was aware of Muslim deprivation and followed the conventional way of addressing it by setting up the Committee.[59] He perhaps understood that a coalition, particularly of secular parties, would present a supporting background to advance this issue. The Congress party, particularly the UPA benefitted out of it, as the results of the 2009 Parliamentary elections would corroborate. Unfortunately, Dr Manmohan Singh has not received as much credit as he deserves for steering this one.

Perhaps he was not interested either because he was not attempting to build a social base for himself or hijack the party. Indeed, the assertive role of Dr Manmohan Singh becomes clear when one looks at the political positioning of Sonia Gandhi and Rahul Gandhi. Gandhis are not unapologetic secularists. Once Narendra Modi's dominance was established, Sonia Gandhi cancelled the Congress Iftar party to shun the Party's allegedly pro-Muslim image. In a panel discussion over the results of Karnataka in 2023 hosted by the Indian Diaspora Group, Washington DC,[60] Sunita Viswanath, a founder of Hindus for Human Rights (HHR) shared that though Rahul Gandhi has been consistent in his criticism of Narendra Modi, he does not utter the word 'Muslim' while attacking the Hindu Right. Unfortunately, many secular leaders are hesitant to utter the 'M' word meaning Muslim on their lips these days, which is a reflection of both the growing dominance of Hindutva politics and the fragile nature of Indian secularism.

After working for 18 months, the 403-paged Sachar Report was submitted in 2006, triggering a global debate. The Commission had the following members: Justice Rajinder Sachar as Chairperson, Dr Abu Saleh Shariff as Member-Secretary, and the members Saiyid Hamid, Dr TK Ommen, MA Basith, Dr Rakesh Basant, and Dr Akhtar Majeed. But there should have been at least two or three women members in the Committee if not more. There are enough competent women available for the job. However, the Chairperson explained this all-men Committee in the *Foreword* of the Report as follows:

> During the Committee's interaction with women's groups, some of them seriously articulated a grievance that it did not have any woman member. The Committee tried to make up for this by convening a half-day meeting with women's groups during its visits to the States. In addition to that, women social activists in larger numbers attended all the meetings of all groups and expressed their points of view and apprehensions in an open and frank manner. Their input was intensive and to the point about various matters

like education, medical facilities, Aganwadi requirements, etc. The Committee also held one full-day meeting in Delhi in July 2006 exclusively for women from all over India .[61]

Even if one appreciates the Chairperson's gesture to rectify the gender bias in the composition of the Committee, it does not dilute patriarchy in any manner. It only suggests that women can represent indirectly, and cannot have a voice of their own. Notwithstanding this flaw, the report comprehensively discusses women's issues.

The report covered a wide range of themes but a few that present adequate light on the analysis of Muslim backwardness are as follows:

1. educational backwardness;
2. employment and credit-related issues;
3. Muslim caste issues and its backwardness.

Chapter Four, 'Educational Conditions of Muslims',[62] presented a detailed comparative analysis with other Socio-Religious Communities (SRC). According to the analysis, a significant disparity between the status of Muslims and that of other SRCs (except SCs and STs) can be noted. For example, both the mean years of schooling and attendance levels of Muslims are low in absolute terms and in contrast to all SRCs, except in some cases of SCs/STs. In several contexts, SCs and STs are found to have overtaken Muslims.[63]

The report further observed that the gap between Muslims and other SRCs is generally higher in urban areas than in rural areas. Two further crucial observations include: 1) Muslim parents are not opposed to or resist the idea of modern education. They are eager to send their children to government schools; 2) Muslim parents' failure to send their girls to schools is not because they are not interested but the challenges to send them to schools are often very high. For instance, often schools are located in faraway places and not easily accessible for girls in the early phases of their education. Other factors that contribute to this sad situation of exclusion include the absence of girls' hostels, the absence of female teachers, and the non-availability of scholarships as they move up the education ladder.[64]

The dropout rates among Muslims, it is further noted, are higher at the level of primary, middle, and higher secondary compared to all the SRCs. The difference in the graduation attainment rates has been widening between Muslims and all other categories since the 1970s. This is both the urban and rural areas. The most significant finding is its claim that only three per cent of Muslim children of school-going age go to Madrasas.[65] Ever since 9/11, the growth of Islamic radicalization has been attributed to the Madrasas education system. According to this study, for example, in West Bengal where Muslims form 25 per cent of the population, the number of Madrasa students is at 3.41 lakhs and is only four per cent of the 7-19 age group.[66] It also sheds light on the popular misconception between Madrasas and Maktabs. The latter is a neighbourhood school, often attached to a mosque, that offers religious education to children who attend other mainstream schools. Combining the estimates of madarsas and maktabs only 6.3 per cent of all Muslim children attend any form of madrasa.[67]

When it comes to employment, firstly, the community is overwhelmingly self-employed; and secondly, there is massive under-representation of the community in employment in various sectors of the economy.

The Muslim workers, the report claims, are more engaged in self-employed manufacturing and trade activities.[68] Further, Muslim workers, it suggests, tend to be more vulnerable in terms of conditions of work (contract length, social security, etc.) because they are concentrated in the informal sector in a big way. Other important findings show interesting employment patterns of Muslims compared to other SRCs and SCs/STs are as follows:

1. The prospect of being in regular non-agricultural employment for male workers is higher for SC/ST and Muslim workers as compared to all other SRCs in rural areas.
2. The prospect of Muslim workers taking up regular work is the lowest, while that of SC/ST workers is the highest among urban male workers.

3. The prospect of undertaking regular non-agricultural employment is the highest among rural SC/ST female workers. This is followed by other minorities and the rest of the SRCs.
4. The prospect of undertaking regular work is the lowest for urban Muslim female workers, and interestingly, the SCs/STs have the highest chances. This is followed by other minorities, Hindu OBCs, and Hindu Upper Castes (UCs).[69]

Obvious questions that arise are: Why are Muslims in the self-employment category instead of public or private employment? Why are they not able to rise above poverty even if they have autonomy of choice in employment? These jobs are described as self-employment and are not economically rewarding. For instance, a vegetable vendor whose net income is very low could fall in the self-employed category. Because, often, Muslims opt for self-employment more out of their failure to find employment in the private or public sector, which is further owing to the prevalence of deep-seated prejudices against the community. Furthermore, to make sense of why the self-employment category is not economically rewarding demands an investigation into credit systems and practices, particularly what the Sachar Report says about it.

Another disturbing trend is the low and insufficient access of Muslims to bank credit, including the priority sector advance (PSA). The average size of the credit is relatively small, particularly compared with other SRCs in public sector banks and private sector banks. Concerning finance, the situation is not any different for institutions, such as SIDBI and NABARD. Part of the reason why this has occurred is also because 'some banks use the practice of identifying negative geographical zones based on certain criteria whether bank credit and other facilities are not easily provided.'[70]

The other theme to which the SCR made a vital contribution is the relationship with institutional poverty that Muslims suffer owing to their caste identities. Islam does not approve of caste but Indian

Muslims do have castes and even have caste practices owing to a lack of Islamization, some would say.

At the policy-making level, the Sachar Report perhaps has made the most prominent identification of this relationship and has recommended measures on how to address them. The chapter 'The Muslim OBCs and Affirmative Action'[71] presents an insightful analysis of this vexed issue alluding to various reports and judicial verdicts.

Based on the analysis of the Kaka Kalelkar Commission (1955) and BP Mandal Commission (1980), which have recognized the presence of castes among Muslims, the Report has argued that the Indian Muslim community has mainly three categories of castes: Ashraf, Ajlaf, and Arzal. The Ashraf category includes all Muslims of foreign blood and converts from higher castes. In Uttar Pradesh, Bihar, and Bengal, Sayyads, Sheikhs, Moghuls, and Pathans are part of the Ashraf category of castes. Another category is Ajlaf which means degraded or unholy and includes those who take part in ritually clean occupations. They are considered as low-ranking converts. Examples of this category are carpenters, artisans, painters, graziers, tanners, milkmen, etc. According to the Census of 1901, the Ajlaf category includes various classes of converts. In Bihar, they are known as Nao-Muslim and in North Bengal as Nasya. It further includes various other groups such as julaha or weaver, dhunia or cotton trader, kulu or oil presser, kunjra or vegetable seller, hajjam or barber, and darzi or tailor.[72]

The third category according to the 1901 Census is Arzal. It comprises castes, such as Halalkhor, Lalbegi, Abdal, and Bediya, and they are the lowest ones.[73] The people of these caste groups have traditional occupations that are identical to their Hindu counterparts in the list of SCs. The Report further states, 'It is widely believed that these communities are converts from the untouchables among Hindus. Change in religion did not bring any change in their social or economic status but they are denied Scheduled Caste (SC) status, which is available to their Hindu counterparts.'[74] Indeed, this exclusion from the SC list dates back to 1936, when the imperial government rejected SC status for Christians and Buddhists of similar origins. Depressed classes such as Halalkhors among Muslims were included but were denied benefits, a denial that has continued according to the Constitutional Order 1950, and its subsequent revisions in 1956 which included Sikhs of this category, and, in 1990, included neo-Buddhists.

The Report recommends affirmative action policies for Muslim OBCs after a comprehensive analysis of existing situations in various states. It argues that the three models of affirmative action policies available are[75]:

1. Seat reservations for the entire community (excluding the creamy layer): Kerala and Karnataka
2. Reservations owing to backward caste/biradari including Muslim groups, covering 95 per cent of its population in Tamil Nadu.
3. Division of Other Backward Castes (OBCs) into backwards and most backwards (MBCs)—with most of the Muslim backwards in the MBC list in Bihar.

The major recommendations included:

1. Setting up a National Data Bank 'to assess afresh the data needs for evaluating conditions of citizens by the SRC status regularly to understand and assess the flow of the development needs.'[76]
2. Setting up an autonomous Assessment and Monitoring Authority (AMA) to evaluate the extent of development benefits which accrue to different SRCs through various programs.
3. Equality of Opportunity Commission (EOC) be set up to look into grievances of the deprived groups in lines of the Race Relations Act 1967.[77]
4. To promote diversity and arrest religious ghettoization, the Committee proposed the construction of a Diversity Index

(DI) that would measure diversity in critical areas such as education, private sector, and housing complex to promote 'composite living spaces.'[78]

5. Finally it has a series of suggestions on how to improve education, particularly higher education and modernization of madrasas, which has been a concern as its curriculum is limited to religious studies.

The major shortcoming of the report is, however, that it is a politically gender-less, and ideologically neutral document. The Report was deliberately politically toned down or ideologically muted, being driven by a naïve assumption that the findings would appeal to all forms of political regimes regardless of their ideological view of Indian Muslims. This assumption was a mistake as the trends since 2014 indicate. In an essay in the *Frontline* under the title, 'Sachar Report: Shaved and Forgotten', former Member Secretary Dr Abu Saleh Shariff wrote, 'Now that the National Democratic Alliance (NDA) is at the helm of the affairs at the Centre, one tends to find either unresponsive governance or often an unfriendly attitude.'[79] And yet the Hindu Right unleashed a massive attack on the document, raising questions about its authenticity and even its relevance.

The Sachar Report was embroiled in controversy even during its preparation. When the data from the armed forces on the proportion of Muslims in the army was sought by the Committee, it was accused of trying to communalize it. On this, Shekhar Gupta raises the following concern, 'If official concerns about the proportional representation of Muslims take root, there can be questions why other minorities, Sikhs and Christians, for example, are over-represented in armed forces. Then you are sucked into a disastrous spiral.'[80] Justice Sachar explained in his foreword, 'The Committee received data from the Navy and Air Force. However, the Ministry of Defense informed the committee that it could supply the data to the Army. It also requested the Committee not to use the data which had already been sent to it by the Air Force and Navy. Thus in the report, wrote

Sachar, the Committee has not used the data received from the Armed forces.'[81]

The Left parties were more aggressive in dismissing the BJP's charges of appeasement. Brinda Karat of the CPI(M) said the report had completely turned on its head the issue of so-called minority appeasement. 'Our party is concerned. The government has now to look into specific components which are indicators of development and to which the community does not seem to have access, like education, employment, bank loans.'[82] The CPI leader Gurudas Das Gupta said the Left was against religion-based reservation but quite clearly, there was an urgent need to take steps.

According to the Annual Report 2019-20 prepared by the Ministry of Minority Affairs (MMA) under the current Modi government, out of 76 recommendations made by the Sachar Committee, 72 were accepted, three were not accepted, and one was deferred.[83] The rejected three recommendations are as follows: 1) enumeration of caste/groups as a part of the decennial census exercise; 2) creation of All India cadre of officers to manage the affairs of State Waqf Boards and Central Waqf Council; 3) having an alternative criteria for admission to facilitate admissions to the most backwards amongst the SRCs in various institutions such as universities and colleges. The recommendation that was deferred was for absorbing Arzals in the SC list or at least in a separate list of MBCs carved out of the OBCs.

While the UPA government responded to it enthusiastically, this enthusiasm slowed down after a couple of years. The fact remains that the early enthusiasm with which the UPA began its attempt to bring about what Tarunabh Khaitan[84] considers a 'paradigm shift' about policymaking towards minorities, particularly Muslims, seems to have lost steam. Heewon Kim raises several concerns in her book, *The Struggle for Equality: India's Muslims and Rethinking the UPA Experience.* She writes 'Yet, within three years of the UPA's election, most of these policy initiatives were put on the back burner. While publicly the Congress-led coalition still professed commitment to these policies, its allegiance was more tactical, symbolic and performative.'[85]

Among all the questions Heewon Kim raises, two are vital to our analysis: What accounts for this about turn? Why did it slow down? She explains it by analysing what she describes as institutional policy analysis. This she elaborates by focussing on the institutionalized opposition to the UPA policies that made them ineffective. Three particular areas, she recognizes, where resistance to these policies arose: first, it arose from the institutionalized Scheduled Caste (SC), Scheduled Tribe (ST) and Other Backward Class (OBC) regimes and lobbies considered guardians of these caste groups' interests. They saw these provisions as encroaching upon their rights and also diluting their institutional structures and legal provisions of reservations; secondly, it was entrenched in the state structures which include civil services and the judiciary. It looks at minority issues as religiously defined and incompatible with the policies of a secular state. Thirdly, it was articulated most forcefully by the BJP and the allied forces of the Hindutva, and some within the Congress party as well. Its primary objective 'was to protect the ideological construction of caste as it is the firm defender of the Constitutional settlement. This opposition rejected the claims of religious identity as a marker of social and economic disadvantage.'[86] While I endorse broadly her set of explanations, I would, however, argue it is mainly the third factor that played a major role in creating the general political climate that led to the UPA regime's diminished enthusiasm for these policies. Though Dr Manmohan Singh was India's Prime Minister and mainly spearheaded the workings of this Committee by giving it complete support from his office, he was aware that he did not have the requisite political capital in the electoral arena. When the BJP and the other entities of the Hindu Right targeted the Sachar Report as an act of vote bank politics, Dr Singh began to withdraw, and the Congress party failed to counter-challenge the BJP and the Hindu Right organizations on this point. It is well known that the Congress and other secular parties were invariably defensive when it came to dealing with the onslaught by the Hindu Right on Indian minorities, particularly Muslims. Such behaviour by secular leadership has given lot of legitimacy to the Hindu Right.

Closer to the end of its second term, the UPA government set up a panel to evaluate its implementation of the Sachar Report headed by noted economist Amitabh Kundu. Its members included PC Mohanan, Amir Ullah Khan, PA Inamdar, Manzoor Alam, Jeemol Unni, Ali Ahmed Khan, and Abdul Shaban. The Committee submitted its interim report in March 2014 to K Rahman Khan, Minister of Minority Affairs (MMA), and found the implementation rather unsatisfactory.[87] The final report was submitted to the MMA under the Modi government a few months later in early 2015 to Najma Heptullah, Minister in charge. Dr Abu Saleh Shariff, member secretary of the Sachar Report, published a book titled *Institutionalising Constitutional Rights*. According to Dr Shariff, his book had two major motivations: firstly, to examine if the Report's recommendations that were supposed to be pursued by various ministries and departments such as labour, human resources, and employment were implemented seriously or not. Not surprisingly, Dr Shariff did not find it satisfactory; secondly, the MMA that was set up in 2006 was seeking to implement various recommendations. After eight long years of its existence, there was no impact assessment or review. According to the author, the 'broad findings of this book and the Post-Sachar Evaluation committee (PSEC) are in tandem and make a strong case for institutionalizing constitutional rights to address the issue of deprivation of the Indian Muslims.'[88]

In India's democratic politics, a great deal of sincerity has been displayed in the setting up of committees by various governments. On the issue of implementation of such committees, there has not been sincerity of most regimes regardless of their ideological complexion. The record of the UPA government on the issue of implementation of the Sachar Report's recommendations is very modest. What is noteworthy is that the UPA government chose to implement some of its recommendations, which has forced the Modi-led NDA government to continue with them, and in some instances, with its ideological spin as was the case with the Multi-Sectoral Development Program (MSDP).

Apart from all these, there is another significant issue that needs to be borne in mind while pondering the development of Indian Muslims. There is a shift in the migration pattern among Indian Muslims, which is not similar or parallel to other religious communities.

TABLE 6.3 Migration Rates (migrants per 1000 population) for Major Religious Groups

	RURAL			*URBAN*		
	Male	*Female*	*Person*	*Male*	*Female*	*Person*
55th round	(1999-2000)					
Hindus	**69**	**439**	**250**	**277**	**442**	**356**
Muslims	49	331	189	159	301	227
Christians	**128**	**332**	**231**	**296**	**402**	**349**
Sikhs	84	533	298	186	468	320
Jains	**37**	**588**	**288**	**212**	**474**	**340**
Buddhists	111	468	285	314	431	369
All	**69**	**427**	**244**	**257**	**418**	**334**
64th round	(2007-08)					
Hindus	**55**	**490**	**267**	**285**	**483**	**380**
Muslims	40	390	211	143	333	234
Christians	**98**	**364**	**230**	**257**	**401**	**334**
Sikhs	52	577	303	196	565	365
Jains	**131**	**554**	**314**	**273**	**527**	**395**
Buddhists	109	524	309	369	538	453
All	**54**	**477**	**261**	**259**	**456**	**354**

Source: Computed from unit-level data 'All' includes other religions, religion not reported etc.

We learn from this table that Muslims record the lowest percentages of migrants in their population in both rural and urban areas among major religious groups. This is for men as well as for women. According to Amitabh Kundu, 'The percentage of migrants among Muslim males has however gone down in both rural and urban areas, along with that of Christians, which is not the case for other communities.'[89] Mr Kundu further observes that this is a matter of serious concern for Muslims since their share of migrants is the lowest across communities.[90] Historically, a vast majority of Muslims have been urban dwellers.

Sachar Report (2006) and the Hindu Right

Two particular strands of criticism were hurled by the Hindu Right at the Sachar Report and its findings. Soon after its publication, the BJP's top leadership as well as some of its mouthpieces such as *The Organizer* attacked the Report as an act of appeasement by the UPA government, and its secular allies as another effort in vote bank politics. Both the phrases, 'appeasement' and 'vote bank politics' have long existed in the political vocabulary of the Hindu Right as a weapon to attack Indian Muslims. The same old weapon the Hindu Right began to deploy to delegitimize the fresh interventions made by the Indian state to address the worsening conditions of Indian Muslims. Another strand of criticism emerged in the response formulated by the Gujarat state government headed by Narendra Modi at the time. For instance, the Gujarat government was not willing to offer scholarships that were started for Muslim students based on the Sachar Committee recommendations. Except the Gujarat government, other BJP governments such as Madhya Pradesh and Rajasthan implemented the scholarship provisions for Muslim students. Interestingly, the Gujarat government took the matter to court.[91]

After a couple of years, however, with Mr Modi's ambition to become India's Prime Minister, he began Muslim outreach. There was some rethinking of his approach, which led to the reframing of his take on the Sachar Report, the results of which were witnessed in the post-2014 regime. As a prime ministerial candidate in 2014 with a campaign slogan of *Sabka Sath Sabka Vikas,* Mr Modi began selectively using the Sachar Report as campaign rhetoric, which encouraged the BJP leadership to take another look at its deplorable approach to the Sachar Report.

Unfortunately, even some senior members of the BJP's top leadership did not apply their minds while spreading the age-old campaign of appeasement against Muslims. They ignored hard facts on Muslim suffering and attributed negative motives to a sincere piece of policy work for the welfare of India's largest and poorest religious minority. For instance, Sushma Swaraj,[92] a distinguished political figure and former Foreign Minister of India, reacted to the Sachar Report by saying that 'it was full of prejudices.'[93] She further argued that Dr Manmohan Singh's attempt to look at the vast Muslim population's root cause of enduring backwardness was another extension of cynical politics that led to India's Partition in 1947. In her words, 'Ironically, 100 hundred years after the first seed of a separate electorate for Muslims was sown in India, which ultimately led to the demand for Partition, a report has come talking of nomination for Muslims.'[94]

Another prominent critic of the Report was Mr Venkaiah Naidu,[95] then serving as the BJP's Vice President and later served as India's Vice President. He announced, 'We don't accept the report which does not have scientific analysis.'[96] He further alleged that a scientific study had also indicated that in seven states including Maharashtra, the percentage of educated Muslims was more than that of Hindus. This report, Mr Naidu warned, would create more divisions and give birth to a new Pakistan and all other communities would also start demanding the same. Mr Naidu even announced that his party would launch the 'Janjagran Abhiyan' from the bloc to district level on issues like the Sachar Report, price hikes, and suicides by farmers from 16 January till May in the year 2007.

What further polarized the debate was a statement by Prime Minister Dr Manmohan Singh, at the 52nd meeting of the National Development Council in December 2006. According to reports, Prime Minister Dr Manmohan Singh said that minorities (Muslims) should have first claim on natural resources.[97] This provoked the BJP to unleash severe criticisms of the Sachar Report and Dr Manmohan Singh's government's intentions. Dr Singh's remark continues to be raised by the BJP leaders. For instance, Prime Minister Narendra Modi said in 2018, 'For the last two days, I am hearing that a *naamdar* leader (a sarcastic reference to Rahul Gandhi) recently said that the Congress is a party of Muslims. I'm not surprised. Even former Prime Minister Manmohan Singh once said that Muslims have the first right over the nation's natural resources.'[98] Given the indiscriminate way allegations of appeasement and vote bank politics is deployed by the Hindu Right to target Muslims, it is plausible, regardless of Dr Singh's remark, that the Hindu Right's attack on Sachar Report would have continued. Dr Singh's remark was just an alibi to make some noise!

In 2006, when the Sachar Report was submitted, Narendra Modi was serving his second term as Gujarat's Chief Minister. He did not take the report or its findings kindly, partly because of his party's ideological understanding of the concepts of majority and minority. For the Hindu Right, the idea of majority and minority is inherently divisive because everyone is a citizen and thus equal in the eyes of the state. Though it sounds like very well-argued egalitarian reasoning, its real problem lies in its unwillingness to accept the distinct nature of the notion of minority rights. Also, because the normative logic of majoritarianism claims that it is inherently non-discriminatory, the Modi government did not implement the central government scholarship for Muslim students in Gujarat. Other BJP-ruled states such as Jharkhand and Chhattisgarh implemented such scholarship schemes.

The Gujarat government's decision not to offer scholarships to Muslim students as recommended by the Sachar Report was brought to the attention of Mr Modi at a presentation made by Zafar Mehmood[99] in 2013, as part of Mr Modi's Muslim outreach. Mr Mahmood made the presentation at the Young Indian Leaders Conclave organized by Citizen of Accountable Governance. Former Chief Minister, Narendra Modi, remained closeted for a day with 150 young participants. Out of the 150, around 30 were from the Muslim community. In his presentation, Dr Mahmood highlighted the plight of the victims displaced by the 2002 riots.[100]

Besides raising issues like the BJP's view on the Sachar Committee, anti-Muslim articles on the BJP's official website, and creating a special cadre for the Waqf board, Mahmood said the central scholarship for minorities was not implemented in Gujarat even though the BJP governments in Chhattisgarh and Jharkhand were implementing such schemes. 'It is very good you said all that and I will consider it. We have come to know the points raised by you. I and my companions in the party will consider it,'[101] Mahmood quoted Modi as saying according to media reports.

What is interesting to learn is as Narendra Modi began to nurture Prime Ministerial ambitions, his attitude towards Muslims or Muslim issues began to change. Mr Zafar Sureshwala[102] played a vital role in working as an interlocutor and helped set up many meetings of Muslims from various walks of life with the then Gujarat Chief Minister Narendra Modi. On the one hand, while Modi was becoming increasingly flexible in his approach to Muslim issues, the approach of the BJP was also becoming less critical and more accommodative around the same time—particularly closer to the 2014 parliamentary elections.

Having attacked the Sachar Committee from the outset, the BJP made a U-turn according to a report published in *The Hindu* on 12 March 2014.[103] The then Party spokesperson, Shahnawaz Hussain, said the Sachar Committee's findings would form the basis of the BJP's policy orientation in the future. On the question of whether the BJP would implement the recommendations of the Committee, he said, 'Modiji has quoted from the report. That means that we take serious notice of the findings of the report. Recommendations are a different matter. The BJP's policy towards the Muslims will be geared towards improving education and health standards besides poverty alleviation.'[104] Thus, Modi's motivated use of the Sachar Report brought some moderation in the BJP's attack on it closer to the 2014 election campaign, but not its ideological position about Muslims.

On the other hand, Indresh Kumar, head of the Muslim Rashtriya

Manch (MRM), used the Sachar Report as a major tool in his dialogue with the Muslim community as he began canvassing for Narendra Modi in 2014. The Rastriya Muslim Morcha boasts of a 32-member national-level committee, and a 250-member national council and is spread across 22 states and 300 districts. He said, 'We found that the Muslim community is receptive to a dialogue away from the media glare and the pressures of so-called secular parties.' As one of the most communally polarized elections in India wound its way to a close, Kumar, who handled the MRM said that the Sachar Report reflected 'the true communal face of secularism.'[105] He said, 'Muslims also feel, once they hear us out, that according to this Sachar report, those who are supposed to hate us have never harmed us and those who offer to speak for us have never benefited us.'[106]

The Sachar Report demonstrated that Gujarat police and other wings of the government had better representation from the Muslim community than formerly communist West Bengal and other states, according to Indresh Kumar. During the election campaign in 2014, there were occasions when Narendra Modi also referred to the Sachar Report. While it is widely known that the MRM is part of the RSS, according to Walter K Anderson and Shridhar D Damle, the relationship is at best ambiguous. Despite the RSS links to the MRM, this organization has never been enlisted in the official list of RSS affiliates. Nonetheless, it was established with help from the RSS and Sanghsarchalak Sudarshan took part in the official launch of MRM on 24 December 2002 and attended every national convention till 2012, the year he passed away. However, Anderson and Damle write, 'Yes the RSS has faced the recurring dilemma regarding how far it should go in supporting the MRM, and how openly it should acknowledge its association.'[107] Curiously, the MRM has started a campaign to promote education among Muslims under the name of a campaign, *Aadhi Roti Khaayenge, Bachchon ko Padhayenge*. It means 'We will eat only half a bread but educate our children.'[108]

After assuming the Prime Minister's post in 2014, Narendra Modi was able to shut down the high-powered policy-making body, India's

Planning Commission. However, the MMA was retained. Najma Hepatulla was appointed the Minister of Minority Affairs. In the early days, she created a controversy with a statement that Indian Muslims are not a minority.[109] The Sachar Report remained part of the conversation, but low on priority.

While the Sachar Report was not on the priority list of the Modi government, some of the programmes for Muslims that were already rolled out by the Dr Manmohan Singh government were continued. Some were diluted or tweaked. For instance, the Modi-led NDA government has renamed and restructured the Multi-Sectoral Development Programme (hereafter MSDP) as Pradhan Mantri Jan Vikas Karyakram (hereafter PMJVK).[110] On the basis of the recommendations of the Sachar Committee Report, the MSDP was launched. Earlier, only those clusters of villages with a minority population at least 50 per cent were considered. Now that has changed. The population criteria have been reduced to 25 per cent and is no longer limited to Muslim minorities. According to the modified policy, the area to be covered under PMJVK would be 57 per cent more as compared to the existing MSDP. The MSDP covered 196 districts. And the present PMJVK covers 308 Indian districts. The Expenditure Finance Committee and Department of Expenditure have recommended the continuation of the programme as PMJVK at the cost of ₹1200 crore for the year 2017-18, ₹1320 crore for 2018-19, and ₹1452 for 2019-20 and the total is ₹3972 crores. According to Zafar Mahmood, 'Though the scheme is for minorities, the basic purpose of it was upliftment of the Muslim community but with the population criteria being brought down to 25 per cent, it means that more districts could be covered and the money could be spent in those districts where the minority population is a mere 25 per cent and the non-minority population would be 75 per cent.'[111] According to Mr Mahmood, the districts which would have a non-Muslim minority population concentration of 20 per cent and five per cent of the Muslim population would be entitled to this scheme. This defeats the purpose. With a greater focus on Muslims, clearly these schemes would have worked better for Muslims. This is not to deny that there are others who deserve attention as well, but such attentions could have been given without denying Muslims their fair share. Muslims' prospect of deprivation in a universal programme meant for all minorities is much higher, which is why Muslim-specific programmes are designed.

Impact of the Hindu Right

The decision by Dr Manmohan Singh-led the government to set up and then implement the Sachar Report has forced the Modi-led NDA government to accept it as a policy document, though it has diluted some of its recommendations. At least a robust template is available to carry this discussion forward. It is also true that the UPA government did not implement the Sachar recommendations with sincerity. As Zoya Hasan, former member of India's National Commission for Minorities (NCM) observed, 'The UPA government's response to the Sachar Committee recommendations has been at best half-hearted, lacking the political will to pioneer bold policies that can overcome structural disadvantages that derive from membership of a minority community.'[112] Had the UPA not adopted the Sachar Report, the Hindu Right might not have made any fresh approach to the Muslim backwardness issue. In that sense, regardless of the lack of enthusiasm by the UPA—the very existence of the Sachar Report is a blessing in disguise.

Prime Minister Modi has been able to close down the Planning Commission. But he or his government has not been able to take similar steps with regard to the MMA or the NCM. Would Mr Modi or any future Hindu Right regime take such an extreme step? It is a matter of speculation. Indeed, there is a high probability that it might happen if the Hindu Right continues to dominate the electoral politics and India's governance structure. But a mere continuation of the UPA approach in this restrictive sense does not imply that there are no differences between the NDA and the UPA or the Hindu Right and the UPA governments. If the BJP is determined for *Sabka*

Vikas, why is it not fielding more Muslim candidates in Parliament and State Assemblies? After all, under-representation is one of the major findings of the Sachar Report. One of the early measures that the newly formed BJP government took in Maharashtra in 2015 under Devendra Fadnavis as its Chief Minister and then in 2017 in Uttar Pradesh under Yogi Adityanath as its chief minister, was to ban cow slaughter.[113] Hundreds of Muslim families are involved in the cattle business, mostly at an individual or small-scale level. These decisions affected their livelihood causing enormous miseries but no remedial steps were taken by the respective state governments. Also, no serious research is undertaken on the gravity of its impact. No effort was made to provide alternative livelihoods for these families by the government in the state or Centre. Some of these issues reveal how the Hindu Right looks at Muslim backwardness issues as well. For secular parties, this has been a non-issue as well.

In recent months, there have been considerable discussions on Pasmanda Muslims and the desire of the BJP's national leadership to address their backwardness. While the Prime Minister has made several statements on this issue, there is limited evidence of any effort by his party or his government. One is receiving mixed signals, which is more of a lip service showing concerns for Muslim backwardness issues rather than substantive interventions. For instance, no minister of the Pasmanda community is inducted at the Centre or state governments, say, of Haryana or Gujarat. The electoral dominance of the Hindu Right has created a new ecosystem within which the debate over Muslim backwardness sounds counter-productive. As Amartya Sen has argued, real development needs to be viewed 'as a process of expanding the real freedoms that people enjoy.'[114] Sen further writes, development calls for 'removal of major sources of unfreedom: poverty as well as tyranny, poor economic opportunities as well as systematic social deprivation, neglect of public facilities as well as intolerance or overactivity of repressive states.'[115] From the point of view of all these parameters, the approach of the Hindu Right regime towards Muslims is disappointing, and the perpetuating of a spiral web of backwardness further among Muslims appears very high.

Notes

1 Kapur, Devesh. 2014. *Diaspora, Development, and Democracy—the Domestic Impact of International Migration from India*. Princeton University Press.

2 While there are always Muslim artists and actors in Bollywood, but the domination of the Khan trio, Shahrukh Khan, Salman Khan, and Amir Khan for more than three decades is not just about their stardom but also it is about their business empire.

3 See, 'Azim Premji is India's "most generous" billionaire for 2nd straight year'. 2021. Available at http://www.thehindustantimes.com (accessed on 10 December 2023).

4 See. Rajan, Raghuram G and Lamba, Rohit. 2023. *Breaking the Mould: Remembering India's Economic Future*. Penguin Random House. Pp. 20-23.

5 See, Sengupta, Somini. 2006. 'Report Shows Muslims Near Bottom of Social Ladder'. Available at http://www.nytimes.com (accessed on 10 December 2023).

6 Jaffrelot, Christophe and Kalaiyasaran, A. 2023. 'Post-Sachar Muslims: Socio-Economic Profile', in Tanweer Fazal, Divya Vaid, Surinder S. Jodhka (Eds). *Marginalities and Mobilities among India's Muslims. Elusive Citizenship*, New Delhi: Routledge. Pp.19-41

7 Ibid.

8 Rehman, Mujibur. 2010. 'Muslim Politics in India and 15th General Election' in *Emerging Trends in Indian Politics: The 15th General Election*. (Ed.) Ajay K Mehra. New Delhi: Routledge. Pp. 133-157.

9 Scholars such as Mohammad Mujeeb have argued that there were Muslim families or Muslim dynasties not average Muslims who ruled India. See Mujeeb, Mohammad. 1967. *The Indian Muslims*. New Delhi: Munshilal Manoharlal.

10 There is considerable literature on Black poverty or discriminations of African Americans.

11 Hunter, WW. 2002. *The Indian Musalmans*. New Delhi: Rupa.

12 Savarkar, Veer. 2019. *Indian War of Independence 1857*. New Delhi: Abhishek Publications. Also, see Sharma, Jyotirmaya. 2019. *Hindutva: Exploring the Idea of Hindu Nationalism*. New Delhi: Context.

13 Subramanian, Lakshmi and Ray, Rajat K. 1991. 'Merchants and Politics: From the Great Moghuls to the East India Company' in Dwijendra Tripathi. (Ed.). *Business and Politics in India: A Historical Perspective*. New Delhi: Manohar. Pp. 19-85.

14 He was working in a Madrasa.

15 Quoted in Ahmed, Rafiuddin. 1988. T*he Bengal Muslims 1871-1906: A Quest for Identity*. New Delhi: Oxford University Press. P.136.
16 See. Hunter, WW. 1876. (2nd ed). A Life of the Earl of Mayo. (London). Originally quoted in Ahmed, Rafiuddin. 1988. *The Bengal Muslims 1871-1906: A Quest for Identity*. New Delhi: Oxford University Press. P. 146.
17 Hunter, WW. 2002. (First published in 1871). *The Indian Musalmans: Are they Bound in Conscience to Rebel Against the Queen?* New Delhi: Rupa Publications. P. 12.
18 Ibid. P. 168.
19 Rehman, Mujibur. 2010. 'Muslim Politics in India and 15th General Election' in *Emerging Trends in Indian Politics: The 15th General Election* (Ed.) Ajay K Mehra. New Delhi: Routledge. Pp. 133-157.
20 The Indian Muslims, it was generally noted, were 'less nimble than the Hindus, were less ready to seize opportunities offered by Western education and less quick to adapt themselves to changing conditions under British rule.'
21 Ahmed, Rafiuddin. 1988. *The Bengal Muslims 1871-1906: A Quest for Identity*. New Delhi: Oxford University Press.
22 Ibid. P.135.
23 Ibid.
24 Paul, Nilanjana. 2022. *Bengal Muslims and Colonial Education, 1954-1947*. New Delhi: Routledge. P. 16.
25 Saberwal, Satish. 2010. 'On the Making of Muslims in India Historically' in *Oxford Handbook of Muslims: Empirical and Policy Perspectives*. (Ed.) Rakesh Basant and Abusaleh Shariff. New Delhi: Oxford University Press. Pp. 37-71.
26 Ibid.
27 For critical understanding of India's economic reform, see Ahluwalia, Isher and Little, IMD. 2012. *India 's Economic Reforms and Development: Essays in Honor Of Manmohan Singh*. New Delhi: Oxford University Press. Joshi, Vijay and Little, IMD. 2018. India's Economic Reforms. New Delhi: Oxford University Press. Also,see, Dreze, Jean and Sen, Amartya. 2020. *An Uncertain Glory: India and Its Contradictions*. New Delhi: Penguin.
28 Gopal Singh Panel Report, Government of India, New Delhi, 1983.
29 Sachar Commission Report, Government of India, New Delhi, 2006.
30 For a substantive analysis on how Muslim lives were impacted after liberalization see, Islam Maidul. 2019. *Indian Muslims After Liberalization*. Cambridge: Cambridge University Press.

31 Mohapatra, Bishnu. N. 2010. 'Minorities and Politics'. *Oxford Companion to Politics in India.* (Ed.) Gopal, Nirja Jayal and Mehta, Pratap Bhanu. New Delhi: Oxford Unviersity Press. Pp. 219-237.

32 Bagchi, Amiya Kumar. 1996. 'Studies on the economy of West Bengal since Independence.' *Economic and Political Weekly.* 33(47).

33 Though Bhartiya Jana Sangh (BJS) was there before, the rise of the BJP brought about a significant change in the political discourses in the country—particularly with regard to Muslims.

34 See Stigltiz, Joseph. 2002. *Globalization and Its Discontents.* London: Penguin; Bhagwati, Jagdish. 2004. *In Defense of Globalization.* New Delhi: Oxford Univrsity Press.

35 See Stiglitz, Joseph. 2002. *Gloablization and Its Discontent.* London: Penguin. P. 8.

36 The origins of the poverty line is an outcome of the research of two economists, VN Dandekar and N Rath from India, who mainly worked in the Gokhale Institute in Pune, Maharashtra. They fixed a minimum consumption line in the 1970s based on a calorie norm., For roughly two decades, that line was used to define the poverty line after making adjustments for price changes for each Indian state. A major controversy arose on poverty line after 1999-2000 NSSO survey. This is mainly because of a change in the survey methodology of the NSSO, based on which official numbers are estimated. Owing to the change in the recall period, the consumption figures and hence the poverty estimates of 1999-2000 were no longer comparable to earlier estimates. This raised questions on the data raising questions over the poverty decline in the 1990s. In 2002, Noble Prize winning economist August Deaton and Jean Dreze wrote a paper applying alternative methodologies. They proved that poverty decline was indeed real which led to the somewhat closure of the debate. See an interesting analysis, Bhattacharya, Pramit. 2013. 'Everything you wanted to know about the poverty debate.' Avaialble at http://www.livemint.com (accessed on 10 December 2023). For a comprehensive understanding, Deaton, Angus and Kozel, Valerie. (Ed.). 2005. *The Great Indian Poverty Debate.* New Delhi: Macmillan.

37 For an understanding of castes among Indian Muslims, see Imtiaz Ahmad (Ed.). 2018. *Caste and Social Stratification Among Muslim in India.* New Delhi: Aakar Publications.

38 Two publications which could be of tremendous value to grasp the history and evolution of India's Planning Commission are: Chibber, Vivek. 2006. *Locked In Place: State Building and Late Industrialization in*

India. Princeton: Princeton University Press; and Frankel Francine, R. 2006. *India's Political Economy 1947-2004: The Gradual Revolution*. New Delhi: Oxford University Press.

39 See Rehman, Shaikh Mujibur. 2017. 'A Rewriting of Nehru?' Available at http://www.thehindu.com (accessed on 10 December 2023). It is crucial to note that when Modi arrived in Delhi as Prime Minister, political commentators mostly compared him with Indira Gandhi.

40 Khalidi, Omar. 2006. *Muslims in Indian Economy*. New Delhi: Three Collective. P. 40.

41 Ibid. Pp. 41-42.

42 Sherman, Taylor. 2023. *Nehru's India: A History of Seven Myths*. Princeton: Princeton University Press. P. 86.

43 Ibid. P. 86.

44 See, Mehta, Vinod. 2015. *The Sanjay Story*. New Delhi: Harper Collins.

45 Khalidi. Omar. 2006. *Muslims in Indian Economy*. New Delhi: Three Essays Collective.

46 Ibid. P. 43.

47 Gopal, Sarvepalli. (Ed.). 1992. *Anatomy of a Confrontation: Ayodhya and the Rise Communal Politics in India*. London: Zed Books Ltd. Also, see Mukhopadhyay, Nilanjan. 2021. *The Demolition and the Verdict: Ayodhya and the Project to Reconfigure India*. New Delhi: Speaking Tiger.

48 Jalan, Bimal. (Ed.) 2004. *Indian Economy: Problems and Prospects*. New Delhi: Penguin.

49 Jaffrelot, Christophe. 1998. *The Hindu Nationalist Movement in India*. New Delhi: Columbia University Press; Hansen, Thomas Blom. 1999. *The Saffron Wave: Democracy and Hindu Nationalism In Modern India*. New Jersey: Princeton University Press; Rehman, Mujibur. (Ed.) 2018. *Rise of Saffron Power: Reflections on Indian Politics*. New Delhi: Routledge.

50 Hasan, Zoya. 2012. *Congress after Indira: Policy, Power and Political Change (1984-2009)*. For a detailed analysis, see chapter 7, 'Co-opting the Minorities.' Pp. 166-192.

51 See, Singh, Prem. 2019. 'Rajinder Sachar, a Life Long Socialist, Showed the True Picture of Indian Muslims.' Available at http://www.indianexpress.com (accessed on 10 December 2023).

52 See, 'Justice Ranganath Mishra Passes Away.' 2012. Available at http://www.newindianexpress.com. (accessed on 10 December 2023).

53 Mukherjee, Aditya, Mukherjee, Mridula and Mahajan, Sucheta. 2008. *RSS, School Texts and the Murder of Mahatma Gandhi: The Hindu Communal Project*. New Delhi: Sage.

54 For a detailed discussion, Kim, Hewwon. 2019. *The Struggle for Equality:*

India's Muslims and Rethinking the UPA Experience. Cambridge: Cambridge University Press.

55 Ibid. P. 71.

56 Interview with Dr Abu Saleh Shariff on 10 February 2007.

57 For an incisive analysis of how it has shaped policy making, see Hasan, Zoya. 2012. *Congress After Indira: Policy, Power, Political Change (1984-2009).* New Delhi: Oxford University Press.

58 For an incisive analysis see, Chandra, Kanchan. 2004. *Why Ethnic Parties Succeed: Patronage and Ethnic Head Counts in India.* Cambridge: Cambridge University Press.

59 For a biographical account of Dr Manmohan Singh and his early life as a policy maker, see Singh, Daman. 2014. *Strictly Personal: Manmohan and Gursharan.* New Delhi: Harper Collins.

60 This panel discussion (online) took place on 10 June, 2023.

61 Sachar Committee Report. Government of India. New Delhi. P. XIII.

62 Ibid. Pp. 49-84.

63 Ibid. P. 84.

64 Ibid. P. 85.

65 Ibid. Pp. 76-78.

66 Ibid. P. 77.

67 Ibid. P. 78.

68 Ibid. P. 106.

69 Ibid. P. 107.

70 Ibid. P. 136.

71 Ibid. Pp. 89-213.

72 Ibid. P. 192.

73 Ibid. Pp. 192-193.

74 Ibid. P. 201.

75 SCR. P. 198.

76 SCR. P. 238.

77 SCR. P. 240.

78 SCR. P. 242.

79 Shariff, Abu Saleh. 2017. 'Sachar Report: Shelved and Forgotten.' Avaialble at http://www.frontline.the hindu.com. (accessed on 10 December 2023).

80 Gupta, Sekhar. 2018. 'Kitney Mussalman Hain: Why this Sachar Committee Question to Army was an abomination.' Available at: http://www.theprint.in (accessed on 30 September 2023).

81 SCR. Foreword.

82 Iyer, Shekhar, Nagi, Saroj and Patranobis, Sutirtho. 2006. 'Sachar

Committee Report full of prejudices: BJP.' Available at http://www.hindustantimes.com (accessed on 30 September 2023).

83 See, *Annual Report 2019-20. Ministry of Minority Affairs.* Government of India, New Delhi. 63-68.

84 Khaitan, Tarunabh. 2008. 'Transcending Reservations: A Paradigm Shift in the Debate on Equality.' *Economic and Political Weekly.* 20(8): 8-12.

85 Kim, Heewon. 2019. *The Struggle for Equality: India's Muslims and Rethinking the UPA Experience,* Cambridge: Cambridge University Press.

86 Kim, Hewwon. 2019. *The Struggle for Equality: India's Muslims and Rethinking the UPA Experience.* P. 10.

87 Sethi, Neha. 2014. 'UPA policies have done little for Muslim enfranchisement: Panel available at: http://www.livemint.com (accessed on 30 September 2023).

88 Shariff, Abualeh. 2016. *Institutionalizing Constitutional Rights: Post-Sachar Committee Scenario.* New Delhi: Oxford University Press. P. 22

89 Kundu, Amitabh. 2019. 'Trends in Mobility In India: issues of labour market integration and exclusion of vulnerable sections of the population.' *Area Development and Policy.* 4(4): 346-366.

90 Ibid. P. 18.

91 See, 'Gujarat government appeal on minority scholarship scheme in SC.' Available at http://www.economictimes.com. 7 May 2013 (accessed on 20 January 2024).

92 Sushma Swaraj (1952-2019) served as India's foreign minister from 26 May 2014 to 30 May 2019 in the Cabinet of Prime Minister Mr Narendra Modi.

93 Iyer, Shekhar, Nagi, Saroj and Patranobis, Sutirtho. 2006. 'Sachar Committee Report full of prejudices: BJP.' Available at http:// www.hindustantimes.com (accessed on 30 September 2023).

94 Ibid.

95 Mr Venkaiah Naidu served as India's Vice President from 2017-2022.

96 'BJP to oppose Sachar Committee Report.' Available at: http://www.zeenewsindia.com. 4 January 2007 (accessed on 20 December 2023).

97 'Minorities must have first claim on resources: PM.' Available at: http://www.economictimes.indiatimes.com December 9, 2006 (accessed on on 20 December 2023); for the entire speech see, 'Controversy: The first claim on resources.' Available at: www.outlookindia.com. 9 December 2009 (accessed on 20 December 2023).

98 'PM Modi slams Congress for "Muslim-party" remark; stop lying, it responds.' Available at: http://www.business-standard.com. 23 July 2018 (accessed on 20 December 2023).

99 Mr Mahmood served as Officer on Special Duty (OSD) to Sachar Committee.

100 These victims were residing in Dhorajinagar and Citizen Nagar on the outskirts of the city. According to Mr Mahmood 200 families were rehabilitated with the help of local Muslim philanthropists. They were residing at the foothill of a one-kilometre long and fifty feet high heap of trash dumped there from all over the city.

101 See, 'Narendra Modi lends ears to the presentation in 2002 riots.' 2013. Available at: http://www.economictimes.indiatimes.com (accessed on 10 December 2023).

102 Zafar Sureshwala is a business man who suffered during the 2002 riot. He reconciled with Mr Modi later and remains one of Modi's most well-known Muslim loyalist.

103 'BJP does a U-turn on Sachar Committee.' *The Hindu*. 12 March 2014.

104 Ibid.

105 Nistula, Hebbar. 2014. 'Rajinder Sachar Committee Report helps RSS connect with Muslims.' Available at http://www.economictimes.indiantimes.com (accessed on 10 December 2023).

106 Ibid.

107 See, Andersen, Walter K, and Damle, Shridhar D. 2018. *The RSS: A View to the Inside*. New Delhi: Penguin Viking. P. 93.

108 Ibid. P. 103.

109 See, 'Muslims are not minorities, Parsis are: Najma Heptullah'. 2014. Available at http//www.timesofindia.com. (accessed on 10 December 2023).

110 Raza, S Khurram. 2018. 'Modi govt changes scheme meant for Muslims to include all minorities.' Available at http://www.nationalherald.com (accessed on 10 December 2023)

111 Ibid.

112 See Hasan, Zoya. 2012. *Congress After Indira: Policy, Power and Political Change (1984-2009)*. New Delhi: Oxford University Press. P.193. Similar conclusions could be found in the writings of other scholars such as Dr Abu Saleh Shariff, etc.

113 On the issue of cow protection movement, see the chapter titled 'Cow Protection Movement' in Vaidik, Aparna. 2020. *My Son's Inheritance: A Secret History of Lynching and Blood Justice in India*. New Delhi: Aleph. Pp. 31-45.

114 Sen, Amartya. 2000. *Development as Freedom*. New Delhi: Anchor. P.3.

115 Ibid. P. 3.

CONCLUSION

'To accept passively an unjust system is to co-operate with that system; thereby the oppressed become as evil as the oppressor. Non-co-operation with evil is as much a moral obligation as is co-operation with good. The oppressed must never allow the conscience of the oppressor to slumber.'

—Dr Martin Luther King Junior, *In Stride Toward Freedom*

In early February 2023 in New Delhi, I was having a conversation with Robert Fuerest, a London-based senior journalist working for *The Economist* for a story on nationalism he was writing at the time.[1]

'How far would they (the Hindu Right) go,' asked Fuerest.

I had no straightforward answer then. I don't have it even now.

Only some crystal gazing here.

India's tectonic shift towards Hindu majoritarianism has made the future of its largest religious minority, Indian Muslims, dark and gloomy. Those who are swayed by slogans like *Sabka Sath, Sabka Vikas, Sabka Vishwas* might find it hard to believe this. Often slogans during elections are just slogans or jumla.

Nevertheless, a conversation with an average Muslim anywhere in India or outside about the state of polity or the position of Muslims in India would make you aware of how concerned or even frightened they are about their future.

An equally important question is: Is there a way out?

As the unabated waves of Hindu majoritarianism sweep through India's vast electoral landscape, the obvious question is: What would happen to the equal rights status for Indian Muslims enshrined in the Indian Constitution?

Will it remain just in the law books or statutes or find meaningful resonance in political rhetoric or public debate? And will it remain in the hearts and minds of India's non-Muslim population—more, specifically, its dominant majority, the Hindus?

Enough incidents have already taken place in India ever since the Hindu nationalist BJP emerged as a politically significant force—first, as a ruling party in various states such as Uttar Pradesh, Madhya Pradesh, Gujarat, Maharashtra etc., and subsequently at the national level from 1998 to 2004. But the BJP's return to power in New Delhi in 2014 presents a completely new face of Hindu majoritarianism. And this new avatar in its hegemonic role is not just about socio-political exclusion, it is also about new forms of violence, degradation, and more importantly, a new form of state response towards incidents such as lynchings or riots in which Muslims continue to be prominent victims.

The Hindu Right organizations and its regimes—often in tandem—choreograph hostile conditions, forcing Muslims to find themselves in confrontation with the state. The result is, what I call, *A State Against Muslims.*

At present, the Muslim community is in the grip of acute despondency reminiscent of its despondency in the post-1857 Mutiny period. There is, however, a massive difference between what Muslims in India are going through now and their post-Mutiny period experience. The post-Mutiny despondency was happening under a colonial state that had no obligation, moral or legal, to care for Indian Muslims. On the contrary, the present despondency is occurring under an Indian state that has a constitutional obligation to stand for the life, dignity, and freedom of every citizen of Muslim heritage and others. Furthermore, another key difference in the approach towards Muslims is: as a colonial regime, the British government demonstrated some semblance of equality in their treatment of Hindus and Muslims as both communities were their subjects, despite harbouring deep suspicion towards Muslims, owing to their massive participation in the 1857 mutiny. That semblance of equal treatment seems to be completely missing in the present era of Hindu majoritarianism.

In today's India, an analysis of various incidents concerning Muslims would suggest that the community is seen as guilty. For Indian Muslims, the core law of modern criminology, 'innocent until proven guilty', is reversed with 'guilty unless proven innocent'. This is also valid for secularists who voice concern for Muslims. The very process of proving oneself innocent is so cumbersome that it becomes a punishment for a targeted Muslim. Take, for example, fact-checker Mohammad Zubair.[2] And there are many more. Often the laws have failed to protect Muslims from violence or take cognizance of their victimhood—as if the laws have fallen silent for them. The community is increasingly seen only as a perpetrator and perpetrator alone.

There are several instances to corroborate these observations. Two cases that immediately come to mind are: the Gurgaon Namaz controversy and the Bikis Bano case.

Gurgaon's Friday Namaz Controversy

In this case, a large number of Muslims in Gurgaon, a city in the state of Haryana and situated adjacent to New Delhi, were deprived of the privilege to offer weekly Friday namaz owing to the consistent threat posed by Hindu Right groups to such an extent that even the Haryana state felt intimidated. The law and order machinery found itself helpless in the face of their threat. Though this remains so far just a Gurgaon issue, it has the potential to become a national issue because Muslims continue to offer namaz in public spaces in many cities and towns. Indeed, there is already a similar case in Delhi. Muslims do not have the resources to build large mosques that could accommodate a growing number of namaz-goers every Friday in various cities and towns in India.[3] Therefore, it reflects Muslim backwardness also—not just in Gurgaon but also in the rest of India. The Friday namaz is a mass prayer like Eid or Bakre-e-Eid namaz and has to be offered in a group as part of Islamic practice, unlike regular daily namaz that can be individually performed. For a congregation, a larger space is required.

According to some estimates, the Muslim population in Gurgaon is somewhat close to five lakh or more. Muslims, like others, have migrated to Gurgaon for livelihood purposes from various parts of India. They are in professions that range from white-collar jobs to security guards, office staff, daily construction workers, auto wallas, mechanics, tailors, and many more types of formal and informal jobs.

Gurgaon city is part of the National Capital Territory (NCT)—one of India's wealthiest cities—and represents some kind of apolitical cosmopolitanism. The Friday Namaz controversy (also called the Jumma Namaz controversy because Jumma is the Urdu name for Friday[4]) began in 2018. Between the Censuses of 2001 and 2011, Gurgaon's population grew by 74 per cent. The influx of labour—in the services sector, information and technology (IT), and communications—has led Gurgaon to become the 56th largest Indian city by population. In terms of wealth, it is ranked eighth. Its per capita income in 2020 was ₹4.6 lakh, nearly three times the national average of ₹1.3 lakh. With its innumerable skyscrapers and malls, Gurgaon presents a panoramic view of a city of neo-rich Indians.

However, this liberal cosmopolitan façade has been shattered since 2018. A few Hindu Right organizations began protesting against the routine practice of Friday namaz by Muslims. The city has only 13 small mosques. They are inadequate for its growing Muslim population, running into lakhs. Muslims used to offer weekly Friday namaz in designated public spaces approved by the administration. Friday namaz has often been offered in public spaces all over India since time immemorial. All non-Muslims have been accommodating and respectful towards this exercise. It barely lasts for two hours. Eid and Bakr Eid namaz which happens once in a year is offered in public places such as roads etc. Often newspaper reports carry photos of Eid namaz being offered on roads in their front pages—a familiar sight for anyone who has grown up in India.

Prior to 2018, there were close to 100 spots in Gurgaon where Muslims peacefully offered Friday namaz. The permission to offer namaz in these designated places was withdrawn owing to systematic protests by Hindu groups. Owing to the pandemic, these protests stopped for a while but resumed again in 2021. These protests caused a great deal of friction and anxiety among Hindus and Muslims, inducing a sense of fear and alienation in the city's corporate world. Consequently, it has shown the fragility of the carefully cultivated apolitical cosmopolitanism.

These protests against the Friday namaz were led by various Hindu Right outfits that worked under an umbrella group called, Sanyukt Hindu Sangharsh Samiti (SHSS).[5] Some organizations include Vishwa Hindu Parishad (VHS), Bajrang Dal, Bharat Mata Vahini, Akhil Bhartiya Hindu Kranti Dal, and others. Some of the hotspots that were in the news were Sector 12, Sector 39, Sector 42, and Sector 53. As the protest continued, the methods of protest and demands also kept changing. According to reports, protesters raised 'Jai Shri Ram' and 'Bharat Mata ki Jai' slogans amid heavy deployment of security personnel. Protesters alleged namaz was being offered 'illegally' by 'outsiders.' Some members of the SHSS performed Govardhan Puja at the Sector 12 site where namaz used to be offered. This is mainly to show Muslims their place—*you cannot offer namaz, but we can perform puja.* They alleged that some of these Muslim groups were Rohingyas, which is neither established nor is the case. Such wild accusations were made to create confusion at different levels.

In November 2021, according to a report, protests took a fresh turn as locals from the villages of Mohammadpur Jharsa, Khandsa, Narsinghpur, and Khatola occupied the designated namaz site near Sector 37 police station and conducted a havan[6] ceremony. The men said the event was meant to commemorate the 26/11 martyrs on the 13th anniversary of the Mumbai terror attacks. A heavy police force was deployed after some locals submitted a memorandum to the Deputy Commissioner opposing namaz on the ground. At noon, over 100 men sat in the open ground where namaz was not allowed and participated in the havan.[7] This was another message to Muslims that Hindus can have their havans here because the country belongs to them, but Muslims cannot offer namaz.

In the early phase of their protests, the demand was to allow the prayer to take place in designated places. In 2018, negotiations between the members of Hindu Right protest groups and leaders of the Muslim community first reduced the number of spots from 100 to 37, and finally, by 2021, all spots were denied. Only the 13 small mosques that already existed were allowed which weren't enough to accommodate the needs of the community by any stretch.

The Gurgaon administration tried to mediate in the early days of the protest in 2018 but began to show helplessness by 2021. The statement by Haryana Chief Minister Manohar Lal Khattar of the BJP government made in December 2021, 'namaz cannot be tolerated in public spaces,' reveals the real intention of the administration.[8]

In M Ismail Faruqui Vs Union of India and Others, 1995, the apex court held that a mosque is not an essential part of the practice of the religion of Islam. It further said namaz by Muslims can be offered anywhere, even in the open space. It ruled that the power of acquisition is available to the State for a mosque like any other place of worship of any religion. The court further said that the right to worship, guaranteed under Article 25 of the Constitution of India, does not extend to the right of worship at 'any and every place'.

On the other hand, a community iftaar was hosted during the month of Ramadan in 2018 to promote inter-religious harmony among Hindus, Muslims, and Sikhs. It was also meant to reflect communal harmony in the face of the demands made by the SHSS. The iftaar was organized by Gurgaon Nagrik Ekta Man and took place at the community centre in Sector 27.[9] Among others, Yashpal Saxena, father of Ankit Saxena,[10] who was killed earlier this year, allegedly by family members of a Muslim girl, also participated.

After the Gurgaon administration withdrew permission for Friday prayers at eight of the 37 sites agreed upon earlier citing objections from residents and Resident Welfare Associations (RWAs), a committee overseeing five gurudwaras offered Muslims their premises for the namaz. Sherdil Singh Sidhu, president of the Gurdwara Sri Guru Singh Sabha, Sabzi Mandi, Gurgaon, explained the decision as follows, 'A gurdwara is the house of the Guru. People from all communities are welcome to come here and pray. If the Muslim community is facing problems in praying at designated sites, they can offer prayers in the gurdwaras. The doors of gurdwaras are open to all.'[11] The five gurdwaras are located in Sadar Bazar, Sector 39, Sector 46, Model Town, and Jacobpura. However, this offer from the Gurudwara did not work out as the Hindu groups put pressure on them. Kulbhushan Bhardwaj, the legal advisor for SHSS, said they distributed 2,500 copies of a book titled 'Guru Tegh Bahadur-Hind ki Chadar' and paid tributes to Guru Nanak Dev. He further admitted that 'they asked the gurdwara committee members not to allow the Muslim community to use gurdwaras for Friday prayers. If the Muslims offer prayers in their houses or mosques, we have no objection.'[12]

In December 2021, Mohammad Adeeb, a former MP, Rajya Sabha, had moved the Supreme Court seeking contempt action against the Haryana Director General of police and Chief Secretary for failing to comply with the court's directions regarding measures to curb communal and violent sentiments that result in hate crimes. Ironically, police lodged a FIR against Mohammad Adeeb and others on a complaint filed by local Hindu activists. These Hindu activists accused them of disrupting communal harmony and trying to grab land, which is a false accusation. The FIR has been lodged against Adeeb, Abdul Haseeb Kashmi, and Mufti Mohammad Salim Kashmi at Sector 40 police station under Sections 153 (wantonly giving provocation with intent to cause riot) and 34 (common intention) of the Indian Penal Code, officials said. The complainants were members of various Hindu outfits.

There is no solution visible to this otherwise manufactured conflict between Hindus and Muslims. If this manufactured conflict is allowed to replicate, it could generate perpetual conflict and endless violence between the two communities in a vast number of cities and towns in India. The narration here shows various facets of Hindu majoritarianism and its operational dimension. Most secular parties have remained largely silent. They are not proactive in fighting for secular India. First, administration-approved designated places were taken off as namaz sites; then the puja and havan were performed in the same site which was denied to Muslims, and then when other religious groups such as Sikhs wanted to provide alternatives, they were threatened. On all of these, the state, and political elites, both secular and non-secular, largely remained silent, and the Hindu Right groups had the last laugh.

'Injustice of Exceptionalism'[13] and the Bilkis Bano Case

During the Gujarat riot in 2002, Bilkis Bano, a Muslim woman from Gujarat, who was five months pregnant was gang raped. In front of her, 14 members of her family were murdered including her three-year-old daughter. Bilkis Bano, who survived, fought the case and, in the end, 11 men were convicted for this heinous crime and were given life imprisonment.

As noted lawyer, Indira Jaising, writes, gang rape is a crime against humanity. The International Criminal Court prescribes a sentence of 30 years for crimes against humanity with no remission.[14] On 15 August 2022, on India's independence day, all the 11 convicts who were serving life sentences were released. This happened only a few hours after the Prime Minister's independence speech from the ramparts of Red Fort, New Delhi, in which he urged Indians to respect women. The Central government approved the premature release of 11 men.[15] The remission was given by the Gujarat statement. State officials explained that the decision to release was made following the procedure in which a government panel approved the remission application. These men—first convicted by a trial court in 2008—had spent more than 14 years in jail and other factors such as good behaviour in prison and their age contributed to this decision. A viral video showed the men lined up outside the Godhra jail and their relatives greeting them with sweets. The most intriguing justification came from a former Gujarat minister and a six-time MLA from Godhra, who said the accused are Brahmins. Brahmins are known to have good sanskaras. He further added that it might have been someone's ill intention to corner and punish them.[16]

The Bilkis Bano Case Timeline (2002 to 2024)[17]

March 3, 2002: Bilkis Bano was gang-raped and her family members were murdered.	May 13, 2022: The Supreme Court directs the Gujarat government to consider the plea of a convict for pre-mature release under its policy of July 9, 1992.	December 17, 2022: Court dismisses her plea seeking a review of its May 13 verdict in which it had said that the state of Gujarat is the 'appropriate government' competent to examine the application for the pre-mature release
December 16, 2003: Supreme Court Orders a CBI inquiry	August 15, 2022: As part of the Gujarat government's remission policy, 11 convicts were released from Godhra jail.	March 27, 2023: Court sends notice to Centre, Gujarat government and others on a plea filed by Bilkis Bano
January 21, 2008: A Special Court convicted 11 men into life imprisonment	August 25, 2022: Top court issues notice to the Centre and Gujarat government on a PIL plea against the pre-mature release.	August 7, 2023: Court starts final hearing on the petition challenging the remission
May 4, 2017: Bombay High Court Upholds the Order.	Nov 30, 2022: Bilkis Bano moves to the Supreme Court challenging the remission.	January 8, 2024: Supreme Court quashes the remission given to 11 convicts.

The matter of this premature release was finally heard by India's Supreme Court. On 8 January 2024, the Supreme Court of India quashed the remission order en masse granted by the state of Gujarat in August 2022. The order delivered by a bench comprising Justice BV Nagarathna and Ujjal Bhuyan described the crime committed by these men against Bilkis Bano as a grotesque and diabolical crime driven by communal hatred. The verdict was also a scathing reprimand of the ruling BJP government in Gujarat for acting in tandem with the prisoners. The verdict said that the Gujarat government did so by usurping the power as the rightful power for this belongs to the government of Maharashtra. According to a Constitution Bench decision in Union of India vs V Sriharan (2015), the appropriate government to consider a remission application is the state where the convicts are sentenced, which is Maharashtra in this case. That is why the Court notes that the BJP government usurped the power from the government of Maharashtra.

It is worth noting here that while releasing these convicts and granting remission, the Gujarat government as well as the Centre ignored notes of dissent given by the Central Bureau of Investigation (CBI) and Special CBI judge. The Special CBI judge noted that 'the crime was committed only on the ground that the victim belonged to a particular community.'

At this point, it is worth recalling the words of Justice Nagarathna, who wrote, 'A woman deserves respect howsoever high or low she may be otherwise considered in society or to whatever faith she may follow or any creed she may belong to. Can heinous crimes against women permit remission of the convicts by a reduction of their sentence and by granting them liberty?'[18]

Hindu Rashtra and the Future of Indian Muslims

For some, India has already become a Hindu Rashtra.[19] Officially though, as per the Constitution, India is still a secular nation.

At this juncture, the most pertinent question is: What might happen to Muslims once India becomes *officially* a Hindu Rashtra?

The political and electoral trends indicate clearly that it is only a matter of time before India is officially declared a Hindu Rashtra.

The question raised above about the fate of Indian Muslims could be addressed in two ways.

Firstly, by looking into what Indian Muslims have already gone through in the BJP-ruled states, particularly in states like Gujarat, Uttar Pradesh, Uttarakhand, Maharashtra, Karnataka, Haryana, Assam, etc., and under the Hindu Right regime that has run India since 2014; or even prior to that, under the Vajpayee era.

Secondly, by drawing parallels with the conditions of minorities (religious, racial, ethnic, etc.) in various countries under various shades of majoritarian regimes. For instance, African-Americans in America; Rohingyas in Burma, or religious minorities such as Hindus/Sikhs/Christians in Pakistan or Bangladesh, Uyghurs in China, etc.[20]

Muslims Under Hindu Right Regimes

The most significant chapter showing the adverse relationship between Hindu majoritarianism and the Indian Muslims begins with Gujarat. With the BJP becoming Gujarat's ruling party in 1995—and the Gujarat riot of 2002 receiving global attention—several changes took place in the state and its behaviour.

For one, the decision was taken by the BJP not to field Muslim candidates on its behalf, which meant no Muslim MLAs from the BJP in the state Assembly and no Muslim in the Cabinet of the Gujarat government. This happened under Narendra Modi as its Chief Minister. Ever since, this tradition has been continued by successive post-Modi BJP regimes in Gujarat. From the vantage point of the BJP, Muslims became a community without a political voice. This is a pattern we saw in the Gujarat government-formed elections after elections in 2002, 2005, 2012, and 2017, and recently in 2023. The exclusion of Muslims from governance and political power structures has become an acceptable practice by the Hindu Right. This practice has become a source of inspiration for the BJP in Parliamentary elections and also in various state elections such as Uttar Pradesh, Karnataka, Madhya Pradesh, Maharashtra, Haryana, Rajasthan, West Bengal, Telangana, Andhra Pradesh, and many more. Overall, the political representation and political voice of the community is substantially reduced and in nearly all BJP states, they have no political voice at all. This trend is likely to continue.

What does this denial or Muslim voicelessness mean in the language of liberal democracy? We are aware of the meaning of the well-known slogan 'taxation without representation is colonialism'. Therefore, the taxation of the Muslim population without their political representation in the political power structure at all levels implies a colonial mindset, a unique form of majoritarian domination with deliberate exclusion. Unfortunately, the complacent secular political forces barely considered it a big issue when it became a policy in Gujarat. Their silence emboldened the Hindu Right to extend its practice to the national level and in states where it occupied power, and that is how it is a national phenomenon. There are occasions when such questions are raised and this is explained away by suggesting how Muslims in Gujarat are doing well in panchayat and city elections. In a country where Muslims have served as India's President, members of the cabinet, and governors, to look at Muslim representation in panchayat and city elections as the indicator of empowerment is, at best, ridiculous. But then this is a sort of trick that the Hindu Right plays in outsmarting secularists in public debate and hiding its anti-Muslim ideology. It would be interesting to see how the loud claim of the Hindu Right to address Pasmanda issues plays out in the coming years. Till now, there is not much evidence.

Another significant implication rests in the state's response to riots and its victims. Hindu-Muslim riots have a long history in India. Enough research is there to suggest that the Indian state has miserably failed—even in its heydays of secular politics—often not just in containing the riot, but also in its post-riot responses. And yet, there were often efforts to reach out to victims, help build reconciliations, etc., and help create enduring post-riot peace. The state did not turn its back completely towards these victims because they happened to be Muslims. Now the response of various Hindu Right regimes has brought about a paradigmatic shift in the state response to riots. Generally, the state often took an active interest in the settlement of victims and their families. In most cases, there was never complete closure and survivors lived with scars but most of them returned to their native homes. They did not have to sell off their ancestral properties or participate in compromise with perpetrators or their representatives. This is the new trend. The Gujarat Riot 2002 and the Muzaffarnagar Riot 2013 are two prominent examples that have set such trends.

After the Gujarat riot in 2002, the sitting Chief Minister chose not to even visit relief camps or colonies where the victims were settled. The Muzaffarnagar riot took place in 2013 when the SP led by Akhilesh Yadav was in power. Since 2017, the BJP government has been in power in the state. Instead of helping the victims in their pursuit of justice, the victims are encouraged to withdraw cases or FIRs, not to return to their places, and opt for new places to settle down, forfeiting their right to live in their native villages. More than 60 such colonies today stand in Muzaffarnagar in Uttar Pradesh, and a majority of them are without basic amenities. There seems to be no interest by the state to help such victims settle down. In the past, post violence, a committee invariably led by a retired judge of the High Court was set up to investigate and prepare a complete report on the causes and recommendations. This is no longer the standard practice with riots in India, which means the government version is the only version. This became apparent in the Delhi Riot 2022 and subsequent riots such as the Nuh Violence 2023 and other big or small riots in various parts of India. Additionally, there are issues about the criminal justice system and how it has been particularly counter-productive in cases of ethnic violence. Vrinda Grover and Soumya Uma's narrative on this, based on their work on anti-Christian violence, is very instructive.[21]

The frequency, nature, and character of riots have gone through radical changes under the Hindu Right regimes. There are cycles of violence taking place in most parts of the country. Often, victims are presented as perpetrators. The most glaring example of this has been the Delhi riots in which a vast number of Muslims were presented as perpetrators though generally they were the main victims of violence according to a report prepared by the Delhi Commission for Minorities (DCM), which was under the Arvind Kejriwal-led AAP government. The AAP government barely even endorsed the report. Silence on the riot is a smarter political strategy to deal with the BJP or the Hindu Right, as many sympathizers of the AAP conveyed to this author.

The other noteworthy aspect of the Hindu Right regime that has implications for Muslims is the significant departure in governance with the introduction of what is known as the bulldozer model (also, bulldozer justice). In this approach, as part of the punishment, a bulldozer is used to demolish the house of the person concerned without following any procedure of law or establishing that the alleged violator is indeed on the wrong side of the law. While there are instances of it being used against non-Muslim citizens, it has been predominantly reserved for Muslim citizens who are alleged to have violated some law. Uttar Pradesh is considered the pioneer of this form of justice but it has become an inspiration among various Hindu Right regimes in other states such as Assam, Madhya Pradesh, and Haryana, too. Though some of the courts have been deeply critical of this approach, it has fallen on deaf ears, demonstrating another evidence of a failure of what I have described as the 'separation of powers' model of liberal democracy in the Indian case.

Another concern of the Hindu Right regime is about the madrasas and their activities. In Uttar Pradesh, there was an attempt by the government to survey the state of madrasas. As an institution, since 9/11, madrasas have been a site of suspicion and there have been clamours for their reform and modernization. Scholarly research by Usha Sanyal, Shriya Aiyer, and Hem Borker presents a positive picture of the role of madrasas even in the context of Muslim women—their supplementary contributions.[22] Some of the concerns by the Hindu Right about madrasas has been to find out how nationalistic they are.

The legality of old mosques and shrines is another area where the Hindu Right regime is eager to intervene. Invariably an attempt is made to ask for legal documents. In Delhi, a list of Muslim shrines and dargahs has now been prepared, for which the state seeks legal documents. In the event of failure to show these documents, properties are seized and structures are demolished.[23] In Gujarat, particularly in Junagarh, this led to violence.[24] In Delhi, a list of hundreds of such sites is under scrutiny.[25]

Another major accusation is about the concerted attempt by

Muslims to engage in religious conversions or what is called love jihad. Muslim youths, it is claimed, are deliberately enticing Hindu girls into having affairs, mainly to convert them to Islam. This allegation is so widespread that young couples are often targeted by vigilante groups. All in all, the Indian Muslim community seems to be a target of various forms of violence. Cow vigilantism has also been unleashed to coerce the community.[26] In a well-researched book titled, *Love Jihad and Other Fictions,* by Sreenivasan Jain, Mariyam Alavi, and Supriya Sharma, several of the high-profile cases are well analyzed and the Hindu Right groups' claims have been debunked.[27]

When all of these accusations and responses by the Hindu Right to Muslim lives, issues, or identity are taken into account, it becomes clear that there is more to it than just stopping the alleged appeasement politics or abuse of minority rights by the governments. The truth is there is a clear-cut agenda of what I have described in the Introduction as the DEISLAMIZATION of India.

Comparison with African Americans

One way to look at the future of the relationships between Indian Muslims and India's evolving majoritarian polity is by comparing it with the experiences of the African American minority in America. From the dark days of slavery to the Black Lives Matter movement, the arduous and painstaking journey of African Americans has confronted countless challenges and experienced multiple forms of human cruelty. Nonetheless, the community continues to fight a remarkable battle for human dignity and human rights. It is widely known how Martin Luther King Jr offered extraordinary leadership and had to pay the price of his life for the cause.

The basic issue is how much of the rights of a Muslim can be taken away from him/her under a Hindu majoritarian state and what type of violence can be unleashed.

In the lives of the African American community, there is living evidence of how cruelty, violence, and degradation can be unleashed on fellow human beings by a dominant social group. Multiple laws have been enacted to control their lives, extract their services, and unleash violence on them with impunity. This sustained violence for centuries has affected the emotional self of African-Americans. But the struggle, in its individual as well as collective form, is not yet over. The consequences of this form of violence on Black people have been enormous. Annette Gordon-Reed, in her book, *On Juneteenth*, presents a fascinating perspective on the fight for equality and human dignity.[28]

Lessons from Violence Against Dalits

While there are insights from the African American experience of possible forms of suffering and degradation the Muslim minority might face in the coming days—and also draw inspiration on how to fight back—there is indeed no need to go that far or to another nation's history to make sense of what Hindu majoritarianism might unleash on Indian Muslims. Valuable insights could also be drawn from India's history and society by looking at the experiences of Dalits or former untouchables in India. Since 1947 there has been constitutional protection of their rights and dignity and yet they face violence and degradation regularly.

The most sophisticated and theoretical narrative is found in the multi-volume writings of BR Ambedkar. It is thus crucial to look into these writings mainly to make sense of what a powerful social group could do to a minority if it has the monopoly of state power—and the minority is perceived as the one with no rights or treated not as equal or even as human beings. The nature and depth of violence towards India's former untouchables cannot be adequately acknowledged with the term untouchability, which I consider deeply inadequate and too soft a term to describe what was unleashed on Dalits for centuries. All of those violent treatments were given to them by fellow Indians, whose descendants we are. Such treatment has led to the conversion of many to leave Hinduism and embrace other religions such as Islam, Christianity, Buddhism, etc. Ambedkar thus argued conversion as emancipation. The Hindu Right seems quite indifferent to understanding the internal issues of Hindu society or caste order.

Unfortunately, not many Dalits have left behind autobiographical works to detail the specific treatments meted out to them, though this trend is changing. Thenmozhi Sundarajan's *The Trauma of Caste: A Dalit Feminist Meditation, Survivorship, Healing and Abolition* (2022)[29] is a good example and there are others.

In his famous essay, *Annihilation of Caste,* Ambedkar shares various forms of atrocities unleashed on Dalits in the name of untouchability. Many such practices are repeated in our society even today. Ambedkar notes the following:

> Under the rule of Peshaws in Maratha country untouchables were not allowed to use public streets if a Hindu was coming along, lest he should pollute the Hindu by his shadow. The Untouchable was required to have a black thread either on his waist or around his neck as a sign to prevent the HINDUS from getting themselves polluted by his touch mistake. In Poona, the capital of the Peshwa, the untouchable was required to carry, strung from his waist, a broom to sweep away from behind himself the dust he trod on, lest a Hindu walking on the same dust should be polluted. In Poona, the Untouchable was required to carry an earthen pot hung around his neck wherever he went for holding his pit falling on earth should pollute a Hindu who might unknowingly happen to tread on it.[30]

Ambedkar further offers more instances that he came across in the media at the time of his writing. According to a report published in the *Times of India* (4 January 1928), high caste Hindus (Kalotas, Rajputs, Brahmins, Patels, Patwaris etc.) in Central India wanted the Balais, an untouchable community, to follow the following rules if they wanted to live among them:

1. Balais must not wear gold lace-bordered pugrees.
2. They must not wear dhotis with coloured or fancy borders.
3. They must convey intimation of the death of any Hindus to the relatives of the deceased—no matter how far away these relatives may be living.

4. In all Hindu marriages, Balais must play music before the processions and during the marriage.
5. Balai women must not wear gold or silver ornaments; they must not wear fancy gowns or jackets.
6. Balai women must attend all cases of confinement of Hindu women.
7. Balais must render services without demanding remuneration and must accept whatever a Hindu is pleased to give.
8. If the Balais do not agree to abide by these terms, they must clear out of the villages.[31]

Crimes against Dalits continue to happen regularly in various parts of India despite stringent laws against those crimes. The Scheduled Caste (SC) and Scheduled Tribes (ST) Prevention of Atrocities Act 1989 was framed to prevent these atrocities, which unfortunately is continuously violated. Some argue that there is no untouchability in India today, but this is not true at all. In a study undertaken by the Ford Foundation, widespread practice of untouchability in both rural and urban India was reported.[32]

Regularly, one comes across various forms of crime against Dalits, reported in national, and to a lesser extent, in international dailies. In its 14 August 2023 issue, the *Outlook* magazine published a report titled, 'Murder, Rape, Humiliation: A Timeline of Atrocities Against Dalits',[33] a list of prominent cases of atrocities against Dalits all over India. A careful reading of these cases would suggest there is not much that has changed between Ambedkar's India of the 1930s and present-day India, despite constitutional protections for Dalits. Most importantly, these short descriptions shed light on the nature of crimes that are committed against Dalits, which as the domination of majoritarian politics grows, might serve as a clue to the nature of violence against Indian Muslims.

Here are some of the cases of atrocities against Dalits prior to and after 2014.

TABLE A: Atrocities against Dalits Before 2014

Date	*Name*	*Nature of Violence*
1968	Keezhvenmani Massacre	44 Dalits were burnt alive by landlords in Nagapattinam district of Tamil Nadu, over a labour dispute as the labourers were demanding higher wages.
July 17, 1985	Karamchedu Killings	Upper castes killed six Dalits in Andhra Pradesh over a minor dispute leading to rape, looting, and displacement.
January 25, 1986	Golana Murders	Four Dalits were murdered by an upper caste mob in Gujarat for planning to build houses on government-allotted land.
December 1, 1997	Laxmanpur Bathe Massacre	58 Dalits were killed by the Ranvir Sena in Bihar over the allegation of the villagers being the sympathisers of CPI (Marxist-Leninist) Liberation.
July 23, 1999	Manjolai Massacre	Dalit labourers protesting for better wages in Tamil Nadu were brutally assaulted by the police, leading to deaths because of police actions.
March 4, 2000	Kambalpalli Incident	Seven Dalits were burnt alive in Karnataka in retaliation for the alleged killing of a member of an upper caste family.
October 15, 2002	Jhajjar Lynching	Five Dalits were lynched to death in Haryana by a mob that believed that they were engaged in cow slaughter.
September 29, 2006	Kherlanji Killing	Four Dalits were murdered in Maharashtra over a land dispute, involving rape and mutilation of genitals.
January 22, 2012	Lathor Burning	Over 40 Dalit homes burnt down in Odisha after a Dalit boy was accused of theft.

(Source: The Outlook Magazine, 14 August 2023)

TABLE B: Atrocities against Dalits in and After 2014

Date	*Name*	*Nature of Violence*
April 7, 2014	Bihar Arson Attack	Upper-caste people burnt down Dalit homes over a land dispute.
September 21, 2014	Jawkheda Khalasa Killings	Three Dalits were killed and their body parts were found in a dry well.
March 2, 2015	Karuvanur Assault	Dalit youth attacked and humiliated by upper caste men in Tamil Nadu.
January 17, 2016	Rohit Vemula's Suicide	Dalit student commits suicide at Hyderabad Central University due to alleged caste-based discrimination.
March 29, 2016	Bikaner Rape Case	Dalit student was raped and murdered in Rajasthan.
March 14, 2017	Telangana Murder	A Dalit man was murdered and his private parts were injured as he got into a relationship with an upper-caste woman.
June 15, 2018	Gujarat Assault	A 13-year-old Dalit boy was attacked for wearing leather shoes.
September 14, 2018	Miryalaguda Killing	Dalit man killed in Telangana for marrying an upper-caste woman.
April 26, 2019	Uttarakhand Murder	21-year-old Dalit was beaten to death for sitting on a chair and eating food prepared by upper-caste residents.
September 14, 2020	Hathras Case	Dalit woman gang-raped and murdered in Uttar Pradesh, cremated without consent of family members.

(Source: The Outlook Magazine, 14 August 2023)

These cases present a somewhat comprehensive portrait of the various forms of violence Dalits have been dealing with in modern India, despite some robust laws to protect them.

In the context of caste, various forms of violence that were directed towards Dalits are or might be directed towards Indian

Muslims. But what majoritarianism does is that it creates a legitimate environment for such forms of violence to be unleashed.

On Minorities in Pakistan and Bangladesh

For the Hindu Right, the persecution and violence that Hindus have been confronting in Pakistan and Bangladesh has been a very dear cause and has inspired them to advocate majoritarianism and seek legitimacy among otherwise secular Hindus. Some may suggest that this is one of the reasons for the passage of the CAA 2019. There is a fair chance such forms of violence are going to be repeated against Indian Muslims by various groups directly or indirectly associated with the Hindu Right.

We may ask whether the present-day anti-Muslim/anti-minority ideology that the Hindu Right nurtures is a result of the persecution of violence and degradation that Hindus and other minorities face in other South Asian countries, such as Pakistan or Bangladesh. To put it differently, can we argue that if our neighbouring countries had been more respectful towards minority rights, the Hindu Right might have recognized Muslims as part of minority rights? These are hypothetical questions. While the sufferings of Hindus or other non-Muslim minorities in Pakistan or Bangladesh have provided some legitimacy in promoting Islamophobia or Muslim phobia in India, there is no guarantee that the Hindu Right would not have pursued its majoritarian political goals in India otherwise. After all, as an organized political movement, it can be traced back to the 1920s, which is much before the Partition or creation of Bangladesh. As I suggested in the Introduction of this volume, the Hindu Right is an ideological movement which would have pursued its majoritarian goals even if there was no Partition. Given that minorities were treated badly in Pakistan and Bangladesh, it only legitimized the Hindu Right's majoritarian campaign. Indeed, the Hindu Right, I would argue, might have even presented imaginary facts as it does about Indian Muslims in present-day India to advance its majoritarian cause. The major reason for this: the Hindu Right believes that India is a Hindu land and Muslims are foreigners.

Some reflection on what is going on in Pakistan and Bangladesh to religious minorities should be instructive. Efforts were made by the national leadership of India and the newly created Pakistan in the early days of Partition to address the religious minority issues so that various minorities were protected from the onslaught of majoritarianism. The most prominent intervention came in the form of what is known as the Nehru-Liaquat Pact in 1950. According to the Nehru-Liaquat Pact both governments would solemnly agree:

> that each shall ensure, to the minorities throughout its territory, complete equality of citizenship, irrespective of religion, a full sense of security in respect of life, culture, property and personal honour, freedom of movement within each country and freedom of occupation, speech and worship, subject to law and morality.[34]

However, as it is widely known, neither democracy in Pakistan[35] evolved nor was the country able to keep itself together, and it finally led to the creation of Bangladesh in 1971, decimating the idea of Two Nation Theory forever.[36] Indeed, India played a decisive role in this process and one of the reasons for India's intervention according to Mohammed Ayoob, was to boost India's secular project.[37] Looking back, neither India hoped to use the Bangladesh creation for its secular project nor the efforts to create conditions for respecting minority rights in neighbouring countries through pacts or agreements worked out. It seems, retrospectively, political developments have worked out for the Hindu majoritarian project in India.

Considerable reporting on the violations of the rights of religious minorities on both sides of India's border is available both in respective national and global media. Among others, valuable insights are found on the deep impact of India's ongoing citizenship debate on the conditions of religious minorities in Farahnaz Ispahani's book, *Purifying the Land of the Pure: Pakistan's Religious Minorities.*[38] At the time of Partition in 1947, almost 23 per cent of Pakistan's population which then included Bangladesh, comprised non-Muslim citizens. The proportion of non-Muslims has since fallen to approximately three per cent.[39] This violence is not limited to religious minorities such as Hindus, Sikhs, and Christians, but also non-Sunni Muslims. The Shia population is roughly 20-25 per cent of Pakistan and has been the victim of violence, so also Ahmadias which is less than one per cent of Pakistan's population and are declared non-Muslims by the Pakistan state. The Ahmadias, also pejoratively called 'Qadianis' or 'Mirzais', had actively supported the demand for Pakistan and one of the sect's members, Sir Zafarullah Khan, was Pakistan's first foreign minister. In 1974, the Ahmadias were officially declared as non-Muslims and Shias were also subjected to similar treatment. These minorities are constantly targeted by suicide bombs, and their worship places are often bombed when filled with worshippers. According to Ispahani, 'The descent began in 1949 with the Constituent Assembly declaring the objective of Pakistan's Constitution.'[40] In East Pakistan, Bengali Hindus were roughly 20 per cent of the population, and they were more educated and actively involved in politics. In the early years, the West Pakistani elite looked at Bengali Hindus as a threat. Likewise, there was a great deal of violence against Hindus and other religious minorities in Bangladesh. According to the most recent Census of 2011, Hindus are 8.5 per cent, Christians are 0.3 per cent, and Buddhists are 0.6 per cent.[41] Some of them come to India as Bangladeshi refugees[42] and many migrated out of the region. While India's Hindu Right has been a consistent champion of these violations, its ability to bring justice to these cases remains limited. The introduction of the CAA is its first major intervention.

Is There a Way Out?

Two political events have played a crucial role in shaping the present predicament of Indian Muslims are: One is Partition and the other is Ayodhya Movement of the 1980s. If Partition made the Muslim identity vulnerable, the resultant creation and existence of Pakistan as a political entity has provided the Hindu Right to raise questions about Muslim loyalty forever—even at the drop of a hat. 'Go to Pakistan' continues to be a favourite jibe the Hindu Right has for

Indian Muslims, though the geopolitics in South Asia has changed and we have another Muslim country, Bangladesh, since 1971. No such jibe as 'Go To Bangladesh' is raised by the Hindu Right! It is another matter that a vast number of India's dominant castes are deliberately plotting their path to the West or Middle East or becoming non-resident Indians (NRIs) anywhere.

On the other hand, the Ayodhya movement has made Muslim identity undesirable in modern electoral politics. Reflecting on the ongoing challenges of Indian Muslims, Ayesha Jalal writes, '[T]he partition of 1947 was no more than a partial solution to the Muslim minority problem in the subcontinent. The point has been made more poignant by the resurgence of communal tensions in India and the repercussions in Pakistan and Bangladesh. Apart from targeting their non-Muslim minorities, citizens of Pakistan and Bangladesh can merely look helplessly across the borders at the plight of India's Muslim minority under siege.'[43] On top of it, there is nothing original about Muslim politics in present India so that a focus on minority rights can emerge. Like mainstream politics, Muslim politics of India has also been dynastic and two major minority universities such as Aligarh and Jamia Millia Islamia do not even hold regular student elections or allow student bodies to operate. As a result, there has always been the issue of positive politicization of Indian Muslims. There is no mechanism or process through which a political class in India that can champion minority rights or care for Muslim causes can be formed. This has deeper political repercussions for Muslim polity and society. As a result, organizations like the AIMPLB or JUH have emerged as big players, which has been counterproductive for secular modern Indian politics.

Furthermore, the role of Muslim elites has been deeply discouraging. What the so-called secular phase of Indian politics, meaning the pre-BJP era, has done is that it has managed to produce some Muslim elites—not just political but also cultural elites. Barring Hamid Ansari,[44] for instance, not many seem to be interested in taking political positions or expressing concerns over the issue of Muslim conditions.[45] In the film world where Muslims have a significant presence, not many raise their voices or articulate their views like Naseeruddin Shah. The Khans of Bollywood are particularly silent, mainly because they fear there will be a backlash against the financial empire that they have built up by the Hindu Right as it holds the state power; likewise, Azim Premji from the corporate world. None of these people are interested in showing concern for justice or the rights of people that could resonate with secular resistance. Some may be expressing concerns in private, but in public, they are all largely silent. Consider this, had Gandhiji remained concerned for his legal career and chose not to participate in the rights of people in South Africa or India, we might have stayed under colonial rule even today. So, the depoliticization of Muslim elites is a matter of grave concern and has tremendous negative repercussions for India's secular polity. That is not true about the African American elites, who are always vocal about their issues or the rights of their community. For instance, Barack Obama can take a position on race and still stand for inclusive politics. But India's Muslim elites sulk.

For Indian Muslims, the options are very limited. As a religious minority, it no longer has a choice to ask for a separate nation—an option it has exhausted with catastrophic consequences with the creation of Pakistan and later Bangladesh. In the contemporary world, it cannot explore radicalization as an alternative as it could be self-destructive. The events associated with 9/11 and the terrorism and violence that followed have had an almost irredeemable impact on the image of Muslims as peace-loving people worldwide. This has galvanized Islamophobia and helped the Hindu Right to legitimize their Islamophobic arguments against Indian Muslims both in India and outside.

For Indian Muslims, challenges regarding their future or political future are an internal issue and they have to deal with them by crafting strategies on their own. They have a lot to learn from Dalit activism or activism of the African American community as well, among others. India is an electoral democracy, and likely to remain so despite possible distortions under Hindu majoritarian regimes. More importantly, India is not Myanmar or Burma. From the point of view of geopolitics and also its global economic status, India is a much sought-after nation—almost indispensable in a multi-polar world. No nation either in the West or elsewhere can afford to ignore India today, and no nation is going to champion Muslim concerns at the cost of its bilateral interests with India. Many Middle Eastern nations have given their highest honour to Prime Minister Modi[46] because it serves their bilateral purposes, or more crudely, their economic interests. In turn, they are rewarded as well, invited as guests on India's Republic Day.

For Indian Muslims, the best option is to explore a possibility with fellow secular citizens of other faiths such as Hindus, Sikhs, Christians, etc. for a secular polity with rights for minorities. As Jan-Werner Muller says, 'Democracy is—after all—not about trust, (be it individual or institutions), it is about efforts.'[47] Post-1947, some efforts were made but those efforts have failed. There were mistakes and lessons can be learnt from them to revive and rebuild a secular polity. In the last 70-odd years, there have also been plenty of good experiences and Indians have to believe that a secular India is possible. In the end, democracy is about the rights of people.[48] Moreover, Indians are deeply connected with the global society and they often enjoy multicultural privileges in various parts of the world, particularly in the multicultural West.

Viewing everything from a historical context, division and further division of Indian Muslims since 1857 and various political projects associated with it—particularly separate homelands like Pakistan and later Bangladesh—has considerably weakened the political capital of Indian Muslims in the continent. Although the Muslim population today in India is more than double what it was at the time of Partition in 1947, its political capital or organizational strength or ability to negotiate its future remains very limited. Remember a note by Lord Dufferin (1826-1902) who wrote in November 1888 that 'Muslims of British India, a nation of 50 million reigned supreme from the Himalayas to Cape Cormorin.'[49]

The challenge for the Indian Muslim community is not just because the Hindu Right political forces are hostile, but because the so-called secular forces are confused and ambivalent. Somehow or the other they consider standing for Indian Muslims or championing Muslim or secular causes as electorally harmful. But results of various state elections whether in Karnataka in 2023, West Bengal in 2021, Himachal Pradesh in 2023, or Telangana in 2023 do not support such perceptions. Political parties taking secular positions have proved to be quite successful not just in winning but containing the Hindu Right. But the challenges that Indian Muslims are facing have become mammoth. As Rafiq Zakaria notes, 'The task is not going to be easy because the communal Hindus have now risen to revive Savarkar's long forgotten thesis of Hindus and Muslims being two separate nations and implement it with a vengeance to outdo even with Jinnah. There are no Gandhis and Nehrus in India now to negate its all effect; the task therefore is most formidable.'[50] Therefore, the Muslim community has to invest considerably to build up goodwill with other communities—with various religious minorities, dominant castes, and also with Dalits. Even today, a large chunk of Indian voters do not subscribe to Islamophobic world views of the Hindu Right. A majority of them could serve as allies for a new India with the potential to build a secular polity. Despite all odds, Muslims have excelled in various walks of life by virtue of their ability and talent—such as art, culture, music, business, etc. Many of them are ambassadors of Hindu-Muslim unity. Such people should become proactive in building a better India which also secures the future of Indian Muslims. In that sense, all is not lost.

The writings of two thinkers could be of tremendous value to Indian Muslims. The first one is by Ambedkar and his slogan of EDUCATE, ORGANIZE AND AGITATE. The second one is from the writings and works of Dr Martin Luther King, Jr in *Where Do We Go From Here: Chaos or Community.* Dr King presented several lessons. In one case, he suggested, African Americans have no option for isolation and they have to work with white folks. As Dr King wrote,

'There is no solution for the Negro through isolation.'[51] Likewise, Indian Muslims need to continue to work with fellow Indians from other faiths. It is necessary to continue to foster solidarity with them and work for a secular polity. The other suggestion that I find useful is that Muslims should work for human rights and its larger cause to build a more humane India. As Dr King Jr wrote, 'We have left the realm of constitutional politics, we are entering the area of human rights.'[52] Given that a majoritarian state will create illiberal conditions to undermine equality provisions, the only way it could be fought back is by stressing on human rights. According to Upendra Baxi, human rights emerge, 'in this era of the end of ideology, as the only universal ideology in the making, enabling both the legitimation of power and praxes of emancipatory politics.'[53]

Though the political future of Indian Muslims is irretrievably threatened, the political possibilities to fight back continue to exist. It calls for solidarity within the community and collaboration with other communities outside as well. After the abrogation of Article 370, when disgraceful statements were made about Kashmiri girls, an Akal Takht Jathedar urged the Sikh community that it is the religious duty of Sikhs to protect the honour of Kashmiri (Muslims) sisters.[54] And there are a vast number of secularists and humanists from the Hindu community who are also part of this struggle. In other words, Indian Muslims—despite adversarial conditions—must continue to have faith in humanity, help build political relationships with various social and religious groups, and defend the rights of their own and others for human dignity. There are still many possibilities. Instead of being intimidated by the Hindu Right offensive, Indian Muslims need to look up to African Americans, Dalits, and others as sources of inspiration as this fight against Hindu majoritarianism is going to be long, and full of challenges. The challenge with Hindu majoritarianism is that it has the infinite potential for what Richard J Bernstein describes as 'radical dehumanization' in a deeply thought essay titled, 'Are Arendt's Reflections on Evil Still Relevant?'[55]

The unfortunate side of the present Indian democracy is most of its secular parties are dynastic—and it has become apparent in political campaign that the Hindu Right seeks to hammer 'dynastic parties' down to establish a public perception that their loyalty lies with their family, not with the country or people so they are less national compared to the Hindu Right. In any case, it is quite apparent that the commitment of these dynastic parties to secular polity is limited and often strategic, some deploying what is generally known as 'soft Hindutva'. For the complete renewal of secular polity that can practice the politics of rights and equality among people of all faiths, there is a need for a new political class. It is going to take time and going to be a long-term goal.

India's new secular polity can be possible only when India restores its democratic habits, places greater emphasis on rights, the idea of human equality, and its electoral democracy moves towards substantive equality. Individuals are appreciated more owing to the 'content of their character' as Dr King Jr would like to put it than their religion or caste or any other form of ascriptive identity. And then the future of Indian Muslims, together with its political future, can blossom. At this point, it calls for struggles against many odds. In other words, the political future of Indian Muslims that would give the community a political voice of its own directly depends on the future of Indian democracy. Without the healthy political future of the world's largest religious minority, Indian Muslims, and Indian democracy will remain incurably wounded.

Notes

1 This conversation took place on 3 February 2023 in New Delhi.

2 'Who is Mohammad Zubair?' Available at: http://www.Indianexpress.com. 28 June 2022 (accessed on 20 September 2022). Mohammad Zubair is the co-founder of fact-checking website AltNews, which Zubair founded, together with Pratik Sinha, in 2017 to fight fake news. In August 2020, Delhi Police had booked Zubair in a POCSO case based on a complaint filed by Priyank Kanoongo, Chairperson, National Commission for Protection of Child Rights (NCPCR). The complaint was about a tweet shared by Zubair on 6 August 2020.

3 Jalali, Ujwal. 2024. 'Delhi Cop kicks men offering namaz on road, suspended.' Available at: http://www.newindianexpress. (accessed on 9 March 2024). Such an incident happened recently in Delhi.
4 Joshi, Aakash. 2022. 'Namaz Controversy: Gurgaon's Corporate Offices and condominiums, and a widening gap.' Available at: http://www.indianexpress.com (accessed on 15 August 2023).
5 This is an umbrella group that led the protest against Friday namaz in public places in Gurgaon. For a detailed report, see. 'Hindu Groups seek immediate ban on namaz at public places: Muslim leaders urge Govt to allot land for building mosques.' Available at: http:// www.thehindu.com. (accessed on 20 September 2023).
6 Havan is a Hindu practice of worship.
7 'Gurugram: Over 100 people conduct havan at site marked for namaz in Sector 37.' Available at: http://www.scroll.in 26 Nov 2021 (accessed on 20 September 2023); Also see, Kissu, Sagarika. 2021. 'Gurugram: Now, Havan at Sector 37 site as namaz protests continue.' Available at: http://www.timesofindia.com (accessed on 20 September 2023).
8 Anand, Utkarsh. 2021. 'Gurugram Namaz Issue: Faith and Public spaces, through the eyes of Indian Courts.' Available at: http://www.hindustantimes.com (accessed on 15 August 2023).
9 Arora, Naina. 2018. 'Gurugrammers relish interfaith iftar gatherings'. Available at: http://www.thehindustantimes.com. (accessed on 15 August 2023) Also, see, Kumar, Ashik. 2018. 'Sanjha Iftar to promote brotherhood.' Available at: http://www.thehindu.com. (accessed on 15 August 2023).
10 Bhattacharya, Somreet and Bhardwaj, Sidharth. 2018. 'Ankit Saxena murder: Girl's family plotted to kill lover and her.' Available at: http://www.timesofindia.com (accessed on 20 September 2023)
11 'By offering gurudwara grounds for namaz in Gurgaon, Sikh community highlights the best in religion in a polarized climate.' Available at: http://www.indianexpress.com. 19 November 2021. (accessed on 15 August 2023)
12 Dhankhar, Leena. 2021. 'Namaz not offered at Gurudwara in Gurugram.' Available at: http://www.thehindustantimes.com (accessed on 15 August 2023).
13 The phrase was used by Viswanath, Neetika in an Oped she wrote in the Hindu newspaper on 20 August 2022. For details see, Vishwanath, Neetika. 2024. 'Justice for Bilkis Bano, questions on remission.' Available at: http://www.thehindu.com (accessed on 10 February 2024).

14 Jaising, Indira. 2014. 'An extraordinary judgement.' http://www.thehindu.com (accessed on 10 February 2024).

15 Pandey, Geeta. 2022. 'Bilkis Bano: India PM's Modi's government okayed rapist's release.' Available at: www.bbc.com.

16 Sharma, Rekha. 2024. 'Doing Justice, reinforcing trust.' *Indian Express*. 10 January.

17 See, 'Bilkis Bano Case Brief: The Timeline, the Key Milestones.' Available at: http://www.indianexpress.com. 9 January 2024 (accessed on 10 February 2024).

18 Quoted in a report by Rajagopal Krishnadas. 2024. 'SC quashes remission granted to 11 men convicted in Bilkis Bano gang rape case.' Available at: htp:// http://www.thehindu.com (accessed on 10 February 2024).

19 For a rich perspective on this see, Jaffrelot, Christophe's chapter titled, 'A Defacto Hindu Rashtra: Indian Style Vigilantism' in Jaffrelot, Christopher. 2021. *Modi's India: Hindu Nationalism and the Rise of Ethnic Democracy*. Princeton: Princeton University Press. Pp. 211- 247.

20 There are many more examples of minorities of various types suffering from difficult experiences under varied political conditions. A few chosen here will offer a broad overview of possible trends that Indian Muslims might go through once Hindu majoritarianism becomes the only game in town.

21 See, Grover, Vrinda and Uma, Saumya. 2017. *Kandhamal: Introspection of Initiative for Justice 2007-2015*. New Delhi: United Christian Forum (UCF) and Media House.

22 See, Sanyal, Usha. 2020. *Scholars of Faith: South Asian Muslim Women and the Embodiment of Religious Knowledge*. New Delhi: Oxford University Press. Also, Iyer, Shriya. 2018. *The Economics of Religion in India*. Cambridge: Harvard University Press. Borker, Hem. 2018. *Madrasas and the Making of Islamic Womanhood*. New Delhi: Oxford University Press.

23 See Aafaq, Zafar. 2023. 'In the Heart of Delhi, authorities take bulldozers to Muslim shrines with little warning'. Available at: http://amp.scroll.in (accessed on 10 February 2024).

24 See, 'Junagarh Violence: One dead, cops injured as mob hurl stones to oppose plan to raze dargah; 174 held.' Available at: http://www.m.economictimes.com. 17 June 2023. (accessed on 10 March 2024)

25 See, Salam, Zia Us. 2023. 'Explained: What is the Tussle between the Central Government and the Delhi Waqf Board?' Available at: http://www.thehindu.com (accessed on 10 February 2024).

26 For an understanding of the place of Holy Cow in the Hinduism, see Jha, DN. 2010. *The Myth of Holy Cow*. New Delhi. Navayana.

27 Jain, Srinivasan, Alavi, Mariyam, and Sharma, Supriya. 2024. *Love Jihad and Other Fictions: Simple Facts to Counter Viral Falsehoods.* New Delhi: Aleph Book Company.

28 Reed-Gordon, Annette. 2021. *On Juneteenth.* New York: Liveright Publishing Corporation. (A Division of WW Norton & Company Limited). Also see Reed-Gordon, Annette 2002. (Ed.). *Race on Trial: Law and Justice in American History.* New York: Oxford University Press.

29 Sundararajan, Thenmozhi. 2022. *The Trauma of Caste: A Dalit Feminist Meditation, Survivorship, Healing and Abolition.* New York: North Atlantic Books.

30 Ambedkar, B. R. 2015. *Annihilation of Caste: Annotated Critical Edition.* New Delhi: Navayana. p. 214.

31 Ibid. P. 215. Balais did not comply, but it led to oppression by upper-caste Hindus on them. They were not allowed to get water from village wells, and not allowed to walk past the land owned by the upper caste Hindus, and Hindus also let their cattle graze in the fields of Balais.

32 Shah, Ghanashyam, Mander, Harsh, Thorat, Sukhdeo, Deshpande, Satish, and Baviskar, Amita. (Ed.). 2023. *Untouchability In Rural India.* New Delhi: Sage Publications.

33 The lists in Table A and Table B are a condensed version of a long list carried by *The Outlook* (14 August 2023). It is compiled by Thallapelli Praveen.

34 Text of Nehru Liaquat Agreement, 8 April. 1950, File No. 20(16)-R/C/50, Ministry of States, Rehabilitation Branch, NAI. Originally quoted in, Raghavan, Pallavi. 2020. *Animosity at Bay: An Alternative History of the India- Pakistan Relationship, 1947- 1952.* New Delhi: Harper Collins. Particularly see, Chapter 2 titled, 'The Nehru- Liaquat Pact.' Pp. 47-71.

35 For important works on Pakistan's history and its contemporary challenges, see. Devji, Faisal 2013. *Muslim Zion: Pakistan as a Political Idea.* Cambridge: Harvard University Press. Fair, C Christine. 2014. *Fighting to the End: The Pakistan Army's Way of War.* New Delhi: Oxford University Press. Raghavan, TCA. 2017. *The People Next Door.* New Delhi: Harper Collins. Jalal, Ayesha. 2017. *The Struggle for Pakistan.: A Muslim Homeland and Global Politics.* Cambridge: Harvard University Press.

36 For an interesting perspective on Partition and its impact, see Kabir, Ananya Jahanara. 2013. *Partition's post-Amnesias.* New Delhi: Women Unlimited.

37 Ayoob, Mohammad. 2021. 'Opportunity of the Century.' *The Strategic Analysis*. 45(6):573-579. It is worth recalling here that Mohammad Ayoob's column, Recognise Bangladesh, was the first in a national daily asking the government to recognize the new country, which it did. For a detailed analysis of the event, see Ayoob, Mohammad and Subraminum. 1972. *The Liberation War*. New Delhi: S. Chand.

38 Ispahani, Farahnaz. 2018. *Purifying the Land of the Pure: A history of Pakistan's religious minorities*. New Delhi: Harper Collins.

39 Ibid. P. 3.

40 Ibid. P. 6.

41 For insight into this minority conundrum in Bangladesh, see, Fair, Christian. C and Patel, Parina. 2023. 'Religious Intolerance in Bangladesh.' in Ispahani, Farahnaz. 2023 .(Ed.). *Religious Majoritarianism in South Asia: Politics of Hate*. New Delhi: Harper Collins. Pp. 212-242.

42 For a detailed analysis of Bangladeshi refugees, see Shamsad, Rizwana. 2017. *Bangladesh Migrants In India: Foreigners, Refugees, or Infiltrators*. New Delhi: Oxford University Press.

43 Jalal, Ayesha. 2020. *The Sole Spokesman: Jinnah, the Muslim League and The Demand For Pakistan*. Cambridge: Cambridge University Press. P. XVII. The book was first published in 1985.

44 For a good overview of Hamid Ansari's view on identity, and rights, see Ansari, Hamid. 2022. *Challenges to a Liberal Polity: Human Rights, Citizenship and Identity*. New Delhi: Penguin.

45 I am mainly alluding to elites, who are non-professional politicians. I am aware that there are many Muslim politicians operating from various political parties.

46 'India's Narendra Modi gets top UAE honour amid Kashmir crisis.' Available at: http://www.aljazeera.com. 24 August 2019 (accessed on 10 February 2024). 'PM Modi conferred Egypt's highest state honour, countries elevate relationships to strategic partnership.' Available at: http://www.indianexpress.com. 25 June 2023. There are also awards from Saudi Arabia, Bahrain etc.

47 See, Muller, Jan-Werner. 2021. *Democracy Rules*. New Delhi: Penguin Random House. P. 185.

48 For a good understanding of minority rights, see Pattern, Alan. 2014. *Equal Recognition: The Moral Foundation of Minority Rights*. Princeton: Princeton University Press.

49 Quoted in Hardy, Peter. 1971. *The Muslims in British India*. Cambridge University Press. P. 1.

50 Zakaria, Rafiq. 2002. *Communal Rage in Secular India.* Mumbai: Popular Prakashan. P. 203.

51 Jr, King, Dr Martin Luther. 2010. *Where Do You Go From Here: Chaos or Community?* Boston: Beacon Press. P. XVI.

52 Ibid. P. XVIII.

53 Baxi, Upendra. 2007. *The Future of Human Rights.* New Delhi: Oxford University Press. P.1.

54 Brar, Kamaldeep Singh. 2019. 'Religious duty of Sikhs to protect Kashmiri girls: Akal Takht Jathedar.' Available at: http://www.indianexpress.com (Accessed on 3 March 2024).

55 Bernstein, Richard J. 2010. 'Are Arendt's Reflections on Evil Still Relevant?' in Benhabib, Seyla. 2010. (Ed). *Politics in Dark Times: Encounter with Hannah Arendt.* Cambridge: Cambridge University Press. Pp. 293-304.

ACKNOWLEDGEMENTS

Once a group of students from the Jawaharlal Nehru University invited me to a panel discussion on Indian Muslims few years ago. It was hosted at India Islamic Cultural Centre, New Delhi. In my attempt to speak something new on the subject, I chose to speak on the political future of Indian Muslims. My talk resonated well with the audience. Ever since, I began mulling over the idea of writing a book on the political future of Indian Muslims in the context of Hindu majoritarianism.

It was a chance meeting with Himanjali Sankar, Editorial Director, and Sayantan Ghosh, Executive Editor at Simon and Schuster India, at a book launch at Bikaner House, New Delhi. Over coffee with both at SDA's Barista, I took the call not just to write the book, but to put it on priority. At the time, I was in the middle of working on a book on the Muslim mind. But I chose to set that aside that evening and embarked on this new book with a clear determination to wrap it up in a year's time. The writing was going well, but then I was hit by Covid which led to hospitalization and interruption in work. When people ask me how the Covid experience was, often I say, 'I had one leg in grave.' Fortunately, I have a new life. It took a while for me to revive interest and resume work. Here I am.

Parts of this book were presented in various conferences and universities. I would like to place my appreciation for Katharine Adeny and Indrajit Roy for being part of a panel discussion at the annual meeting of the British Political Studies Association, where I presented some parts of this work. Also, I am especially thankful to

Ayesha Jalal for her invitation to deliver a talk at Tufts University, Boston, USA. Also, to John Echeverri-Gent for his invitation to speak at the University of Virginia, Charlottesville, USA. Mehr Farooqui, Neeti Nair, and Richard Cohen made my visit to Charlottesville a very memorable experience. Geeta Patel from UV has always been very supportive and encouraging of my work as well. Also, grateful to Rumela Sen for her invitation for a talk at the Columbia University, USA. No doubt, these presentations and discussions that followed with scholars and students have been invaluable. Christophe Jaffrelot, Steve Wilkinson, Justin Jones, Zoya Hasan, and A Kalaiyrasan were always prompt in sharing their works, some of which I have used in this book.

For bringing clarity to my understanding of the Indian Muslim question and general politics that has shaped this puzzle, there are some scholars, journalists, and friends who I would like to acknowledge: Romila Thapar, Upendra Baxi, Martha Nussbaum, Barbara Harris-White, Bernard Hykel, Amrita Basu, Upinder Singh, Sayida Hameed, Shruti Kapila, Mohammad Ayoob, James Chiriyankandath, Shikha Mukherjee, Robin Lewis, Rochana Bajpai, Wilfried Swenden, Taylor Sherman, Ravinder Barn, Eleanor Newbigin, Dipesh Chakravarty, Lisa Wedeen, Ilyse R Morgenstein Fuerst, Nandini Deo, Vrinda Grover, Prabir Sen, Rajiv Bhatia, Tuktuk Ghosh, NC Saxena, Rani Mullen, Rumela Sen, Manan Ahmed, Jean Muller, Smruti Koppikar, Arunabh Ghosh, Akeel Bilgrami, Zoya Hasan, Ananya Vajpeyi, Mohsin Alam, Yaseer Arafat, Razi Aquil, Charu Gupta, Vinay Lal, Jyotirmaya Sharma, Sakuntala Banaji, Radhika Bordia, Mimi Chaudhury, Raphel Susewind, Amitabh Kundu, Bishu Mohapatra, Vidhu Verma, Dwaipayan Bhattacharya, Maidul Islam, Pallavi Raghavan, Hilal Ahmad, Nazima Perveen, Irfan Engineer, Amir Ali, Tanvir Aijaz, Gautam Menon, Nicolas Gravel, Narendra Kumar, Anil Nauriya, Sumita, Debjani, Aftab Alam, Razi Raziuddin, S Zainuddin (Aligarh), Santosh Raghavan, Aparna Vaidik, Ali Khan, Anwar, Mohammad Wajihuddin, Asmer Ali Baig, Aftab Alam (Aligarh), Balveer Arora, John Dayal, and many others.

At Chomsky, Prof Tanuja, Arvinder, Prashant, Arvind, Samarendra, and others have been very supportive.

As a personal friend, Daman Singh, has always been very encouraging and supportive.

Some of my other personal friends include, Dr Thom Wolf, Linda Wolf, Nishant Jain, Sherebanu Frosh, Prashanto Sen, Saif Mehmood, and others who have been supportive of my work. Special thanks to Keith Topping who continues to encourage me even after his shift to Singapore.

Among my students, Abida, Haider, Ali, and Shashwata Dashora were helpful, but special thanks to my doctoral students Malka, Thafseer, Alfaz, Jaseemul, Illaiha, and Smita for their research-related assistance during the writing process.

In the long hours of writing and rewriting, my beautiful Ammijan (whenever she came to live with me) would provide a constant supply of fruits, snacks, and tea at my work table. I am glad that she won't tease me any more by saying, 'Well, you have been saying you will complete the book in next couple of weeks for the past one year or so!'

I am glad it is done.

Last but not the least, I have deep gratitude for the editorial team of Simon and Schuster India, particularly its CEO, Rahul Srivastava, and Megha Mukherjee for their contribution in the making of this book.